READINGS IN LANGUAGE STUDIES

VOLUME 4

LANGUAGE AND SOCIAL JUSTICE

INTERNATIONAL SOCIETY OF LANGUAGE STUDIES

READINGS IN LANGUAGE STUDIES

VOLUME 4

LANGUAGE AND SOCIAL JUSTICE

EDITED BY
MIGUEL MANTERO
JOHN L. WATZKE
PAUL CHAMNESS MILLER

A PUBLICATION OF THE
INTERNATIONAL SOCIETY FOR LANGUAGE STUDIES, INC.

Copyright © 2014

International Society for Language Studies, Inc.
2885 Sanford Ave SW, #21186
Grandville, MI 49418
USA

All rights reserved.

ISBN 978-0-9779114-7-9

Library of Congress Control Number: 2008927091

Text layout by Julie Wernick Dallavis

Cover art comes from the original painting *Emma*, by Hector Rolando Garza. Cover art reproduction of the painting used with permission from the artist. He may be reached at hgarza26@gmail.com.

This book was printed on acid-free paper.

Printed in the United States of America.

Para mis padres—MM

For LDB, BEW, GSW, and TLW—JLW

For Fr. Andrew Marr, whose friendship and guidance changed my life—PCM

CONTENTS

Introduction ix

LANGUAGE, CULTURE AND SOCIAL JUSTICE

1. Language Ideologies in an Anglo-Controlled Bilingual Charter School: A Teacher's Reflections — *Malathi Iyengar* — 3

2. Differences in Expressions of Social Justice Evidenced in College Students' Fables — *Bettina Murray* — 23

3. Creating Russian-American Identities in Recent American Fiction: Two Perspectives — *Julia Stakhnevich* — 47

4. Qué revolú: The ¡Atrévete y Dilo! Campaign and Language Legitimation in Puerto Rico — *Ashlee Civitello and Elaine M. Shenk* — 59

5. Idiomaticity and Language Use: A Sociolinguistic Investigation in the Philippines — *Yvonne Velasco* — 83

LANGUAGE TEACHING PRACTICES, PEDAGOGY, AND SOCIAL JUSTICE

6. Intersections of Study Abroad, Social Capital, and Second Language Acquisition — *John Schwieter and Aline Ferreira* — 107

7. Ableism and Social Justice in Higher Education: GTAs Readiness and Attitudes Towards Accommodating Students With Disabilities — *Muriel Gallego and Carey Busch* — 129

8. Multicultural Social Justice Education through the Lens of Positioning: English Language Learners in K-12 Contexts — *Hayriye Kayi-Aydar* — 147

9. Social Justice through Critical Language Pedagogy in the Heritage Language Classroom — *Ariana Mrak* — 161

10. Non-Native Teachers and English Language Teaching: Critical Social Choices in the Mexican Context — *Gerrard Mugford* — 179

11	A Transformative Educational Experience in San Andrés, Colombia *Maria Montoya, Carol Dean, and Diane Mancini*	197
12	College English Instructors' and Students' Preference for Types of Written Corrective Feedback on Expository Compositions: Challenges, Inequalities and Opportunities *Janet Oab*	215
13	Doing Critical Pedagogy in Neoliberal EFL Spaces: Negotiated Possibilities in Korean Hagwons *Gordon West*	231
14	Cross-Cultural Equity: Pathway for Impoverished and Marginalized Students in Two-Way Bilingual Immersion Programs *Ana Hernández and Annette Daoud*	247

LANGUAGE POLICY AND SOCIAL JUSTICE

15	Language rights for Mexican Americans and the Treaty of Guadalupe Hidalgo *Eduardo Faingold*	271
16	Language Policy and Social Justice in Québec *Patrick-André Mather*	283
17	Analysing Language Policy Texts: A Two-Pronged Approach *Dilhara Premaratne*	291
18	The Discursive Construction of Pro-Nuclear Ideology post-3/11: A Critical Discourse Analysis of the Oi Reactors Restart Decision *Nicholas Drane*	307

Index	321
About the Editors	325
About the Contributors	327

INTRODUCTION

The International Society for Language Studies has its origins in a grassroots effort to bring together multiple disciplines around issues of language, power and identity. In 2002, a group of international scholars began planning a conference that would eventually grow to forty papers, representing such diverse fields as medicine, law, education and linguistics, presented the following year in St. Thomas, Virgin Islands. This fledging "society" was further advanced through its incorporation as a 501c(6) non-profit with the vision of founding a volunteer-based organization of scholars and practitioners committed to critical, interdisciplinary, and emergent approaches to language studies. Fast forward to 2014. We celebrated our tenth year anniversary just two years ago, and the tenth volume of the society's official journal, *Critical Inquiry in Language Studies* (published by Taylor & Francis), was published. Our first conference in Asia was successfully organized this year in Akita, Japan, and planning of the eighth conference is underway. International membership continues to grow. Throughout this period of growth, the society has remained focused on providing a means to disseminate the important scholarship of its membership. This fourth volume of the *Readings in Language Studies* series, focused on language and social justice, represents the society's continued efforts to provide peer-reviewed fora as a reflection of its mission.

Readings in Language Studies, Volume 4: Language and Social Justice presents international perspectives in several thematic sections. The book's first section focuses on Language, Culture and Social Justice (Chapters 1-5). In Chapter 1, Iyengar initiates the section by examining the ideologies of linguistic anonymity and authenticity underlying the daily pedagogical, organizational, and interpersonal practices of an Anglo-controlled bilingual charter school in a low-income, black-and-brown "'hood" within a major California city. While academic instruction in and through two or more languages can be a powerful tool for promoting social justice, this chapter calls attention to the fact that bilingual/multilingual school programs also have the potential to perpetuate social and linguistic injustice—in this case, by reifying and institutionalizing hegemonic language ideologies. Murray offers a study in Chapter 2 in which Freshmen (N= 131) from varied cultural backgrounds in college communications courses received instruction in composing fables over a semester. Students wrote creative short stories concluding with a lesson. Students who lived in the United States over 17 years expressed social justice experiences differently than did those whose primary language was Spanish. Long-term residents of the United States expressed significant concern over discrimination and economic hardships while Spanish-speaking students, regardless of length of residence, were significantly concerned with prejudice and negative influences. Stakhnevich's essay, Chapter 3, examines themes of immigration and identity in the recent novels by Lara Vapnyar and Irina Reyn, both Russian-American translingual authors. The projected hybrid Russian-American personas created by Vapnyar and Reyn for their female protagonists are intimately connected to the writers' personal journeys and reflect their own understanding of what it means to be Russian on the American soil. She argues that their different vantage points outside of Russia and within the immigrant Russian community distinguish their voices and showcase divergent perspectives on what it means to be Russian-American in the twenty-first century. Chapter 4, by Civitello and Shenk, focuses on the intent and impact of the *¡Atrévete y dilo!* radio campaign in Puerto Rico in its presentation and affirmation of a uniquely Puerto Rican Spanish by analyzing patterns and discourse collected through interviews with twenty Puerto Ricans living on the Island. Results showed that although most participants were unfamiliar with the campaign, they demonstrated strategies of language legitimation of lexical variants, including loanwords from English. Velasco's discussion in Chapter 5 seeks to answer whether social class differences are filtered through schools or whether classroom processes amplify the differences between the groups of college learners employing a quantitative method using a cross-sectional design involving four college freshman classes coming from different socio-economic and regional backgrounds. Through a test of idioms, results of the study reveal that several differences in the interpretation of data may be attributed to the learning conditions of students. These results therefore highlight the need for scholars to frame investigations in the context of social development.

The second section of the volume focuses on language teaching practices, pedagogy, and social justice (Chapters 6-14). In Chapter 6, Schwieter and Ferreira report on a study in which English (L1) language learners of Spanish (L2) and French (L3) participated in a short-term L2 study abroad experience. In particular, the study explored the development of linguistic and social variables including self-ratings of language abilities, L2 socialization, identity construction, and the development of social capital. In addition to the language history questionnaires and Language Contact Profile, open-ended interviews were conducted. The results demonstrated significant growth in self-ratings of language abilities in the L2, as expected, but also revealed a significant decline in some L3 abilities. The language contact data highlighted the importance of interaction with native speakers in the community along with the ability to make connections between classroom learning and real-life application. The responses to the open-ended interviews suggested that participants not only recognized that they would be able to apply what they have learned abroad to social aspects in their everyday lives, but they also realized a potential increase in value and social power from having participated within a unified learning community abroad. Chapter 7 presents Gallego and Busch's investigation, operating on the premises of Social Justice Education and the need for faculty advocacy in order to guarantee that every student, regardless of their placement within a specific group, is granted access to higher education, and the resources to navigate through college. Their chapter focuses on the interdisciplinary work of providing training to graduate students serving as foreign language teaching assistants (GTAs). By means of a survey (completed by 107 participants) distributed across several institutions of higher education in the U.S., they analyze the readiness

GTAs display concerning instructing and accommodating students with disabilities. Kayi-Aydar draws, in Chapter 8, on the literature on positional identities of English language learners (ELLs) and positioning theory (e.g., Davies & Harre, 1990, 1999) and provides a critical discussion regarding how ELLs position themselves and are positioned by others in the second language (L2) culture and society. Analyzing the ways ELLs are positioned in K-12 contexts, she describes what social justice should mean in the education of ELLs. In light of the literature, implications for classroom teachers, researchers, and policy makers are offered. Chapter 9 presents Mrak's model for Spanish for heritage speakers' courses that includes instructor training and curricular development, drawing on two approaches to teaching heritage languages (HL) in use today: second dialect acquisition (SDA) and critical language awareness (CLA). Both have been criticized, the former for dictating appropriateness of use to the different varieties in a speaker's linguistic repertoire and the latter for depriving students of the prestigious variety. This new model combines both of the current approaches into a critical pedagogy that informs students on linguistic variation, prejudice, and prestige and provides the tools they will need to decide their linguistic future on their own terms. Mugford's chapter (Chapter 10) sheds light on English language teachers in Mexico, who are generally non-native speakers and are trained in how to teach American English using imported methodologies and textbooks. His chapter investigates whether these teacher-training programs adequately prepare teachers to respond to students' social, cultural and educational needs. To identify Mexican teachers' attitudes towards English-language teaching, he interviewed 115 teacher trainees and 201 English-language students to determine whether teaching objectives are in touch with students' needs. With another group of 26 teacher trainees, he analyzed these results, which suggest that English-language teaching rarely answers local needs and is heavily focused on satisfying global language concerns. In Chapter 11, Montoya, Dean, and Mancini describe a one-semester course entitled "Experience in San Andrés, Colombia" which offered undergraduates cultural and linguistic immersion through service-learning. Through observations and interactions with the diverse communities of the island, students experienced first-hand how social context influences community development; they also planned and engaged in activities with community members that reflected their own culture and traditions. Student and community feedback demonstrated that this cross-cultural service-learning experience was mutually beneficial. Connections and information gained from this opportunity will continue to serve as the building blocks for long-term academic and social development between the College and the San Andrean communities. Oab's Chapter 12 studies the preferred types of written corrective feedback on expository compositions by the participants. Its objectives are to determine the forms of errors in the compositions they think warrant corrective feedback and what types of written corrective feedback (WCF) are most useful. As revealed in the study, an important dimension that emerged in the investigation is the apparent asymmetrical social structure imposed by the educational system as teachers and students' attempts to negotiate not only meaning but also power relations in the classroom context. In the case of social justice, practitioners need to be sensitive to the cultural, political and social climates of both students and teachers to create equal opportunities for learning. West, in Chapter 13, reports on a teacher's evolving critical pedagogy praxis in a neoliberal EFL context. As part of a larger study encompassing multiple teacher research projects over a two year progression toward critical pedagogy, this chapter shares a narrative detailing negotiated syllabi and participatory curriculum development in a private language institute in Seoul. The neoliberal context of EFL education in South Korea is set to contextualize the study and draw attention to this context for further research. The challenges and successes of critical pedagogy are discussed along with responses to critiques of critical pedagogy in neoliberal and EFL settings. The final chapter in this section, Chapter 14 by Hernández and Daoud, describes the cross-cultural equity of peer interactions between low socioeconomic Hispanic/Latinos who are native Spanish speakers (NSS) and middle class White English native speakers (NES) in a Two-Way Bilingual Immersion (TWBI) program in southern California, USA. The research examines the students' interactions during their Spanish social studies instruction in grades 6-8. The study revealed the students' cross-cultural dispositions through their sociolinguistic interactions in Spanish and English. The analysis of an interpersonal disposition survey and the teacher's reflection demonstrated positive as well as strained relationships pertaining to cross-cultural equity and equal status of languages during student interactions.

The final section of the volume, Language Policy and Social Justice (chapters 15-18), examines the intersection of these two areas of study. Faingold, in Chapter 15, explains that as a result of the Mexican-American War (1846-1848), Mexico lost more than half of its territory to the U.S. through the Treaty of Guadalupe Hidalgo (1848). The consensus among scholars of the Treaty is that the language rights of Mexican Americans in the Southwest are protected by it, especially by Article IX. However, a close reading of the Treaty reveals that neither Article IX nor any other article is designed to protect the linguistic rights of Mexican Americans in the annexed territories. He argues that the Treaty of Guadalupe Hidalgo is not the correct legal instrument to protect the language rights of Mexican Americans. Rather, stronger arguments can be made under the 14th Amendment of the U.S. Constitution and more modern civil rights legislation, such as Titles VI and VII of the Civil Rights Act of 1964. In Chapter 16, Mather explores how Québec has adopted strict language laws that promote the use of French as the main or exclusive language of business and government in the province. This chapter analyzes aspects of Québec's language policies over the past 4 decades, and the effects of these policies on economic and social justice in the province. The main argument is that even though language laws have failed to impose French as the sole language in Québec, they have allowed Francophones to achieve greater economic success, increased rates of bilingualism among Anglophones and immigrants in the province, and reduced the income gap between linguistic communities in Québec. Premaratne argues in Chapter 17 that while social justice issues can be caused by language policies, it is usual for top-down language planners to attempt to conceal such issues in policy documents. She maintains that rigorous text analysis is necessary to reveal how information is controlled in language policy texts and how communication is used strategically to manage public opinion. To this end, the chapter looks at two analytical frameworks—Cooper's language planning accounting scheme (1989) and Fairclough's critical discourse analysis framework (2003) - that can be used together effectively to reveal how public opinion is shaped in language policy texts to bring about policy change. Lastly, in Chapter 18, Drane offers a critical discourse analysis of seven online news sources covering the Oi reactors restart decision in June 2012. These were the first reactors in Japan to go online following the March 11th 2011 earthquake, tsunami, and nuclear crisis. The perspective of individuals and groups opposed to the restart are discursively deflected through strategies of over-lexicalization and unequal quotation patterns while convenience and economic necessity are framed as neutral social values. Structurally the analysis is informed by systemic functional linguistics, particularly notions of transitivity and thematic foregrounding. Multiplicity of opinions are entombed ("Japan", "the government", "greens", "critics"), creating a dehumanized discourse.

Since its inception, ISLS has had as its mission the bridging of disciplines around language studies with a particular emphasis on critical theory. With few venues, the Society, with its conference, journal and publications initiative, now stands as a major advocate for this paradigm. *Readings in Language Studies, Volume 4,* represents contemporary issues, theory, and practices in language studies around issues of language and social justice. Volume 5, scheduled for publication in 2015 will continue to focus on emergent international perspectives in these areas, as they relate to society, and Volume 6, scheduled for publication in 2016, will focus on the intersection of language and community. These forthcoming volumes, as well as future volumes will further the Society's core mission and the work of its membership.

LANGUAGE, CULTURE, AND SOCIAL JUSTICE

CHAPTER 1

LANGUAGE IDEOLOGIES IN AN ANGLO-CONTROLLED BILINGUAL CHARTER SCHOOL:
A Teacher's Reflections

Malathi Michelle Iyengar
University of California–San Diego

The present paper examines the ideologies of linguistic anonymity and authenticity underlying the daily pedagogical, organizational, and interpersonal practices of an Anglo-controlled bilingual charter school in a low-income, black-and-brown "'hood" within a major California city. Though informed by theoretical insights from linguistic anthropology, this paper is not an ethnographic study; it is a personal essay by an elementary school teacher.

My stance here dispenses with a generations-old precedent in education studies: the (gendered) split between, on the one hand, those whose voices are most often heard regarding educational matters (i.e., those who are permitted to speak authoritatively about education, those who control education, those who profit from educational institutions, those who are permitted to blithely pass judgment upon the work of education) and, on the other hand, those who actually perform the *embodied labor* of teaching. The standpoint from which I write is the standpoint of the theoretically-informed teacher. While there is abundant educational research and theory that positions teachers as *objects* of knowledge (or of "investigation"), we need more studies that recognize teachers as *producers* of (theoretical as well as substantive) knowledge about education. My standpoint is that of the laborer who thinks.

One thing I found myself thinking about frequently during a recent school year, when I worked as a bilingual teacher in a multiage K-2 classroom at a charter school in a ghettoized region of a sprawling metropolis in California, was the impact of particular language ideologies upon the life of the school. Woolard (1998) defines *language ideologies* as "representations, whether explicit or implicit, that construe the intersection of language and human beings in a social world." Importantly, language ideologies "are not about language alone. Rather, they envision and enact ties of language to identity, to aesthetics, to morality, and to epistemology" (p. 3). Language ideologies inform the ways in which speakers *use* (or don't use) language, and the ways in which speakers *perceive* (or ignore) and *engage with* (or avoid) other speakers (or those who are presumed to be speakers) of particular languages and language-varieties. Language ideologies also intersect and interact with other ideological constructions, notably race.

Anonymity and Authenticity

Woolard (2008) suggests that the legitimation of language in "modern western societies" is often anchored in one of two interrelated ideological constructions, which she terms *authenticity* and *anonymity* (p. 303). The ideology of authenticity, says Woolard,

> locates the value of a language in its relationship to a particular community. That which is authentic is viewed as the genuine expression of such a community, or of an essential Self. Within the logic of authenticity, a speech variety must be perceived as deeply rooted in social and geographic territory in order to have value. For many European languages, these roots are in the mountain redoubts of peasant folk purity. For [some U.S. language varieties], the roots are often located in the soulful streets of the urban ghetto or *barrio*, where the real folks are said to be busy "keepin' it real." (p. 304)

Authenticity involves markedness: "authentic" speech is a marked form— be it a marked "language" per se, a marked grammatical usage, a marked set of lexical items, a marked accent, etc. Social indexicality comes into play here, as a language is taken as indexical of a certain group of people, and an individual speaker's use of that language is thus taken as indexical of his or her relationship to that group.

While Woolard's use of the term "authenticity" specifically refers to the value afforded to a language via its link with a specific (marked) group of people, it is also worthwhile to consider the colloquial use of the word "authentic" to suggest the "True," the "Genuine" ... the natural, honest-to-goodness, unadulterated Real Thing. Hence, I suggest, a speaker's intentional deployment of "authentic" language not only relies upon the association of the language with a specific group of people, but also asserts that the speaker's relationship to that group is a "real" (authentic) relationship, a "natural," spontaneously-arising relationship, rather than a formal or studied one. (Of course, the use of a linguistic form widely viewed as indexical of a certain group of people can also be deployed with vari-directional double voicing, thereby indexing the fact that the speaker is actually *not* a member of the group, or is in fact mocking or deriding the group.)

Under the ideology of linguistic *anonymity*, in contrast to that of authenticity, a linguistic form derives authority precisely because it is imagined to be free of ties to any specific group of people; it is an unmarked form, it is *everybody's* language ... or it *should* be everybody's language, it *would* be everybody's language, if only those stubborn fools who don't speak it would reform their foreign/low-class/uneducated ways. Of course, as Woolard (along with numerous other scholars, notably Bourdieu) points out, no linguistic variety has ever emerged as a people-less entity; if a language is regarded as an "anonymous," culturally-neutral, pure civic language, this illusion in fact rests upon (and reinforces) the language's hegemonic status. "Standard" English, for instance, is certainly not equally available or accessible to everyone (even within English-speaking societies), nor does every speaker of this variety bear the same cognitive/affective/political relationship to it. Following Bourdieu (1982, 1991), Woolard (2008) notes that hegemonic linguistic forms are not *actually* anonymous, but are *misrecognized* as such. "Under misrecognition, listeners recognize the authority of a dominant language, but fail to recognize the historical developments and the material power differences between groups of people that underpin that authority" (p. 307). Schools, as Bourdieu has pointed out, play a significant role in producing and perpetuating this misrecognition, both by drawing attention away from the historical and structural factors that have enabled the dominant positioning of a particular language, and by presenting dominant linguistic forms as objectively "good" and "correct."

In order to provide some background for my discussion of the operation of these language ideologies, I turn now to a brief sketch of the school site where I observed them.

Urban Renaissance: A Snapshot

The Urban Renaissance Charter School (All proper names—personal as well as institutional—have been changed) was founded in 2000 by two wealthy, white Teach For America[1] alumni, Allison Wheeler and Tim Aldridge. When the first campus opened in 2000, the founders described the school in terms of a social justice mission: Urban Renaissance would be located in a poor urban area and would provide bilingual instruction, something which had been made unavailable to the vast majority of California students after the 1998 passage of Proposition 227. Over the years, the school has consistently enrolled two distinct populations of students: working class students of color (some English-speaking and some Spanish-speaking) from the surrounding neighborhood, and wealthy white Anglophone students whose parents personally know the founders and/or are attracted to the school's "philosophy."

Enrollment for the 2010-2011 school year totaled 571 students in K-8 and 87 students in the newly-opened Urban Renaissance high school. In terms of demographics, K-8 enrollment for that academic year was reported as follows: 71.1% "Hispanic or Latino," 13.7% "White," 10.3% "Black or African American," and 1.1% "Asian." 66% of students qualified for free or reduced-price lunch (a lower figure than the local school district as a whole, in which 69.7% of students qualified). The other 34.4 % of Urban Renaissance students ranged from "middle-class" to very wealthy—with a significant number of students coming from the city's most exclusive neighborhoods, featuring homes with seven-figure price tags.

Since its inception, Urban Renaissance has been billed by its founder-directors as a "Dual Immersion" bilingual school. The school's curriculum, however, does not fit the general definition of dual-immersion (or its usual synonym, "two-way immersion") adhered to by university-based researchers, the California Association for Bilingual Education (CABE), and the Center for Applied Linguistics (CAL). CAL maintains an extensive directory of two-way immersion programs in the U.S. In order to be included in CAL's two-way immersion directory, a program must meet a number of explicit criteria. The local school district of the city where Urban Renaissance is located includes three schools with dual-immersion programs that meet these criteria and are thus listed in CAL's directory. One of these district schools, Salazar Elementary, is also located in the "Central Focus Area," in the same neighborhood as one of the Urban Renaissance K-8 campuses. (The term "Central Focus Area" was coined by the city council, which deems the area to be in need of "targeted investment" in order to ward off "blight.") Urban Renaissance and Salazar are about a five-minute drive or a fifteen-minute walk apart. The program at Urban Renaissance is indeed "bilingual"; however, unlike the district-run Salazar Elementary, it does not meet CAL's definition of two-way immersion and hence is not included in the CAL two-way directory. Nevertheless, the Urban Renaissance website and the founders' publicity pitches grandly declare that Urban Renaissance is a "Dual Immersion" school.[2]

The observations upon which this paper is based were made during a recent school year. During that year, I taught full-time at Urban Renaissance, generally spending 10-11 hours per weekday on campus, as well as attending various weekend meetings, fundraisers, and other events such as the mandatory overnight team-building retreat at a mountain campsite. Like the other teachers, I conducted home-visits with a number of students' families during the year. I also lived in the Central Focus Area; many of the Urban Renaissance students were my neighbors.

I should note that I was only involved with Urban Renaissance for one academic year: I came to the charter school after having been laid off from another school district (where I'd been teaching in a 90/10 dual-immersion program) due to budget cuts; and, the following year, left the classroom in order to go "back to school" myself, in my thirties, as a PhD student in Ethnic Studies. I have since kept in touch with several of my former students and their parents, who have become close friends. These students had all left Urban Renaissance by the time they were in second grade, and they all recently completed fifth grade at the district-run bilingual program in the same neighborhood. I have not had any contact with Urban Renaissance since leaving the school.

What follows, then, are some theoretical interventions into the study of ideologies of linguistic anonymity and authenticity, based upon personal observations made by a single teacher over the course of a single school year at a particular bilingual charter school. We might characterize the methodology behind this essay as a sort of auto-ethnography, since I am essentially writing about my personal experiences with particular language ideologies in the context of my work as a teacher. My own preferred term for this approach, however, is *labor as method*.

Anonymity and Authenticity, English and Spanish

That English in the context of Urban Renaissance (as in every other U.S. school) held the hegemonic status of the unmarked code—that English, in other words, possessed authority-via-anonymity—requires no elaboration here. All the students had to learn English. All of the teachers and administrators had completed university degrees at English-medium institutions, with the single exception of a part-time music teacher from Cuba, who also spoke English, though his formal education had been completed in his home country. English was a "must."

Spanish, the "other" linguistic medium of instruction, possessed no anonymity-value. It was distinctly *not* a requirement for "everybody." What I mean here is not simply that U.S. *society* doesn't make Spanish a "requirement," but that the *school*—despite making a claim to the "dual immersion" label—actually didn't make the language a requirement for all students. English-speaking elementary students did not receive Language Arts instruction in Spanish—the only subjects which Anglophone students learned through Spanish were Math, a half-hour "Homeroom" period, an hour-long "Art" period held once per week, and a half-hour "elective" course held three times a week. Spanish-dominant students were separated from English-dominant students during Language Arts and "elective" periods, receiving Language Arts instruction in Spanish and an elective geared for English learners.

But the uneven allocation of instructional hours in the two languages, and the fact that students were separated by language for literacy instruction, only tell part of the story. When I say that Spanish was "not required" at Urban Renaissance, I refer not only to instructional hours, but also to attitudes. The school culture distinctly revolved around an idea of Spanish as an "extra" for Anglophone students—something potentially desirable but not required. For example, Anglophone students felt no need to attempt to speak in Spanish during the periods supposedly designated for that language, and were also free to speak what Hill (1995, 2008) calls "Mock Spanish."

After working at Urban Renaissance for a few months and having multiple opportunities to interact with the older students who had been attending the school for a several years, I began to realize that—much to my surprise—most of these students demonstrated very little knowledge of Spanish. I refer now to the students who came from monolingual Anglophone homes. Not only could many of these students barely produce a complete sentence of spoken Spanish, they also had little receptive language. At first I assumed that the seventh and eighth-grade students who didn't speak much Spanish must have transferred into Urban Renaissance from monolingual schools during the past couple of years, in the fifth or sixth grade. I was wrong: it turned out that most of these students had been at Urban Renaissance since the early elementary grades—since kindergarten, even. How could they have learned so little of a language they had supposedly been "immersed" in for so many years? I decided to ask Annette, a teacher who had been working at Urban Renaissance for longer than I had. I asked for her impressions of the Spanish-acquisition of the students who started Urban Renaissance as English monolinguals—how much Spanish, I asked, did these students typically learn by the seventh or eighth grade?

"Well," Annette answered frankly, "some of them get really into it and learn a lot of Spanish, but a lot of them just ... don't, really."

I had to wonder about this teacher's seemingly untroubled attitude towards the obvious disparity between the values afforded to the two languages in this so-called "dual-immersion" setting. While English was clearly "everyone's" duty and requirement, Spanish was apparently more of an optional pastime: students didn't really have to pay attention to the language unless they just happened to be "into" it.

It is instructive here to note parents' stated reasons for sending their children to Urban Renaissance. Very few of the Anglophone parents ever mentioned the "bilingual" nature of the school as a primary reason for having chosen to send their children to Urban Renaissance. This fact stands in great contrast to most dual-immersion programs—school programs which parents specifically select *because they want their children to be educated in two languages*. In the case of Urban Renaissance, parents did not seem to view bilingualism or bi-literacy as central components of the curriculum or as primary reasons for enrolling their children in this particular school. Parents who lived near the school usually expressed that they had chosen

Urban Renaissance because of its convenient location. Some parents also needed the free daycare the school provided—children could be dropped off at seven in the morning and stay until six in the evening, giving parents up to eleven hours of free daycare if needed. Parents from wealthier areas—indeed, there was a significant population of very wealthy students at Urban Renaissance—frequently expressed that they had chosen the school because of its "philosophy"—particularly with regards to the "freedom" their children had there, in contrast to the rigid rules enforced at other schools. Some of these parents merely tolerated the "bilingual" aspect of the school, in the same way that they tolerated the undesirable (to them) location. Other Anglophone parents did appreciate the bilingual component, but did not consider it a serious priority or a major aspect of the curriculum. A typical comment from one of these parents would be: "I love the freedom my son has at Urban Renaissance. He has a lot of energy, and I love that they let him be himself and don't punish him or make him sit still all day. I'm also thrilled that he's at a school where he can learn music, art, and Spanish."

In one case, a teacher reported to me that at an end-of-year conference, the parents of one Anglophone kindergarten student had been "shocked" to learn "how much Spanish their child had been hearing" at school all year. These particular parents had not only enrolled their daughter at Urban Renaissance at the beginning of the school year, but had also been to the campus numerous times, attended three extensive conferences during the year, and had regular phone contact with their child's homeroom teacher. I was baffled as to how these parents had managed to miss out on the fact that they had enrolled their child in a "dual-immersion" bilingual school.

Students from Spanish-speaking families didn't seem to fair much better than Anglophone students in terms of their progress in Spanish language arts during their time at Urban Renaissance. Things like standard spellings, accent marks, etc., were basically absent from their writing—which was quite understandable, since a number of the teachers also failed to use standard spellings and accent marks in their own writing, visible on the white-boards and handmade posters around the rooms.

Of the school's two founder-directors (both of whom had been among the primary teaching staff for several years, before becoming full-time administrators), only one—Allison—spoke Spanish. Tim had much difficulty even pronouncing Spanish names. When Roberto, the recently-hired music teacher from Cuba, was absent one day from a staff meeting, Tim shared with the rest of us the joke he'd made up to help him remember the man's name: *What do you call a Cuban with a rubber toe? Rober-to!*

Allison was very proud of the fact that she had learned Spanish as an adult. She liked to tell the story of how she'd gotten her first bilingual teaching job, a position as an upper-grade teacher at a district-run school in another large city. At the time, she'd had a Spanish-speaking daycare provider who took care of her son during the day. She therefore possessed a good amount of daycare-related Spanish language. Going to the interview for this bilingual teaching job, she had been nervous about fielding questions in Spanish, afraid she might not understand them or have the vocabulary to formulate adequate answers. She went to the interview, and it was conducted almost entirely in English. Only the final question was in Spanish, and—what luck!—it turned out to be a conversational sort of question about her son! And so she happily answered, using all the vocabulary she knew. She got the job.

Of course, I have no way of verifying to what extent this story was actually true. What is interesting for the purposes of this paper, however, is not so much whether the story was *true*, but the fact that Allison was so happy about telling it. It is difficult to imagine anyone getting a bilingual teaching job—or any teaching job—in the U.S., if all they can talk about in *English* is sippy-cups and diapers. In Allison's mind, however, it was perfectly fine to apply for and obtain a job that involved giving academic instruction in Spanish, while knowing full well that her Spanish was quite limited. One wonders how well she would have been able to actually *do* this job. But this question clearly did not impinge upon her enjoyment of the story.

Though clearly emphasizing that she had not grown up in a Spanish-speaking family or community, and had instead learned Spanish as an adult in California, Allison also frequently made a point of stating that she had "never taken a Spanish class." It seemed like an odd thing to make public assertions about, in the context of running a bilingual school. It certainly is not possible to be a public school teacher in the U.S.—much less a school director – if one has "never taken an English class." And it would be strange indeed to see a U.S. educational institution—again, bilingual or otherwise—in which one director spoke no English, another could speak English but had no formal education in the language, English spelling and writing conventions were neither here nor there, and students didn't even have to bother learning English if they weren't really "into it." All this is to point out that, despite the "dual immersion" label, English and Spanish did not have anything close to equal status at Urban Renaissance. English had authority-via-anonymity; Spanish did not.

But if Spanish was not afforded anonymity-value within the context of Urban Renaissance, this did not mean the language was simply de-valued, or value-less. Rather, Spanish possessed and provided a different type of value: authenticity value. Let us recall Woolard's definition of authenticity: the ideology of linguistic authenticity "locates the value of a language [or language-variety] in its relationship to a particular community. That which is authentic is viewed as the genuine expression of such a community, or of an essential Self." Recall also the colloquial connotations: *authentic* is natural, uncontrived. Real.

If English was (required) for *everyone*, Spanish was of and for a particular group of people. Who were these people? Were they defined by ethnicity—Mexicans, Mexican-Americans, Chicanos, Latinos? Not necessarily, in fact. The use of Spanish within the context of Urban Renaissance *could* in some cases be taken as indexical of ethnic identity, but I'm going to suggest that Allison's use of Spanish— and, in particular, a specific "type" of Spanish—was intended to index something else about herself and her school. The indexical value of Spanish, for Allison, lay in its association with what Woolard calls "the soulful streets of the urban ghetto or *barrio*, where the real folks are said to be busy 'keepin' in real.'" Throughout the years of Urban Renassiance's existence, there had been several charges—some from teachers employed at the institution—that the charter school, despite being geographically located in the "ghetto," did not really understand or respond to the perspectives and needs of the students and families living there. Allison had become very invested in demonstrating that, although she was distinctly not from an "urban ghetto or barrio," she bore a true (authentic) connection to those who were.

Rather than encourage the use—let alone the explicit teaching—of a "standard" academic version of Spanish, Allison preferred to use "street" Spanish, and to reject Spanish usages that she thought sounded formal or official. During one staff meeting, for example, she asked whether anyone knew how to say "light switch" in Spanish. One teacher offered "interruptor." Although no other word was supplied, Allison refused to take up the offer of "interruptor." Instead she made a face and repeated—with a type of vari-directional double-voicing indicating a rejection of the word as too formal and therefore not a truly authentic lexical item—"¿¿*Interruptor??*"

Allison frequently used vari-directional double-voicing to indicate her rejection of a particular linguistic form or utterance. When, on one occasion, a teacher used the word "amamantando," meaning "breast-feeding," Allison later repeated this expression with vari-directional double-voicing, drawing a verbal caricature of snooty scientific formality.

Within this context, the school director's statement, "I've never taken a Spanish class" becomes, not a confession, but a sort of boast. What she asserted with this statement, I suggest, was that she had learned *real*, authentic Spanish in the real, authentic way, rather than in the inauthentic context of an academic course.

While English held authority-via-anonymity at Urban Renaissance, Spanish was not afforded any anonymity-value; however, it did possess a potential authenticity-value, upon which one could draw in order to assert the legitimacy of one's connection to the "ghetto/barrio" environment in which Urban Renaissance had placed itself. Bucholtz's (2003) definition of *authentication* becomes useful in describing Allison's use of Spanish. Authentication, says Bucholtz, "is instantiated through the assertion of one's own or another's identity as genuine or credible"; the opposite of authentication is *denaturalization*, "the phenomenon whereby an identity is held up as inauthentic or unreal" (Bucholtz, 2003, pp. 408-409). As a wealthy Anglo running a bilingual school in a "ghetto/barrio" environment, Allison used strategies of linguistic authentication to authorize herself and her school as appropriate mediators of life and learning in the Central Focus Area.

More on Indexicality: Anonymous Bodies, Authentic Names

Two brief stories about names:

(1)

The first person one would encounter upon entering the Urban Renaissance building was the front office receptionist, a Mexican American woman in her late twenties or early thirties, whose name was spelled M-A-R-Y. This woman had been working at Urban Renaissance for several years, and played a vital role in the school's day-to-day operations. Everyone associated with Urban Renaissance pronounced her name as in Spanish: *Mari*. When I began working at the school, Allison introduced this woman to me—as to everyone—as *Mari*.

Hence, I assumed that her name was to be pronounced as *Mari*. This Spanish pronunciation of the receptionist's name was used by everyone, regardless of whether it was in the context of an English utterance ("Where is *Mari* today?") or a Spanish utterance ("¿Dónde está *Mari* hoy?"). Speakers who could not or would not pronounce the Spanish "r" still kept the "ah" sound of *Mari*, rather than use the English pronunciation *Mary*. None of this seemed the least bit odd to me, since I assumed that everyone at Urban Renaissance was pronouncing, or attempting to pronounce, this woman's name the way she herself wanted it pronounced. One day, however, I heard this woman introducing herself to a group of visitors: "My name is *Mary*." Upon hearing the Anglicized version of the name, I assumed that Mary/Mari felt pressured to alter the pronunciation of her name in order to accommodate the visitors, a group of monolingual Anglophone men in suits. Later, however, I learned (from a teacher's assistant who had known Mari/Mary for many years because the two belonged to the same close-knit church community) that in fact this woman did indeed call herself *Mary*, her parents had named her *Mary*, her family members all called her *Mary*, her church members and other personal friends called her *Mary* … in short, everyone in this woman's life, outside of Urban Renaissance, called her *Mary*. Her name was *Mary*. In the context of Urban Renaissance, however, Allison had seen fit to re-name her *Mari*.

(2)

One young teacher, hired at Urban Renaissance the same year I started working there, was named E-V-A. Everyone at Urban Renaissance used the Spanish pronunciation for her name, *Eva*. One day, at a faculty meeting, this teacher raised her hand to make a comment, and Allison called on her using the English pronunciation of her name, with long "e," *Eeva*. Actually, Allison stated the woman's full name, as follows: "*Eeva—Montes—Matthews*." These three names were pronounced with vari-directional double-voicing, in a manner indicating that Allison was ironically quoting something or someone. She then explained, in the tone of an insider who both understood and disowned the fact, "That's what it says on your answering machine – 'You have reached *Eeva—Montes—Matthews*.'"

"Well," the teacher replied, "that is my name."

This teacher was one of those who (again like me) left at the end of the year. She took a new job at a different school. Another teacher, Jessica, also left at the same time and found work at the same school as Eva/Eeva. I ran into Jessica at a conference the following year, and we chatted for a while. Then, knowing that Eva/Eeva was working at the same school as Jessica, I asked, "So, is Eva here?"

"Yeah, she's around here somewhere," Jessica replied, then added abruptly, "Do you know her name is *Eeva*?"

"*Eeva*?" I repeated the English pronunciation.

"Yes, that's her name, *Eeva*. She was only called *Eva* at Urban Renaissance. You know," she added somewhat bitterly, "that's how it was there. Allison thought it sounded more ... *Latina*."

I include these two stories here because they illustrate a further point about the strategies of authentication practiced at Urban Renaissance. To explain what I mean here, I will first suggest that a name is the single most obvious point at which language meets the body. A name functions as an index of the person who inhabits a particular body.

Note that only Latina bodies were subject to the sort of re-labeling practices described above. None of the Anglo teachers' names were changed at Urban Renaissance. Only Latina teachers, such as Eva and Mary, were re-named by Allison. Note also that this re-labeling took place in both languages—in other words, the woman whose name was spelled "E-V-A" was *always* and *only* "Eva" at Urban Renaissance; she was not just "Eva" in the context of Spanish utterances and "Eeva" in the context of English. The re-labeling was also not a voluntary process—as demonstrated by these anecdotes, both of these employees continued to refer to *themselves* by their given names (with the given pronunciation), even after they had been re-labeled by Allison—and even after the entire school (including the students, who addressed teachers and other adults by first names) followed Allison's lead and proceeded to address both women by the Spanish versions of their names throughout the year (or, in Mary's case, for several years).

What was the point of this re-labeling of particular bodies? I would suggest that what was happening at Urban Renaissance might be read as a process of *sign-construction authentication*. In the context of a bilingual school environment in which Spanish has authenticity-value but no anonymity-value, and in which the founders and directors of the school are wealthy Anglos, the presence of Latina bodies at the school becomes a source of legitimacy for the program, since Latinas in such a context are "authentic" speakers of the authentic language. But in order for this legitimating process to work, these Spanish-speaking urban Latinas must have authentic Spanish names.

A Spanish-sounding name ("Eva," "Mari") serves as an icon for "Spanish" as a language; this is the first sign-relationship involved in the process I'm describing. When this iconic Spanish name indexes a Latina body, a second sign-relationship is created. The Latina teacher with a Spanish-sounding name is read as an *authentic* Spanish speaker. Then, through the creation of a third sign-relationship, the authentic speaker becomes an icon representing the school itself. This whole process is what I'm calling "sign-construction authentication." These various iconic and indexical relationships between name, language, body, and school served an authentication function for Urban Renaissance.

Naturally I am not implying that this process was planned or premeditated by anyone. Rather, I am suggesting that the notion of sign-construction authentication can function as a helpful analytic for making sense of the apparently senseless practice of a school director re-naming her employees.

Language, Education, and Social Justice

Founded during the post-227 era, when ELL students were being subjected to subtractive "English Only" submersion programs, the bilingual Urban Renaissance could easily be read as a social justice project. At the same time, the language ideologies in operation at the school distinctly reflected and perpetuated linguistic *injustice*. The problem was not just that the school claimed to be operating a "Dual Immersion" program even though the instructional model did not fit any recognized educational definition of dual immersion. It was also that English and Spanish were assigned completely different roles and statuses. English was afforded "anonymity" value, while Spanish was a marked language that was afforded value only through "authenticity," and was policed for adherence to particular notions of authenticity, so that it could be deployed in the service of conferring a particular type of authenticity on the school itself. This compartmentalization of languages and their functions was clearly more detrimental to students from Spanish-speaking families than to those from English-speaking families. Further, the fact that these language ideologies were forcibly plastered onto the racialized and gendered bodies of particular *teachers* raises alarming questions about what these ideologies "do" to small *children* who inhabit racially-marked bodies within such spaces.

In conclusion, let me reiterate that these are the observations of a teacher. As a bilingual teacher, I am in no way opposed to the idea that education in and through two (or more) languages can be an important tool for promoting social justice. Unfortunately, bilingual education—like monolingual education—can also reinscribe language ideologies that promote social injustice. Researchers in education and applied linguistics have alerted us to the potential benefits and the potential dangers of dual-language immersion in particular. In 1997—just a few years before Urban Renaissane was founded—Guadalupe Valdes issued an important "cautionary note" regarding dual-immersion. Valdes noted that while dual-immersion, like other forms of bilingual education, can be a successful and beneficial model, it also runs the risk of reproducing some of the same inequities (along intersecting lines of language, income, and race) commonly observed in monolingual school settings. We should also note that, while dual immersion is an increasingly popular educational model, it is also a completely unregulated term. Most parents are not well-versed in bilingual education research; most families do not know about the CAL directory or the scholarly definition of dual immersion. If a school's promotional materials—as in the case of Urban Renaissance Charter—proclaim that the school is "Dual Immersion," then parents are likely to believe that dual immersion education is what their children will be getting if they choose that school.

Given the fact that legitimate dual immersion programs still run the risk of reproducing social and linguistic inequity, along with the fact that families choosing schools for their children are subject to the type of "false advertising" use of the Dual Immersion label seen at Urban Renaissance, it is clear that more research and education are needed if the DI model is to realize its potential in terms of social and linguistic justice. The perspectives presented here suggest several directions for future research. To name just a few:

- *Race and racism in dual immersion programs.* There is a need for more research into how ideologies of language are interwoven with ideologies of race within the context of particular dual-language immersion school programs, with attention to how racialization shapes processes of language socialization in the classroom. How do racial assumptions and subtly racializing messages affect students' unfolding relationships to the languages of instruction? How can we better understand the unique challenges present in dual-immersion programs where linguistic identities (e.g. Spanish-mothertongue vs. English-mothertongue) are aligned with racial identities and economic categories (e.g. brown vs. white, working-class vs. middle class)? How, in such settings, might racial microaggressions and the racialization of language impact children of color whose dominant language is also the "minority" language? How might these children's affective relationships with their "minority" mothertongues be impacted by these types of school settings? Research should also examine the effects of racialized discourses, and particularly of racial microaggressions, upon *teachers* in such programs. Several young female teachers "of color" at Urban Renaissance complained that many of the wealthy Anglo parents treated them as service providers rather than as knowledgeable professionals. Some parents seemed to feel that they should interact with certain teachers in the same way they interacted with their children's nannies—issuing instructions, evaluating performance, interrupting instructional time with various demands, etc. One teacher simply complained: "They think they're *better* than us." This teacher, prior to joining the faculty of Urban Renaissance, had worked for several years in a dual-language program entirely devoted to serving low-income students of color, and noted that she had never faced this type of systematic disrespect from parents at her prior school. The behavior of many of the Anglo parents seemed to suggest that they had developed certain settled expectations about the types of interactions they should have with brown, Spanish-speaking women. We need to know more about how these racialized interactions, along with racial microaggressions and linguistic microaggressions (parents speaking "Mock Spanish," singing "La Cucaracha," etc.) affect teacher morale and consequently impact student outcomes.

- *Language varieties and the purposes of bilingualism.* It would be helpful to have more site-specific research examining the question of *which language varieties* are used in particular dual-immersion programs, what purposes are served by privileging those particular varieties, and what the benefits and drawbacks are for the different constituencies involved. Again, this question is not "about dual-language immersion" per se; issues of language variety are handled differently in different settings, hence the need for situated analyses of particular dual-language school-community sites. In the case of Urban Renaissance, Allison's reification of "street" Spanish as authentic language prompts us to ask *whose interests were being prioritized* in the program: While Anglophone students could potentially experience a sort of extra-curricular additive value by learning "street" Spanish at Urban Renaissance, Spanish-speaking students did not need to attend a bilingual school in order to learn "street" Spanish. The lack of attention to academic Spanish raises the question of just what the Spanish-speaking students were actually gaining linguistically by attending Urban Renaissance. On the other hand, teachers in some dual-language programs may find that an over-emphasis upon "standard" language is detrimental within the specific circumstances of their schools, or that stakeholders do not even agree upon what exactly constitutes the proper academic standard for the languages in question—hence the need for critical site-specific inquiries in this regard.

- *Bilingual models and terminologies.* I have noted that Urban Renaissance used the "Dual Immersion" label but did not actually employ the instructional model designated (in research-based educational literature) by this label. I have also noted that both personal observations and quantitative measures (e.g. test scores) point to the failure of Urban Renaissance to actually inculcate meaningful bilingualism and bi-literacy in most of the students enrolled. At the same time, anecdotal evidence suggests that there are some bilingual programs that depart from the standard models of dual-language instruction *and are successful.* Again, this anecdotal evidence points to the need for site-specific research. Why and how might particular programs depart from the standard models, and what types of outcomes do these programs produce? What specific conditions necessitate departures from the standard models, and what are the benefits and drawbacks for the specific communities being served? It would also be useful to have some broad-based studies that examine the ways in which particular terminologies around bilingual education ("dual immersion," "two-way immersion," "developmental," "foreign language immersion," and even "bilingual" itself) are currently being used, misused, strategically reconfigured, contested, etc., in actual school environments.

To address these types of questions, we need *sustained, site-specific, detail-oriented* research into everyday life in schools and classrooms that implement—or claim to implement—dual language immersion (and other bilingual instruction of various sorts). I suggest that teachers be included as partners—not merely positioned as objects of study or as ethnographic informants—in this research. A teacher's observations at a school site do not necessary qualify as ethnography (unless the teacher is also a trained ethnographer and has IRB approval); nevertheless, these observations can provide uniquely valuable information about—among other things—how a particular model is functioning in terms of day-to-day practice. Teachers have important theoretical insights and substantive knowledge about the work we do every day. Scholars should take these insights seriously, and make a space within the research community for teachers to present our perspectives *on our own terms*; a teacher's insights need not be interpolated into or subsumed under the project or agenda of some other "researcher" who has more official status as such. My hope is not only that these observations about language ideologies will be of use to teachers and other scholars working to promote social justice through multilingual education, but that they will also demonstrate that an essay by a teacher can make an important contribution to the world of theory.

Notes
1. Founded in 1989 by Wendy Kopp, Teach For America recruits recent college graduates to teach for two years in under-resourced urban and rural schools. Kopp initially outlined the idea for such a program in her undergraduate honors thesis in sociology at the Woodrow Wilson School of Public and International Affairs at Princeton University. The idea behind the program is not to recruit trained teachers for the schools in question, but to attract recent graduates who might not otherwise have considered teaching; these graduates are to be enticed into the two-year teaching commitments by the idea of becoming part of an elite "corps" of young people whose mission is to—in the organization's words—"lead an educational revolution in low-income communities across the country" (Teach For America website, http://www.teachforamerica.org/our-mission, accessed 3/30/2014). Kopp, a member of Princeton's *Business Today,* garnered support from Union Carbide, Morgan Stanley, and Mobil Corporation in order to launch the project described in her thesis ("How Teach For American Became So Powerful," *The Washington Post,* 10/22/2012, http://www.washingtonpost.com/blogs/answer-sheet/wp/2012/10/22/how-teach-for-america-became-powerful-2/). Teach For America "corps members" receive five weeks of training during the summer prior to starting employment, and are then placed in teaching positions in districts across the country. Analysts point out that this process entails the displacement of experienced, credentialed teachers in order to make room for the "corps members"—a situation which creates opportunities for the corps members themselves (who often use their two-year experience with the organization as a launch-pad for profitable careers in business, government, and other fields), but is detrimental to students and to the teaching profession. Critics also point out that the organization promotes a narrative of public school failure which encourages the privatization of public education, and that many of the organization's most prominent "alumni" are heavily involved in school privatization (Kretchmar et al., "Mapping the terrain: Teach For America, charter school reform, and corporate sponsorship." *Journal of Education Policy,* February 2014). The founder-directors of Urban Renaissance were Teach For America corps members in the mid-1990s; hence, scholarly critiques of *current* Teach For America policies and discourses are not necessarily relevant to a discussion of Urban Renaissance. It is worth noting, however, that the Urban Renaissance founder-directors were heavily invested in a narrative of failure regarding the local district schools, frequently asserting that the neighborhood schools were

"bad" (this was the word Allison used) and promoting a heroic image of Urban Renaissance Charter as saving children from these (in Allison's words again) "bad schools."

2. CAL's criteria for Dual Language Immersion include "Integration: Language-minority and language-majority students are integrated for at least 60% of instructional time (and ideally more) at all grade levels" and "Instruction: Content and literacy instruction in English and the partner language is provided to all students, and *all students receive instruction in the partner language at least 50% of the instructional day at all grade levels.*" (CAL Two-Way Immersion Homepage, http://www.cal.org/twi/ Accessed 2013—7-31.) The program at Urban Renaissance did not meet these guidelines.

References

Bourdieu, P. (1982). *Ce que parler veut dire: L'économie des échanges linguistiques* [What speaking means: The economy of linguistic exchanges]. Paris: Fayard.

Bourdieu, P. (1991). *Language and symbolic power.* Cambridge, MA: Harvard University Press.

Bucholtz, M. (2003). Sociolinguistic nostalgia and the authentication of identity. *Journal of Sociolinguistics, 7*(3), 398-416.

Hill, J. H. (1995). Mock Spanish: A site for the indexical reproduction of racism in American English. *Language & Culture: Symposium 2.* Retrieved from http://language-culture.binghamton.edu/symposia/2/part1/

Hill, J. H. (2008). Language, race, and white public space. *American Anthropologist, 100*(3), 680-689.

Valdes, G. (1997). Dual-language immersion programs: A cautionary note regarding the education of language-minority students. *Harvard Educational Review, 67*(3), 391-429.

Woolard, K. A. (1998). Language ideology as a field of inquiry. In B. Schieffelin, K. Woolard and P. Kroskrity (Eds.), *Language ideologies: Practice and theory* (pp. 3-47). New York: Oxford University Press.

Woolard, K. A. (2008). Language and identity choice in Catalonia: The interplay of contrasting ideologies of linguistic authority. In K. Süselbeck, U. Mühlschelegel and P. Masson (Eds.), *Lengua, nación e identidad: La regulación del plurilingüismo en España y América Latina* [Language, nation and identity: The regulation of pluralingualism in Spain and Latin America], (pp. 303-324). Madrid: Iberoamericana.

CHAPTER 2

DIFFERENCES IN EXPRESSIONS OF SOCIAL JUSTICE EVIDENCED IN COLLEGE STUDENTS' FABLES

Bettina Murray
City University of New York

Objectives

Reports indicate that linguistically diverse students face unusual challenges meeting literacy requirements (Abbate-Vaughn, 2009; ACT, 2006; Lo Bianco, 2003). Numerous researchers contend that instruction is especially effective when it becomes "culturally relevant" and connects the curriculum to students' historical traditions (Carmmarota, 2007; Delgado-Bernal, 2002). Study objectives were to examine the differences in students' expressions of social justice and to empower the students through increased self-expression and engagement with literacy.

Theoretical Framework

This study was founded on critical pedagogy (Freire, 1970, 1973; Giroux, 2009), theories of social constructivism (Vygotsky, 1978), and ethnic epistemology (Delgado-Bernal, 2002; Sleeter, 2012). Critical educators believe that the educational system has the power to strongly influence students' thinking processes and to enable them to have greater control of their own destiny. These pedagogues maintain that education is not neutral but a source of constant struggle over what is considered to be a valid and legitimate source of knowledge (Freire, 1973). Social constructivists emphasize the importance of social interaction and stress the process by which learners are assimilated into the entire learning community (Vygotsky, 1978). Ethnic epistemology is an extension of critical and social constructivist philosophy which supports learning strategies that focus on social justice issues and are based upon students' personal experiences and cultural knowledge (Gonzalez, Moll & Amanti, 2005). This philosophy fosters student self-empowerment and the enhancement of literacy skills through the use of culturally relevant strategies (Delgado-Bernal, 2002). Paris (2012) takes this approach a step further and argues that in order to achieve a "culturally sustaining pedagogy" students should be involved in meaningful social justice activities not only within their classrooms but also within their communities.

Participants

The majority of the participants were college freshmen and sophomores who had come right out of high school to pursue a four year college degree and they were the first generation in their family to attend college. Sixty percent of the participants were female. Students were placed into a required communication course because they had failed the college entrance test in reading. The communications course concentrated on college literacy skills and critical thinking. Approximately 47% of the students had resided in the United States for 17 or more years. Over 86% of the students directly experienced economic hardship and received federal or state financial aid through either the Tuition Assistance Program (TAP) or Search for Education, Elevation and Knowledge (SEEK) program which provides state aid to students based on their taxable income or that of their families if living at home. The Pell Grant, which is a federal needs-based grant, also financially assisted dependents whose family income met the low-income requirements. In most cases financial assistance covered all of the students' expenses. The college was located in a large urban setting, and in addition to a minimum college course load of 12 credits, approximately 30% of the students held part time jobs. The participants were from diverse regions of origin with 55% of the group stating in the survey that they were Hispanic and that Spanish was their first language, even though 6 of these students said they were born in the United States (Appendix 2A). In addition to the students born in the United States who identified themselves as Hispanic, there were groups of students whose primary language was Spanish from Mexico (5), the Caribbean (47) and Central or South America (14) (Appendix 2A). These 72 Spanish-speaking students were referred to in this study as Hispanic and fit the description of this term used by the 2010 United States Census Bureau. The 2010 U.S. Census Bureau uses the term Hispanic to refer to a person of Cuban, Mexican, Puerto Rican, South or Central American or other Spanish culture regardless of race. The Spanish-speaking students in this study match this description of Hispanic. Students from the continent of Asia (33) represented the second largest region of origin for the student participants (Appendices 2A and 2B).

Research Questions

The researcher, who was the professor, had noted over a period of years that the students in the communications courses represented many cultures and countries. Upon observation of the students' short stories the researcher was interested in the diversity of topics presented and the students' varied interpretations of social justice issues. The fable writing exercise commenced initially as a creative writing lesson in which students were encouraged to draw their own conclusions about situations that might prove to illustrate a lesson or moral. (Appendix 2C). Numerous pedagogues maintain that student learning is fostered when individual expression is stimulated and students are encouraged to draw upon their prior cultural and linguistic experiences (Carreira, 2004; Kondo-Brown, 2010; Rodriquez, 2010).

1. Did students express concerns about social justice issues in their fables and, if so, what were these expressions?
2. If students expressed concerns about social justice issues, were these expressions related to their cultural and linguistic heritage or to the length of time they had been in the United States?
3. Did the creative exercise of writing short fables appear to stimulate the students' self-expression?

Procedures

The researcher, a professor in the communications program, conducted a survey with the students which asked them a number of demographic questions primarily related to their family origins and linguistic heritage. Students regions of origin according to their self-descriptions are indicated in Appendices 2A and 2B. Students were introduced to the elements of the fable genre (Calkins, Ehrenworth, Khan, Mooney; 2010; Kimbell-Lopez, 1999) at the commencement of a three month semester. Examples of fables were given from many cultures (Ashliman, Jones & Rackman, 2003; La Fontaine, 2002; Zipes, 1992). After initial instruction students were required to write their own unique fable that ended with some kind of ethical principle or lesson they wished to impart to the reader (Appendix 2C). The researcher and her two assistants, who were adjunct professors in the same program, categorized the fables according to the topics and lessons they discussed. A statistical procedure (the Shure factor as cited in Tuckman, 1999) was used to establish an objective level of agreement between the professors. An inner rater-reliability of 90% was attained. Students wrote about numerous topics which were separated under several general headings: stories relating to family issues, the rewards of hard work, instances where assistance was received from unexpected sources, the problems of greed and excessive ambition, the consequences of having too much or too little confidence, the results of poor decision making, and the problems of being deceived by appearances.

Topics on subjects related to social justice were very popular, although quite varied, with approximately 1/2 of the class expressing concerns on themes related to this subject. Fables that were identified as having social justice topics fell into the following categories: feelings of prejudice, acts of discrimination, dealing with inner moral struggle, wrestling with attitudes of equity or revenge, coping with economic hardship and dealing with negative influences. In this study, feelings of prejudice were expressed as sentiments of dislike for a person or group because of race, sex, or religion (*Prejudice*, Merriam-Webster, 2013), whereas acts of discrimination described the actual practice of unfairly treating a person or groups of people differently from other people or groups of people (*Discrimination*, Merriam-Webster, 2013).

Fables that dealt with inner moral struggles illustrated issues where the protagonist was engaged in an inner battle before making the choice between what was considered to be right or wrong. Situations that illustrated dealing with poverty and lack of food or shelter fell under the category of coping with economic hardships. Concerns about falling under the effects of negative influences contained stories in which individuals were influenced by bullying, drugs and/or alcohol, gangs, or simply got into trouble for not obeying their parents. Appendix 2B further defines the most frequently used social justice categories and provides an additional overview of students regions of origins. The results section of this paper provides samples of the students' fables.

Upon the completion of their fables, students were asked to mention where they or their families were from and to share their stories with their classmates. They were also encouraged to discuss the lesson they posed at the conclusion of their fables and to state the reason it was important to them. At the completion of the three-month semester students were given a questionnaire in which they were asked to write their reactions to the fables exercise. Appendix 2D provides samples of these student reactions to the fables exercise.

Data Sources

Students' region of origin, choice of topic, and the lesson or moral of each fable were analyzed through the use of the data gathered from students in the initial survey. Predictive Analytics Software (PASW) was used to conduct frequency analyses and Chi-square tests were used to examine research questions one and two (Table 2.1). Chi square tests were specifically computed to study the categories of social justice, students' region of origin, and being Spanish-speaking or being in the United States for seventeen years or more. Students written responses to the fable writing were gathered, and their reactions to the sharing of their fables with classmates were noted.

Results

Chi square tests determined that the overall category of Social Justice and its components; prejudice, discrimination, economic hardship and negative influences were associated with region of origin and being Spanish-speaking or being in the United States for seventeen years or more. Being in the United States seventeen years or more was associated with increased use of the Social Justice topics of discrimination ($p=.03$) and economic hardship ($p=.05$). Spanish-speaking participants were more likely to use topics of prejudice ($p=.005$) and negative influences ($p=.01$) than non-Spanish-speaking participants (Table 2.1).

The results shown in Table 2.1 suggest the word "prejudice" may be more linguistically and culturally meaningful to the Spanish-speaking participants (Paris, 2011), just as "discrimination" connotes a specific meaning to long term residents of the United States. Drug abuse and bullying are cited as examples of negative influences in the Hispanic population in the United States (Science Daily, 2007).

Table 2.1

Presence of topics associated with being in the United States for seventeen years or more and being Spanish-speaking

TOPIC	n^a (%) USA 17+ Years	n^a (%) Not USA 17+ Years	χ^2	df, N	p
Discrimination	6 (9.8)	1 (1.4)	4.56	1, 131	.03
Economic Hardship	7 (11.5)	2 (2.9)	3.78	1, 131	.05
	Spanish-speaking	Non-Spanish-speaking			
Prejudice	14 (19.4)	2 (3.4)	7.80	1, 131	.005
Negative Influences	8 (11.1)	0 (0.0)	6.64	1, 128	.01

Note. ^{a} indicates the number of students using the topic

Supporting Explanation of Study Results Section
Significant Topics Expressed by the Group of Students in the USA 17 Years or More

Discrimination. Six out of the seven students who expressed concern over discrimination (*p*=.03) were born in the United States. Further research is needed to determine if students who grew up and were educated in the United Sates might be more familiar with the word *discrimination* and had heard the topic discussed in school. These students' fables described situations where people in authority had acted in a discriminatory way or particular individuals were targeted by the police or airport security to receive negative treatment.

The following are example excerpts from fables from students who were born in the United States. These students were products of the American School system.

Male student expresses concern about discrimination due to *color*:

It was Saturday night in the Bronx and I was walking home from my girlfriend's house. I saw a black man driving a yellow Hummer. A police car and the yellow Hummer stopped at the same time at the light in front of me. The policemen in the squad car saw a black man driving the Hummer so they stopped him. They asked the guy in the Hummer for his driver's license, and they looked over the entire car. They could find nothing. People get discriminated against because of their color.

Male student expresses concern about discrimination *because of his looks*:

There was a town in New York where rats had long pointy tails. Every rat in the town had the same physical features. A small rabbit lived there that had big blue eyes, no tail, sharp claws and a deep voice. The rats would go around eating the rabbit's food and knock his home down and steal his personal things. Then they decided to kill the rabbit and loot his place again. The rats told the others that they killed the rabbit because of his looks and said that anyone who didn't look like them didn't belong. Sometimes differences cause resentment and unfair treatment.

Female student born in the United States expresses concern about discrimination by authority figures due to *how they look*:

A group of guys went to the airport in their regular clothes. The security there didn't know that they were soldiers going home on vacation. The one guy who looks like an Arab gets stopped and had to show everything in his luggage and clothes. He shows them his ID and he says, "I love this country." They say "sorry, we didn't know that." You cannot tell how a person feels by how they look.

Economic Hardships. These students were also more likely to portray situations of economic hardship ($p=.05$). Further research is needed to determine if longer-term residents in the United States are sensitive to issues relating to poverty as they have been more exposed to the challenges and contrasts of economic and class structure in American society. Several students referred in their fables to the loss of home, job or even lack of food. Aries and Seider (2005) maintain that lower income students struggle with feelings of powerlessness and exclusion in both elite and state colleges.

The following are example excerpts from fables from students who were born in the United States. These students were products of the American School system.

Male student expresses concern that *some people need to get along on very little*:

> It was a hot sunny day and all the animals in the kingdom were so thirsty and they could not find any drinking water. The lion on the other hand was guarding a little puddle of water just for him to drink and not to share with anyone else. After an hour passed there was half of the water he began with, the lion started to cry. A monkey came over to him and asked him, "What is the matter?" The lion told him that he only has half a puddle left. The monkey said all the animals in the kingdom wish they could have just one drop. Some people need to get along on very little, other people need a lot.

Female student expresses concern that *she knew the hardships of poverty*:

> A husband and a wife had been married for over 25 years. They loved each other dearly. But at this time in their marriage, the husband lost his job, and the wife was the only one supporting the family. The husband felt useless. His heart would ache watching his beloved tired from work. One day the wife's relative came with news that her mother left her over $25,000. The couple was so happy. The husband took some money to buy lots of stuff instead of paying the back rent. He brought more and more with his wife's permission. She could not say no to the love of her life even though she knew the hardships of poverty and was afraid they would live on the streets. The money went lower and lower. There was nothing left but for the wife to work hard for the family again. Hang on to what you can get, money has a way of disappearing.

Female student states *watch out or you will always be poor*:

> One day the frog found out that he was getting a check in the mail and decided he wanted to go shopping. He had been pretty poor and lived in a shabby dwelling in a dirty swamp. The lion kept telling him don't spend the money until you have it. The frog didn't listen and borrowed money from all his friends and promised he would pay them all back. The frog went out and spent hundreds of dollars. As time went on the frog never got his check. He called and told the bank, and they said he wasn't receiving a check that it must have been a mistake. He was so upset that he didn't listen to the lion. How was he going to pay back his friends? Now he's back in the shabby hole. Watch out or you will always be poor.

Significant Topics Expressed by the Group of Spanish Speaking Students

Prejudice. Fourteen out of sixteen students described issues concerning situations of prejudice significantly more ($p=.005$) than did the non-Spanish-speaking group. Data from a random survey (N=2,081) conducted by the University of Wisconsin (2003) on attitudes about race and American identity found that 84% of the Hispanics surveyed felt that prejudice in favor of Whites caused the Whites to have an advantage in society.

Although the words prejudice and discrimination are often used interchangeably, Spanish-speaking students in this college study wrote fables involving incidents of prejudice and the use of the word *prejudice* with greater frequency ($p=.005$) than did non-Spanish-speaking students. The Pew Center reported that 60% of Hispanics surveyed in 2010 believe that prejudice and discrimination against them is a major problem, up from 54% in 2007 (Wides-Munoz, 2010). Further research is needed to determine the root causes of prejudice perceived by Spanish-speaking students.

The following are example excerpts of fables written by the Spanish-speaking students:

Female student from Puerto-Rico expresses concern over treatment of Hispanics and *illegal immigrants*:

> *There was a fancy girl who only had white friends. She went to a school with Hispanics and black people, but she hung out with the white people because she came from a family that only had white friends. Some of her white friends were friendly with the other kids, but she told them they were wasting their time. She told them that these people were a bunch of illegal immigrants and that they shouldn't talk to these people who didn't even speak correct English. One day she was walking in the street in the back of the school and a group of kids from all different backgrounds started punching her because of her attitude. This Hispanic guy by the name of Jose showed up and scared them off. She decided that all Hispanics were not so bad. Maybe we should give other people a chance.*

Male student, family from Puerto Rico, expresses concern over prejudiced treatment and says *to fall on prejudice is a shock*:

> *Once upon a time there was a black wolf who lost his way from his pack because of a bad snowstorm. He did not know where to go. While he searched for any kind of familiar scent, he heard a howl from afar. He howled back at them. He followed the howling until he came upon a pack of gray wolves that were relaxing in their*

habitat. One of the gray wolves heard the black wolf and approached him in a threatening manner. You don't howl just like us, you don't look just like us." The black wolf became frightened because all he wanted was some company. The gray wolf asked, "Does it look like any of your kind live here? Now leave or else!" The other gray wolves began growling at him. The black wolf was sad and left without a word. He had to travel alone never able to find his way back to his pack. To fall upon prejudice like this came as a shock. "It should be all right just to be a wolf, shouldn't it?" he said to himself.

Female student from the Dominican Republic says *jealousy and prejudice can be hurtful*:

Once upon a time there was a lioness named Sarahi who had beautiful hair that all other lionesses wanted. The other lionesses wanted to style and make their hair look as good as hers. Sarahi had a best friend name Marie. Marie was a tiger with attractive stripes across her body. Marie's mother said stay away from Sarahi, she is not from your kind. "That lioness may be pretty with wild hair but those animals are not as striking as we are. They want to be king of the jungle but they are just trying to take us over." When Marie returned home, she quickly went to the pharmacy and grabbed the ingredients needed for a hair die. With the recipe in the book she mixed the water, dirt and leaves. When she finished it, she went to Sarahi's house and gave it to Sarahi and told her that it would make her hair grow longer. The next day, Sarahi woke up and looked in the mirror. She had no hair and began to cry. Still she decided to go to school. As she walked into her class, the class looked shocked and whispered and laughed at her. Sarahi saw Marie pointing at her and laughing at her with the others. Sarahi was devastated because she realized Marie's mixture was what made her hair fall out. She knew Marie was jealous of her and was prejudiced about her because her mother said, "We have too many of that that kind of animal in this place already." Jealousy and prejudice can be hurtful.

Negative Influences. Spanish-speaking participants in this college study were extremely conscious of the negative influences ($p=.01$) in their environment that might adversely impact their success. Many of the Hispanics in this study live in poor urban environments where gangs and drug use are a constant danger. A 2011 report from the University of Michigan cited that 49% of Hispanic parents rated drug abuse as their greatest concern, and 37% of these parents surveyed also feared bullying. These concerns rated higher for the Hispanic population surveyed than it did for the Whites or Blacks. Sociologist Scott Akins maintains that "substance abuse increases among recent Hispanic immigrants as they replace their traditional cultural beliefs with those of white Americans" (Science Daily, 2007, p. 1). The eight college students in this study who were concerned about the consequences of negative influences were Spanish-speaking ($p=.01$). Although a higher percentage of the students in the study were female (60%), it is interesting to note that six out of eight of the students who wrote about negative influences in their fables were female. Further current research is suggested to determine why Spanish-speaking college women in this study were more likely than men to express concern over negative influences.

Female Spanish-speaking student from Puerto-Rico expresses concern about bullying and says *if you are really tough, you are tough inside*:

> *Buba was an elephant bully. He thought since he was so big he could bully everyone. He would always tease the other animals by calling them wimps, making fun of their size and by spraying water on them with his trunk. Then one day a small mouse who was tired of being picked on screeched loudly at Buba in a shrill way. Buba looked all over before he saw the little mouse. When he saw the mouse he ran up on top of a boulder and shouted "go away." The mouse said now you know what it is like to be bullied. You may act big and tough but the smallest thing can scare you. You are really tough when you are tough inside.*

Female Spanish-speaking student, family from the Dominican Republic, expresses concern about negative influences and says *stay away from bad people*:

> *In the Bronx, NY, there was a girl name Sharlene. She lived in a burgundy building on the third floor. Sharlene was sixteen and a freshman in high school. The only problem with her was that she always wanted to hang out with kids that were older that her and they were always bad influences. One Friday night Sharlene's friend Brianna invited her to a party. They were both desperate to go, but little did they know that at the party everyone was between the ages of eighteen and twenty. Sharlene told her mother she was going to stay at Brianna's house. When they arrived at the party nothing seemed to be right. A real big fight broke out and the party had just started. Then the five boys fought at the scene, but the party continued. Sharlene and Brianna still stayed at the party. Every time Sharlene's mother called her she would run out of the party and tell her that she was fine and that she would go home in an hour. While the girls finally walked out of the building at 2:00am in the morning the boys that had the fight were downstairs with guns. They shot everyone who exited the building. Sharlene got shot in her*

torso. Her friend got shot in the knee and her shoulder. The mother got the call from Lincoln Hospital, she was devastated. Stay away from bad people. Bad people cause bad things to happen.

Female Spanish-speaking student from South America says *watch who you hang out with*:

Once upon a time there was a rabbit that had two friends that were troublemakers. They would steal carrots from other rabbits, break into houses and sell the stolen carrots so they can buy their drugs. The rabbit on the other hand was a good rabbit. He never stole from anybody, broke into their houses and never took any food from them to feed any habits. All he did was hangout with these two bad rabbits. The other rabbits from the village automatically thought bad about him. Every time the rabbit would walk to the park the other rabbits would walk away from him or would try to keep their children from talking to him. The rabbit was upset that he was playing alone and decided to go home. Along the way the rabbit would think, "Why is it that nobody likes me?" Why is it that nobody lets their kids play with me?" After a while the rabbit came to the conclusion that his friends were giving him a bad name. So he decided that he wouldn't hang out with them. Instead he decided that he would help everybody around the village with their groceries and talk to the other rabbits. Little by little everybody trusted him. He became the happiest and best liked rabbit around the village when he went to the park everybody was there to play with him. If you want to get ahead in the world, watch who you hang out with.

Male Spanish-speaking student from Mexico says *if you hang out with the wrong crowd you will get into trouble*:

A boy named Adrian was always a good kid. He had a good childhood and never suffered until he started hanging with the wrong crowd. He thought he was cool by hanging with the gang bangers and drug users. Little did he think that the crowd he always followed never cared for him. One day he was with the crowd, they were all smoking weed outside a building, and he was just sitting there talking. They all saw a police car around the block and threw the blunt out but when the officer came to ask the kids questions, they all blamed Adrian. Adrian had also started to sell weed and he had two bags in this pockets, but he had forgotten about them. When the officers searched him, they took him in. He thought he had been cool, but he got arrested instead of all the others. Don't hang with the wrong crowd. It will catch up with you.

Overview of Student Observations as Stated on the Student Questionnaire

The fable writing exercise appeared to be received in a positive way by the majority of students. There were also frequent comments which indicated that students acquired new insights about their classmates when they shared their stories. Several expressed initial difficulty when trying to articulate their stories in English but stated that they felt more confidence in their ability to express themselves by the end of the semester. The overall responses to the student questionnaire asking students their reactions to the fable writing exercise were positive with 70% of the students saying they enjoyed the exercise. See Appendix 2D for examples of students' responses to the questionnaire.

Limitations

The study was limited due to the nature of the participants in a college setting and may vary in different settings. The nature of this research does not account for individual differences as students were categorized into groups according to general regions of origin, and dominant topics chosen from students' fables were then selected for further investigation.

Implications and Suggestions for Future Study

It appeared that Spanish-speaking students maintained particular concerns regarding their status as it pertained to social justice issues in the United States. It is possible that students from other linguistic backgrounds might reflect different concerns and interpretations of social justice as they perceive it from their culture. A future study might investigate this issue as it relates to students of varied linguistic cultures.

Scholarly Significance

Students from differing cultures were interested in social justice issues, but they used distinct expressions to identify these concerns. It is recommended that teachers become more sensitive to linguistic differences among students and assist learning by employing a culturally sustaining pedagogy which fosters activities that build from students' personal experiences and "funds of knowledge" (Gonzalez, Moll & Amanti, 2005). The fable genre appeared to empower students to further express themselves and discuss matters pertaining to their sense of ethics and fair treatment. This study supports proponents of critical pedagogy who maintain various modes of literacy and approaches to instruction should be embraced in a democratic society so students may achieve their highest potential.

References

Abbate-Vaughn, J. (2009). Addressing diversity. In Filippo, R. F., & Caverly, D. C. (Eds), *The handbook of college reading and study strategy research* (pp. 289-313). New York: Taylor Francis.

ACT. (2006). *Reading between the lines: What the ACT reveals about college readiness in reading.* Washington, DC: Author. Retrieved from http://www.act.org/research/policymakers/pdf/reading_report.pdf

Aldridge, M. (1997). *Critical thinking: Thinking with proverbs, reasoning by analogies.* New York: Kendall Hunt.

Aries. E., & Seider, M. (2005). The interactive relationship between class and identity and the college experience: The case of lower income students. *Qualitative Sociology, 28*(4), 419-443.

Ashliman, D. L., Jones, V. S., & Rackman, A. (2003). *Aesop's fables.* New York: Barnes and Noble Classic Series. (Original text *Aesop Fables* derives from V.S. Vernon Jones's edition published by W. Heineman, 1912)

Calkins, L., Ehrenworth, M., Khan, H. A., & Mooney, J. (2010). *Constructing curriculum* (pp. 242-255). Portsmouth, NH: Heinemann.

Cammarota, J. (2007). A social justice approach to achievement: Guiding Latina/o students toward education attainment with a challenging, socially relevant curriculum. *Equity & Excellence in Education, 40*(1), 87-96.

Carreira, M. (2004). Seeking explanatory adequacy: A dual approach to understanding the term "heritage language learner." *Heritage Language Journal, 2*(1), 1-25.

Delgado-Bernal, D. (2002). Critical race theory, Latino critical theory, and critical raced-gendered epistemologies: Recognizing students of color as holders and creators of knowledge. *Qualitive Inquiry, 8*(1), 105-126.

Discrimination. (n.d.). *Merriam-Webster.com.* Retrieved from http://www.merriam-webster.com/dictionary/discrimination

de la Fontaine, J. (2002). *Love & folly: Selected fables and tales of LaFontaine* (M. Ponsot, Trans.). New York: Welcome Rain Publishers.

Freire, P. (1970). *Pedagogy of the oppressed* (M. B. Ramos, Trans.). New York: The Seabury Press.

Freire, P. (1973). *Education for critical consciousness.* (M. B. Ramos, trans.) New York: Continuum Publishing.

Giroux, H. (2009). The attack on higher education and the necessity for critical pedagogy: In Macrine, S. (Ed.), *Critical pedagogy in uncertain times: Hopes and possibilities* (pp. 11-26). New York: Palgrave-Macmillan.

Gonzalez, N., Moll, L. C. & Amanti, C. (2005). *Funds of knowledge: Theorizing practice in households and classrooms.* Mahwah, NJ: Erlbaum.

Kimbell-Lopez, K. (1999). *Connecting with traditional literature: Using folktales, fables, and legends to strengthen students' reading and writing.* Needham Heights, MA: Allyn & Bacon.

Kondo-Brown, K. (2010). Curriculum development for advancing heritage language competence: Recent research, current practices, and a future agenda. *Annual Review of Applied Linguistics, 30,* 24-41.

Lo Bianco, J. (2003). Multiliteracies and multiculturalism. In Cope, B., & Kalanis, M. (Eds.), *Multiliteracies: Learning and the design of social futures* (pp. 92-105). New York: Routledge.

Paris, D. (2011). *Language across difference: Ethnicity, communication and youth identities in changing urban schools,* Cambridge: Cambridge, University Press.

Paris, D. (2012, April). Culturally sustaining pedagogy: A needed change in stance, terminology, and practice. *Educational Researcher, 41*(3), 93-97.

Prejudice. (n.d.). *Merriam-Webster.com.* Retrieved from http://www.merriamwebster.com/dictionary/prejudice

Rodriquez, D. (2010). Storytelling in the field: Race, method, and the empowerment of Latina college students. *Cultural Studies-Critical Methodologies, 10*(6), 491-507.

Science Daily. (2007, Aug. 13). *Hispanic drug use rises in US culture.* Retrieved from http://www.Sciencedaily/.com/releases/2007/08/070812173257.htm

Sleeter, C. (2012, May). Confronting the marginalization of culturally responsive pedagogy. *Urban Education,47,* 562-584.

Snyder, T. D., & Dillow, S. A. (2011). *Digest of education statistics* 2010 (NCES 2011-015). Washington, D.C.: U. S. Department of Education.

Tuckman, B. W. (199). *Conducting education research* (5th Ed.). Fort Worth, TX; Harcourt Brace.

United States Census Bureau. (2010). *Overview of race and Hispanic origin: 2010.* Washington, D. C.: Department of Commerce, Economics and Statistics Administration. Retrieved from http://www.census.gov/prod/cen2010/briefs/c2010br-02.pdf

University of Michigan Medical School. (2011, Aug. 15). Child health evaluation and research unit. Ann Arbor, MI: Author. Retrieved from http://www.uofmhealth.org/news/top-ten-national-poll-0815

University of Wisconson Survey Center. (2003). *The role of prejudice and discrimination in American's explanations of Black and disadvantaged White privilege.* Madison: University of Wisconsin. Retrieved from https://docs.google.com/viewer?a=v&q=cache:ktmilghGkRMJ:www.racialequitytools.org/resourcefiles/u

Vygotsky, L. S. (1978). *Mind in society: The development of higher psychological processes.* Cambridge, MA: Harvard University Press.

Wides-Munoz, L. (2010, Oct. 28). Hispanics increasingly fear immigration blacklash: Pew Hispanic Center. *Associated Press.* Retrieved from http://www.salon.com/2010/10/28/us-hispanics-immigration/

Appendix 2A

Students' Regions of Origin
Based on Students Self-Description

Regions of Origin	Spanish Speaking	Non-Spanish Speaking	Students/ Percentage
North American (NA)			13 / 9.9%
United States Spanish Speaking	6		
United States Non-Spanish Speaking		2	
Mexico	5		
Caribbean (CAR)			54 / 41.3%
Dominican Republic	35		
Puerto Rico	12		
Haiti		4	
Jamaica		2	
Antigua		1	
African (anyplace on the African continent) (AFR)			4 / 3.0%
Ghana		2	
Egypt		2	
Asian (A)			33 / 25.2%
India		3	
China		23	
Bangladesh		1	
Korea		2	
Hong Kong		2	
Viet Nam		2	
Central/South American (C-SA) (countries south of Mexico and the mainland)			16 / 12.2%
Peru	3		
Ecuador	7		
Belize		1	
Guyana		1	
Columbia	4		
European (Eur) (includes Eastern Europe)			11 / 8.4%
Poland		2	
Italy		2	
Russia		3	
Albania		1	
Ukraine		1	
England		2	

Note. Total 131 Students

Appendix 2B

Differences in Students' Expressions of Social Justice:
Discrimination, Prejudice, Economic Hardship, Negative Influences

Number of students, Percent of sample

Social Justice Issues	judgments of equity/revenge	moral struggles	discrimination	prejudice	economic hardships	negative influences
	13, 10%	14, 11%	7, 5.3%	16, 12.2%	9, 7%	8, 6%

Student Origins Count	African	Asian	Caribbean	European	North American	Central/South American
	4	33	54	11	13	16

Spanish-speaking	17 Yrs+ In USA
72	61

61 students (47%) resided in the USA for 17 or more years
72 students (55%) were Spanish-speaking

Students came from numerous countries with 55% identifying themselves as having Spanish as their first language, 51% of the students chose topics and morals dealing with issues of social justice

Explanation of the categories of Social Justice Issues:
- Judgments of equity or revenge: Acts students thought were merited by a previous action which might include revenge
- Moral struggle: Any battle for justice within oneself or between two or more forces
- Discrimination: An actual behavior or act toward an individual or a group of people
- Prejudice: A negative attitude towards an individual or social group
- Economic hardships: The state of being poor, penniless dressed in rags and/or dying of starvation
- Negative influences: A situation or individual influenced by bullying, gangs and/or drug and alcohol abuse

Summation of the Results:

The study indicated that whether students resided in the United States for 17 years or more, or had arrived more recently, that both groups were interested in issues of social justice, although their interpretations varied. Students who had been in the United States 17 years or more expressed a significant concern over discrimination and economic hardships. Spanish-speaking students were uniquely concerned about the effects of prejudice and negative influences on their success in society whether they had arrived recently or been in the United States 17 years or more.

Appendix 2C

Lesson Plans

Lesson I: Understanding the Fable Genre

Overview

Topic: Teacher instruction on the reading and analysis of fables.
Purpose: To provide practice in reading a fable and interpreting the author's implied lesson or moral that is illustrated by the fable.
Activities: Read short fables possibly by Aesop (Zipes, 1992) or LaFontaine (2002), and have students guess what they think the author intended for a lesson. See sample fable entitled *The Hen and the Cat* as an example.

Hearing that a hen was laid up sick in her nest, a cat paid a visit out of sympathy. After creeping up to her, he said. "How are you, my dear friend? What can I do for you? Do you need anything? Just tell me, and I'll bring you anything in the world you want. Just keep up your spirits, and don't be alarmed."

Thank you said the hen. "Just be good enough to leave me, and I'm sure that I'll soon get well again." (Zipes, 1992, p. 62).

Lesson Objectives

General objectives are to have students understand the fable genre and to practice interpretations of the morals of fables through oral discussion.

Instructions for the teacher:
The teacher will:
1. Discuss some of the characteristics of a fable and that some go back to classical antiquity and that many of them have been passed down by word of mouth. The fable may or may not use personification and human frailties may have been easier to discuss without naming names. The multicultural society of today has brought with it many versions of the same fable heard in a variety of languages and cultures, each perhaps with a different twist (Aldridge, 1997). Some insights are

provided on the background of fables and myths on pp. 242-255 in the text by Calkins, Ehrenworth, Khan & Mooney (2010).

2. Read *The Hen and the Cat* (Zipes, 1992, p. 2), and then ask students what they think the moral might be. Student answers will vary, and there should be several interpretations and wordings of the moral are acceptable. The teacher should not give her/his own interpretation of the fable but encourage the students to do this.

3. Commence a general discussion of what the fable genre is about and let the students take the lead in making suggestions.

4. Read three or four short fables with the entire class without giving any direct summation of the supposed moral. In Zipes (1992) book of selected fables by Aesop there are many good illustrations of fables for reading, see examples *The Horse and the Stag* (p.128) or *The Horse and the Frog* (p. 97). Fables by LaFontaine (2002) also provide many good examples and Ashliman, Jones and Rackman (2003) provide good sources.

5. Students are then asked to interpret the morals of the fables provided. Some possible student interpretations of the fables might be written on the chalkboard.

6. Point out that there is frequently more than one interpretation for the fable. Other features to note are the tone of the fable, whether or not personification was used and the choice of the author to use certain animals to tell the tale.

7. Explain that the lessons provided by the fable may sometimes be contradictory and that they may have been reinvented or superimposed by a variety of authors to suit their own purposes. There is frequently more than one interpretation for the fable.

Materials: Zipes (1992) book of selected fables by Aesop. A copy of *The Hen and the Cat* (Zipes, 1992, p. 62) may be provided. Further material by La Fontaine (2002) may be used for additional examples if necessary. Chalk and a chalkboard would be helpful.

Lesson II: Fable Writing

Overview

Topic: Teacher instruction on the writing and analysis of fables.
Purpose: To have the student write an original fable of their own creation
Activities: Group review and discussion of the fables that the have been presented in Lesson I.

Class Assignment in the Writing of An Original Fable
Lesson Objectives

General objectives are to have students review and understand the fable genre and to write a fable of their own creation.

Instructions for the teacher:
The teacher will:
1. Review the characteristics of a fable, and ask students to think of a topic to write about which might provide any kind of a lesson or moral. The teacher should not give her/his own list or interpretation of morals or lessons about which the student might write. These suggestions should come from the student.
2. Mention to the students that any event in their daily lives or the lives of their friends is suitable for a topic, and tell them that the story does not have to be true or factual.
3. Circulate amongst the different students in the class, and if they are showing difficulty in starting to write, then ask them what they are thinking of writing about. Talk to students independently. If they say they are having difficulty in finding a suitable topic, ask them if they have any situations or circumstances that would make a good short story about which they could write.
4. Do not share any of the individual student's ideas with the rest of the class or let students do group work when writing the fables. One of the purposes of this exercise is to have students express any concerns that are personal or individual to them and to come up with original ideas.
5. Remind students that their fables should conclude with a lesson.

Materials: Students should have paper and pencil or access to a computer in order to complete the written aspects of this assignment.

Appendix 2D

Examples of Comments Written by Students on the Questionnaire (Distributed at the Conclusion of the Fables Exercise)

Seventy percent of the students wrote positively about the fable writing experience. Approximately 35% of the group noted that they believed they gained confidence in how to express themselves or mentioned that they enjoyed talking about themselves and the reasons they chose the particular lesson they did to share with their classmates.

Questionnaire given to students
Please write down in a few sentences giving your reactions to the exercises we did on fable writing. You will not be graded on these responses. The purpose of your responses is to help the teacher in planning future lessons.

Examples of students' comments:
"I liked the fable writing we did in class as it made me think of some good lessons to talk about to the other students. I read my fable to them during class and some students said they liked it."

"I think the lesson on the stories with a moral was more interesting than I thought. I thought at first that it was too much like things I did in middle school, but I found out that some people wrote some complicated stories and you had to analyze them to get the point."

"This was good inference practicing. The professor said we need work in making inferences because they are harder than understanding the straight facts. I know we have to do inferences on the ACT reading test. I have to pass it this time. I think I will now."

"I told a lot about myself with this story with a lesson. After hearing from other people, I see they wrote a lot about experiences too. I liked talking about my experiences and it was good for me to express myself in English. I was force to talk English to the other students and I had to write in English too. I am use to talking in Spanish but the professor said I must do small group work with only English speakers and writers. At first this annoys me but I got to like the other people. I think I learn something in this class about other people and about talking to them in English."

"The fable stories from other people in the class were good. Some of them talked about brave actions and some talked about weak actions. I liked sharing the stories with the other people. They came from all over and their stories were different. English is not my first language so this assignment was not too easy. People seemed to like my story and asked me about myself and where I was born and my country before this one. I made friends in this class."

"When I was young I read some stories like the fables we wrote. My grandmother took me to church and I heard some there. My fable was about myself and I talk about an experience I had when I was young. I learn a lesson and I want to tell it to the class. It took a lot of time to do all this but I like learning about the other students. Some of them don't speak very good English but they did try and they listen which is good. The professor talks a lot about summarizing. She makes us practice getting to our point and speaking out in a clear voice. I speak in English now. More than I did before."

CHAPTER 3

CREATING RUSSIAN-AMERICAN IDENTITIES IN RECENT AMERICAN FICTION:
Two Perspectives

Julia Stakhnevich
Bridgewater State University

When writers choose to express their creativity through the medium of another language, they experience an unparalleled freedom "to go beyond the familiar words of the tribe" (Kellman, 2000, p. x). Such freedom provides a necessary estrangement, or *otstranenie* as Victor Shklovsky (1965) calls it that energizes their creativity. By separating themselves from the natural form of expression in the language of their childhood, they see the world more clearly; thus, fulfilling the purpose of art (at least, as it was understood by the Russian Formalists), which is "to impart the sensation of things as they are perceived and not as they are known" (p. 11). At the same time, "the emancipatory detachment of writing in another language" is not without its dangers: one of which is the perception that it is "not only painful but unnatural, almost matricidal" (Kellman, 2000, pp. 2-3).

This double-edged sword of translingualism translates into conflicting audience reception: translingual writers can ride the wave of exotic popularity among the audiences of their adoptive land, while, at the same time, their choice of a language other than their native tongue "undermines their status as genuine representatives of a specific ethnicity" (Wanner, 2008, p. 663). With their authenticity in question, translingual writers, then, must find a veritable way to express their attachment to the new country while not completely disregarding the old one. They must forge "a new reality in which the claims of the new world and the old find at least a tenuous balance" (Stavans, 2009, p. xxi).

As translingual writers, these individuals can fashion their own hybrid identities by retaining, rejecting, and/or acquiring various identity features and negotiating them with their intended audiences (Wanner, 2008, p. 662). Their first language does not completely disappear; neither does their first culture. Using the repertoire of both languages and cultures in various measures, they exercise agency to create unique voices that both distinguish them from and enmesh them in their two cultures. Some authors feel that they are on the cusp of both culture and language, crossing the borders back and forth; others feel that they belong to neither and attempt to create their own space outside of traditional demarcations.

This essay examines themes of immigration and identity as they emerge in two recent novels: *Memoirs of a Muse* (2006) by Lara Vapnyar and *What Happened to Anna K.* (2008) by Irina Reyn using the conceptual framework of translingual writing. I argue that these works by the Russian-American translingual authors provide a unique glimpse of how individuals outside of Russia interpret what it means to maintain or retain, perhaps involuntarily, some degree of Russianness on American soil. The projected hybrid Russian-American personas created by Vapnyar and Reyn for their female protagonists are intimately connected to the writers' personal journeys and reflect their own understanding of what it means to remain Russian outside of Russia. I claim that their different vantage points outside of Russia and within the immigrant Russian community distinguish their voices and showcase divergent perspectives on what it means to be Russian-American in the twenty-first century. Both have chosen to capitalize on, what Adrian Wanner (2008) called, the exotic allure of the Russian literary brand (p. 663), focusing on the interpretations of female experiences in the Russian-Jewish communities of New York.

To claim their right to tell these stories, they employ a strategy of blurring the boundaries of fiction and reality. Their cultural authenticity is established through the marketing of their books that highlight similarities in their heroines' experiences with those of the writers: the blurbs on the dust jackets and the interviews with the authors underline Reyn's and Vapnyar's Russian immigrant status. Readers learn that like Anna K., Reyn immigrated with her family when she was seven and lived in Rego Park during her formative years. Vapnyar was born in Moscow and came to the States in her late teens with limited English and, like her protagonist, Tatiana Ruper, settled down in New York. The publishers make sure that these similarities are brought to the forefront and exhibited as evidence that the writers have a tangible connection to Russia that adds authenticity to their voices.

In general, both novels received favorable reviews in the United States. Reyn's novel is described as "a pitch perfect rendering of the life of newly arrived Russian immigrants" (Cone, 2008, p. 66), whereas Vapnyar is praised for writing "a knowing, irreverent, and toothsome ode to the imagination, a power that all too often leads us astray (Seaman, 2006, p. 42). Some of the critics feel compelled to commend Vapnyar on her language skills, an observation which seems to be reserved only for foreigners. For example, Caryn James (2006) called her a fast language learner who "writes ridiculously well in English" (p. 31). No similar remarks were made about Reyn's English, whose early immigration afforded her, at least in the eyes of the critics, an undeniable ownership of the English language. While Vapnyar is still identified as the exotic Other who writes surprisingly well in the language that still doesn't belong to her, Reyn is recognized as a cunning cultural anthropologist with an insider perspective, who, according to Lynne Sharon Schwartz's blurb on the novel's dust jacket, "knows her subject—Russian-Jewish immigrants in New York City—inside out, and casts a skeptical glance at their habits, aspirations, and thwarted destinies."

On the surface, Reyn and Vapnyar share lots of similarities: both are Jewish, both are immigrants from Russia, both are English as a Second Language speakers, both are female. Both position themselves *vis a vis* their American readership as Russian enough to offer authentic insights into the intricacies of Russian worldview with its anachronisms, contradictions, and exotic allure. But, upon a closer examination of their personal journeys and their works, it becomes clear that they have different vantage points from which they observe and comment on the formation of contemporary hybrid Russian-American female immigrant identities.

Vapnyar, who immigrated to the United States in her late teens, was old enough to have a solid understanding of Russian cultural values. She is looking at the immigrant experience from the outside in, symbolically still clothed in her Russian garb; her Tanya refuses to get rid of a herringbone coat that she brought from Moscow, even if it is a telltale sign of a poor Russian émigré.

This is an allusion to Gogol's *The Overcoat* (1842): Tanya hangs on to hers as a protective shield against the unknown, whereas Gogol's Akaky Akakievich is ashamed of his coat and scrimps and saves for a better one, thus, hoping for some recognition in society. For Vapnyar, this is a way to establish a strong affinity, albeit in the English language, with the Russian literary tradition of humanism following in the assertion attributed to Fyodor Mikhailovich Dostoyevsky that "We all have come out from Gogol's *The Overcoat*."

Reyn, on the other hand, is describing the Russian-Jewish community of Rego Park not as an outsider cast there by the powers of fate, but as one who fully belongs, who came to the United States so young that her experiences of Russian culture are but fleeting memories of her childhood. A person who is intricately enmeshed in the life of the residents of Rego Park, she exerts a moral authority to take Americans on a tour of life as experienced by "sausage immigrants", with humiliating details of discount shopping addictions, public admonitions of strangers, and herring sandwiches.

Using a chronological approach, Reyn Americanizes key elements of Tolstoy's *Anna Karenina*: we see a reinvented meeting of Vronsky (David in Reyn's book) and Anna at Penn Station, witness David and Anna's fatal attraction at a New Year's party in the Chagall restaurant at Brighton Beach, and are forewarned of Anna K.'s imminent demise under a subway train by the narrator's description of Anna's childhood fascination with trains.

Vapnyar uses a more complex approach to her story-telling: *Memoirs of a Muse* is written in the voice of Tanya Ruper, who begins her story by introducing Apollinaria (Polina) Suslova, Dostoyevsky's lover. Throughout the novel, Tanya is telling two stories: one of her own life and the other of Polina, who serves as Tanya's foil in the quest to become a great man's muse. Tanya's search eventually leads her to immigrate to the United States where she hopes to find that one Great Writer whom she could inspire to create literature in the manner of Dostoyevsky. Tanya conceptualizes immigration as an escape from the reality of wifehood and motherhood, an escape that comes just in time to prevent Tanya from succumbing to a life of "cracked nipples... a shiny ring and a fat sleepy baby" (pp. 66-68).

In the center of both novels is a female protagonist who believes in the mythology of a muse: the desire to be an object of adoration and, subsequently, inspiration to a great artist. In Tanya's case, aspiring to be a muse rather than a wife and a mother is a quiet challenge to the Soviet *status quo*: a society where gender equality has been openly proclaimed, but never achieved. Locked within her Soviet upbringing, Tanya is left to ponder whether to accept the life of a passive female who is rendered insignificant but is held in high regards as a symbol of a happy and healthy Soviet family, or to become a social outcast, a mistress, a woman scorned by society but wanted and loved by the artist whom she inspires.

In giving these limited choices to her protagonist, Vapnyar makes an insightful comment about the insincerity of the Communist regime in its treatment of women: lauded in public as equal to men, in everyday life Soviet women were coached to lead a lifestyle that emphasized marriage and motherhood as the ultimate achievement in life. That is not the route that Tanya wants to take; her route is to become an inspiration to a great man. This choice, although different from that of the majority, still puts Tanya in a secondary position, an idea that she is able to grasp only after several years of living in New York with Mark, a man she once thought was her great writer.

Anna K.'s motivation to be a muse stems from her "hazy fantasy" (p. 9) of a life best portrayed in Woody Allen's Manhattan flicks with loft apartments and "those stimulating dinner parties dropping names like e.e. cummings, Kierkegaard, Dostoyevsky, Bergman" (p. 8). In Anna's view such dreams separate her from the "sausage immigrant" milieu which she longs to escape: after all, when in Rego Park she finds her uniqueness in "thinking she was the only Russian immigrant to moon over Heathcliff from Wuthering Heights" (p. 9). However, outside of Rego Park, she considers herself special because of her immigrant status: she is the exotic Russian transplant, her immigration is a gift to others, a magical quality that sets her apart among native-born Americans, a uniqueness that could help realize her purpose in life, which is to inspire men to create great works of literature.

Neither heroine lives up to their muse aspirations: Anna K. ends her life because she cannot live outside of the 19th century Russian sensibilities, whereas Tanya sees the falsity of the muse myth and abandons it. When confronted with an uneasy choice of reinterpreting her life and moving to the cornfields of Iowa with her lover or returning to live with her parents in Rego Park, Anna K. feels lost between the two worlds and is not able to make amends with either: she is not American enough to live in Iowa, yet she is not Russian enough to bear living in Rego Park. As a failed muse unable to adapt to new reality, Anna K. is left with no other option but to follow the tragic fate of Tolstoy's heroine. Reyn allows her protagonist the agency to end her life, but not to change it.

Tanya, on the other hand, eventually sees her relationship with the artist she intends to inspire for what it really is: being a kept woman for a neurotic author whose work is shallow and trite. In Vapnyar's novel, Tanya's failed bid to be a muse is akin to the alienation that immigrants experience upon their introduction to a new, unfamiliar society. It is only with the help of her American friends, two elderly neighbors, that Tanya is able to escape this situation. Vapnyar offers her heroine a mechanism to become successful in immigration by creating new meaningful relationships with others, relationships that are built outside of the confines of the muse myth. Tanya's journey through immigration leads her to a much more proactive worldview where she has the agency to act and recreate herself.

Ultimately, Vapnyar's novel tells an immigrant story of empowerment found in oneself, found in the new environment granted by immigration, an escape that Tanya fights for, first quietly and tentatively; but as her realization of the falsity of the muse myth grows stronger, so does her determination to become someone on her own terms. At the end of the novel, Tanya realizes that "immortality doesn't do you any good" (p. 205), but imperfect happiness with your work and your family might. And, that's what she attempts to find in America.

Vapnyar ends her novel with Tanya learning that she is a *bona fide* muse to a female painter, Vera Mielich, a reclusive lesbian neighbor in Mark's apartment building: this serendipitous realization of Tanya's dream doesn't require any sacrifices on the pyre of creative genius. Tanya's 'great' writer, Mark, who practically enslaves her both mentally and physically, is rendered creatively impotent, whereas the lesbian painter, although considered by others in the building to be mentally unstable, is capable of seeing Tanya's distress and fears and successfully expresses these emotions on canvas. Vapnyar suggests that it is not gender that matters, but the depth of emotion and the bond that people develop. It is through these meaningful connections that Tanya is able to overcome her limitations and adjust to living within her two cultures and two languages.

Vapnyar's humanistic message transcends the confines of immigration and the patriarchal world order, the very cornerstones upon which Reyn relies to craft her retelling of *Anna Karenina*. In Reyn's novel, Anna K.'s world is demarcated: the immigrant community represents the world of immutable tradition, a world that might feel suffocating for those who can function independently in a larger community. Adept at living outside of the immigrant community, these individuals, usually children of immigrant parents, still feel a strong pull toward the traditions in which they are raised. These traditions are not necessarily those of reading Pushkin and Dostoyevsky; most likely, the traditions in question are the survival skills that immigrants develop in their new land. This is why Reyn uses being cheap and rude, publicly admonishing strangers, an avoidance of positive sentiments, a lack of consideration for others, and racist attitudes in describing Anna K.'s community.

Reyn's account of Rego Park is written from the position of a child of immigrants who sees the unflattering qualities of her parents, but fails to empathize with their alienation and attempts to survive by their wits in a new country. Like her Anna K., Reyn is comfortable in the larger American world where Russianness becomes an exotic currency. The author describes her protagonist as being stuck in immigration by proxy with her parents who exhibit behaviors marking them as the Other. And, understandably, Anna K. doesn't want to be labeled as such: she feels comfortable outside the immigrant community, but the pull to come back is always there. Reyn's account of the immigrant life is not a happy-ending story of well-adjusted immigrants; instead, it is a painful story of never finding the exact fit, of never belonging to either community.

The qualities that Anna associates with being Russian are full of stereotypes: Russians are portrayed as vodka-loving people who have "a fatalistic binary mentality—things tended to be wonderful or terrible" (p. 15). No matter how much Anna K. tries to be American (meaning loving, rational, polite), she has "shards of the Russian soul" (p. 15) lodged in her as if by being born in Russia, Anna lived through an explosion that left her traumatized and lacking in comparison to 'normal' Americans in some significant ways. Thus, no immigration can save her substandard soul. Yet Anna K. confesses to "playing the immigrant card"; it is her story "that never failed her, the story that always sucked them in" (p. 18). She knows that being a Russian immigrant, the one educated in the States with a slight, nearly untraceable accent, is a cultural capital she can cash in. When she claims her Russianness, it is often for utilitarian purposes: seducing yet another aficionado of Russian lit or getting an easy A. What this accomplishes, though, is to present herself as a person she really is not: she is much more comfortable with her American persona, but admitting to it would make her commonplace and boring. Instead, she would rather pose as the exotic, beautiful woman from the country of the ever-lasting winters, vodka, and great literature, although America is Anna K.'s home and Woody Allen's universe of Manhattan is where she longs to live. The uneasiness that Anna feels about her hyphenated identity initially stems from the Soviet anti-Semitism: "In the Russian language, one was either a "Russian" or a "Jew" (one annihilated the possibility of the other)" (p. 41). It is further reinforced by her alienation in immigration, the cultural loss, and the inability to make meaningful connections with others without resorting to pretence.

Anna's cultural loss must have not happened at once: Reyn offers a glimpse into the process when she introduces Anna K. as a seven-year-old immigrant child in school where she was being bullied and taken advantage of by other kids because the only English word that she knows is "No" (p. 45). This early, painful memory of being "an easy target… naïve, pigtailed, Soviet" (p. 45) is juxtaposed with Anna's recollections of her teenage years when she manages to make her Russian accent into an asset, not a blemish:

> Anna was happy to note that her Russian accent and freshly scrubbed, nectarine smoothness attracted their attention at once. She was always the first to raise her hand, answers at her fingertips (p. 22).

These two memories highlight the contradictory nature of Anna's immigration, showing how she suffered for what she was when she first arrived in the States (a child who didn't speak English) and how, eventually, she learns to use immigration to her advantage. As many other immigrant children, she wants to belong so badly in her new social and linguistic environment that she has to shed her old self, with its culture and language, only retaining what amounts to a shtick used to impress, to seduce, and to control.

For the adult Anna K., Russianness is a cross to bear with its melodramatic tendencies, limitations set by great but outdated 19th century novels, and the reprehensible public behaviors of Rego Park, all separated from a larger narrative of America, a narrative that Anna desperately wants to be a part of, but is unable to commit to. Tanya Ruper, on the other hand, treats her Russianness as a launching pad in a quest to find meaning in life; she is not afraid of change and learns through trial and error how to survive on her own in immigration. Vapnyar's novel fits the definition of a traditional narrative of success by a person who immigrates as an adult, "a story of an ultimately happy fate, as initial hardships yield to a comfortable and perhaps gently ambivalent adaptation to life in the United States" (Stavans, 2009, p. xxi).

Reyn's book is a story by and of a person who immigrated in her early childhood: "those who immigrate as children often possess a kind of double consciousness, allowing them especially sharp insights into the ongoing struggle between native and adopted cultures that strikes at the core of the immigrant's being" (Stavans, 2009, p. xxii). *What Happen to Anna K.* is a novel about those who are forced to navigate between the land that adopted them and the land of their parents. Their ancestral land, whose language they may or may not remember, is both legendary and ugly, a blessing and a curse, a land that does not lie before them, but is always there when they turn their head; no matter how hard they try, Russia is the country that won't go away.

Both writers are conscious of their American readership and use their understanding of readers' expectations to their advantage. For example, to add to the authenticity of their protagonists, Vapnyar and Reyn insert words in Russian here and there, all easily understandable within the context. Cultural references are also re-thought and re-imagined for better audience reception. For example, Vapnyar on several occasions makes necessary adjustments in her text to ensure that her readers get the meaning without having to deal with additional cultural explanations that could make a novel too heavy in footnotes. For instance, when Tanya describes the portraits of several great Russian writers lining the walls in her mother's room, she compares Tolstoy's bearded likeness to "a mean Santa Claus" (p. 6). In actuality, little Tanya would not know who Santa Claus was, but would be familiar instead with Father Frost who also boasts of a long white beard, but brings presents to kids on New Year's Eve instead of Christmas. On a different occasion, when Vapnyar mentions the grades in Tanya's Russian school and university, she uses the American letter grade system in place of five-point Russian grades (p. 41). Such necessary cultural substitutions result in the normalization of the text, connecting it to its audience without overwhelming them with too many exotic details.

In her novel, Reyn draws the audience's attention to the importance of names and naming as cultural markers of identity. She frequently comments on the right and wrong pronunciations of Anna's name, and in one scene we witness how Anna is praised by her grade school teacher in Russia with "Very good, Anna Borisovna, very good" (p. 22). Readers with an understanding of how patronymic names work in Russian would catch the improbability of a school teacher addressing his students with a combination of a full first name and a patronymic: this type of address is reserved as a sign of respect only toward someone who is older and/or of a higher social status. This cultural gaffe works as an effective characterization of Anna K.: it demonstrates that the adult Anna K. is out of touch with basic assumptions behind Russian cultural values, which she must have possessed as a young child in Russia, but lost through her years in the US.

Although both novels deal with the themes of immigration and creation of Russian-American hybrid identities, the result is different. Reyn writes based on her understanding of the American readership and is eager to draw from the well-known stereotypes about Russian immigrants and Russia in general. This essentialist approach to identity, whether intentional or not, serves the purpose of the book: to recollect the immigrant journey of a child and to explore how her early experiences in childhood and adulthood are closely intertwined with the sense of loss, alienation, and the desire to belong, all related to her immigrant status. Anna's naïve misunderstanding of Russianness and her reliance on commonplace stereotypes in the description of what it means to be Russian serve as a veritable backdrop to a person who was taken out of the Russian milieu early on in her life, but had to resort to its familiar contours without having an opportunity to fully understand it as an adult.

Vapnyar, too, writes for her English-language readers, but does not rely on stereotypes; instead, she uses her novel as a textual space to connect American readers with Russia, its people, and their cultural values by creating characters that are flawed, but with flaws that go beyond any particular ethnicity or nationality. In Vapnyar's world, the readers are faced with humanity in its various representations: Soviet, Russian, American, Russian-American, straight or lesbian. As a writer, she strives to stay above essentialism and to share with her audience the complexities involved in having multiple identities, a challenge and a gift that we all face living in the postmodern world.

Vapnyar and Reyn offer their own distinct interpretations of what it means to be Russian, or, at least to keep Russia as part of one's identity on American soil. Each narrative is told from a different vantage point outside of Russia and within the immigrant community, resulting in divergent perspectives on what it means to be Russian-American. Notwithstanding the differences in the conceptualizations of Russian-American identities, both authors see immigration as a key element in the identity of their protagonists that affords them a special lens to see Russia from a distance in their own way and to re-imagine Russianness as an important cultural construct guiding their narratives.

Finally, stepping away from the particulars of Russian-American journeys and the venues of professional creative writing, I agree with Canagaranjah (2012) in that the conceptual framework of translingualism provides a useful, powerful, and innovative lens not only for the analysis of literary works, but also, and perhaps more importantly, for the instruction of adult ESL writers. ESL teachers need to recognize that their multilingual students use different vantage points to merge their languages and sociocultural values in creative, unique, and often unexpected ways while negotiating their multiple identities in writing. ESL learners will benefit from writing instruction that stems from the understanding of the hybrid nature of their multilingual competencies. Their voices transcend the limits of one language and one culture, constructing new identities and unique varieties of English as they engage in writing activities. The application of the translingual framework to ESL writing pedagogies will help teachers gain important insights into their students' linguistic choices and encourage educators to value the uniqueness of translingual voices.

References

Cone, E. (2008). Review of the book *What Happened to Anna K.*, by I. Reyn. *Library Journal*, 133(121), 66.
Gogol, N. (2000). *The overcoat*. (J. Forsyth, Trans.). London, UK: Bristol Classical Press. (Original work published 1842)
Canagarajah, S. (2012). *Translingual practice*. New York: Routledge.
James, C. (2006). Review of the book *Memoirs of a Muse*, by L. Vapnyar. *Publishers Weekly*, 253(927), 31.
Kellman, S. G. (2000). *The translingual imagination*. Lincoln, NE: University of Nebraska Press.

Stavans, I. (2009). Introduction. In I. Stavans (Ed.), *Becoming Americans: Four centuries of immigrant writing* (pp. xix-xxiii). New York: The Library of America.
Reyn, I. (2008). *What happened to Anna K.* New York: Simon & Schuster.
Seaman, D. (2006). Review of the book *Memoires of a Muse*, by L. Vapnyar. *Booklist, 102*(1215), 42.
Shklovsky, V. (1965). Art as Technique. In L. T. Lemon & M. J. Reis (Eds.), *Russian formalist criticism: Four essays* (3-24). Lincoln, NE: University of Nebraska Press.
Vapnyar, L. (2006). *Memoirs of a muse.* New York: Vintage International.
Wanner, A. (2008). Russian hybrids: Identity in the translingual writings of Andrei Makine, Wladimir Kaminer, and Gary Shteyngart. *Slavic Review, 67*(3), 662-681.

CHAPTER 4

QUÉ REVOLÚ:
The ¡Atrévete y Dilo! *Campaign and Language Legitimation in Puerto Rico*

Ashlee Dauphinais Civitello
University of Puerto Rico-Rio Piedras

Elaine M. Shenk
Saint Joseph's University

Introduction

Spanish is an official or national language in twenty-one countries, and thus dialectal variation is frequently a topic of discussion among its speakers, dialectologists, and linguists. In terms of dialectology, Puerto Rican Spanish is part of a broader category of Caribbean Spanish, with a clear relationship to the Spanish(es) spoken in Cuba and the Dominican Republic. The history of language use and contact in Puerto Rico is politically, socially, and historically complex, owing to a colonial history with both Spain and the United States, as well as its current Commonwealth status in relationship with the United States (see for example, Barreto, 2001; Duany, 2002, 2005; DuBord, 2007; Mazak, 2008; Ortiz López, 2000; Pousada, 2008; Rúa, 2002; Torres, 2007; Torres González, 2002; Vélez, 2000; Zentella, 1999). In addition to an extended contact with English, Puerto Rican Spanish is also enriched by contact with lexical items from both Taíno and a variety of African languages. The complexity of this situation impacts the ways in which Puerto Rican Spanish is perceived *vis-à-vis* other varieties of Spanish. This paper analyzes the role and impact of a radio campaign about language among a limited sample of Puerto Ricans living on the Island through semi-structured interviews in which they discussed both the campaign and issues relevant to the legitimation of a uniquely Puerto Rican Spanish.

Theoretical Framework

The evaluation of language varieties is typically dependent not on linguistic factors but rather on socially- or politically-determined values. It is common to hear ideologies that disparage 'non-standard' or non-dominant varieties, and/or that privilege specifically identified 'standard' varieties (Delpit, 2008; Lippi Green, 2011). Efforts to alter these statuses are sometimes made through legislative or educational policy at an official level, but notably these can also happen through unconventional means in the public sphere (Heller, 1996; Jaffe, 2001; Swigart, 2000). Although linguistic inquiry takes a decidedly descriptivist framework—that is, identifying and describing language varieties in neutral terms—this framework typically does not filter into conceptions of language in the public sphere, and linguists may not circulate research to those outside their discipline or even outside academia, both due to their own objectives for their research as well as perhaps to a lack of training as to how to do so (Reaser & Adger, 2007).

In recent years, materials that facilitate language and dialect awareness and that overtly counter discriminatory language ideologies have been developed for non-academic audiences. These include (a) books or other printed materials, such as the Center for Applied Linguistics digests, *Spoken Soul: The Story of Black English* (Rickford & Rickford, 2000), *American Voices: How Dialects Differ from Coast to Coast* (Wolfram & Ward, 2006); (b) video documentaries, such as *Voices of North Carolina, Lumbee English, Mountain Talk, and Spanish Voices* (Hutcheson & Wolfram, 2008); *Los castellanos del Perú* and *Las lenguas del Perú* [*The Spanishes of Peru* and *The Languages of Peru*] (Proyecto PUCP, 2007); *Do You Speak American?* (Cran, 2005); and *American Tongues* (Álvarez & Kocher, 1987); and (c) curricular materials specifically designed to accompany video or audio resources in the classroom, such as the curriculum for *Do You Speak American?* (Reaser, Adger, & Hoyle, 2005). Blogs on language and linguistics topics also circulate linguistic research more informally in the public sphere.

In 2010, the *Puerto Rican Academy of the Spanish Language* (ACAPLE) released the *¡Atrévete y dilo!* [Go Ahead and Say It!] campaign, a series of fifty thirty-second public service announcements highlighting seventy-five words that were identified as part of Puerto Rican Spanish. The *¡Atrévete y dilo!* campaign was on its surface designed to counteract negative evaluation of Puerto Rican Spanish in its legitimation of specific features of the spoken vernacular—a legitimation not only of Spanish *vis a vis* English on the Island, but also of a uniquely Puerto Rican Spanish, which demonstrates unique phonological, morphological, lexical, and syntactic features. The campaign officially lasted over a month, but several radio stations continue to play the announcements today. Some were played by contract and others as public service, principally on AM radio stations. The presentation of lexical items in many cases was accompanied by etymological information. In the words of ACAPLE Director Dr. José Luis Vega, the spots "contribute to strengthening the knowledge and pride in Puerto Ricans about the Spanish of Puerto Rico" (ACAPLE, 2010, translation by authors). The campaign also produced a compact disc that was sent to schools throughout the island, and was additionally made available for purchase. As a branch of the Real Academia Española, the "Academia Puertorriqueña de la Lengua Española promotes the correct usage, the conservation, and the study of Spanish in the context of the cultural history of the country, from its origins to its most recent manifestations, and represents Puerto Rico internationally to its sister Academies" (ACAPLE, 2010, translation by authors). The funding for the campaign came from a grant from the Puerto Rican Foundation of the Humanities and the National Foundation for the Humanities; the ACAPLE also receives funds from educational workshops and courses for which they charge a fee (Salmonte García, 2010).

As Reaser and Adger (2007) urge, there is clearly a place for materials such as these to be accompanied by curricular guides for use in education. This paper investigates the impact of the radio campaign *beyond* educational arenas and in the public sphere through the framework of Critical Discourse Analysis (CDA), which allows us to map various forms of analysis onto one another (Fairclough, 2003, 2009; van Dijk, 2001, 2009; Wodak & Meyer, 2009). As fits a CDA approach, the historical and sociopolitical framework of Puerto Rico's historically colonial relationship to Spain (and as a result, to the Real Academia Española) as well as currently to the United States (and the accompanying Spanish-English language contact) is crucial to understanding what is occurring as a backdrop to the radio campaign. Additionally, a CDA approach requires the coordination and overlapping of analyses of how specific spoken and written texts (e.g., the campaign announcement texts) are produced and distributed, with discourse about those texts (e.g., the discourses voiced about those texts in the semi-structured interviews), thus moving between a micro- and macroanalysis of text and context. As we will see in the section detailing our findings, the participants' discourse both legitimizes and delegitimizes certain forms of language, and forms of legitimation are both reproduced and resisted in their discourse (Bourdieu, 1991; Fairclough, 2009; Foucault, 1982; van Leeuwen, 2007).

In concordance with the theme of this volume on the intersections of language and social justice, we note Labov's call for linguists "to use their linguistic knowledge to address language-related social issues" (1982, pp. 172-173), more recently affirmed by Wolfram (2008, p. 2) who points out that "our professional training as sociolinguists should, in fact, be used to address language-related social and educational inequality".

Methodology

The materials and data analyzed in this paper come from the following sources: (a) fifty ¡*Atrévete y dilo!* radio spots aired in Puerto Rico, and (b) twenty semi-structured interviews conducted with Puerto Ricans regarding the campaign's impact. Initial exploration of the campaign's effect as evidenced in the media and internet blogs uncovered some discourse relevant to the campaign, some of which made active efforts to counter linguistic insecurity among Puerto Ricans about Puerto Rican Spanish, but which did not appear to engender extended online interaction on the topic. Thus the current research focused on discourses present in data collected through the interviews carried out with Puerto Ricans living on the Island.

These semi-structured interviews included specific questions related to the campaign and linguistic attitudes held about Puerto Rican Spanish. The process was designed to elicit responses to these questions, as well as to encourage informal conversation on questions related to the ¡*Atrévete y Dilo!* campaign and Puerto Rican Spanish. Interviews varied in length from five minutes to an hour, with an average length of around twenty minutes, depending on how much the participant elaborated on his or her responses. The interviews mainly occurred at the homes of the participants or in a public place such as a café, and were carried out by the first co-author of this article. All interviews were conducted in Spanish, except for a few instances of participant code-switching.

The interviewees were recruited using the snowball method of participant selection, in which the researchers selected an initial set of participants through a pre-existing social network of Puerto Rican speakers to which the researchers had access. These participants then recruited other potential participants for study from among their own social networks. Participants were selected in such a way to have demographic diversity in the study, as shown in Table 4.1.[1]

Table 4.1
Participants by Gender and Geographic Region

	San Juan/Metro	Interior	West	South	Total
Men	3	2	4	0	9
Women	4	1	4	2	11
Total	7	3	8	2	20

The participants also varied in age (18-81 years old), educational level (from having completed third grade through having completed a Ph.D.), and the number of years residing outside Puerto Rico (from never having lived outside Puerto Rico to fourteen years residing off the Island).

Appendix 4A shows the variety of topics that the interview questions addressed. The interviews began with a request for demographic information, such as age, educational level, place of residence and birth, and the number of years that the participant lived outside of Puerto Rico. Questions were then asked regarding familiarity with the ¡Atrévete y Dilo! campaign. If the participants were aware of the campaign, more specific questions were then asked. If not, the interview continued with questions about the Academia Puertorriqueña de la Lengua Española and its impact on the lives of Puerto Ricans. The fourth and final set of questions dealt with more general topics outside of the campaign regarding attitudes about Puerto Rican Spanish and anglicisms. The interviews often lent themselves to discussion of other related topics that were not part of the originally specified list of questions but often contributed to the larger discussion at hand.

The recordings were then transcribed by the second co-author, with both co-authors collaborating on several segments of the recordings that were unclear. The interviewer contributed contextual information from notes and memory of each interview to clarify the data where the voice recording was muffled. Common thematic patterns were identified, and each co-author then coded the transcriptions separately to quantify the responses related to each theme. The individual findings from each co-author were discussed, compared and contrasted, which the co-authors then combined to devise the final list of findings. Specific examples were highlighted from various participants to explore these themes within the context of the interview and the sociopolitical context on the Island. These examples were examined for strategies of legitimation and delegitimation of lexical items identified as Puerto Ricanisms and Anglicisms, paying specific attention to linguistic resources such as stress, repetition, and word choice, among others, to further understand and contextualize claims made by participants. The examples chosen for inclusion here were then translated into English through collaboration by both co-authors.

Findings and Analysis

This section presents the patterns observed in the interviewees' responses alongside a critical analysis of the interviewees' discourses on Puerto Rican Spanish. One of the clearest findings of this study is that participants were unfamiliar with the ¡Atrévete y dilo! campaign. Of the twenty Puerto Ricans interviewed for this study, fifteen had not heard of the campaign, and of the five who claimed to have heard of it, four could not describe its topic or objective. Only one of the twenty interviewees associated the campaign's objective with a topic related to language. However, even his responses demonstrated knowledge based more on his understanding of ACAPLE's work than with the specific objectives of the campaign itself, when he was asked about his reaction to the content of the announcements:

(1)
M27[2]: Bueno realmente, que tratan de, de en—de **meter el lenguaje en una caja**. Y realmente no porque el lenguaje es una—la evolución propia del— del mismo humano.

*M27: Well really, they try to, to in—to **put the language in a box**. And really that's not because language is a—the actual evolution of—of the human being itself.*

This participant articulated clearly a rejection of what he perceived to be the objective of the campaign—that of controlling language in a way that is antithetical to how language evolves based on human usage—and made a strong association between this attempted control and the work of ACAPLE. When asked who he thought had created the campaign and what its purpose was, he responded as follows:

(2)
M27: Bueno me imagino que los que se creen que tienen el poder del dellenguaje pues la Real Academia. [...] E: concientizar, que el humano está diciendo disparates.

M27: Well I imagine that those who believe themselves to have the power of of the language well the Real Academia. [...] Um: to bring awareness, that humans are making up words.

This participant later acknowledged that he had not 'seen' any of the announcements, confirming that his responses were not based on the content of the announcements themselves, nor even on the stated objectives of the campaign, but rather on the knowledge of prior and/or current work of the Academy. Although it must be acknowledged that the sample size for this research was relatively small, the campaign clearly did not appear to have had a significant impact on this group of Puerto Ricans.

Nevertheless, some level of familiarity with the work of the Academy as expressed above was highlighted by a number of participants. Of the twenty interviewees, eighteen had heard of, or were familiar with either ACAPLE or its parent organization, the Real Academia Española (see Table 4.2). Ten affirmed that they had heard of, or were familiar with, ACAPLE as an organization, although there were differing levels of recognition among them. Eight of those ten knew about ACAPLE's work, even though three initially stated that they did not know what ACAPLE did, but then went on to demonstrate familiarity with some aspect of its work; the remaining two had heard of the organization but did not know anything further than that.

When asked to define or describe ACAPLE's mission/work, fourteen of the twenty participants articulated a variety of responses that coalesced around several language-related topics. Responses were coded for any mention of the following topics—several participants mentioned more than one aspect of ACAPLE's work, thus responses reported in Table 4.3 do not equal an even twenty responses. Seven participants associated ACAPLE with rules, correctness and standardization; four participants stated more generally that ACAPLE worked with language or the study of language; and four participants connected ACAPLE with the publication of a dictionary along with the acceptance or rejection of vocabulary items. Fewer participants associated ACAPLE with pronunciation of words (2 participants) and with "dialect" (1 participant). Six participants were either unfamiliar with ACAPLE's mission or did not respond directly to this issue.

Table 4.2
Familiarity with ACAPLE/RAE

	Total n=20
Familiar with ACAPLE and/or RAE	18
Familiar with ACAPLE's work	10
Familiar with RAE, but not ACAPLE	8
Completely unfamiliar with ACAPLE / RAE	2

Table 4.3
Participants' View of the ACAPLE's Mission/Work

	No. of participants who mentioned topic
Rules, correctness, standardization	7
Language/study of language	4
Dictionary, accept/reject vocabulary	4
Pronunciation	2
Dialect	1
No direct response/unfamiliar with mission	6

Given the level of familiarity or understanding of the mission of either ACAPLE and/or RAE, participants were then asked to articulate what effect these institutions had on Puerto Ricans, and on themselves personally, in their daily lives. A clear pattern in the responses focused on the relevance of these institutions in academic and professional environments, as seen in Table 4.4.

Table 4.4
Participants' Perspectives on Effect of ACAPLE/RAE in Daily Lives

	No. of participants who mentioned topic
Education/writing/profession	9
Correction, resolving disagreements	3
No effect	3
Unfamiliar with ACAPLE's mission	6

Although it is conceivable that the first two categories listed in the table could be interpreted as related categories, many participants did not articulate the importance of the academies as helping to distinguish "correct" and "incorrect" speech patterns as a whole, but rather as helping within very specific domains related to education and their professions, and specifically developing what is often referred to in linguistics as stylistic variation and/or convergence within an accommodation theory model. These participants typically presented the Academy's role in helping them to develop a professional register or style that would be appropriate in a professional identity, but notably did not disparage the alternate variation that serves as the norm in a more informal setting among close peers. This kind of discourse is seen in the following example:

(3)
M25:Sí. Para: bueno me sirve—de hecho la necesito para, como, preparaciones y **como profesional**, me sirve para formar mi propio negocio. Uh, expresarme bien, con el público. Y hay distintas maneras de expresarse pero cuando por ejemplo hablamos del trabajo yo **no voy a expresarlo así "mera, ¿qué es la que hay?"** o sea— no se puede o sea no es el mismo um, la misma forma de hablar de expresarse. Tiene que ser como algo má:s uh que se—**cierta manera profesional.** No sé."

M25: *Yes, for me it helps, in fact I need it for, like, my formation and **as a professional**, it'll help me to set up my own business. Uh, speak effectively, with* the public. And there are different ways of speaking but when for example we're talking about work, **I'm not going to say "Yo, what up?"** I mean, you can't do that. I mean it's not the same um, the same way of speaking of expressing yourself. It has to be like something more, uh that—**a certain professional manner**. I don't know.

In (3), the participant clearly sets out the connection between what the ACAPLE does for him and his professional goals, such as expressing himself well with the public in his (future) business. Although on the surface he states the unacceptability of a particular phrase "mera, ¿qué es la que hay?"/*Yo, what up?* in the professional workplace, he nevertheless points out the existence of this phrase within the context of his assertion that there are different ways of expressing oneself and that thus there must be a context in which this kind of expression is also valid. This consciousness of style-shifting within the linguistic repertoire represents at a minimum the normalization of a more popular way of speaking as compared to professional circles, while it potentially represents a more active stance of legitimation of non-Academy-approved ways of speaking for other contexts.

A second major objective in the current research was to explore the connotations of specific lexical items found in Puerto Rican Spanish that were highlighted in the campaign. These included words such as *revolú*, *zafacón*, and *fracatán*. The first word can be translated roughly as a disorder or, alternatively, can reference a 'coolness' factor. The other two words, respectively, mean 'trashcan' and 'a large quantity'. Aside from one participant (who, it should be noted, was 81 years of age) who found these words to be 'unpleasant', nearly half (9/20) of the participants simply stated that these words were 'common' or 'normal' for Puerto Ricans, as seen in Table 4.5.

Table 4.5
Connotations of Revolú, Zafacón, and Fracatán

	No. of participants who mentioned topic
Common or normal	9
Puerto Rican origin/identity	7
From the past	1
Unpleasant	1

In fact, many interviewees experienced some level of surprise when asked this question. Seven of the twenty participants referenced a connection to a specifically Puerto Rican identity or origin for these words:

(4)
F24: Ese tipo de palabras a mí me viene a la mente que **son boricuas**.

F24: *For me, that type of words it seems to me that they* **are Puerto Rican**.[3]

In fact, when the interviewer pushed the participants to clarify, beyond the open-ended responses, whether words such as *revolú, zafacón,* and *fracatán* were specifically used primarily in Puerto Rico or whether they were also common in other Spanish-speaking countries, sixteen respondents confirmed the strength of the connection to Puerto Rico, responding that they were very Puerto Rican in nature. The four who were unsure how to answer this question cited their lack of experience either travelling or living in other countries or the fact that they did not know people from other Spanish-speaking countries. The exploration of perceived perspectives on Puerto Rican Spanish was also subject to this limitation. When participants were asked to articulate their perspectives on the status of Puerto Rican Spanish relative to other dialects of Spanish, many of them both what other people think as well as what they themselves believe—thus making it difficult to quantify their responses. Specific nationalities (e.g., Colombians and Spaniards) were particularly recognized as being more critical of the Spanish spoken by Puerto Ricans. Again, as above, at least four participants did not know what others' perspectives about Puerto Rican Spanish were, and four additional participants never responded directly to the question at all, as shown in Table 4.6.

Nevertheless, although at least eight participants referenced negativity in others' perceptions of Puerto Rican Spanish (bad/incorrect speech/pronunciation), several presented those stereotypes but almost immediately rejected them. This was sometimes done outright, but at times the form of the response indicated its function, as in (5). Here the participant is specifically referencing the borrowing of words from the English spoken in the United States, but she chooses to portray this borrowing in decidedly positive terms, alluding to the results of such borrowing in terms of enrichment and accommodation.

Table 4.6
Outsiders' perceptions of Puerto Rican Spanish

	No. of participants who mentioned topic (No.>20)
Bad/incorrect speech/pronunciation	8
'Sung' speech	3
Normal dialectal variation	3
Speak fast	1
No direct response	8

(5)
F58: El español puertorriqueño está **bien enriquecido** por una gran cantidad de de idiomas (risa) y de palabras porque este: por ejemplo **cogemos palabras** de Estados Unidos o de inglés y **las acomodamos muy perfectamente** al español.

F58: *Puerto Rican Spanish is **really enriched** by a great quantity of languages (laughter) and of words because, um, for example **we take words** from the United States or from English and **we accommodate them quite perfectly** into Spanish.*

Set in a context where borrowings from other languages, particularly from English, are sometimes viewed as something *impure* or less than ideal, this participant's contestation of that viewpoint portrays Puerto Rican Spanish in purely positive terms, where borrowing shows linguistic wealth and richness. In this discourse, Puerto Ricans are agentive, actively taking ('cogemos'/ *'we take'*) the words from English into Spanish (i.e., they do not just appear automatically) and then accommodating them *perfectly* into Spanish (i.e., they are not corrupting Puerto Rican Spanish). This discourse implies a particular skill set that Puerto Ricans have—that of flexibility and adaptation. Notably, her laughter in this section indicates her awareness of the counter discourse (that borrowing from other languages might not be perceived by everyone as 'enriching' those languages). Nevertheless she legitimates the borrowing of English words into Puerto Rican Spanish. This participant was not alone in portraying language contact in Puerto Rico in positive terms. In (6) we also see a legitimating discourse related to language contact, as the participant chooses to highlight the advanced nature of Puerto

Ricans in terms of their language use in comparison with speakers of other languages:

(6)
M26:El—**estamos más avanzados** que todos los demás porque **el lenguaje del futuro es Spanglish**. Sí. Todo el hemisferio de nosotros va a hablar eso y el otro va a hablar chino [...] Pues me imagino que depende del país que le pregunte, pero **según los españoles me imagino que hablamos súper mal**.

M26:*The-* ***we're more advanced*** *than all the rest because* ***the language of the future is Spanglish****. Yes. Our whole hemisphere will be speaking that and the other half will be speaking Chinese [...] Well I imagine that depends on the country where you ask, but* ***according to Spaniards I imagine we speak super poorly****.*

This participant particularly chooses to identify Puerto Rican Spanish with Spanglish, and goes further to index the backwardness of anyone who might not be comfortable with either the idea or the reality of this kind of language contact. What is particularly interesting, after his forceful presentation of the strength and inevitability of Spanglish as a future dominant language variety, is that he proceeds to directly reflect back on the question and to recognize the stereotype, in this case highlighting Spaniards as the voice of critique. The recognition, however, that borrowings (and/or codeswitching) may be one of the reasons why Puerto Rican Spanish is sometimes perceived negatively by Spanish speakers from other countries did not dissuade this sample of Puerto Ricans from clearly 'owning' the Anglicisms present in daily speech. When asked whether Anglicisms such as 'party', 'wikén' [weekend], 'ticket', or 'chequear' [to check on/out] belong to/are part of Puerto Rican Spanish, the majority of participants (17/20) responded definitively that they are, as seen in Table 4.7:

Table 4.7
Status of Anglicisms: party, wikén, ticket, chequear

	Yes	No	No direct answer
Are Anglicisms part of Puerto Rican Spanish?	17	2	1

Even those participants who stated that Anglicisms are *not* part of Puerto Rican Spanish qualified their answers. One participant clarified that not only did Anglicisms belong to Puerto Ricans, but that they were an accepted and normal part of ordinary speech, using the example of 'jangueo', adapted and borrowed from the English expression 'hang out':

(7)
F63: Como nuestras. Sí. O sea como el jangueo. Explicarles que son de otros lugares qué es un jangueo entonces yo también ¡lo bonito es que ellos también lo utilizan después! (risa) [...] Pero en lo demás esas palabras así como las que tú estás diciendo que son anglicismos, yo las veo **norMALes**. Yo las veo **BIEN. BIEN**. El idioma tiene que crecer. Tiene que ser cambiante también. Para mí está **bien**.

F63: *As ours, yes. That is, like "jangueo". Explaining to people from other places what is a "jangueo", then me too. What's cool is that they end up using them too! (laughter) [...] But overall those words like the one's you're saying that are Anglicisms, I see them as* **NORmal**. *I see them as* **perfectly fine, perfectly fine**. *The language has to grow, it has to change too. For me* **it's okay**.

The stress (indicated here by use of capital letters on 'norMAL' and 'BIEN. BIEN') and repetition in her discourse emphasizes even more clearly the weight of her perspective. Like the participant in (5), her laughter here also references a potential counter discourse—the disapproval of outsiders for a word such as 'jangueo'—but she emphasizes the eventual acceptance and use by foreigners of terms such as this when they live among and interact with Puerto Ricans. This understanding of Anglicisms as reflecting a process of adaptation into Puerto Rican Spanish and also as a natural part of daily speech patterns was reflected by the number of times these themes were mentioned by the participants, as seen in Table 4.8.

Unlike the stereotype referenced for non-Puerto Rican Spanish speakers, very few (3/20) of the participants in this study portrayed Anglicisms negatively, and even these latter participants still recognized that the Anglicisms are part of Puerto Rican Spanish. In fact one of the participants who expressed the strongest negative reaction to these words used the word 'essay' himself without comment ("Ya zafacón para mí es bastante normal. Desde pequeño—pero revolú no no no escribiría revolú en en un *essay*." ["For me

Table 4.8
Connotations of Party, Janguear, Wikén, Ticket, Chequear

	No. of participants who mentioned topic (No.>20)
Adaptation/adoption of words/Puerto Ricanisms	10
Normal/natural/daily life	9
Corruption/harm/laziness/bad habits	3
Influence from the U.S./political factors	3
Youth/slang	2
Inaudible response	1

zafacón is really normal. Since I was little—but revolú I wouldn't write revolú on an essay."] *M25*) and additionally switched completely to English at one point to express himself:

(8)
M25: En mi opinión hay muchos factores porque, quizás yo puedo venir de una familia boricua y, me mudo a Estados Unidos comienzo a utilizar las palabras, se sigue, como sucede a todos se sigue propagando y luego sucede con un ecuatoriano que comienza a decir wikén, este: **el otro que usa todos los anglicismos pero no creo que esté correcto.** En todo caso que sea algo más latino una de las lenguas romances que—
INT: Sí. Pero por ejemplo si los niños hoy en día pues siempre escuchan wikén—
M25: Lo lo van—
INT: Y quizás o janguear y nunca saben que vienen del inglés? Entonces para ese niño, o sea ¿cómo tú cómo tú ves tú ves esa palabra en ese con— dado eso?
M25: **Wow. (2.0) Got me there. (4.0)**

*M25: In my opinion there are many factors because, maybe I might come from a Boricua family and, I move to the United States I start using the words, time goes on, like it happens to everyone it continues spreading and later it happens with an Ecuadoran who starts to say weekend, um: **another who uses all the Anglicisms but I don't think it's correct**. In any case it might be some more Latin one of the romance languages that—*
INT: Yes. But for example if children today well they always hear weekend—
M25: They're going to—
INT: And maybe or janguear and they never know that it comes from English?

Then for that child, I mean, how do you how do you see you see that word with that with— given that (reality)?
M25: **Wow. (2.0) Got me there. (4.0)**

The campaign markedly did *not* include many Anglicisms (the exceptions to this were *mapo*, from *mop*, and *asignación*, commented on as having come from the English *assignment*). Participants were thus asked why they thought the campaign had not chosen to include Anglicisms such as these, given the strong response that they were part of Puerto Rican Spanish, alongside words such as *revolú*, *zafacón*, or *fracatán*. Of the twenty participants, seven highlighted the objectives of the Academy in defending Spanish and not promoting Anglicisms; three simply stated that these words were part of another language.

Table 4.9
Explanation of Why Anglicisms Were Not Included in Campaign

	No. of participants who mentioned topic (No.>20)
Defense of Spanish/Not promoting Anglicisms	7
Part of another language	3
Informal/street language	2
Politics	2
Uncommon words	1
Campaign authors don't care	1
Unsure	1
Did not answer question directly	5

Two participants highlighted the informal nature of the words (although many words included in the campaign were also highly informal). Five participants did not answer the question directly and one was unsure. In the example that follows, the participant repeats the phrase "me imagino" ["I imagine"], a distancing strategy that makes a clear distinction from her own beliefs:

(9)
F28: Bueno **me imagino** que están intentando de limpiar el—el idioma. Que no van a, a promover ese tipo de palabras, **aunque son—es lo más que se usa**. Pero: **será** por eso. Tratando de: enseñarnos otro tipo de palabras **más cultas (risa) me imagino.**

F28: Well *I imagine* that they're trying to 'clean up' the—the language. That they're not going to promote those types of words, **although they are—it is what is used most.** But, it **might be** due to that. Trying to teach us other kinds of *'more educated' words (laughter), I imagine.*

The use of the verb "será" in Spanish is interpreted either as a simple future tense (it will be) or as a mode of possibility (it might be), according to context. Here the participant's discourse makes use of expressions of uncertainty to indicate that she does not share the perspective of the need to "clean up" the language, given her affirmation that Anglicisms are indeed what are frequently used. This can be contrasted with several participants who simply presented the reality of the words coming from English as obvious fact, as in (10):

(10)
M25: Porque vienen de otro de otro lenguaje. No son derivadas del mismo lenguaje.

M25: *Because they come from another language. They're not derived from the same language.*

As can be seen here, participants articulated a clear distinction between what the ACAPLE must want to do through the campaign while simultaneously legitimating the commonly held perspective on the full inclusion of Anglicisms in Puerto Rican Spanish.

Conclusions

This paper contributes to current research on the application of sociolinguistic and dialect awareness principles by investigating the impact of materials designed for a non-specialist audience outside academic settings. Like many of these materials, the stated objective of the *¡Atrévete y dilo!* campaign was to increase pride in a uniquely Puerto Rican variety of Spanish, and perhaps, by association, presumably to counter internal linguistic insecurity. This paper suggests that among the participants involved in this study, the impact of the campaign was minimal due to a generalized lack of familiarity with the campaign, its objective, and its content. It drew out limited discourses in the public sphere online that openly countered some Puerto Ricans' linguistic insecurity, but these too did not constitute an extended interaction. Nevertheless, the findings suggest that despite the fact that nearly all of the participants were unfamiliar with the campaign, many of them are actively countering negative ideologies and actively legitimating Puerto Rican Spanish, albeit not in response to the campaign.

The most uncertainty, in general, seems to lie with Anglicisms used in Puerto Rico, but the campaign does not take an overt stance in favor of or against them. However, the fact that only two of seventy-five examples were Anglicisms seems to be a relatively covert stance against them, in contrast to a strong view from our participants that these words belong to Puerto Rican Spanish and are a normal and natural component of the language spoken on the Island. Interestingly, in comparison with this first campaign, as this research was being conducted, the ACAPLE launched a second campaign of twenty-five announcements titled, "El español nuestro de cada día" ["Our Daily Spanish"] in May of 2013 with the ending tagline *Dilo bien. Dilo mejor.* [Say it well. Say it better]. This campaign has a clearly prescriptivist approach, criticizing Anglicisms as well as phonetic and syntactic characteristics of Puerto Rican Spanish, such as the use of *aplicar* for *solicitar*, or *llegastes* for *llegaste*, representing efforts, in the first case, to avoid so-called "false cognates" (aplicar [apply]) and, in the second case, to avoid stigmatized verbal morphology for the second person singular preterite (-*astes* instead of -*aste*). It must be recognized that the current study involved a small sample size; thus, directions for future research include expanding the scope of the population sample, as well as to explore the objective and impact of this second campaign.

Notes
1. Geographic region was determined by taking into account various factors including both place of birth and place of residence. For example, participants such as university students who were temporarily residing in the metro area, but still considered another region their home, were tallied as being from the latter

region, especially due to the frequency with which they travel between the two areas.
2. Interviewees are identified here and throughout the text according to their gender (M=male, F=female) and age—e.g., M27 is a 27-year old male.
3. The term 'Puerto Rican' was chosen here for lack of a better translation into English, although the terms *boricua* and *Puerto Rican* are not exact synonyms. *Boricua* can be understood within a broader context as indicating a sense of pride and/or nationalism in one's identity as Puerto Rican.

References
Alvarez, L., & Kolker, A. (1987). *American tongues*. New York: Center for New American Media.
ACAPLE (Academia Puertorriqueña de la Lengua Española). (2010). Academia Puertorriqueña de la lengua española lanza campaña 'Español puertorriqueño: ¡Atrévete y dilo!' [Puerto Rican Academy of the Spanish Language releases campaign 'Puerto Rican Spanish: Go ahead and say it!]. Retrieved from *http://www.academiapr.org/index.php?option=com_content&view=article&id=154: espanol-puertorriqueno-iatrevete-y-dilo&catid=78:noticias&Itemid=71.*
Barreto, A. (2001). *The politics of language in Puerto Rico*. Gainesville: University Press of Florida.
Bourdieu, P. (1991). *Language and symbolic power*. Cambridge: Polity.
Cran, W. (2005). *Do you speak American?* Video documentary. Washington, DC: MacNeil-Lehrer Productions.
Delpit, L. (2008). *The skin that we speak: Thoughts on language and culture in the classroom.* New York: The New Press.
Duany, J. (2002). *The Puerto Rican nation on the move: Identities on the island & in the United States.* Chapel Hill: University of North Carolina.
Duany, J. (2005). The rough edges of Puerto Rican identities. *Latin American Research Review, 40*(3), 177-190.
DuBord, E. (2007). La mancha del plátano: Language policy and the construction of Puerto Rican national identity in the 1940s. *Spanish in Context, 4*(2), 241-62.
Fairclough, N. (2003). *Analyzing discourse: Textual analysis for social research*. New York: Routledge.
Fairclough, N. (2009). A dialectical-relational approach to critical discourse analysis in social research. In R. Wodak & M. Meyer (Eds.), *Methods of critical discourse analysis* (pp. 162-186). London: Sage.
Foucault, M. (1982). The subject and power. In H. Dreyfus & P. Rabinow (Eds.), *Michel Foucault: Beyond structuralism and hermeneutics* (pp. 208-226). Chicago: Chicago University.
Heller, M. (1996). Legitimate language in a multilingual school. *Linguistics and Education, 8*(2), 139-57.
Hutcheson, N., & Wolfram, W. (2001-2008). *The North Carolina language and life project* (video documentaries). Raleigh: North Carolina State University.
Jaffe, A. (2001). Authority and authenticity: Corsican discourse on bilingual education. In M. Heller & M. Martin-Jones (Eds.), *Voices of authority: Education and linguistic Difference* (pp. 269-296). Westport, CT: Ablex.

Labov, W. (1982). Objectivity and commitment in linguistic science. *Language in Society, 11,* 165-201.
Lippi Green, R. (2011). *English with an accent: Language, ideology, and discrimination in the United States.* New York: Routledge.
Mazak, C. (2008). Negotiating *el difícil*: Uses of English text in a rural Puerto Rican community. *CENTRO Journal, 20*(1), 51-71.
Ortiz-López, L. (2000). "Proyecto para formar un ciudadano bilingüe": Política lingüística y el español en Puerto Rico [Project to form a bilingual citizen": Language policy and Spanish in Puerto Rico]. In A. Roca (Ed.), *Research on Spanish in the United States: Linguistic Issues and Challenges* (pp. 390-405). Somerville, MA: Cascadilla. Pousada, A. (2008). Functions and valorization of language in Puerto Rico: Introduction. *CENTRO Journal, 20*(1), 4-11.
Proyecto PUCP. (2007). *Las Lenguas del Perú, Los castellanos del Perú* [Peru's languages, The Spanishes of Peru]. Video documentaries. Lima, Perú: Pontifical Catholic University of Peru.
Reaser, J., Adger, C. T., & Hoyle, S. (2005). Curriculum for *do you speak American?* Washington, DC: MacNeil-Lehrer Productions. Retrieved from www.pbs.org/speak/education
Reaser, J., & Adger, C. T. (2007). Developing language awareness materials for nonlinguists: Lessons learned from the *Do you speak American?* curriculum development project. *Language and Linguistics Compass, 1*(3), 155–167.
Rickford, J. R., & Rickford, R. J. (2000). *Spoken soul: The story of Black English.* New York: John Wiley & Sons, Inc.
Rúa, P. J. (2002). *La encrucijada del idioma* [Language at the crossroads]. San Juan: Instituto de Cultura Puertorriqueña.
Salmonte García, L. (2010). *Regresan los seminarios de la Academia Puertorriqueña de la Lengua Española* [Seminars return to the Puerto Rican Academy of the Spanish Language]. Universia Puerto Rico. Retrieved from http://noticias.universia.pr/tag/ACAPLE/
Swigart, L. (2000). The limits of legitimacy: Language ideology and shift in contemporary Senegal. *Journal of Linguistic Anthropology, 10*(1), 90–130.
Torres, L. (2007). The politics of English and Spanish aquí y allá (Puerto Rico). In K. Potowski & R. Cameron (Eds.), *Spanish in contact: Policy, social and linguistic inquiries* (pp. 81-99). Amsterdam: Benjamins.
Torres González, R. (2002). *Idioma, bilingüismo y nacionalidad* [Language, bilingualism, and nationality]. San Juan: U. de Puerto Rico.
van Dijk, T. (2001). Critical discourse analysis. In D. Shiffrin, D. Tannen, & H. Hamilton (Eds.), *Handbook of discourse analysis* (pp. 352-71). Oxford: Blackwell.
van Dijk, T. (2009). *Society and discourse: How social contexts influence text and talk.* Cambridge: Cambridge University.
van Leeuwen, T. (2007). Legitimation in discourse and communications. *Discourse and Communication, 1*(1), 91-112.
Vélez, J. (2000). Understanding Spanish-language maintenance in Puerto Rico: Political will meets the demographic imperative. *International Journal of the Sociology of Language, 142,* 5-24.
Wodak, R., & Meyer, M. (Eds.). (2009). *Methods of critical discourse analysis.* London: Sage.
Wolfram, W., & Ward, B. (Eds.). (2006). *American voices: How dialects differ from coast to coast.* Malden, MA: Blackwell.

Wolfram, W. (2008). Language diversity and the public interest. In K. King, N. Schilling-Estes, J. J. Lou, & B. Soukup (Eds.), *Sustaining linguistic diversity: Endangered and minority language and language varieties* (pp. 187-202). Washington, D. C.: Georgetown University Press.

Zentella, A. C. (1999). Language policy/planning and U.S. colonialism: The Puerto Rican thorn in English-Only's side. In T. Huebner and K. Davis (Eds.), *Sociopolitical perspectives on language policy and planning in the USA* (pp. 155-71). Philadelphia: John Benjamins.

Appendix 4A
Interview Guide Document (translation)

A. **Demographic Information**
   1. Gender
   2. Age
   3. Educational level completed
   4. Place of birth
   5. Current place of residence
   6. Number of years lived in Puerto Rico
   7. (If applicable) Number of years lived outside of Puerto Rico/Where

B. **¡Atrévete y Dilo! Campaign**
   1. Have you heard any of the radio spots of the ¡Atrévete y Dilo! campaign? *(If not, skip to question 8)*
   2. When you heard the content of these spots, what reaction did you have?
   3. Have you ever talked about the content of the spots with a family member or friend? What was his/her reaction?
   4. Do you know who made that campaign available?
   5. In your perspective, what was the purpose of the campaign?
   6. Do you think the campaign was successful in terms of this goal? Why (not)?
   7. Is there anything that could have improved or expanded the impact of the campaign?
   8. Are you familiar with the mission of the Academia Puertorriqueña de la Lengua Española? With which aspects?
   9. What effect does the Academia have in the lives of Puerto Ricans? In your life?

C. **Questions about Puerto Rican Spanish**
   1. The radio spots included linguistic, historical, and cultural information about a series of words such as *revolú, zafacón, yunta,* and *fracatán*. What connotations do these words hold for you?

2. Are these specifically Puerto Rican words or are they commonly used in Spanish in any region?
3. In your opinion, what is the status of Puerto Rican Spanish in relation with other dialects of Spanish? Can you explain your answer?
4. What opinion is held in other parts of the Spanish-speaking world about Puerto Rican Spanish?
5. In your opinion, is it important to change people's perspectives about Puerto Rican Spanish? Why (not)? What would be the most effective way of doing so?
6. Are Anglicisms part of Puerto Rican Spanish? What connotation do words such as "*party, janguiar, wíken, ticket, chequear, enigüei/ anyway*"? Are these also Puerto Rican words? Why do you think the Academy does not include them in its campaign?

CHAPTER 5

IDIOMATICITY AND LANGUAGE USE:
A Sociolinguistic Investigation in the Philippines

Yvonne Pedria Velasco
Carlos Hilado Memorial State College

Introduction

It is widely believed that private schools are generally academically superior to public schools. Figlio (1997) for example, found that private schools in the United States outperform public schools and spend less per student than do their public school counterpart. In a World Bank sponsored study conducted in developing countries (Dominican Republic, Tanzania, Thailand, Colombia and the Philippines) it has been shown that, while basic education in the developing countries is free or almost free, parents who are educated and/or employed would choose to pay for their children's education in private schools (Jimenez, Lockheed & Pacqueo, 1991). A principal finding of the World Bank study is that, given student background, students in private schools generally outperform their public school counterparts on standardized mathematics or language tests, or both. Whether private or public, there is a prominence conferred to education and the multifarious ways with which it has influenced a number of factors in the lives of people: education largely and increasingly determines an individual's job choice and income (Danziger & Reed, 1999), and whom one will marry (Kalmijn, 1991). It has more impact than any other factor, possibly excepting wealth, on whether one participates in politics, what one believes politically, and how much political influence one has (Verba, 2001). The impact of education permeates almost every aspect of society.

In the local setting, not many studies have been conducted to investigate whether the government of the Philippines has extended the full equality of educational opportunity to students studying in public schools (in terms of approximating the kind of facilities that are available to private education). Although initiatives to equalize opportunities for both the public and private sectors are in place, with the mandate in Republic Act 9155 passed in 2001 stating that:

> It is hereby declared the policy of the State to protect and promote the right of all citizens to quality basic education and to make such education accessible to all by providing all Filipino children a free and compulsory education in the elementary level and free education in the high school level.

What is not resolved is that for choice programs like post-secondary education, students studying in private schools appear to have the advantage in terms of educational experiences: with competent faculty and sophisticated facilities available to them, and which are not as easily available to public school students.

With the impact of education in language-educational outcomes relative to language being more desirable in private education, language education would benefit from an inquiry into those aspects of language studies that are influenced by socioeconomic indicators, despite the finding that variations in socioeconomic status, within a reasonable range, did not reverse the effect of private education (Jimenez, Lockheed & Pacqueo, 1991); although, interestingly, the magnitude of the private school advantage substantially decreases with lower socioeconomic status. Because language use pervades social life, the elements of social life constitute an intrinsic part of the way language is used. How participants define the social situation, their perceptions of what others know, think and believe, and the claims they make about their own and others' identities will affect the form and content of their acts of speaking (Krauss and Yue Chiu, 2012). Any communication belongs to a social context that constrains the kind of linguistic forms the language users use. Bruner (1990) suggests that "The symbolic systems that individuals used in constructing meaning are systems that were already in place, already 'there,' deeply entrenched in culture and language. They constituted a very special kind of communal tool kit whose tools, once used, made the user a reflection of the community" (p. 11). One can derive an important body of information about how others think from their social category memberships. Language, particularly speech, contains information about the social categories to which a speaker belongs, and serves as a rich source of data for impression formation. The words one use and the way one articulates them mark the social categories associated with the speaker. Quite independently of what we say, our speech tells others a great deal about us: our age, gender, geographic origin, and socioeconomic status (Krauss and Yue Chiu, 2012). Accordingly, one's preference for a particular linguistic form assigns him/her to a particular social class.

Social Class

The nature of the relationship between social class and language, specifically, language variation has been an enduring focus in sociolinguistics. When including social class variables in quantitative analyses, many variationists have followed a set of empirical traditions from sociology that determine an individual's position in a discrete social class by using scales that draw upon factors like income, education, and occupation (Mallinson, 2007). According to Mallinson, little consensus has been reached over how to theorize or measure class, making it both a conceptual and methodological hurdle. Ash (2002) expressed his consternation when he said that social class is a central concept in sociolinguistic research, that it is ironic that social class is often defined in an ad hoc way in studies of linguistic variation and change, and individuals are placed in a social hierarchy despite the lack of a consensus as to what concrete, quantifiable independent variables contribute to determining social class. To conceptualize and operationalize social class, variationists drew on one advancement in sociology in the past: the socioeconomic index. In Labov's (1966) study, a respondent was given a score on a socioeconomic index constructed as part of a sociological survey; it accounted for the person's years of education, the occupation of the family breadwinner, and family income. Wolfram's (1969) study employed Duncan's (1961) Socioeconomic Index (SEI). Erik Olin Wright, in the Encyclopedia of Social Theory (2003), asserts that few concepts are more contested in sociological theory than the concept of class. Confusion exists over what class means. In general, "class" invokes understandings of economic inequality. Yet, different theoretical approaches to class as economic inequality entail different agendas of class analysis (Mallinson, 2007). Wright reviews five such approaches:

1. class as subjective location,
2. class as objective position within distributions,
3. class as the relational explanation of economic life chance,
4. class as a dimension of historical variation in systems of inequality, and
5. class as a foundation of economic oppression and exploitation.

These theoretical approaches to social class keep up with Labovian sociolinguistics tradition that has long contended that language use is shaped by social forces (Krauss and Yue Chiu, 2012). Bernstein's (1977) sociolinguistic code theory examined the relationships between social class, family and the reproduction of meaning systems (code refers to the principles regulating meaning systems). For Bernstein, there were social class differences in the communication codes of working class and middle class children; differences that reflect the class and power relations in the social division of labor, family and schools. Adlam (1977), following Bernstein, advanced the notion that social relationships determine linguistic code. He proposed the following: family relations are fundamental, the socialisation of middle class children differs from that of working class children, families from different social classes have different attitudes towards and relationships with their children, and these differences lead to working class children having access to restricted codes and middle class children having access to both restricted and elaborate codes.

The current study examines the possibility that language variation occurs between designated classes, hypothetically constructed following Hoadley's (2006) framework of classification, by the way they comprehend idiomatic expressions. This is a departure from what has been a tradition in testing for language variation which usually makes use of phonological differences between subjects. It is assumed in the current study that idiomaticity is a marked choice of language use, implying that the use of idioms can be a possible area to test for language variation between groups. There is a dearth of studies with regard to language variation between students in public and private schools that makes use of idiomaticity as the test, to tease out a possible criteria to establish a link between idiomaticity and social class.

Idiomaticity and Second Language Learners

Pawley and Syder (1983) designate idiomaticity as a native-like selection of expressions. They introduced the notion of speech formula, which is a conventional link of a particular formal construction and a particular conventional idea. The term formula, then, could be taken to mean an idiomatic expression. In Pawley and Syder's view, all genuine idioms are speech formulas, but not all speech formulas are idioms. In psycholinguistic terms, accepted by the two scholars, true idioms are such speech formulas that are semantically non-compositional and are syntactically non-conforming. To Fillmore et al., (1988) an idiom is that which one has to know over and above rules and words. The latter definition breaks away from how language is traditionally viewed: that language involves two types of knowledge, rules and lexical items. For a non-native speaker of English, it is quite challenging to attain a status of idiomaticity based on Pawley and Syder's definition. A native speaker of a language will have learned standard ways of expression, which can consist of more than one word or certain clausal constructions, and can, over time, become memorized. With constant use, these expressions become readily available to the native speaker. Retrieving more or less ready-made combinations of words requires less mental effort than composing an utterance word for word (Wray, 2000). Apparently, frequency of use and economy would explicate the idiomaticity of native speakers of English. From the non-native learner's point of view, however, the use of idiomatic expressions is rather problematic. Idioms are difficult to translate because the meaning isn't literal. In other words, one can't necessarily derive the idiom's meaning by using just the words in the phrase. Certain cultural differences might also influence one's understanding of the expression. Unlike native speakers of English who typically just "know" the meaning of an idiom even if the origin isn't understood, non-native speakers need to understand the meaning of idioms, which requires some logic and knowledge of the origin of the phrase. Idioms are so idiosyncratic that they are either learned or refrained from and, as a result, non-native speakers, without much instruction on idioms are left on their own to develop their own idiomaticity.

Furthermore, it is possible that idiom comprehension may possibly locate non-native speakers as learners of English in the social scale. Hypothesizing on the belief that upper income families generally speak more English, and have more exposure to native speakers (i.e., personal acquaintances and media, their knowledge of idioms may be somewhat more sophisticated in that their utterances could include more idioms than those in lower income families. Second language learners of English have to acquire a multitude of conventionalized phrases and native-like proficiency could be difficult to attain. Yet, there are learners who come close to developing such ability. In Wiktorsson's study (2003), in which the frequencies of conventionalised multiword combinations in essays by Swedish university students of English and by native speakers were compared, it was found that there were no differences as to quantity. However, a comparison between essays by less advanced Swedish learners of English (i.e., upper secondary students) and university students showed that the more advanced the students were, the more idioms their essays contained. Conversely, this suggests, that the better students are at English, the more idioms they are likely to know. To those students generally belonging to upper income families who mostly speak English at home, as well as inside and outside of the classroom, it is possible that so many fixed expressions litter their everyday conversation that they receive little explicit instruction concerning conventionalized word combinations. These expressions seem to be picked up fairly effortlessly by them because the meaning of these expressions is already there, suggesting that no new meanings are to be learned. The question of how students from lower income families fare in the use of idioms vis-à-vis those students from upper income families, and whether such use of idioms correlates with SES, looms in the background.

Idioms and Fixed Expressions

Idioms are according to McMordie (1983) "a number of words which taken together, mean something different from the individual words of the idiom when they stand alone" (p. 4).

Consequently, idioms should not be broken up into their elements because they are sometimes referred to as fixed expressions (Cowie and Mackin, 1984). According to Baker (1992) states that idioms and fixed expressions are frozen patterns of language which allow little or no variation in form and, in the case of idioms, often carry meanings which cannot be deduced from their individual components. Strässler (1982), who chose the pragmatic route, defined the idiom as a functional element of language, namely, as a pragmatic phenomenon, (i.e., something that is judged from the point of view of the language user). Coulmas (1981), who worked on the concept of routine formulas, posits that an adequate description of a community's sociolinguistic behaviour must include: (1) idiomaticity, (2) routine, and (3) collocability, which are considered to be significant properties of expression. According to Coulmas, every member of a speech community can distinguish routine utterances from idiosyncratic ones. Since idioms are constructed with particular kinds of formulas, which are semantically and syntactically very often complex, to speak 'with proper idiomaticity' does require the use of formulas of various types. He concluded that if idioms were treated as units, then they must be semantic, not lexical.

The Relationship Between Social Class and Student Performance

The relationship between social class and student performance contextualizes the current study: that data could provide information as to whether social class differences are filtered through schools or whether classroom processes amplify the differences between the groups of college learners. Student performance is herein represented by an idiom comprehension test to be able to infer the relationship between the variables of social class and performance. A number of studies in the sociology of education deal with the relationship between social class and student performance and with how the inequalities are sustained: Bowles & Gintis, (1976) expounded on the concept of social reproduction focusing on the implications for economic relations. Inequality is continually socially reproduced in schools because a dominant group's ideology permeates the whole education system. Students from lower class families who aim to succeed must confront the material inequalities created by unequal funding arrangements (less sophisticated classroom facilities, inadequately-trained teachers, less exposure to media and linkages to business/employment opportunities, etc.). On the other hand, for middle and especially upper class children, maintaining their superior position in society requires little effort. They have access to higher quality instruction and in this way, the continuation of privilege and wealth for the elite is made possible. Bourdieu and Passeron (1997) focused on cultural reproduction. According to Bourdieu, the educational systems function in such a way that they legitimize class inequalities whereby success in education is facilitated by the possession of cultural capital: the familiarity with the dominant culture in a society, and especially the ability to use educated language. Assuming that all students possess cultural capital makes it very difficult for lower-class students to succeed in the educational system (Bourdieu and Passeron, 1997). The present study seeks to explore if there exists a difference that can be gleaned from the performance of students from upper income families than from those coming from lower income families by way of language, routine utterances from idiosyncratic ones, here designated by the way they comprehend idiomatic expressions.

Theoretical Framework

Acker (2006) suggests that class-related instantiations of inequality are observed and measured by paying attention to class-related social divisions. She states, "This conceptual move suggests a shift in terminology—we are enmeshed in class relations, not located in class structures" (p. 47). As Acker suggests, we can observe and measure class by paying attention to class-related social divisions, which are constituted by norms, lifestyle, status displays, and consumption habits. Second, we can observe and measure how images and symbols (language is included here) also constitute and reinforce these class-related social divisions. Third, we can focus on how these class-related social divisions are created, are gendered and raced, and change over time. Finally, we can interpret how these class-related divisions connect to what Acker calls "regimes of inequality," that shape social practice and that are constituted with different bases of inequality, degrees of visibility, legitimacy, hierarchy, participation, and ideology. In the current study, while it is obvious that class is recognized at first blush to be exclusively determined by the participants' higher education institution, it is relatively reasonable enough a sub-categorization. Following Acker, it is conceivable, that based solely on this differential access, one may situate the participants in a specific social class as determined by their idiomaticity.

Bernstein's (1977) class codes also figure in this study. Bernstein's sociolinguistic code theory was developed into a social theory examining the relationships between social class, family and the reproduction of meaning systems. Code refers to the principles regulating meaning systems. For Bernstein, there were social class differences in the communication codes of working class and middle class children, differences that reflect the class and power relations in the social division of labor, family and schools. Based upon empirical research, Bernstein distinguished between the restricted code of the working class and the elaborated code of the middle class. Restricted codes are context dependent and particularistic, whereas elaborated codes are context independent and universalistic. Following this argument, this study is committed to test whether language variation, using idioms as the linguistic feature, could yield a significant link between public and private university students.

Finally, Trudgill (2000) affords this study a structure to build on when he said that the position of the speaker in the society is often measured by the level of education, parental background, profession and their effect on syntax and lexis used by the speaker. An important factor influencing the way of formulating sentences is the social class of the speaker; thus, there has been a division of social classes suggested in order to make the description accurate. For Trudgill, there are two main groups of language users, mainly those performing non-manual work identified as the "middle class", while those who perform some kind of manual work are "working class". The additional terms "lower" and "upper" are frequently used in order to subdivide the social classes (Trudgill, 2000). Therefore, it is plausible to hypothetically subject the participants to classes so that differences between upper middle classes can be compared with lower working classes. In the study, the four groups of participants shall be hypothetically assigned to sub-categories so that comparisons can be made that shall make the arising descriptions from the results of the study as accurate as Trudgill (2000) so recommends.

Objectives of the Study

This study seeks to investigate the way freshman college students from four higher education institutions comprehend and discriminate appropriate use of idiomatic expressions. Specifically, the answers to the following questions are sought:

1. What is the level of comprehension of idiomatic expressions of the college freshman students from the private higher institutions and the public higher institutions?
2. Is there a significant relationship between the levels of comprehension of idiomatic expressions of students from the private higher institutions and the public higher institutions?

3. Is there a significant difference between the levels of comprehension of idiomatic expressions of students from the private higher institutions and the public higher institutions?

Methodology

Design

The study employed the quantitative method using a cross-sectional design involving four college freshman classes, coming from different socio-economic and regional backgrounds. The quantitative aspect of the study was realized with the use of a 10-item test on idioms that form the basis for interpretation relative to the hypothetical subcategories herein described.

Participants

Four college freshman classes from four different higher education institutions (HEIs) served as the participants of the study. The participants' ages range from 16 to 19 with a mean age of 18. The English proficiency level of the participants is at the least average; this is considering the fact that all four higher education institutions from where the participants were studying have institutional admission requirements consisting of an admission protocol (written test and an oral interview). The minimum English proficiency level requirement for admission for all HEI is average. Classes were selected purposively considering the schedule availability of the English instructors. The following is a brief description of the higher education institutions (HEIs) from where the participants were selected and the tests administered. The hypothetical classification of the participants, with a brief description of each, is provided below:

- HEI1 is a state college located in the province of Negros Occidental, with four campuses spread across Negros and mostly caters to the lower socio-economic families of the province. Average tuition per unit is 150 php (www.chmsc.edu.ph).HEI2 is a government-funded school located in the City of Manila. It receives subsidy from the local government, and like HE2 is patronized by those belonging to the middle to lower middle-income families. Average tuition per unit is 145php (www.plm.edu.ph).
- HEI3 is a private school, located in the City of Manila. Some of its degree programs were commended by the Commission on Higher Education (CHED) as abiding to the standards of excellence in education. Average

tuition per unit (based on the lowest available figure) is 2,279 php (www.dlsu.edu.ph).

- HEI4 is a private school, located in the City of Manila, right across from HEI3. It is owned by the same organization that owns HEI3. Average tuition per unit is 1,827 php (www.dls-csb.edu.ph).

The table below shows a comparison of the tuition fees per unit/hour of the four HEIs comprising the participants' schools in the study.

Table 5.1
Tuition fee per unit of the four HEIs

HEI1	HEI2	HEI3	HEI4
P150.00	P145.00	P2,279.00	P1,827.00

Framework for Classification

The study employed the classification framework implemented by Hoadley (2006) in her study where she classified schools with students coming from working class backgrounds as lower income and those schools with students coming from affluent families and neighborhoods as upper income. This following sub-categorization is proposed based on average tuition per unit, and the reason that the kind of school one goes to is dependent on how much income a family earns. Trudgill's (2000) model which recommends that divisions of "upper" and "lower" classes shall be made in order to generate accurate descriptions also lends support to this classification. It is thus on these considerations that the four HEIs were ascribed categories in the following manner:

1. Upper income–HEI3 and HEI4
2. Lower income–HEI1 and HEI2

There were 25 respondents coming from each of the four HEIs with an aggregate total of 100 respondents ($n=100$).

Instrument

The instrument used was a researcher-made questionnaire consisting of 10 items, whereby common idiomatic expressions were couched in sentences. The idiomatic expressions used in the test were generated after due consultation with three inter-raters. There were 15 idioms which were subjected to a rankings test as to the likelihood of their being understood by the students as perceived by the three inter-raters, with 1 being most likely, and 15 least likely. The inter-raters were graduate students in doctoral programs who were themselves college instructors. This process of selection and consequent elimination narrowed down the idioms to 10: the number of test questions that the researcher deemed to be reasonable enough to provide an initial finding.

Pilot Testing

Since the test was researcher-made, it warranted a pilot test to establish its validity and reliability. Content validity was established by the approval made by the three inter-raters who made the selection of idioms for testing and declaring the sentences to be grammatically correct. To test for reliability, the 10-item test was piloted in one of the random freshman classes of HEI1 and the reliability coefficient was obtained. The coefficient alpha (Cronbach's alpha) was used to determine test-score reliability. After running the results using computer software, the instrument was found to have a reliability coefficient of 0.82. Coefficients at or above .80 are often considered sufficiently reliable (Webb, Shavelson, & Haertel, 2006), and thus on this basis the researcher-made instrument is deemed reliable.

Data Collection

The study took place in August of academic year 2013-14. The tests were administered by faculty members of the respective HEIs to one of their freshman classes. The test lasted for a maximum of 15 minutes. The researcher retrieved the questionnaires, scored them and subjected them for statistical treatment.

Procedure

After proper research conventions were observed (permissions, schedules, orientation as to the protocols for the conduct of the test, etc.), the selected faculty members administered the 10-item test that took approximately 15 minutes to complete. The faculty members retrieved the questionnaire and submitted the same to the researcher for scoring, statistical treatment, and interpretation.

Scoring

Comprehension. The measure of comprehension was elicited by having the respondents choose from a set of two choices pertaining to the applicable meaning of the sentence containing the idiomatic expression. Of the two choices, one was the correct response, which, if accurately chosen, showed that the respondent understood the meaning of the idiomatic expression couched in the sentence. The scores were designated descriptors so as to concretize the numerical depiction: 9-10= *Excellent*, 7-8= *Very good*, 5-6= *Average*, and 4 and below = *Below average*.

Data analysis. The idiom test administered to the 100 participants was scored using an answer key which was verified by the other two inter-raters to be correct. Since the questionnaire required correct answers, the scores after checking the test were computed to obtain the mean scores as a descriptive measure. To find for correlations between classifications, the Pearson r was used to appropriately infer from the results. To test for significant difference, the Independent Samples t Test was performed using computer software.

Results and Discussion
Comprehension Level of Idiomatic Expressions of College Freshman Students

Table 5.2 displays the mean scores for both upper income and lower income class. Comprehension is quantified in terms of the number of correct answers the students made in the 10-item test. As can be gleaned from the results, the mean score obtained by the upper income class is 8.16 (sd = 2.004). This mean score is described as *Very Good*. The lower income class obtained a mean score of 8.20 (sd = 1.716), which is .04 higher than the upper income class, and still described as *Very Good*.

Table 5.2 reveals that the comprehension levels of both the upper and lower class as *Very Good* indicate that the participants have a good grasp of the selected idioms' meaning and can spot the context with which the idioms were used. A *Very Good* level of idiom comprehension gives the impression that idiomaticity in both lower and upper classes has probably been mastered. An assumption could be made that idioms had been integrated into previous formal instruction, or that it could have been learned from other sources.

Table 5.2
Comprehension level of idiomatic expressions of college freshman students

Classification	Mean	N	Std. Deviation
Lower class	8.20	50	1.761
Upper class	8.16	50	2.004
Total	8.18	100	1.877

A Pearson Product-moment correlation was run to determine the relationship between the mean scores of the students from the lower and upper class. With a significant value set at $p > .05$, the result showed that there exists no significant relationship between the mean scores of the upper and the lower classes ($r = -0.142$, $N = 50$, $p > .05$). Table 5.3 illustrates the results.

Table 5.3
Relationship between the comprehension levels of the upper class and lower class

		Lower class	Upper class
Lower class	Pearson Correlation	1	-.142
	Sig. (2-tailed)		-.324
	N	50	50
Upper class	Pearson Correlation	-.142	1
	Sig. (2-tailed)	-.324	
	N	50	50

$p > .05$

A statistical correlation was run to establish the strength of relationship between social class and idiom comprehension. It is contended that idiomaticity and social class are not necessarily independent variables but may possibly interact in a significant way. The absence of a statistically significant relationship between social class and idiom comprehension, which the data yield, precludes one from inferring that social class has a relative effect on the performance of the participants.

Table 5.4

Differences in comprehension levels between the upper class and lower class

	Levene's Test for Equality Of Variances		t-test for Equality of Means				
	F	Sig.	t	df	Sig. (2-tailed)	Mean Difference	Std. Error Difference
Equal variances assumed	.163	.687	.106	98	.916	.040	.377
Equal variances not assumed			.106	96.41	.916	.040	.377

As described in Table 5.4, the mean scores for both classes were subjected to an Independent Samples *t* Test to determine if a significant difference exists between the upper class idiom comprehension scores and the lower class idiom comprehension scores. The test was calculated using a computer software. An equal variances *t* test failed to reveal a statistically reliable difference between the mean scores of the upper class and lower class (t (98) = 0.106, p = 0.916). What this means is that the two classes did not outperform each other in the idiom comprehension test: the level of performance of both classes is relatively the same. The diminutive difference in the mean scores between classes ($m = 0.14$) could be attributed to a host of possible factors ranging from small class sample, choice of idioms, few test questions, among others. Since the levels of performance of both classes on the idiom comprehension test are somewhat similar, one can infer that class differentiation did not contribute to performance of the participants on the test.

The findings of the study showed that both upper and lower classes performed equally well in the test. Both classes obtained a comprehension level of *Very Good*, which suggests that in that particular year level, although belonging to different socio-economic backgrounds, the participants have at the very least mastered idiomatic expression comprehension based on the 10-item test. When the results were subjected to a statistical treatment to allow for inferences, results showed that there exists no significant relationship between the two mean scores, which discourages further comparisons (i.e., idiomaticity between the two classes). When scores were subjected to correlations to obtain significant differences, the results showed that there exist no significant differences between the upper and lower classes. What this implies is that although it may seem that the lower class outperformed the upper class with a meagre mean difference of .04, this figure is not significant to warrant a generalization that the lower class participants are better in terms of their ability to comprehend idiomatic expressions. This finding goes back to what Trudgill (2000) has to say about social class, that an important factor influencing the way of formulating sentences or language use is the social class of the speaker. This study has suggested that two different classes of students from four different socio-economic/regional backgrounds performed equally well on an idiom test. There is no inference that can be made as to whether idiomaticity is dictated by social class, as there exists no significant difference in the mean scores of both classes.

There are, however, constraints to the study that the researcher admits as limitations. Since socio-economic status is a basis, there could have been elicited a demographic profile that could locate the participants in the socio-economic scale by asking them to indicate on the questionnaire the annual family income averaged on a monthly basis ideally to get at a general idea. The limited number of test items that could remarkably capture idiom comprehension could also be a possible limitation. Furthermore, it is apparently necessary to have the idioms graded according to level of difficulty and familiarity to participants.

Wiktorsson (2003), previously mentioned in this study, asserted that the better students are in English, the more idioms they are likely to know. Following this observation, it would be ideal to administer an English

Proficiency Test prior to administering the idiom test so that it would reveal the linguistic profile of the participants and thereafter make some inferences about the students' proficiency and their idiomaticity in relation to social class.

Conclusion/Implications to Language Teaching

The present study investigated the potential of students' idiomaticity through idiom comprehension as a test to find language variation between classes. It was found that social class does not affect performance in the idiom comprehension test; also, college freshman students from public and private schools performed equally well in the idiom test.

However, the idiomaticity of students, in spite of the rather positive level of the students' performance, needs to be given attention too if the language teachers are to capture the culture that is attached to the English language. It is undoubtedly not easy to teach idioms due to the rather idiosyncratic nature of these expressions and therefore language teachers need to devise strategies and methodologies for teaching these expressions, even in the college level. Idiomaticity is understood to be an almost native-like selection of expressions (Pawley and Syder, 1983), and teaching students to be cognizant of the way native speakers speak by understanding, and possibly, using idioms in their utterances would pave the way for a communication process that is free from vagueness, ambiguity and imprecision.

What follows, a teaching model for idiomatic expression, is an attempt to include idiomaticity in the language curriculum that is currently being applied in the Philippine classroom. This is a model that the researcher crafted, the impetus of which was derived from the literature that deals with idioms and fixed expressions peculiar to the culture of the native speakers of English, and also the seeming difficulty second language learners' encounter when dealing with idioms.

As Figure 5.1 depicts, the issue about the teaching of idioms for second language learners can apparently be traced to the attitudes of nonnative teachers of English towards idiom teaching, that it would be best for nonnative teachers of English to start to *identify personal perceptions about idiom teaching* first. Their perceptions about the task would largely influence their decision about whether to teach or not to teach them, regardless of whether or not such subject matter is included in the learning outcomes of

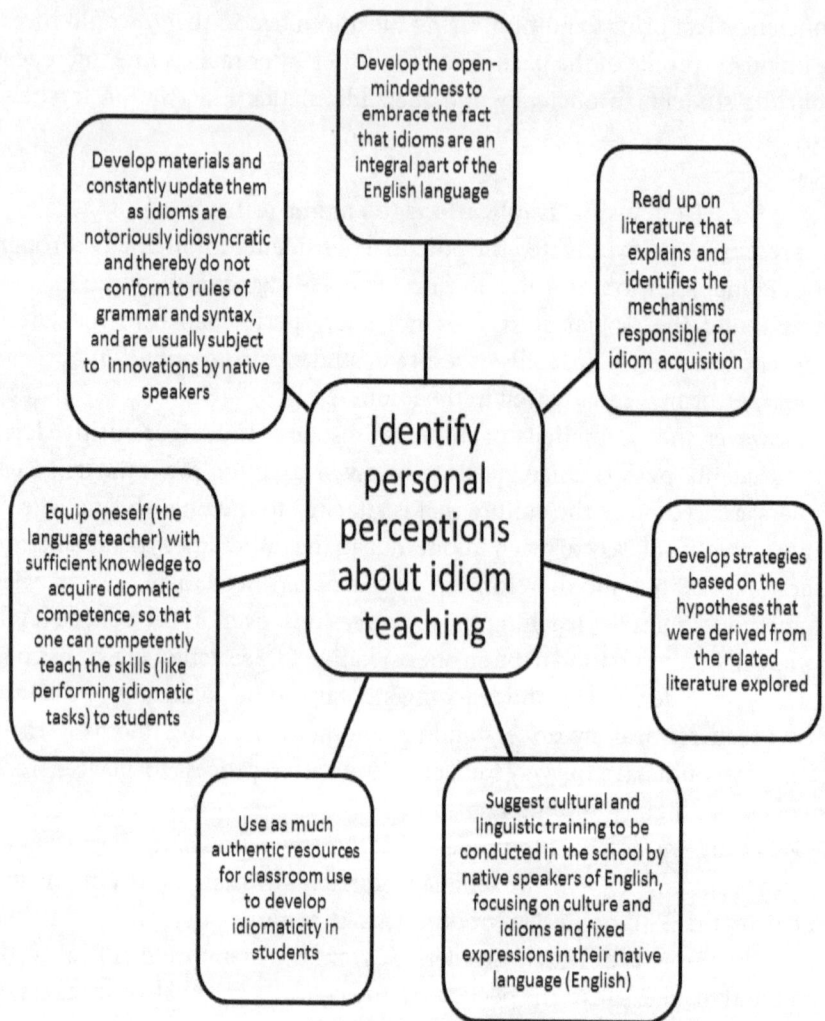

Figure 5.1. A Teaching Model for Idiomatic Expression

the language curriculum. When nonnative teachers of English themselves find difficulty comprehending idioms, it would dictate the way they would implement the English language curriculum. Instructional decisions as a matter of the teacher's creative choice may sometimes fail to be faithful to the language curriculum prescribed by the Department of Education, thus the role of teachers' perceptions about idiom teaching occupies the central role. Teachers must learn to concede and develop the open mindedness to embrace that idioms are an integral part of the English language. When the fence of prejudice is down, the way to idiom instruction is facilitated. It would help when the topic about idiom teaching is included in a best practices forum so that teachers can learn from one another and can self-assess their respective personal capabilities. Once, the prejudice about idiom teaching has diminished, one way of fostering successful teaching of these linguistic units is to read up on literature that explains and identifies mechanisms responsible for idiom acquisition. Would repetition help? Would consistently drilling students on these linguistic items help facilitate their acquisition? Would exposure to media help? These are questions that are answered by research literature and would invariably help in understanding the successes and failures of students in idiom comprehension and use. Going a bit further, and more importantly, nonnative teachers need to equip themselves with idiomatic competence. Without this competence, teaching idioms is difficult to pull off because these linguistic expressions are not available for literal translation and are quite idiosyncratic. Exposure to authentic media content from native speakers could be a good way of updating one's idiom base and could lend the nonnative teacher of English, whether teaching in the private or public school, the necessary tools to effectively teach the language.

References

Acker, J. (2006). *Class questions: Feminist answers*. New York: Rowman and Littlefield.
Adlam, D. S. (1977). *Code in context*. London: Routledge & Kegan Paul.
Ash, S. (2002). Social class. In Chambers, J. K., Trudgill, P., and Schilling-Estes, N. (Eds.), *The handbook of language variation and change* (pp. 402–422). Malden, MA: Blackwell.
Baker, M. (1992. *In other words: A coursebook on translation*. London: Routledge.
Bernstein, B. (1977). *Class, codes and control: Towards a theory of educational transmissions* (2nd ed.). London: Routledge and Kegan Paul.
Bowles, S., & Gintis, H. (1976) *Schooling in capitalist America*. New York: Basic Books.
Bruner, J. (1990). *Acts of meaning*. Cambridge, MA: Harvard University Press.
Bourdieu, P., & Passeron, J. C. (1990). *Reproduction in education, society and culture*. Thousand Oaks, CA: Sage.
Coulmas, F. (1981). Idiomaticity as a problem of pragmatics. In Parret, H., and Sbisa, M. (Eds.), *Possibilities and limitations of pragmatics* (pp. 139-152). Amsterdam: Lawrence Erlbaum Associates.
Cowie, A. P., Mackin, R., & McCaig, I. R. (1975-1984). *Oxford dictionary of current idiomatic English, 1-3*. Oxford: Oxford University Press.

Danziger, S., & Reed, D. (1999). Winners and losers: The era of inequality continues. *Brookings Review, 17*, 14-17.

Dowling, P. (1998). *The sociology of mathematics education: Mathematical myths/pedagogic texts*. Falmer: London.

Duncan, O. (1961). A socioeconomic index for all occupations. In A. Reiss (Ed.), *Occupations and social status*. New York: Free Press.

Figlio, D., & Stone, J. (2012), Are private schools really better? In Polachek, S. W. and Tatsiramos, K. (Eds.), *35th anniversary retrospective (Research in Labor Economics*, Volume 35, pp. 219-244). Bingley, UK: Emerald Group Publishing Limited.

Fillmore, C., Kay, P., & O'Conner, J. (1988). Regularity and idiomaticity in grammatical constructions: The case of "let alone". *Language, 64*, 501-538.

Gerwitz, S., & Cribb, A. (2003). Recent readings of social reproduction: Four fundamental problematics. *International Studies in Sociology of Education, 13*(2), 243-259.

Jimenez, E., Lockheed, M., & Paqueo, V. (1991). The relative efficiency of private and public schools in developing countries. *The World Bank Research Observer, 6*(2), 205-218.

Hoadley, U. (2006, April). *The reproduction of social class differences through pedagogy: A model for the investigation of pedagogic variation*. Paper presented at the Second Meeting of the Consortium for Research on Schooling, Capetown, South Africa.

Kalmijn, M. (1991). Shifting boundaries: Trends in religious and educational homogamy. *American Sociological Review, 56*(6), 786-800.

Krauss, R., & Chiu, A. (2012). Language and social behavior. In Gilbert, D., Fiske, S., and Lindsey, G. (Eds.), *Handbook of social psychology* (4th ed., pp. 41-88). Boston: McGraw-Hill.

Labov, W. (1966). *The social stratification of New York City*. Washington, DC: Center for Applied Linguistics.

Mallinson, C. (2007). Social class, social status and stratification: Revisiting familiar concepts in sociolinguistics. *University of Pennsylvania Working Papers in Linguistics, 13*(2), 149-163.

McMordie, J. S. (1983). *English idioms and how to use them*. Moscow: Vyschaja Shkola.

Morrow, R., & Torres, C. (1994). Education and the reproduction of class, gender, and race: Responding to the postmodern challenge. *Educational Theory, 44*, 43-61.

Pawley, A., & Syder, F.(1983).Two puzzles for linguistic theory: Nativelike selection and nativelike fluency. In Richards, J. C. and R. W. Schmidt, R. W. (Eds.) *Language and communication* (Volume 7, pp. 191-226). London: Longman.

Republic of the Philippines. (2001, August 11). *An act instituting a framework of governance for basic education, establishing authority and accountability, renaming the department of education, culture and sports as the department of education and for other purposes.* (Republic Act No. 9155) Retrieved from http://www.lawphil.net/statutes/repacts/ra2001/ra_9155_2001.html

Strässler, J. (1982). *Idioms in English: A pragmatic analysis*. Tübingen: Günter Narr.

Trudgill, P. (2000). *Sociolinguistics: An introduction to language and society*. England: Penguin Books.

Verba, S. (2001). *Political equality: What is it? Why do we want it?* Cambridge, MA: Harvard University.

Webb, N., Shavelson, R., & Haertel, E. (2006). Reliability coefficients and generalizability theory. *Handbook of statistics* (Volume 26). London: Elsevier.

Wiktorsson, M. (2003). *Learning idiomaticity. Lund Studies in English 105*. Stockholm: Almqvist & Wiksell.

Wolfram, W. (1969). *A sociolinguistic description of Detroit negro speech.* Washington, DC: Center for Applied Linguistics.

Wray, A. (2000). *Formulaic language and the lexicon.* Cambridge: Cambridge University Press.

Wright, E. (2003). Social class. In Ritzer, G. (Ed.), *The encyclopedia of social theory.* Thousand Oaks, CA: Sage Publications. Retrieved from http://www.ssc.wisc.edu/~wright/Social%20Class%20--%20Sage.pdf

LANGUAGE TEACHING PRACTICES, PEDAGOGY, AND SOCIAL JUSTICE

CHAPTER 6

INTERSECTIONS OF STUDY ABROAD, SOCIAL CAPITAL, AND SECOND LANGUAGE ACQUISITION

John W. Schwieter
Aline Ferreira
Wilfrid Laurier University

Introduction

Assuming that language is regarded as a concrete reality of relations between people from which social capital manifests itself (Clark, 2006), this study aims to investigate whether a short-term study abroad (SA) experience can help to increase how adult language learners rate their social capital, as well as how they reflect on their changing identities and language development during the experience. Quantitative analyses were conducted on self-ratings of language abilities of a sample of 14 English (L1) language learners of Spanish (L2) and French (L3) at the beginning and conclusion of a SA experience in Spain. Additionally, responses from open-ended interviews at the conclusion were qualitatively analyzed to explore social issues such as identity, socialization, and social capital. This chapter will first discuss the notion of social capital followed by a brief review of literature of the linguistic benefits of SA and how such benefits may lead to social development of the self within learning communities (Schwieter, 2013a). Following this background, the present study is outlined and the results and implications are discussed.

Background

Social Capital
Social capital, the object that pertains to the structure of the relationship between economic and human capitals (Portes, 1998), is similar to other

forms of capital since there is a conscious or unconscious expectation of future returns once an investment is made (Adler & Kwon, 2002). However, social capital is distinct from other forms of capital because it develops and resides in social relationships (Robison, Schmid, & Siles, 2002) and within specific groups and communities. According to Clark (2006), social capital consists of networks of relationships available to individuals and groups, as well as in the environmental and cultural conditions in which those networks are carried out. Under these assumptions, language can be viewed as a type of wealth-accumulation, a concrete example of the substance of social capital, which is formed by all communication systems between people. Social capital is a value of social interaction and is essentially a mediated phenomenon, guided by language, which is a fundamental matter in human contact. Language is a mode, a form, a concrete reality of relations between people. Those relations become productive given that language has the potential to produce coordinated activities and shared understandings, resulting in positive outcomes (ibid).

Capital, by itself, is a type of power and social capital has been argued to be accumulated power. According to Bourdieu (1986), the original power of capital is its capacity to generate worth or value. Individuals and groups are able to obtain and add productive value from the cultural contexts of the networks to which they have access (Clark, 2006). In bilingual or multilingual communities, needless to say, the language in which this is conducted plays an important role. It seems plausible that bilinguals who are able to utilize the possibilities of socializing in two or more languages may have a unique access to social capital. For language learners seeking to become bilingual, an excellent way to help facilitate these social benefits is through a SA experience in which they not only gain linguistic competence but they also develop and bolster social capital and other attributes such as global citizenship (Davidson & Lehmann, 2005; Paige, Fry, Stallman, Josić, & Jon, 2009; Tarrant, 2010).

Short-Term Study Abroad
There are many reasons that motivate students to study in another country including the desire to learn a non-native language, to travel, to increase job opportunities, to be in contact with native-speakers of the L2, to personally and culturally enrich oneself, to gain course credit, to make new friends, among others (Badstübner & Ecke, 2009; Castañeda & Zirger, 2011).

Regardless of the rationale, it cannot be denied that there are linguistic and non-linguistic benefits. In fact, according to Davidson (2007), "language acquisition at the highest levels of proficiency is generally not possible without a substantial immersion experience in the target culture" (p. 277). As a result, recent studies have shown increased interest in a number of issues including language use and proficiency development (Badstübner & Ecke, 2009; Mendelson, 2004; Schwieter & Kunert, 2012; Smith, Giraud-Carrier, Dewey, Ring, & Goreet, 2011) and personal development such as sensitivity to language and cultural issues (Schwieter & Kunert; Shively, 2010). Other studies have begun to investigate language socialization in general, which is argued to be a complex process of language practice that is affected by several variables including motivation, attitudes, interlocutor attributes, among others (Isabelli-García, 2006). These variables are modulated by social networks, which play an important role in measuring social capital (Coleman, 1988; Lin, 2001).

In general, fairly little attention has been placed on the effects of time spent abroad on L2 proficiency development (Davidson, 2010; Schwieter, 2013b) or on L2 socialization (Isabelli-García, 2006; Smith et al., 2011). Short-term SA programs are becoming increasingly popular in North American universities given that a semester- or year-long option may either be financially unfeasible or may delay graduation and program requirements (for a further discussion on other hurdles of studying abroad, see also Department of Education, Science, and Training, 2004; Otero & McCoshan, 2006; Sussex Centre, 2004; Vande Berg, 2003). The Institute for International Education (2010) furthermore demonstrates that among students from the US who studied abroad in 2010, 55% did so for a relatively short duration (i.e., less than 8 weeks), 41% studied abroad for one semester (i.e., 3-4 months), and only 4% did so for an entire year. While there is far more to be studied when comparing shorter- and longer-term SA experiences, it is clear that there is merit to Dwyer's (2004) and Schwieter's (2013b) claim that in terms of the length of the SA experience, "more is better," but "some is better than none."

Benefits of Short-Term Study Abroad
Results from Allen and Herron's (2003) study revealed significant gains in L2 proficiency in only a six-week SA experience. Milleret's (1990) study

additionally pointed out that US students who studied in Brazil for six weeks significantly improved their speaking skills on average from an intermediate-mid to an intermediate-high level. Furthermore, Schwieter's (2013b) study reported on the development of L3 lexical robustness during a three-week L3 SA experience. Lexical robustness is an important psycholinguistic aspect of global proficiency in which the greater automaticity of word retrieval is due to the familiarity with and frequency of its access (Schwieter & Sunderman, 2008, 2009). The results demonstrated a significant increase in L3 lexical robustness. Interestingly, language learners with lower levels of L3 lexical robustness at the beginning of the SA experience realized more gains in lexical robustness than learners with higher pre-departure levels, demonstrating the ability for SA to potentially jump-start non-native lexical development.

Schwieter and Klassen's (2013) study examined lexical and morphosyntactic development among English language learners of Spanish during a three-week SA experience similar to Schwieter's (2013b). A lexical robustness measure (Schwieter & Sunderman, 2008, 2009) and production and comprehension tasks were conducted prior to and at the conclusion of a SA experience to investigate the development of nominal gender and number agreement among English language learners of Spanish (Montrul, Foote, & Perpiñán, 2008) and the correlation of such development to growth of lexical robustness. The results suggested that lexical and morphosyntactic development do not necessarily go hand-in-hand. In fact, in line with Schwieter's study, L2 learners with lower levels of lexical robustness prior to SA realized a significantly greater increase in lexical robustness than their more proficient counterparts. Contrary to these effects, neither the improvement of lexical robustness nor the level or prior knowledge of gender and number morphology affected morphosyntactic development in this respect. Studies looking at linguistic development thus far have demonstrated fruitful preliminary results when it comes to understanding the development of various linguistic abilities (phonetic, lexical, morophosyntactic, pragmatic, etc.).

In terms of nonlinguistic benefits such as academic attainment, career impact, and intercultural development, Dwyer's (2004) study revealed no significant differences between shorter- and longer-term SA experiences. However, Davidson and Lehmann (2005) argue that at early levels, short-term experiences can provide beginning learners with the motivation they need to continue acquiring the language. Yager (1998) suggests that short-term SA experiences encourage learners to get the most out of their brief stay by maximizing their out-of-class contact with the L2.

As discussed in Schwieter and Kunert (2012), language development from having interacted with native speakers of the L2, mostly when living with a host family, are among the most valued benefits of SA. In all, a SA experience is argued to stimulate communicative interaction and cultural enrichment (Kruse & Brubaker, 2007) and to hold the potential to form relationships that result in social capital which, differently from most other forms of capital, does not tend to emphasize what people possess individually (Smith et al., 2011).

Social Capital and Study Abroad
Social capital is based on individuals' relationships, attributes, and available resources (Smith et al., 2011). The relationships can be based on explicit social networks—built from explicit connections that are made through an intentional action—or implicit affinity networks based on inherent similarities. Because language learners participating in SA naturally share implicit affinities (e.g., the desire to learn the L2) and, at the same time, are able to establish explicit connections (e.g., help peers to cope with culture shock), it is assumed here that social capital goes hand-in-hand with SA experiences. Previous studies have shown that developing social networks with native speakers while abroad via volunteer work, part-time employment, social interactions, etc., can facilitate language acquisition (Isabelli-García, 2006; Whitworth, 2006). In the same way, it is believed that students living in an immersion setting with a host family will develop social relationships that will help development L2 proficiency and social capital. This is expected given that Schwieter and Kunert's (2012) study, which also explored issues of identity development during a SA experience, demonstrated that learners were indeed able to reflect on identity development "when expressing feelings of newly-found confidence, not only about their conversational skills in the target language, but about being global citizens" (p. 11). The learners also reported gains in cultural sensitivity and the ability to adapt to different situations.

Clark (2006) makes an attempt to reconcile language with the notion of social capital, which is formed in cultural and environmental conditions.

Cultural capital, in its fundamental state, presupposes embodiment, and its accumulation is a result of labor, which costs time, that must be undertaken by the investor (Bourdieu, 1984). Although learning an L2 is labor- and time-intensive, it facilitates the development of human relationships and social capital. When learners decide to take part in a short-term SA experience, they are immersed in a cultural environment in which the social networks will operate in the non-native language, such as trust and reciprocity of their members (Clark), contributing to a better development of the L2 acquisition process. As mentioned above, social capital refers to the resources embedded within the interpersonal relationships that, during the SA experience, can be accessed via the host family and community (see also Castañeda & Zirger, 2011; Portes, 1998). It is believed that the SA experience helps students to creatively display and explore themselves, which may have a significant impact on L2 development. In this sense, this study investigates, by means of a pre- and post-test questionnaire and open-ended interviews during a short-term SA experience in Spain, whether the productive value of relationships among a group of students is bolstered and leads to L2 development and positive reflections of language socialization.

Present Study

The present study aims to examine language learners' reflections on language development and their experiences adapting to and socializing within the L2 community. We anticipate that the context of the short-term SA experience will increase a language learner's social capital and, as a consequence, facilitate L2 acquisition, which is usually a key objective for learners who take part in this sort of program. In this study, 14 students spent five weeks in Spain during which they enrolled in an intensive Spanish language and culture course. The participants were also involved in various situations in which they socialized in Spanish in naturalistic settings with native speakers of Spanish. For instance, because they were living with host families, they took part in conversations in Spanish during most of the time they spent at home.

As mentioned at the beginning of this chapter, we interpret language as an essential part of human relationships that results in the productive value called social capital (Clark, 2006; Schwieter, 2013a). SA experiences offer learners plenty of opportunities to establish such relationships. The ability for students to take advantage of their existing social capital and strengthen it is an essential component of any short-term SA experience, enabling language and culture development once it is freely shared with students (Castañeda & Zirger, 2011). In the present study, the participants' discussions of social capital were analyzed through student reflections in open-ended interviews. Below, we describe the participants, methodology, and data analyses.

Participants
The participants who took part in the study abroad experience in Spain were undergraduate students from a medium-sized, English-speaking university in Canada. These 14 participants were English (L1) language learners of Spanish (L2) of which 10 were females and 4 were male. Prior to this study, the participants had been enrolled in L2 university courses anywhere from 1 to 4 semesters. Additionally, the participants had some knowledge of French (L3), but in all cases, their Spanish was more advanced than their French. For the sake of anonymity, all participants were assigned a participant number (e.g., P1, P2, etc.) and are referred to as such throughout the present study.

Method and Procedure
Before departure, participants completed a language history questionnaire (see the Appendix of Schwieter, 2013b, for a complete version) which served to elicit vital information regarding language use and self-ratings of proficiency in English (L1), Spanish (L2), and French (L3). Upon arriving in Spain, the participants spent five weeks of approximately 80 hours of instruction of Spanish grammar and conversation in addition to cultural sessions that focused on intensive language learning and contextualizing upcoming visits to cultural sites (see also Schwieter & Kunert, 2012).

On the final day of the SA experience, the participants once again completed a language history questionnaire in addition to an adapted version of Freed, Dewey, Segalowitz, & Halter's (2004) Language Contact Profile. The latter is designed "to assess second language contact for students entering and completing language study programs in various contexts of learning" such as immersion contexts (p. 349). Also on the final day of the SA experience, an open-ended interview was conducted individually with participants to gather their reactions to the SA experience in terms of their feelings on fitting in and adapting to a new environment (e.g., host family, school, community, etc.) in addition to how this will apply to their lives back home. This structured interview also sought to explore the extent to which the SA experience facilitated the development of social capital. The following are the questions that were posed in the open-ended interviews:

1. Discuss your experiences socializing in Spanish throughout the SA experience.
2. Discuss your feelings on fitting in and adapting to a new environment. Did you feel a part of your host family? The school? The community?
3. With which aspects of Spanish culture do you feel you identified most?
4. Do you think you have changed as a person from this SA experience? If so, in what ways? If not, why not?
5. What aspects of this short-term SA experience can you see yourself applying to your social life once home?
6. Discuss your role as a team member within the social environment of this SA experience. Do you think that your learning experience was facilitated alongside your peers?
7. How has this SA experience (and its social learning environment) helped you creatively display and/or explore yourself?
8. Did this SA experience help increase how you would rate your social capital?

Data Analysis

Language development is measured by comparing participants' self-ratings of language abilities prior to and at the conclusion of the SA experience as elicited from the language history questionnaires. Language contact is explored by analyzing averages and trends that participants reported in their Language Contact Profile (Freed et al., 2004). In terms of the open-ended interviews, the researchers transcribed all interviews and employed a content analysis (Marshall & Rossman, 2010), which Schwieter (2011) argues is "a holistic and systematic way of examining forms of communication to document patterns objectively" (p. 39). The transcriptions were first analyzed thematically and subsequently coded according to three prominent themes related to language and social issues. In the following, we first discuss language development and language contact. We then present some key findings related to language socialization, identity, and social capital that were reported in the open-ended interviews.

Discussion of Findings
Language Development

The language history questionnaire in the present study provided the opportunity for participants to rate their own language abilities on a ten-point Likert scale. This questionnaire was administered both at the beginning and conclusion of the SA experience to explore any possible changes in how participants estimated their English, Spanish, and French language abilities. Table 6.1 displays the data that was elicited from the questionnaire.

Table 6.1

Mean and standard deviations (in parentheses) for self-ratings of language abilities in English (L1), Spanish (L2), and French (L3) at the beginning and conclusion of study abroad

	At beginning	At conclusion	Difference	T	p
English (L1)					
Reading	9.86 (.53)	9.79 (.57)	-0.07	1.84	0.33
Writing	9.71 (.82)	9.50 (.85)	-0.21	1.38	0.19
Speaking	9.93 (.27)	9.79 (.43)	-0.14	1.42	0.17
Listening	9.93 (.27)	9.86 (.36)	-0.07	1.00	0.34
Comfort level of expression	9.71 (.61)	9.89 (.29)	+0.18	1.09	0.29
Spanish (L2)					
Reading	5.64 (1.86)	6.14 (2.25)	+0.50	1.83	0.09
Writing	5.04 (2.08)	5.68 (1.81)	+0.64	1.95	0.07
Speaking	4.68 (2.09)	5.79 (1.80)	+1.11	3.33	0.01
Listening	5.79 (1.92)	7.00 (2.04)	+1.21	2.79	0.02
Comfort level of expression	4.64 (2.24)	5.36 (2.13)	+0.72	2.50	0.03
French (L3)					
Reading	5.43 (2.56)	4.82 (2.54)	-0.61	2.71	0.02
Writing	4.79 (2.22)	4.11 (2.42)	-0.68	2.11	0.06
Speaking	4.71 (2.43)	4.04 (2.26)	-0.67	1.80	0.09
Listening	5.00 (2.25)	4.46 (2.62)	-0.54	1.36	0.20
Comfort level of expression	4.21 (2.51)	3.64 (2.44)	-0.57	1.59	0.14

Note. The scores represent the participants' self-assessment of their language abilities based on a 10-point scale (1=least proficient, 10=most proficient). Standard deviations are presented in parentheses.

Table 6.2
Mean and standard deviations (in parentheses) for self-ratings of language contact

	Days per week	Hours per day
1. Spoke in Spanish outside of class with fluent Spanish speakers.	6.23 (1.01)	2.12 (1.00)
2a. Spoke in Spanish with instructor.	4.29 (1.77)	1.71 (1.42)
2b. Spoke in Spanish with friends who are fluent Spanish speakers.	3.64 (2.34)	1.11 (.76)
2c. Spoke in Spanish with classmates.	4.57 (2.16)	1.68 (1.30)
2d. Spoke in Spanish with strangers.	4.14 (2.24)	.89 (.54)
2e. Spoke in Spanish with host family	6.21 (1.25)	1.82 (.96)
2f. Spoke in Spanish with service personnel	4.00 (2.91)	.82 (.52)
3a. Used Spanish outside of class to clarify classroom-related work.	3.64 (2.73)	1.29 (1.31)
3b. Used Spanish outside of class for directions or information.	3.93 (1.82)	.79 (.45)
3c. Used Spanish outside of class for superficial/brief exchanges with host family	6.50 (1.02)	1.57 (1.22)
3d. Used Spanish outside of class for extended conversations with host family	5.25 (2.39)	1.43 (.80)
4a. Tried to use things learned inside the classroom in situations outside of the classroom.	6.00 (1.47)	1.29 (.77)
4b. Took things learned outside the classroom back to the classroom for questions or discussion.	4.36 (2.27)	1.32 (.96)
5a. Spoke a language other than Spanish or English.	1.29 (2.46)	.21 (.25)
5b. Spoke Spanish to native or fluent speakers of Spanish.	5.43 (2.44)	1.82 (1.38)
5c. Spoke English to native or fluent speakers of Spanish.	3.50 (2.93)	1.04 (1.01)
5d. Spoke Spanish to nonnative speakers of Spanish.	5.21 (2.33)	1.32 (1.16)
5e. Spoke English to nonnative speakers of Spanish.	6.50 (.85)	2.79 (1.44)
6a. Overall reading in Spanish outside of class.	5.14 (1.88)	.79 (.45)
6b. Read newspapers in Spanish outside of class.	1.07 (1.07)	.54 (.44)
6c. Read novels in Spanish outside of class.	.64 (1.28)	.25 (.41)
6d. Read magazines in Spanish outside of class.	1.14 (1.46)	.46 (.58)
6e. Read schedules, announcements, and menus in Spanish outside of class.	5.57 (1.79)	1.07 (.49)
6f. Read e-mail and webpages in Spanish outside of class.	2.14 (2.21)	.75 (.94)
6g. Overall listened in Spanish outside of class.	6.36 (1.50)	2.86 (1.67)

6h. Listened to television and radio in Spanish outside of class.	4.50 (2.95)	.89 (.74)
6i. Listened to movies or videos in Spanish outside of class.	1.07 (1.27)	.42 (.48)
6j. Listened to songs in Spanish outside of class.	4.21 (2.69)	1.18 (.82)
6k. Listened to catch other people's conversations in Spanish outside of class.	5.43 (2.62)	1.14 (.79)
6l. Overall wrote in Spanish outside of class.	2.64 (2.02)	.75 (.70)
6m. Writing homework assignments in Spanish outside of class.	4.89 (1.90)	1.50 (.76)
6n. Wrote personal notes or letters in Spanish outside of class.	1.86 (2.32)	.57 (.62)
6o. Wrote e-mail in Spanish outside of class.	.79 (1.42)	.25 (.41)
6p. Filled in forms or questionnaires in Spanish outside of class.	1.04 (1.82)	.32 (.41)
7. Spoke in English outside of class.	7.00 (.00)	3.71 (1.41)
8a. Read newspapers, magazines, or books; watched movies, TV, or videos in English outside of class.	2.14 (2.18)	.75 (.77)
8b. Read e-mail or webpages in English outside of class.	5.43 (1.87)	1.43 (1.59)
8c. Wrote e-mail in English outside of class.	3.79 (2.55)	1.04 (.77)
8d. Wrote personal notes or letters in English outside of class.	2.64 (3.05)	.71 (.62)

Note. The days per week scores represent the participants' estimate on a 0-to-7 point scale (choosing from zero to seven days). The hours per day scores represent the participants' estimate on a 5-point scale (choosing either 0-1 hours, 1-2 hours, 2-3 hours, 3-4 hours, or 4-5 hours). Standard deviations are presented in parentheses.

As can be seen in Table 6.1, it is not surprising that participants' native language abilities in English were not affected by the SA experience. However, the same cannot be said for their two non-native languages. As expected, Spanish reading, writing, speaking, and listening skills and comfort level of expression in Spanish were positively impacted by the SA experience, corroborating the results discussed in Schwieter (2013b) that shows that lexical robustness and self-ratings of language abilities significantly increase in a short-term immersion experience. Interestingly, the results of the self-ratings show that participants felt as though some of their French language abilities were negatively affected from the short-term experience in Spain. Although these findings were also reported in Schwieter (2013b), the latter study additionally demonstrated that pre- and post-measures of lexical robustness did not reveal attrition. Nonetheless, in both the present study and Schwieter (2013b), native speakers of Language X who are familiar with more than one foreign language (e.g., Languages Y and Z) feel less proficient in Language Y when participating in a study abroad experience in Language Z. This claim has been confirmed both when Language Y is the L2 and Language Z is the L3 (Schwieter, 2013b) and when Language Y is the L3 and Language Z is the L2 (present study).

Language Contact
Who are the stakeholders that facilitate meaningful interaction in the target language during SA experiences? What is the extent of their interaction and what modes of communication (i.e., reading, writing, speaking, etc.) are utilized? To gather information reporting on the exposure to and interaction with the target language, each participant completed a Language Contact Profile (adapted from Freed et al., 2004) at the conclusion of the SA experience. A summary of the findings from the adapted Language Contact Profile can be seen in Table 6.2.

From Table 6.2, it is apparent that learners in the present study daily participated in meaningful interaction with native speakers as shown in Questions 1, 2e, 3c, and 5b. In most cases, this included conversation with host families and other community members. This interaction no doubt helps to explain why participants felt as though their speaking and listening abilities grew more than reading and writing, which also demonstrates that perhaps more reading and writing practice is needed during the SA experience. For instance, although participants reported reading on average 5.14 days per week in Spanish, more careful observation of the *type* of reading revealed that nearly all of this reading practice was with menus at restaurants. Furthermore, even though the learners reported writing nearly 3 days per week, this seemed to be confined to homework assignments and not so much writing e-mail, essays, journals, or personal correspondence. Further studies may wish to try to balance the assessments and activities in which SA learners participate in order to maximize the potential for development across all language abilities. Finally, it is worth noting that Questions 4a and 4b demonstrate that SA experiences provide language learners with the unique opportunity to be able to integrate and try out academic (formal) language learning in real-life situations and to discuss or clarify real-life experiences back in class. This certainly is yet another important area of language contact that supported L2 acquisition and socialization.

Language and Social Issues
Based on the responses gathered from the open-ended interviews, three main themes emerged including language socialization, identity, and social capital. Overall, only one participant (P8) expressed difficulties with regard to socializing in Spanish throughout the SA experience due to what he/she felt was "not enough pre-existing knowledge of the L2." Other than this comment, the participants had experienced anxiety at the beginning, but they felt more comfortable because they realized that they were progressing in the L2, and "ended up enjoying it" (P4). Although there was one student who reported feeling as though he/she could not express her/himself in Spanish at all, the rest of the group expressed that socialization "definitely assisted their Spanish language learning" (P6).

Difficulty adapting to the new environment was also reported, but most participants claimed that this attenuated as time passed by and they began to feel integrated into the community and school. Some aspects of the culture were reported to be very dissonant, especially regarding the food and the pace of life. The participants also felt as though they improved in terms of their appreciation and tolerance to other cultures, in addition to their ability to think critically about their own culture and personality and to develop a new appreciation for things that may have once been taken for granted. They also considered that learning together regardless of individual preferences brought benefits to the overall learning experience.

Many participants reported that the SA experience helped them to think deeper about themselves after having succeeded in dealing with unexpected situations, new people, and ways of life in another language. P2 and P5 stated that after the SA experience, they were rethinking their future career paths. P5 even went on to comment that he/she thought that SA should be a requirement of all undergrads because of its "profound impact on how one views oneself." Gaining cultural knowledge and confidence helped to facilitate the adaptation to the new situations and to be more extroverted in the L2 when meeting new people.

Language Socialization

From the interviews, it was clear that participants recognized the importance of language socialization throughout the SA experience. Socializing in Spanish occurred primarily because students lived with native Spanish-speaking families who were instructed not to speak in English with the participants. As such, learners were pushed to interact in Spanish during the time they spent in the houses, even though sometimes the interaction was facilitated by a peer who may have known more Spanish or may have helped translate into English any vital information that was misunderstood. P13 reflected: "I enjoyed the experience. It was filled with consent interaction. Whether with host families, classmates, teachers, or business owners, there was not much time to be alone. I learned to listen and try to pay closer attention to everything around me, even though my speaking and comprehension abilities were still weak."

However, because of the rather low L2 proficiency level of some participants, they reported difficulties trying to socialize in the L2. Even though it was encouraged to speak in the L2 with other L2 language learners because "they were learning as well" (P11), many times participants felt as they were simply at a lack for words and could not express themselves, as described by P8: "I struggled to socialize in Spanish because I felt like I could not express myself and therefore could not show who I am as a person...if I had not been able to use any English to help my Spanish, I would not have formed any significant friendship at all."

Although this comment points out that having a low L2 proficiency level may be an obstacle for learners to socialize in the L2 while studying abroad, it should be noted that this was the only instance in the interviews in which a participant reported feeling unable to express him/herself because of low L2 proficiency level. On the contrary, participants commonly felt that simply making an attempt to socialize in Spanish—regardless of the accuracy of their output—helped them to adapt faster and more smoothly to the new environment. P3, who had only taken one semester of Spanish before the SA experience, described: "adapting to a new environment was very intimidating at first but then got easier. I went from not having much prior Spanish knowledge to being completely immersed into the culture and language." Later in P3's interview, he/she mentioned that the social environment helped to overcome the language difficulties: "everyone was very accepting and willing to help me with the transition. My host family was very accommodating. The school and staff there were incredible and there was a great support system. The faculty members from our university back home were always with us abroad and were excellent leaders who were always reliable and willing to help when needed." The sense of integration into the target community helped students to accelerate the process of adaptation not only for beginning learners as seen in P3's comment, but also among intermediate learners, who seemed to comment more frequently on how comfortable they felt with the host family, the school, the community, and their ability to adapt to a new environment.

The sense of a unified learning community was constantly mentioned and positively regarded by the participants as reported in Schwieter and Kunert (2012). P9 described that throughout the time abroad: "all my peers and I learned together, we all experienced the same awkwardness and class hours. I was team member by contributing in my class, being out with my peers, and trying to make sure everyone was happy, comfortable, and safe." P10 similarly stated: "being with my peers has helped so much because whether it is about school or other problems, you always have someone to talk to." P14 also reported: "learning alongside peers is a more efficient way for me to learn a language, especially considering the fact that language is a communication tool and social tool. The entire experience would have been more difficult mentally if I had been abroad by myself learning the language." From the interviews, it was apparent that a strong unity underpinning the SA experience fostered a sense of community that helped to minimize the effects of cultural shock, which was rarely mentioned by the learners. This is not to say that the participants relied too heavily on their non-native speaking peers. In fact, quite the opposite was reported in their Language Contact Profiles, which suggested, and the interviews validated, that the learners participated in ample interaction with native or near-native speakers.

Language and Identity
Regarding identity and personal effects that the SA experience had on the learners, several issues emerged. For example, a few of the participants felt as though the pace of life abroad seemed to complement their personalities and preferences in that people in Spain take the time for "siestas," which is uncommon in North America. P8 stated: "I identified most with the

relaxing slow-paced culture—where to-go cups were unheard of. I am late for everything at home so I liked that that is almost expected in Spanish culture. I also loved the 'have-fun' kind of culture that is more 'work to live' rather than 'live to work'. Life abroad seemed to fit me nicely." For many of the participants, these unexpected feelings of being able to identify with a new language and culture—and sometimes almost more so than their home language and culture—were new and uncharted given that this was the first experience abroad. P3 reported that after the SA experience, he/she has seen an incredible growth in himself: "I think that just being abroad is the richest knowledge of all. I have not only expanded my Spanish knowledge but my real-life and world knowledge has grown immensely. When traveling abroad you need to learn to become more independent and responsible. My independence, knowledge, sense of my surroundings, and view on life have changed incredibly."

According to P8, whose first time abroad was the present study, the experience has made him/her decide to change some aspects of his/her behavior: "after living abroad and sharing experiences with others, I've learned more about myself and will work on changing the things about myself that I have seen in others or on being more like the things that I've grown to appreciate in others." This sort of comment was reported repeatedly by the students, who generally voiced that they would be more aware of their actions and traits once home. In terms of language development, they reported a desire to maintain contact in Spanish with the friends they made in Spain and one participant jokingly stated: "Now I want all my friends and family back home to watch Spanish television and films with me all the time" (P8).

The SA experience in the present study helped students to become more independent and aware of what they are capable of in the L2. P12 reflected: "[after studying abroad,] I see myself fearless speaking Spanish when given the opportunity. One cannot be afraid to make mistakes because that is how we learn. Also, I will stop using English as a crutch when caught in a jam speaking Spanish. I feel that these two faults are made far too often by Anglophones learning a new language." Socializing with native speakers was commonly viewed as a fear that was overcome, as clearly stated by P9: "I also proved to myself that I could be with strangers and make friends and not feel lonely. I feel like a more open person." In the same way, the experience not only helped P4 to be more open to meeting new people, but it also has helped him/her to reconsider future plans: "this experience has helped me to realize that it is easier to talk to and get along with others than before. It also helped me to realize my passion for culture, language, and helping others." This comment suggests that the SA experience has provided the learners with an opportunity to explore their identity in a new language, culture, and environment, and to bring to light things that leaners were not aware they were capable of accomplishing.

Language and Social Capital
As previously addressed, social capital is a value of relationship, which is accomplished by means of language. The SA experience reported in this chapter modified the way some of the participants viewed themselves as a member of a learning community requiring responsibilities while providing benefits. P3 stated: "I have learned more about how to work and live within a group of people and how to be independent, smart, and responsible. Exploring the new ways of life, language, and culture has given me a new sense of appreciation as well as a more positive outlook on life and all that it has to offer. I also feel like I can do more in society now that I have more Spanish skills." In a similar way, P10 noted: "in a new group you either need to be able to adapt to it, or be on your own for the whole trip. Gaining the knowledge and confidence needed to adapt to new situations made me realize that I am worth more to myself. I think that in the future, socially speaking, this study abroad experience will make me a more valuable employee and culturally-sensitive human being."

From the interviews, participants realized that meeting new people and making new international connections would lead to an increase in social capital. Realizing and valuing the fact that they were part of a united learning community was also a common theme mentioned in the interviews. In some ways, they felt stronger as a group than alone. As pointed out by P15, "this experience helped to show me how important it is to have people around you. And showed me how beneficial it is to talk to people that are going through the same things. I'm sure that all of us feel as though we can return home feeling as though we have something to share and offer to society."

In all, the open-ended interviews uncovered several social benefits as participants reflected back on the SA experience. Not only did many report that the experience had changed them positively as a person, but more importantly, several reported that they would be able to apply what they have learned to social aspects in their everyday lives. Most importantly, participants recognized the value and social power of learning an L2 within a learning community abroad, a notion which suggests evidence of the development of social capital.

Conclusion

This chapter has discussed a study in which language learners of Spanish participated in a short-term SA experience in Spain. The objective of the study was to examine language proficiency development, language contact, and social issues such as L2 socialization, identity construction, and the development of social capital. In terms of language development, as interpreted from the participants' self-ratings of language abilities, participants rated their L2 abilities significantly higher at the conclusion of the SA experience. However, these differences were only marginally significant for L2 reading and writing skills. Interestingly, participants also felt as though by the end of the SA experience, their L3 reading and writing abilities had significantly decreased and their L3 speaking abilities had marginally decreased. These results should neither be surprising (Schwieter, 2013b) nor alarming, as they most likely reflect decaying-like effects of not practicing a weak non-native language.

The Language Contact Profiles highlighted the importance of interaction with native speakers. The SA experience sets up a context in which learners can emphasize a real-life interface between what they formally learn and how they apply it to real-life situations. The exchange of learning goes back and forth between formal learning abroad (i.e., intensive L2 classes abroad) and the learner's life in the SA community. The Language Contact Profiles additionally validated the lack of exposure to L2 reading and writing practice. Future studies may wish to encourage more reading and writing practice activities during SA experiences, in particular personal reflections (e.g., SA diaries) which could be shared and read by peers.

Several social issues emerged from the open-ended interviews. First of all, learners recognized the importance of socialization in the success in adapting to and living in another language and culture. They felt as though they must be open to participating in activities that encourage social interaction in order to realize a smooth transition and rewarding experience. L2 socialization was easier because confidence and comfort levels were raised due to the unity of the SA group. They truly felt supported and not alone in this "once-in-a-lifetime-experience" (P12). When reflecting on the SA experience and identity development, many participants reported that they had changed and developed as a person. They pointed out several characteristics that they envisioned themselves adapting once back home. A few of the participants even discovered that the SA experience had introduced them to a lifestyle, language, and culture that suited their personalities more. In all, participants in the SA experience saw themselves as more open-minded, worldly, and "fearless to speak in the L2" (P3). Finally, from the interviews it was apparent that participants had realized the value of learning another language via a SA experience given that they felt as though they could go back home and do more with their new language abilities and would have access to more social and professional opportunities. Several participants also believed that the SA experience had provided them with the ability to adapt to and succeed in new situations that life would continue to bring them.

As demonstrated in the present study, SA experiences have the potential to make significant improvements in language abilities through heightened interaction with native speakers that can be brought back to SA classes (and similarly, what is learned in SA classes can be applied to real-life situations outside the classroom). Just as important are the many social benefits that learners attain from participating in SA experiences such as the development of socialization skills in a non-native language, identity construction and personal reflection, and the realization that learning another language has the potential to increase social capital. Future studies are needed to continue investigating these complex issues, potentially directly comparing SA experiences to traditional classroom settings. It is without a doubt that much can be learned at the intersections of SA, social capital, and L2 acquisition.

References

Allen, H., & Herron, C. 2003. A mixed-methodology investigation of the linguistic and affective outcomes of summer study abroad. *Foreign Language Annals, 36*, 370-85.

Badstübner, T., & Ecke, P. (2009). Student expectations, motivations, target language use, and perceived learning progress in a summer study abroad program in Germany. *American Association of Teachers of German, 42*, 41-49.

Bourdieu, P. (1986). The forms of capital. In J. Richardson (Ed.), *Handbook of theory and research for the sociology of education* (pp. 241-246). New York: Greenwood Press.

Castañeda, M., & Zirger, M. (2011). Making the most of the "new" study abroad: Social capital and the short-term Sojourn. *American Council on the Teaching of Foreign Languages, 44*, 544-564.

Clark, T. (2006). Language as social capital. *Applied Semiotics, 8*(18), 29-41.

Coleman, J. (1988). Social capital in the creation of human capital. *The American Journal of Sociology, 94*, S95.

Davidson, D., & Lehmann, S. (2005). A 25-year longitudinal analysis of the language careers of ACTR study abroad alumni. *Russian Language Journal, 55*, 193–221.

Davidson, D. (2007). Study abroad and outcomes measurements: The case of Russian. *Modern Language Journal, 91*, 276-280.

Davidson, D. (2010). Study abroad: When, how long, and with what results? New data from the Russian front. *Foreign Language Annals, 43*, 6-25.

Department of Education, Science, and Training. (2004). *Study abroad and study exchange systems in industrial countries*. Canberra, Australia: Author.

Dwyer, M. (2004). More is better: The impact of study abroad program duration. *Frontiers: The Interdisciplinary Journal of Study Abroad, 10*, 151-163.

Freed, B., Dewey, D., Segalowitz, N., & Halter, R. (2004). The language contact profile. *Studies in Second Language Acquisition, 26*, 349-356.

Freed, B., Segalowitz, N., & Dewey, D. (2004). Context of learning and second language fluency in French. *Studies in Second Language Acquisition, 26*, 275-311.

Institute of International Education. (2010). *Open doors: Report on international educational exchange*. New York: Institute of International Education

Isabelli-García, C. (2006). Study abroad social networks, motivation, and attitudes: Implications for second language acquisition. In M. Dufon & E. Churchill (Eds.), *Language learners in study abroad contexts* (pp. 231-258). Clevedon, UK: Multilingual Matters.

Kruse, J., & Brubaker, C. (2007). Successful study abroad: Tips for student preparation, immersion, and postprocessing. *Die Unterrichtspraxis/Teaching German, 40*(2), 147-152.

Lin, N. (2001). *Social capital: A theory of social structure and action*. Cambridge, UK: Cambridge University Press.

Marshall, C., & Rossman, G. (2010). *Designing qualitative research*. Thousand Oaks, CA: Sage.

Mendelson, V. (2004). *Spain or bust? Assessment and student perceptions of out-of-class contact and oral proficiency in a study abroad context*. Unpublished doctoral dissertation, University of Massachusetts at Amherst.

Milleret, M. (1990). Evaluation and the summer language program abroad: A review essay. *The Modern Language Journal, 74*, 483-88.

Montrul, S., Foote R., & Perpiñán, S. (2008). Gender agreement in adult second language learners and Spanish heritage speakers: The effects of age and context of acquisition. *Language Learning, 58*, 503-553.

Otero, M., & McCoshan, A. (2006). *Survey of the socio-economic background of ERASMUS students: Final report*. Birmingham, UK: ECOTEC Research and Consulting.

Paige, R., Fry, G., Stallman, E., Josić, J., & Jon, J. (2009). Study abroad for global engagement: The long-term impact of mobility experiences. *Intercultural Education, 20*(1), S29-S44.

Portes, A. (1998). Social capital: Its origins and applications in modern sociology. *Annual Review of Sociology, 24*, 1-24.

Robison, L., Schmid, A., & Siles, M. (2002). Is social capital really capital? *Review of Social Economy, 60*, 1-24.

Schwieter, J. W. (2011). Migrant Hispanic students speak up: Linguistic and cultural perspectives of low academic attainment. *Diaspora, Indigenous, and Minority Education: An International Journal, 5*(1), 33-47.

Schwieter, J. W. (2013a). The foreign language imagined learning community: Developing identity and increasing foreign language investment. In D. Rivers & S. Houghton (Eds.), *Social identities and multiple selves in foreign language education* (pp. 139-155). London: Bloomsbury Academic.

Schwieter, J. W. (2013b). Immersion learning: Implications for non-native lexical development. In J. W. Schwieter (Ed.), *Studies and global perspectives of second language teaching and learning* (pp. 165-185). Charlotte, NC: Information Age Publishing.

Schwieter, J. W., & Klassen, G. (2013). Lexical and morphosyntactic development in a short-term study abroad experience. *Open Journal of Modern Linguistics, 3*(4), 360-366.

Schwieter, J. W., & Kunert, S. (2012). Short-term study abroad and cultural sessions: Issues of L2 development, identity, and socialization. In P. C. Miller, J. Watze, & M. Mantero (Eds.), *Readings in Language Studies, vol. 3: Critical Language Studies: Focusing on Identity* (pp. 587-604). New York: International Society for Language Studies, Inc.

Schwieter, J. W., & Sunderman, G. (2008). Language switching in bilingual speech production: In search of the language-specific selection mechanism. *The Mental Lexicon, 3*(2), 214-238.

Schwieter, J. W., & Sunderman, G. (2009). Concept selection and developmental effects in bilingual speech production. *Language Learning, 59*, 897-927.

Shively, R. (2010). From the virtual world to the real world: A model of pragmatics instruction for study abroad. *Foreign Language Annals, 43*, 105-125.

Smith, M., Giraud-Carrier, C., Dewey, D., Ring, S., Gore, D. (2011). Social capital and language acquisition during study abroad. In L. Carlson, C. Hoelscher, & T. Shipley (Eds.), *Proceedings of the 33rd Annual Conference of the Cognitive Science Society*. Austin, TX: Cognitive Science Society.

Sussex Centre for Migration Research, University of Sussex, and the Centre for Applied Population Research, University of Dundee. (2004). *International student mobility*. Issues Paper commissioned by HEFCE, SHEFC, HEFCW, DEL, DfES, UK Socrates Erasmus Council, HEURO BUTEX, and the British Council.

Tarrant, M. (2010). A conceptual framework for exploring the role of studies abroad in nurturing global citizenship. *Journal of Studies in International Education, 14*, 433-451.

Vande Berg, M. (2003). Rapporteur report: Study abroad and international competence. Paper presented at *Global Challenges and U.S. Higher Education*, Duke University.

Whitworth, K. (2006). *Access to learning during study abroad: The roles of identity and subject positioning*. Unpublished doctoral dissertation, The Pennsylvania State University.

Yager, K. (1998). Learning Spanish in Mexico: The effect of informal contact and student attitudes on language gain. *Hispania, 81*, 898-913.

CHAPTER 7

ABLEISM AND SOCIAL JUSTICE IN HIGHER EDUCATION:
GTAs Readiness and Attitudes Towards Accommodating Students With Disabilities

Muriel Gallego
Carey Busch
Ohio University

The core tenant of social justice can be described as guaranteeing that access and resources be fairly distributed amongst all individuals regardless of their place within a traditionally oppressed group (Fouad, Gerstein, & Toporek, 2006). The path to a society that strives for equality and justice requires extinguishing all forms of oppression (Adams, 2000; Wronka, 2008), a process that could be facilitated by extensive advocacy, community outreach, broad discussion and fundamentally having an understanding of the impact that oppression may have on members of an oppressed group.

The pre-established relationship of subordination/domination, intrinsic to any situation of oppression, extends beyond the commonly addressed issues of ethnicity, race, and socioeconomic status, which have been traditionally contemplated within the "multiculturalism lens". A social justice framework is therefore more inclusive in that it also recognizes marginalization due to gender, sexual orientation, country of origin, native language versus second language, physical or psychological impairment, or the combination of two or more of these elements. The *status quo* in the U.S. has been established on the values of white, Eurocentric, able, educated, middle-upper class, heterosexual, native English-speaking, men, determining that those individuals who belong to the dominant group inherently receive privileges. In spite of the advancement made in the last decades towards providing equal access for all to higher education, there is still a significant dropout rate, mainly for minority students (ethnic, racial, LGBT, low-income, non-Christian, working, and disabled) who experience first hand the consequences of disenfranchising (Kozol, 2005).

Working at the theoretical, interdisciplinary intersection of Universal Instruction, Social Justice Education and Critical Multicultural Education is said to offer an inclusive perspective to understand and overcome, in a more holistic way, all forms of oppression (Hackman; Pliner & Johnson, 2004). This theoretical collaboration is essential in order to shift from focusing on the individual and placing him/her in the margins, as the one who requires additional, differential, or specialized attention. Pushing for those who are marginalized to adapt to the center is making the individual responsible for adapting to and functioning in a reality that does not represent him/her, and only contributes to isolation and therefore, more marginalization.

This investigation operates on the premises of Social Justice Education and the need for faculty advocacy in order to guarantee that every student, regardless of their placement within a specific group, is granted access to higher education, and the resources to navigate through college. By means of a survey distributed across several institutions of higher education in the U.S., we analyze the readiness GTAs in "faculty-like" positions display concerning instructing and accommodating students with disabilities.

Ableism and Social Justice in Higher Education

Although the people with disabilities were not included in initial laws passed for other marginalized groups in the late 1960's, the first legal protection was offered with the passage of Section 504 of the Rehabilitation Act in 1973 (P.L. 93-112). This legislation required federal employers and those receiving federal funding, including public and private institutions of higher education whose students utilize federal financial aid, to guarantee physical and programmatic access to people with disabilities. Despite this legislation, in 1978 only 2.6% of students in higher education were reported to have a disability (Cook, Rumrill, & Tankersley, 2009; Salzberg et al., 2002). Nearly 30 years later The National Center for Education Statistics reported that this percentage of students with disabilities had grown to 10.8% (Snyder & Dillow, 2012).

While the described changes in enrollment continued to follow an ascending trend that indicates that more students with disabilities are gaining access to higher education, this is still not happening at an equitable level to people without disabilities. The American's with Disabilities Act (ADA; P. L. 101-336) was passed in 1990 to expand the reach of Section 504 to private employers and buildings with public access. While the ADA did not fundamentally alter the need for colleges and universities to provide equal access, it renewed the awareness that not enough was being done to assure the rights of people with disabilities. *The ADA 20 Years Later* (Kessler Foundation and National Organization on Disability, 2010) reported that 19% of people with disabilities have graduated from college compared to 27% of their non-disabled counterparts. Although these figures have increased for both groups (up from 14% in 2004 for people with disabilities and up from 25% in 2004 for people without disabilities), there remains a gap of 8% suggesting that ableist attitudes still remain in higher education and individuals with disabilities are being denied equal opportunity. According to Wolanin and Steele (2004), students with disabilities have entered the list of marginalized groups in higher education, along with racial and ethnic minorities, women, and low-income students and have been subjected to a culture that undervalues their potential and contributions (Castaneda & Peters, 2000).

The approach to disability in higher education has been largely grounded in a medical model which weighs judgment on the severity of an underlying medical condition as well as the creation of a dependent relationship with "expert" professionals (Smith, Reynolds & Rovnak, 2009). A social model of disability focuses on the consequences of exclusion as a result of social inadequacies and aspires to assure people with disabilities are not excluded as a result of social and attitudinal barriers (Gabel & Conner, 2009). Additionally, Smart (2007) asserted that the shift away from a medical model of disability will empower individuals with disabilities, facilitate collaboration among professionals, and bring disability out of the realm of the "expert" into general discussion.

This social paradigm is consistent with the concept of social justice and can be applied to support the faculty and GTAs in providing equitable opportunities for students with disabilities. It has been reported (Cook, Rumrill, & Tankersley, 2009), that faculty members in higher education manifest their lack of essential knowledge concerning the implementation of accommodations for students with disabilities. However, in spite of their unpreparedness, they are still expected to provide such accommodations in their classes. This could be potentially more difficult for GTAs due to their lack of overall experience. Additionally, many of the GTAs in American universities are foreign-born and might be used to different practices, or no practices at all concerning students with disabilities (Chalupa & Lair, 2000).

Earlier studies have revealed that faculty are apprehensive regarding the provision of accommodations; especially those adjustments that demand more of their time or imply modifications such as extra credit, grammar, spelling, etc. (Bourke et al., 2000; Cook, Rumrill, & Tankersley, 2009; Houck et al., 1992; Jensen et al., 2004; Matthews et al., 1987; Nelson, Dodd, & Smith, 1990; Sparks, 2009). Faculty that are either reluctant to provide accommodations or to inform themselves as to how to better assist students with disabilities, are perpetuating social inequities. Both intentional and unintentional acts of injustice are manifested in the hands of those members of the privileged group (Crethar, Torres Rivera & Nash, 2008). Unintentional injustice tends to be more frequent and it becomes materialized when inequities, inequalities, denied access, and discrimination are overlooked, disregarded, and even perpetuated by the privileged group.

Operationalizing a social justice framework requires the underlying understanding of how stressful and harmful said injustices could be and that the focus should be placed not on "fixing" the dis-abled body, or having the dis-abled individual adapt to a given condition or environment, but rather correcting the injustice, or the oppressive situation (Kelsey, 2012). Social justice requires subscription to the notion that one's personal context will impact one's view and that, particularly as a person who is not part of the oppressed group, one must involve the people impacted by oppression in order to avoid perpetuating the systemic oppression by the dominant group (Bryan, 2000). Guaranteeing the provision of ample opportunities for training and social advocacy is important for both the preparation of faculty and GTAs and the success of undergraduate students with disabilities as well as for the prevention of injustice.

In foreign language instruction, many of the lower-division core courses are multi-section and are overseen by a faculty member and commonly taught by non-tenured instructors and GTAs. Overall training for those in charge of teaching multi-section courses is normally provided either by the department or the university, which may or may not include information concerning accommodating students with disabilities. It has been shown that faculty members improve their willingness and are more responsive towards accommodating students with disabilities if they are aware of the existence of the office responsible for students' accessibility, and feel supported (Bourke, Strehorn & Silver, 2000). Therefore, providing ample opportunities for training educators to work with students with disabilities (being in the form of mandatory sessions, voluntary sessions, one-on-one advising, phone consultation, etc.) is a determining factor for both the preparation of faculty and GTAs and the success of undergraduate students.

Although a body of research exists to discuss the development of GTAs concerning teaching methods, their advancement in professional development, and their responsibilities as a part of both the student body and the faculty (Brandl, 2000; Byrnes, 2001; Chalupa & Lair, 2000; Fox, 1993; Melin, 2000; Rankin & Becker, 2006; VanValkenburg & Arnett, 2000; Wildner-Bassett & Meerholz-Haerle, 1999), less attention has been given to the training (or lack thereof) imparted regarding the implementation of adjustments for students with disabilities. Furthermore, studies conducted concerning faculty readiness and disposition to work with students with disabilities have mainly focused on professors or lecturers, but information concerning GTAs attitudes and readiness is rather scarce.

In addition to elucidating various aspects of GTAs' attitudes, knowledge, and readiness concerning instructing and accommodating students with disabilities, this chapter discusses the importance of a social justice perspective in the training of GTAs. It also offers suggestions as to how to include GTAs in a social justice movement that is inclusive of efforts to end systemic oppression of people with disabilities.

Methodology

An online survey was conducted in institutions of higher education across the country to gather impressions from foreign language GTAs who teach one or more sections of a multi-section course. Lower-division multi-section language courses were chosen because they present a peculiar situation for a myriad of reasons: 1) they are normally instructed by novice GTAs; 2) GTAs do not generally make decisions independently; as these courses are directed and supervised by the Language Program Director (LPD); 3) language GTAs in American universities are normally required to undergo a pre-service orientation and in-service workshops or meetings.

With this in mind, the following research questions guided the investigation:

1. Do GTAs teaching multi-section language courses and LPDs directing them, reveal a satisfactory level of readiness to implement accommodations for students with disabilities?
2. Do GTAs receive ample training on accommodating students with disabilities and the legal mandates and expectations?
3. Do LPDs guarantee that training concerning students with disabilities is provided to GTAs?

Participants
A total of 107 participants, 76 GTAs and 31 LPDs, from institutions of higher education across the country completed the survey. The responses were anonymous; however, some demographic data were collected including: language taught, years teaching, levels taught, institution, and experience with students with disabilities. Participants indicated a wide range of experience either teaching or working with students with disabilities. As per languages and levels taught, there were GTAs teaching elementary, accelerated elementary, intermediate, low-advanced, in Spanish, German, French, Portuguese, Russian, and Italian, and the corresponding LPDs directing those languages and levels taught.

Survey Design
Even though the core was common to GTAs and LPDs, some of the questions were constituency specific, as they referred to, for example, either training received or training provided. Therefore, the survey was administered separately. It was designed in order to highlight systemic issues in providing equal access in the foreign language classroom and also contained questions intended to assess the quantity and quality of resources available for GTAs concerning, training, the implementation of accommodations and advocacy.

The survey was composed of 29 questions, most of which followed a five-point Likert-scale type as well as a lesser amount of open ended or YES/NO questions. Questions were both positively and negatively phrased and all Likert scale questions were randomized throughout the survey, followed by questions addressing level taught, current institution, and method of training received, which were fixed at the end of the survey.

Data Collection and Analysis
There were several measures taken in order to promote and increase participation in the study. First, the FLASC-L listserve of the American Association of University Supervisor and Coordinators (AAUSC) was used to reach a significant number of institutions. Second, a search was conducted through different language department websites and individual e-mail addresses were retrieved. Finally, personal colleagues and nearby institutions were also contacted. Every time the invitation was extended, the purpose of the survey was explained along with a brief description of the research. After data collection, simple frequency calculations were conducted to determine the percentage of respondents selecting a given answer.

Results

The majority of our GTA participants indicated a maximum of 6 years of experience teaching undergraduate students in a multi-section language course. Expectedly, more than one third (36.0%) expressed having taught for 1-2 years with slightly more (38.7%) teaching between 3-5 years and only 8% for 6-10 years. Contrarily, LPDs had much more experience teaching. The majority (83%) claimed 10 years of experience and 40% of them also stated they had 10 years experience directing a language program.

With regards to our first research question, almost half of the GTA participants (45.3%) indicated confidence about their knowledge of disabilities. It should be noted, however, that although almost half of the participants indicated familiarity with the concept and the necessity of accommodating students with disabilities, the other half did not. GTAs are not (and should not be) expected to provide a definition of a concept that is not within their scope of study or research. However, understanding the concept of disability and all that it encompasses, is of great importance within a social justice paradigm, and to help faculty in the process of promoting the establishment of institutions that provide equal access for all.

Furthermore, many of the participants offered responses to the open-ended portion of this question and were able to provide a definition of disability. However, some of these definitions raised the question as to whether participants lack awareness concerning biases, display prejudice, or lack of knowledge. What follows are examples of definitions provided by participants.

> "When a student has difficulty learning in a typical way…"
> "When different students have issues that affect the acquisition of course materials within a range that is considered typical."
> "When a student is unable to learn normally in an academic setting…"

A review of these definitions demonstrates an orientation towards a medical model view of disability that relies on the "normal vs. abnormal" and "typical vs. atypical" dichotomy. This inclination towards the medical model creates greater potential to exclude students with disabilities from educational opportunities and perpetuate social injustice (Gabel & Conner, 2009).

Responses to the remaining questions seem to indicate confusion concerning policies and the implementation of accommodations. Those perceptions and percentages regarding impressions towards easiness to comprehend or implement accommodations, maintaining academic integrity, and readiness to provide accommodations, both from GTAs and LPDs are summarized in Table 7.1.

What guided the investigation, contemplated in our second research question, was to elicit whether GTAs receive either pre-service or in-service training concerning students with disabilities. We were particularly interested in determining how and by whom GTAs are trained and mentored. Results indicate that one third of our participants affirm having received training about accommodating students with disabilities and more than half (50.6%) indicated a lack of training. Moreover, with regard to training facilitated by the LPD, almost half (48.0%) stated not having received any. This indicates that while there is a significant percentage of GTAs who are being trained, there is a great deal of work to be done with respect to training opportunities. Table 7.2 and 7.3 respectively provide a summary of the responses to questions regarding training and mentorship received by GTAs and offered by LPDs.

Table 7.1

GTA and LPD knowledge, attitude and preparedness

	SA		A		N		D		SD		Total	
	GTA	LPD	GTA	LPD	GTA	LPD	GTA	LPD	GTA	LPD	GTA	LPD
How to implement academic accommodations for students is easy to understand.	11 14.7%	6 19.4%	35 46.7%	15 48.4%	16 21.3%	8 25.8%	12 16.0%	2 6.5%	1 1.3%	0	75 100%	31 100%
Policies concerning students with disabilities are clear to me.	9 12.0%	8 25.8%	35 46.7%	18 58.1%	11 14.7%	1 3.2%	15 20.0%	3 9.7%	5 6.7%	1 3.2%	75 100%	31 100%
I am uncertain of the policies regarding students with disabilities	4 5.3%	0	18 24.0%	2 6.5%	7 9.3%	4 12.9%	34 45.5%	14 45.2%	12 16.0%	11 35.5%	75 100%	31 100%
Providing accommodations for students with disabilities puts other students at disadvantage.	2 2.7%	1 3.2%	5 6.7%	0	9 12.0%	2 6.5%	31 41.3%	17 54.8%	28 37.3%	11 35.5%	75 100%	31 100%
Accommodations for students with disabilities compromise the objectives of my course.	1 1.3%	2 6.5%	3 4.0%	0	13 17.3%	5 16.1%	36 48.0%	17 54.8%	22 29.3%	7 22.6%	75 100%	31 100%
I find a good balance between accommodating students with disabilities and maintaining course objectives.	11 14.7%	7 22.6%	37 49.3	13 41.9%	20 26.7%	9 29.0%	5 6.7%	1 3.2%	2 2.7%	1 3.2%	75 100%	31 100%

Note. SA=Strongly Agree, A=Agree, N=Neutral, D=Disagree, SD=Strongly Disagree, GTA=Graduate Teaching Assistant, LPD=Language Program Director

Although only 12.0% and 33.3 % (strongly agreed and agreed, respectively) of our GTA participants indicated having discussed policies during training, the percentages are higher for our LPD participants, who stated that policies are indeed discussed (25.8% strongly agreed and 41.9% agreed). More discrepancies are apparent regarding whether GTAs and LPDs discuss the implementation of accommodations. In this case, 24% of the GTAs strongly agreed, while 30.7% agreed. On the other hand, 35.5% of the LPDs strongly agreed and 41.9% agreed. Lastly, most GTAs indicate that they seldom discuss performance of students with disabilities with their respective LPDs, while LPDs indicate the contrary.

Table 7.2
Training received by GTAs about students with disabilities

	SA	A	N	D	SD	Total
Discussing policies concerning students with disabilities is part TA training.	9 (12.0%)	25 (33.3%)	12 (16.0%)	20 (26.7%)	9 (12.0%)	75 (100%)
Discussing policies concerning students with disabilities is not included in my TA training.	8 (10.7%)	16 (21.3%)	11 (14.7%)	27 (36.0%)	13 (17.3%)	75 (100%)
When making decisions regarding accommodations, I discuss the situation with my LPD.	18 (24.0%)	23 (30.7%)	16 (21.3%)	13 (17.3%)	5 (6.7%)	75 (100%)
My LPD and I regularly discuss performance of students with disabilities.	4 (5.3%)	15 (20.0%)	21 (28.0%)	16 (21.3%)	19 (25.3%)	75 (100%)
Performance of students with disabilities is not discussed with my LPD.	10 (13.3%)	17 (22.7%)	14 (18.7%)	23 (30.7%)	11 (14.7%)	75 (100%)

Discussion

Topics such as maintaining academic integrity were perceived similarly by both our GTAs and LPD participants. In addition, both groups considered that providing accommodations for students with disabilities does not put other students at a disadvantage. However, some salient discrepancies between how issues were perceived by the two groups of participants require attention. The first is the fact that many of the GTA participants indicated not having been trained concerning the policies and the implementation of accommodations, while many of the LPD participants claim to have provided training.

Second, GTAs and LPDs adduced certain confidence concerning their knowledge of policies and legal mandates, yet a significant percentage indicates a degree of confusion as to how to implement the accommodations. This could determine that the equal access those accommodations are supposed to ensure, is in reality not being provided consistently. Moreover,

Table 7.3
Training offered by LPDs about students with disabilities

	SA	A	N	D	SD	Total
Discussing policies regarding students with disabilities is part of training provided for new TAs.	8 (25.8%)	13 (41.9%)	7 (22.6%)	2 (6.5%)	1 (3.2%)	31 (100%)
Discussing policies concerning students with disabilities is not included in my training for new TAs.	0	5 (16.1%)	5 (16.1%)	10 (32.3%)	11 (35.5%)	31 (99.8%)
When making decisions regarding accommodations, TAs and I discuss the situation.	11 (35.5%)	13 (41.9%)	3 (9.7%)	2 (6.5%)	2 (6.5%)	31 (100%)
TAs make decisions regarding accommodations independently.	0	5 (16.1%)	3 (9.7%)	10 (32.3%)	13 (41.9%)	31 (100%)
Training about students with disabilities has been provided to TAs in the courses I coordinate.	6 (19.4%)	7 (22.6%)	6 (19.4%)	11 (35.5%)	1 (3.2%)	31 (100%)
TAs do not receive training from our department on how to assist students with disabilities.	3 (9.7%)	11 (35.5%)	5 (16.1%)	6 (19.4%)	6 (19.4%)	31 (100%)
I regularly check with TAs regarding performance of students with disabilities.	1 (3.2%)	11 (35.5%)	5 (16.1%)	11 (35.5%)	3 (9.7%)	31 (100%)
Performance of students with disabilities is not discussed with TAs.	1 (3.2%)	3 (9.7%)	5 (16.1%)	16 (51.6%)	6 (19.4%)	31 (100%)

unawareness and confusion as to how to go about implementing accommodations and interacting with students with disabilities could influence the willingness to fulfill their responsibility.

This leads to uncertainty as to whether or not: a) the implementation of accommodations is too complex to understand; b) existing lack of training that not only includes an overview of the expectations but also a practical guide for the implementation of accommodations.

Third, confusion concerning how to implement accommodations could be attributed to the fact that slightly over half of our participants did not consider themselves informed enough on the topic of disabilities. This could have serious consequences since lack of awareness and knowledge might lead to the development of preconceptions with regard to students' behaviors, abilities, and performance. Therefore, being aware of institutional policies, yet not understanding what constitutes a disability and how this should be addressed in and out of the classroom could imply severe complications. If GTAs (as any other faculty member) are required to adjust courses and classroom procedures based on certain criteria about concepts that are unknown and foreign to them, this could certainly generate a great deal of frustration.

A fairly low number of GTAs (30%) stated having received a general training concerning students with disabilities. In contrast, 42% of LPDs claimed that training had been provided to GTAs while 38% admitted they had not. This indicates that, whereas efforts are evident and training is indeed carried out to some extent, there is still much to be done. Additional issues that should be evaluated are how to articulate the training, what content to cover, who should be responsible for the implementation of such training, and when training is likely to be most effective.

When taking into account that some of the GTAs that claim to have received very little (to non existent) training are still indicating a significant level of familiarity with policies, it calls into question what information GTAs are receiving and how it might impact their ability and attitude towards implementing accommodations. Perhaps policies posted are readily comprehensible and accessed independently by GTAs or they are operating with generalized information that may or may not be accurate. If GTAs are operating with information that may not be fully accurate, it is possible that the expectations of accommodating students are not being fully met and injustices for students with disabilities are being perpetuated.

Implications and Recommendations

The results of this study indicate that efforts concerning the advancement of social justice, equality and accessibility for many foreign language programs in higher education are being made. However, preparing GTAs and faculty to be part of the social justice paradigm concerning ableism might still be in the beginning stages.

Previous research indicated that opportunities for GTAs' professional growth are rather scarce and less has been said regarding their readiness and attitudes concerning instructing students with disabilities. Findings of this study revealed yet another aspect that is lacking from their development, not only concerning their future careers as professors, but also about the quality of education they provide during their years as graduate instructors. These findings could then be considered as a platform to understand the dimensions of GTA preparation, which includes their ability to face challenges such as implementing accommodations for students with disabilities and to delineate teaching strategies that are inclusive of diverse students and their needs. Preparing GTAs to be part of the overall plan of improving social justice implies instilling in them the sentiment of self-evaluation, to first perceive biases and any unintended perpetuation of the *status quo*. GTAs could subsequently identify any instances of oppression and understand that social justice goes beyond just raising awareness, building on the principles of movement and action.

While several participants of this study claimed knowledge concerning policies in their institutions, they also manifested some degree of confusion as to how to implement the accommodations. Consequently, we subscribe to advocating for ongoing training (Jensen et al., 2004; Rao & Gartin, 2003; Scott & Gregg, 2000) and suggest the design of programs that contemplate the necessity of socially just institutions.

As reported in this paper and in line with data from previous studies (Houck et al., 1992; Rao & Gartin, 2003; Sparks, 2009; Shaw & Scott, 2003), most institutions provide training to faculty members concerning students with disabilities; however, there are some complications as to how to implement the recommendations offered during such training. Scott and Gregg (2000) suggest important steps that faculty members should take into consideration, such as discussing particular needs with students, making the requested adjustments without compromising the academic integrity of the course, and being aware of those students who might not be registered but might benefit from a referral. We additionally recommend implementing a system of periodic consultation between LPDs and GTAs in order to determine the performance of students with disabilities and to establish the results of the training programs.

Concerning informative sessions or programs to raise awareness or educate faculty members, results of this study and also those of Jensen et al. (2004) indicate that there is a great need to take an interdisciplinary approach in order to offer an integral program that helps faculty members and GTAs design activities, materials, and a universal teaching style that serves the necessity of an heterogeneous population (Nelson, Dodd, & Smith, 1990). Increasing training opportunities or enhancing existing ones could potentially improve GTAs in-service performance and their future professional development, but it ultimately has a significant impact in the quality of life, retention and outcomes before and after graduation of undergraduate students with or without documented disabilities.

It is then recommended that all faculty members (and more importantly novice GTAs) be offered training that includes a detailed and accessible explanation of disabilities and legal matters (Scott & Gregg, 2000) as well as an overview of accommodations and referral procedures. However, if as indicated by our data, GTAs can recognize the easiness of the policies, we suggest that training shift towards a social justice perspective. Offering GTAs an understanding of the impact of various disabilities and the marginalization of people with disabilities in education not only supports the effective implementation of academic adjustments, it fosters an attitude of valuing those with different abilities. More practical information can be provided related to producing adjustments without compromising academic integrity, understanding hidden or invisible disabilities, how to functionally implement the different accommodations, and establishing academic strategies that are inclusive of every type of student. The suggested approach for the training programs could have a positive long term effect since having faculty and GTAs that are well prepared to implement a universal design of instruction will determine less need for course substitutions or waivers.

In the case of GTAs in multi-section language courses, they could access training concerning students with disabilities through two avenues: 1) via their LPD; 2) via the Student Accessibility Services. However, even when the LPD is in charge of GTA training and the facilitation of their professional development, he/she cannot be expected to provide preparation concerning, for example, specific instructional techniques that contemplate the needs of students with disabilities. Rather, it is essential that the LPD officiate as the connection between GTAs and staff at Accessibility Services, as well as sustaining the responsibility of being in charge of the transmission of information. Concurrently, Accessibility Services is to provide guidance and training to faculty members regarding the implementation of accommodations and to offer support of students with disabilities as indicated by the Association on Higher Education and Disabilities (AHEAD).

Even though faculty members are required to understand that it is their responsibility to implement the accommodations, Scott and Gregg (2000), Shaw and Scott (2003), and Salzberg et al. (2002) revealed that faculty tend to show reluctance to voluntary participation in training mainly due to lack of time. While GTAs do have time constraints as well, they are required to participate in pre-service orientations and in-service meetings and workshops. These meetings could potentially be the first venue in which a consciousness-raising plan can be presented in order to further address more detailed preparation during their in-service orientation.

GTAs in faculty-like positions are responsible for the provision of equal access in the classroom; however, it should be guaranteed ultimately by the LPD as the person who oversees the multi-section course. Additionally, as the GTAs' mentor, the LPD should set the example and take part in the consciousness raising process by implementing a system that allows him/her to assure policies are being followed. Consequently, the proactivity of the LPD will determine the degree of success in the implementation of accommodations and in the training of GTAs.

The advantage of raising awareness amongst GTAs and requiring them to participate in training programs is twofold: to enhance the quality of education they provide to undergraduate students and to prepare them for their future endeavors as faculty members. Additionally, while serving to help GTAs better understand the "big picture" regarding the oppression of people with disabilities, it potentially fosters the development of a sense of urgency for including disability rights in social justice advocacy and fundamentally, in the professional development of those who will educate both able and disabled students.

Limitations and Future Research

It is important to note the exploratory nature of the present study and that the results drawn should be evaluated contemplating its limitations. First, the low number of participants impedes the generalization of the results. Therefore, even when we targeted different institutions, the findings only reflect the realities of the participants in the study and might not be extended to all GTAs and LPDs across the country. Future research should stand to advance our general understanding of GTAs' and LPDs' readiness and attitudes towards implementing accommodations, by focusing on obtaining responses from various institutions. It is also recommended that a larger sample include research, hybrid, and teaching universities, together with junior or community colleges and liberal arts colleges. Follow-up studies seeking to gather large numbers of responses may also allow for greater statistical comparison.

In addition to advancing knowledge on the questions and conclusions we provide, other questions have emerged. Potential areas for expansion include identifying avenues for the creation and execution of training around instructional strategies and teaching styles as well as exploring particular outcomes of the proposed interactive model of pre-service and in-service training. Moreover, further investigation is needed to establish whether providing that type of training has a long-term impact in the performance of students with disabilities and in the development of GTAs as future professors.

Conclusions

This study investigated GTAs and LPDs preparation and attitudes with respect to implementing accommodations for students with disabilities. It also examined the training (or lack thereof) received by GTAs and provided by LPDs. Our findings indicated that GTAs and LPDs maintain an overall positive attitude concerning the accommodations for students with disabilities, and understand this does not constitute a hindrance to the academic integrity, nor does it put other students at a disadvantage. Responses also revealed some inconsistencies related to how certain aspects, such as the provision of training, were perceived by GTAs and LPDs, indicating that even when training is indeed provided, there is yet much more to accomplish concerning this issue.

Closing the gap between the responsibility and reality of guaranteeing equal access will continue to grow in importance in college or university classrooms as the number of students with documented disabilities is expected to grow. An interdisciplinary approach to the advancement of socially just institutions of higher education is, therefore, of utmost importance.

References

Adams, M. (2000). Conceptual frameworks. In Adams, M., Blumenfield, W. J., Castaneda, R., Hackman, H. W., Peters, M. L, & Zuniga, X. (Eds.) *Readings for diversity and social justice* (pp. 1-9). New York: Routledge.

Americans with Disabilities Act 1990, Pub. L. 101-336, 104 Stat. 327.

Bourke, A. B., Strehorn, K. C., & Silver, P. (2000). Faculty members' provision of instructional accommodations to students with LD. *Journal of Learning Disabilities, 33,* 26-32.

Brandl, K. K. (2000). Foreign language TAs' perceptions of training components: Do we know how they like to be trained? *Modern Language Journal, 84,* 355-371.

Bryan, W. V. (2000). The disability rights movement. In Adams, M., Blumenfield, W. J., Castaneda, R., Hackman, H. W., Peters, M. L, & Zuniga, X. (Eds.) *Readings for diversity and social justice* (pp. 324-330). New York: Routledge.

Castaneda, R., & Peters, M. L. (2000). Ableism. In Adams, M., Blumenfield, W. J., Castaneda, R., Hackman, H. W., Peters, M. L, & Zuniga, X. (Eds.) *Readings for diversity and social justice* (pp. 319-323). New York: Routledge.

Chalupa, C., & Lair, A. (2001). Meeting the needs of international TAs in the foreign language classroom: A model for extended training. In Rifkin, B. (Ed.), *Mentoring foreign language teaching assistants, lecturers, and adjunct faculty. Issues in language program directions: A series of annual volumes* (pp. 119-142). Boston: Heinle.

Cook, L., Rumrill, P. D., & Tankersley, M. (2009). Priorities and understanding of faculty members regarding college students with disabilities. *International Journal of Teaching and Learning in Higher Education, 21,* 84-96.

Crethar, H. C., Torres Rivera, E., & Nash, S. (2008). In search of common threads: Linking multicultural, feminist, and social justice counseling paradigms. *Journal of Counseling and Development, 86,* 270-287.

Fouad, N. A., Gerstein, L. H., & Toporek, R. L. (2006). Social justice and counseling psychology in context. In Toporek, R. L., Gerstein, L. H., Fouad, N. A., Roysircar, G., Israel, T. (Eds.) *Handbook for social justice in counseling psychology: Leadership, vision, and action* (pp.1-16). Thousand Oaks, CA: Sage.

Fox, C. A. (1992). Toward a revised model of TA training. In Walz, J. C. (Ed.), *Development and supervision of teaching assistants in foreign languages* (pp. 191-207). Boston: Heinle.

Gabel, S. L., & Conner, D. J. (2009). Theorizing disability: Implications for social justice in education. In Ayers, W., Quinn, T., & Stovall, P. (Eds.) *Handbook of social justice in education* (p. 381). New York: Routledge.

Houck, C. H., Asselin, S., Troutman, G., & Arrignton, J. (1992). Students with learning disabilities in the university environment: A study of faculty and student perceptions. *Journal of Learning Disabilities, 25,* 678-684.

Jensen, J. M., McCrary, N., Krampe, K., & Cooper, J. (2004). Trying to do the right thing: Faculty attitudes toward accommodating students with learning disabilities. *Journal of Post Secondary Education and Disability, 17,* 81-90.

Katz, S., & Watzinger-Tharp, J. (2008). Toward understanding the role of applied linguistic in foreign language departments. *Modern Language Journal, 89,* 490-502.

Kessler Foundation/National Organization on Disability. (2010). *The ADA 20 years later: The 2010 survey of Americans with disabilities.* Retrieved from http://www.2010DisabilitySurveys.org

Leyser, Y. (1989). A survey of faculty attitudes and accommodations for students with disabilities. *Journal of Postsecondary Education and Disability, 7*, 97-108.

Matthews, P. R., Anderson, D. W., & Skolnick, B. D. (1987). Faculty attitude toward accommodations for college students with learning disabilities. *Learning Disabilities Focus, 3*, 46-52.

Melin, C. (2000). Beyond language courses and into the college classroom: TAs and the full scope of undergraduate teaching. *Die Unterrichtspraxis, 33*, 7-13.

Nelson, R., Dodd, J., & Smith, D. (1990). Faculty willingness to accommodate students with learning disabilities: A comparison among academic divisions. *Journal of Learning Disabilities, 23*, 185-189.

Nelson, R., Dodd, J., & Smith, D. (1991). Instructional adaptations available to students with learning disabilities at community vocational colleges. *Learning Disabilities, 2*, 27-31.

Rehabilitation Act of 1973, Pub. L. 93-112, 87 Stat. 355.

Rao, S., & Gartin, B. (2003). Attitudes of university faculty toward accommodations to students with disabilities. *The Journal for Vocational Special Needs Education, 25*, 47-54.

Scott, S. S. (1997). Accommodating college students with learning disabilities: How much is enough? *Innovative Higher Education, 22*, 85-99.

Scott, S. S., & Gregg, N. (2000). Meeting the evolving education needs of faculty in providing access for college students with LD. *Journal of Learning Disabilities, 23*, 158-167.

Scott, S., & Shaw, S. (2003). New directions in faculty development. *Journal of Postsecondary Education and Disability, 17*, 3-9.

Smart, J. F. (2007). The promise of the international classification of functioning, disability, and health (IFC). In Dell Orto, A. E., & Power, P. W. (Eds.), *The psychological and social impact of illness and disability* (pp. 582-595). New York: Springer Publishing Company.

Smith, S. D., Reynolds, C. A., & Rovnak, A. (2009). A critical analysis of the social advocacy movement in counseling. *Journal of Counseling & Development, 87*, 483-491.

Snyder, T. D., & Dillow, S. A. (2012). *Digest of education statistics 2011* (NCES 2012-001). Washington, DC: National Center for Education Statistics, Institute of Education Sciences, U.S.

VanValkenburg, J., & Arnett, C. (2000). The professionalization of teaching assistants: Can it be accomplished? *Die Unterrichtspraxis, 33*, 7-13.

Wildner-Bassett, M. E. (1993). "Poof! You're a teacher!": Using introspective data in the professional development of beginning TAs. In Walz, J. C. (Ed.), *Development and supervision of teaching assistants in foreign languages* (pp. 153-169). Boston: Heinle.

Wronka, J. (2008). *Human rights and social justice*. Los Angeles: Sage.

CHAPTER 8

MULTICULTURAL SOCIAL JUSTICE EDUCATION THROUGH THE LENS OF POSITIONING:
English Language Learners in K-12 Contexts

Hayriye Kayi-Aydar
University of Arkansas, Fayetteville

Introduction

The fields of Second Language Acquisition (SLA) and Applied Linguistics have experienced a social turn within the past twenty years challenging the traditional and longstanding views of SLA and encouraging scholars to focus on notions such as self, discourse, and identity (Mantero, 2007). Numerous scholars have examined how identities were negotiated in local contexts, in moment-by-moment development of interaction. In order to understand identity negotiation, they have explored how learners positioned themselves and others, with certain rights and obligations, through conversation in local contexts. With an increasing attention on local context, the term positioning, referring to a momentarily dynamic construction of identities, has gained more attention.

Drawing on social and positioning theories (e.g., Davies & Harre, 1990; Erickson, 2004; Holland et al., 1998) a number of scholars have focused on power relations in classrooms and provided descriptions of the classroom contexts and speech events for understanding classroom participation. Their findings have been eye-opening in terms of demonstrating how English language learners were positioned in English dominant discourse communities in ways that native speaker peers or teachers limited their access to classroom discussions and activities (e.g., Bashir-Ali, 2006; DaSilva-Iddings,

2005; Duff, 2002; Hunter, 1997; Martin-Beltrán, 2010; McKay & Wong, 1996; Miller, 2000). Since the goal of the social justice education is "full and equal participation of all groups in society that is mutually shaped to meet their needs" (Adams et al., 1997, p. 1), it is important to understand how ELLs are positioned in educational settings and how their self- and other-positionings influence their participation and access to learning opportunities. Focusing on the K-12 classroom contexts, in the following section I first define social justice education, review related literature on positioning, and then revisit the notion of multicultural social justice to discuss further what it should mean in the education of ELLs.

Multicultural Social Justice Education

Adams et al. (1997) argue that "social justice includes a vision of society in which the distribution of resources is equitable and all members are physically and psychologically safe and secure" (p. 1). In order for social justice to occur, individuals should "have a sense of their own agency as well as a sense of social responsibility" (p. 1). Rooted in social reconstructionism, multicultural social justice education deals with oppression and social structural inequality based on language, race, social class, gender, and disability and aims to "reconstruct society toward greater equity" (Banks & Banks, 2012, p. 51). In multicultural social justice education, students are encouraged to take an active role in their own education, while teachers are expected to create "empowering, democratic, and critical education environments" (Hackman, 2005, p. 103). Banks and Banks (2012) describe four practices that are unique to multicultural social justice education:

1. Democracy is actively practiced in the schools.
2. Students learn how to analyze institutional inequality in their own life circumstances.
3. Students learn to engage in social action so they can change unfair social processes.
4. Bridges are built between various oppressed groups (e.g., people who are poor, people of color, and White women).

That is, multicultural social justice education does not simply focus on difference or diversity but pays attention to "systems of power and privilege that give rise to social inequality" (Hackman, 2005, p. 104). Students are encouraged to critically examine oppression so that they can find opportunities for social actions in the service of social change (Hackman, 2005).

Oppression operates at different levels—individual, cultural, and institutional. According to Adams et al. (1997), oppression fuses "institutional and systemic discrimination, personal bias, bigotry, and social prejudice in a complex web of relationships" (p. 4) and denotes "constraints that significantly shape a person's life chances and sense of possibility" (p. 4). Through oppression and hierarchical relationships, privileged groups benefit from the disempowerment of subordinated or targeted groups. Hackman (2005) further argues that "social justice education requires an examination of systems of power and oppression combined with a prolonged emphasis on social change and student agency in and outside of the classroom" (p. 104). Given the increasing diversity in schools in countries such as the United States, England, and Australia where the numbers of ELLs are increasing rapidly, it is important to understand how ELLs, who come from diverse cultural and linguistic backgrounds, gain access to power and exercise agency in educational settings? How do they deal with power and oppression? How do they become agents? How are oppression, power, and agency interact with their access to learning opportunities in the school environment?

In the rest of this chapter, I aim to address these questions by examining, in light of the literature, the unique ways in which oppression is manifested through positioning as well as differentials of power in educational settings that are linguistically and culturally diverse. Given that "diversity and appreciation of differences are inextricably tied to social justice and the ways that power and privilege construct difference unequally" (Adams et al., 1997, p. 4), it is important to understand how linguistically and culturally diverse learners access to power in classroom settings and how they are viewed by their domestic, non-ELL peers. This understanding is important because, if ELLs are recursively assigned non-powerful and non-agentic positional identities in the classroom environment, they may never be empowered to analyze institutional inequality in their own life circumstances, change unfair social processes, or build bridges between themselves and more powerful groups, which are all essential and necessary for multicultural social justice education to survive (Banks & Banks, 2012).

Positioning, Identity, and Social Justice Education

Identity plays a significant role in social justice education. Goals of multicultural social justice education are achieved only when diverse (cultural) identities are recognized, accepted, and appreciated. Drawing on Gee (2008) and Norton (2000), I define identity as multiple presentations of self which are (re)constructed in and through social interaction across social contexts and demonstrated through actions and emotions. Identities are shaped by power relations amongst speech communities and individuals. While people form or construct identities as they wish to be perceived by others, sometimes they take on identities imposed on or assigned to them by other people. They constantly ask the question "are the perceptions that others have of me true, and do they reflect what I know to be true of myself?" (Mantero, 2007, p. 4). Identity negotiation occurs when people are expected to take on or reshape their identities. This negotiation is indeed influenced by a variety of factors such as "the repertoire and importance of social identities that a person has, the setting in which one is located, and the actions and influence of other people in those settings" (Deaux, 2001, p. 9). When the negotiation is successful, people may form new identities or (re)construct their existing selves. These identities are validated as individuals position themselves or are positioned by others across time and settings. That is, "as people negotiate identities, they take-up, assert, and resist identity positions that define them" (Reeves, 2008, p. 35) For example, Martina, one of the participants in Norton's study (2000) was socially positioned as an immigrant woman in her work setting in Canada where she felt uncomfortable speaking English with native speakers and positioned herself as "stupid" and "inferior". However, as a mother, she successfully used English against false claims by her landlord in order to protect the rights of her family, for whom she was responsible. In different contexts, Martina positioned herself differently. In one, she was clearly defining herself as inferior, while in another she asserted herself as a successful user of English. Therefore, power relations, contextual conditions, and her roles all played a role in her taking-up, asserting, or resisting positional identities.

The fields of SLA and Applied Linguistics have seen an increasing number of studies on identities of second language (L2) learners (see Block, 2009; Ricento & Thomas, 2005) and language teachers in the past two decades. Identity research has mostly used ethnographic case studies to explore how L2 users form and negotiate identities in work settings (e.g., Gordon, 2004; Kim, 2007) as well as classroom or school environments (e.g., Duff, 2002; Miller, 2007). The majority of identity research explored how learners negotiated multiple and sometimes contradictory identities with regard to the L2 writing process and the process of learning to write (e.g., Abasi, Akbari, & Graves, 2006; Fernsten, 2008). Another major area focused on assimilation, resistance, and rejection (Pavlenko, 2002). For example, Bashir-Ali (2006), in an ethnographic study, reported that a female student from Mexico went to extreme measures in an attempt to assimilate in the dominant social culture of her school. Bashir-Ali (2006) indicated how this Mexican female refused to speak her native language in public, distanced herself from other students of her own Mexican ethnic background, and insisted on being identified as an African American in order to become part of a collective powerful social identity in that school. Similar findings were found by McKay and Wong (1996) who demonstrated how Chinese students resisted their powerless positions as "ESL learners" and tried to reposition themselves.

Numerous scholars whose work is situated in post-structural SLA research have examined how identities were formed and negotiated in local contexts in moment-by-moment development of interaction. In order to understand identity negotiation, they explored how learners positioned themselves and others with certain rights and obligations through conversation. For these scholars, positioning has become a powerful tool in exploring dynamic concepts, such as identity, agency, and power. Because positioning allows or limits individuals to say or do things, it has consequences for social actions. For example, positioning a student as a legitimate member in a group work is at the same time giving the right to that individual to contribute positively to group work. Positioning him/her as illegitimate member, on the other hand, would mean denying him/her the right to make contributions, share ideas, or even perhaps to speak up. Since positioning comes with rights, duties, and obligations, individuals can become powerful or non-powerful, agentic or non-agentic, competent or incompetent, depending on the positions assigned to them.

Studies using the concept of positioning have provided insights into classroom participation outside of language learning environments. Studies in mainstream classrooms have mostly focused on social positioning and explored how social positions of students who come from certain racial or ethnic backgrounds have been constructed in classroom activities and how those positions interacted with their learning. For example, Antwan and Chris, two African American students in Maloch's study (2005), were positioned as passive and incompetent by their classmates as these students did not recognize Antwan and Chris's conversational moves, which seemed to be inconsistent with the norms of the classroom. However, their social positions changed positively over time due to the teacher's strategic and timely scaffolding.

In the following section, I provide a brief and yet comprehensive and critical overview of studies on positioning of ELLs in mainstream classrooms. A clear understanding of how ELLs are positioned by their classroom teachers and domestic peers is critical in order to create more equitable educational policies and practices for linguistically and culturally diverse classrooms.

Positioning of ELLs in Mainstream Classrooms

A number of researchers explored the asymmetric power relations between English language learners (ELLs) and domestic students in primary and secondary schools. These studies have indicated that ELLs were marginalized and denied access to learning opportunities in mainstream classrooms either due to their limited skills in the target language or school practices.

The literature shows that ELLs are recursively positioned as learners with learning deficits or low cognitive abilities, which negatively affect their academic performance as well as attitudes toward school and classroom practices (Ajayi, 2006; Pavlenko & Norton, 2007). One striking example was provided by Pavlenko and Norton (2007). In a Canadian public school, a Japanese learner of English is positioned negatively once a classmate yells at her, "Are you deaf or ESL?" (p. 43). This and similar incidents indicate how English speaking students might impose "linguistic domination by denying access to classroom social practices to those who do not have the linguistic capital and consequently condemn them to silence" (Ajayi, 2006, p. 475). For example, Ajayi (2006) reported that English-only students in three middle schools in the United States dominated and ridiculed Hispanic students in various school practices, which severely limited opportunities for them to practice language. Marginalization experienced by those Hispanic students were clearly evident in their comments: "What I dislike about schools is that some students make fun of other students speaking (English)" (p. 475), "I don't like students in my school because they speak English and think they are all that" (p. 474), and "Because you don't speak English, they think you are not cool" (p. 474). Similarly, Miller (2000) reported that Asian immigrant students in an Australian high school lost the chance to speak English in their classes and became isolated as their Australian classmates did not understand their foreign accent and were unwilling to communicate with them.

In addition to linguistic dominance, various school practices also marginalize ELLs as shown by the literature (DaSilva Iddings & Katz, 2007). Ajayi (2006) argues that in American contexts

> knowledge, culture, history and social practices of the minority groups are treated as illegitimate and excluded from the school curriculum. Furthermore, their linguistic and social practices are measured against the 'legitimate' practices of the dominant group—the monolingual and monocultural American Eurocentric curricula and consciousness (Will 1989 cited in McCarty et al 2003). (p. 470)

In a study by Duff (2002), for example, teaching practices including pop-culture and other textual and media based references engaged and united domestic students who were able to project identities that they wanted, and shared their interests and experiences in a Canadian social studies class. The same practices, on the other hand, excluded most of the ESL learners who were unfamiliar with these cultural tools. Thus, the choice and practices within the curriculum positioned ESL learners as outsiders or outcasts. Similarly, Hunter (1997) portrayed the multiple and conflicting identities of a Portuguese child, Roberto, who was positioned as an outsider as the contents of his writing did not match the interests of other boys' stories in a 4th grade classroom–his family-centered topics contrasted with their media-based fantasy adventures. However, Roberto was able to become an accepted member of his gender group in 5th grade when new students joined the class and collaborated with him on writings which included pop-culture elements.

Besides non-ELLs, classroom teachers influence identity construction or negotiation of ELLs. The literature suggests that the teachers' views of their roles with regards to ELLs affect their teaching practices, pedagogical approaches, and ELLs' classroom participation. In a number of studies, teachers were observed to assign unwanted identities to ELLs (e.g., "low learners" in DaSilva-Iddings, 2005; "worst" students in Harklau, 2000).

For example, DaSilva-Iddings (2005) provided us with a clear picture of how ELLs were positioned in an English dominant discourse community and how native speaker peers and general education teachers limited their access to classroom practices including classroom discussions and activities. Constantly oppressed and marginalized by their native speaker peers and positioned as 'low learners' by one of their teachers, these second grade students could not gain the same rights to participate as the local students. In a study conducted by Yoon (2007, 2008), Mrs. Young, one of the teacher-participants, provided ELLs with learning opportunities by drawing them into literacy activities, encouraged their participation by inviting them to share their experiences, and addressed their cultural and linguistic differences in meaningful ways. Her positive attitudes and beliefs towards ELLs as well as classroom practices not only positively shaped her teaching but also mainstream students' perceptions toward ELLs. As a result, mainstream peers positioned ELLs as resourceful and intellectual, rather than powerless and inferior. Such positioning assigned by their classmates increased ELLs' participation and interaction in the class. In contrast, the other teachers, Mr. Brown and Mrs. Taylor, who believed that teaching ELLs was not their main responsibility, played a passive role in supporting ELLs' needs. As a result, Mr. Brown's mainstream students resisted accepting ELLs as legitimate partners, and Mrs. Taylor's students showed indifference towards the ELLs. In brief, the ELLs' positioning of themselves as powerful or powerless fluctuated depending on their interactive positioning, with teachers taking the leading role and students mirroring teachers' attitudes. In a related study, by analyzing teacher identity negotiation through positioning theory and the concept of investment, Reeves (2008) analyzed the case of a secondary English teacher in the United States, Neal, who negotiated identity positions for himself while assigning positions to his students. Neal positioned himself as a natural and highly competent teacher while he positioned ELLs like any other student, which resulted in his refusal to make linguistic accommodation for ELLs during instruction. Reeves argues that Neal's stance on ELLs and undifferentiated instruction are indicative of an assimilative approach in the education of ELLs and concludes that while positioning ELLs like every other student is problematic, so, too, could be the positioning of them as "dramatically different from other students" (p. 39). Overall, this and other studies emphasize that although learners may resist an assigned identity by their teachers or peers, ELLs in mainstream classrooms have limited power to do so (Harklau, 2000; Reeves, 2008).

Revisiting Multicultural Social Justice Education for ELLs

The literature reviewed in this chapter shows that, in many mainstream classrooms, teachers or peers negatively position English language learners (ELLs), as ELLs speak limited English and are not familiar with the pop-culture around which the classroom activities center. ELLs are recursively positioned as low-performing students in the media and elsewhere, which is detrimental to their identity development in the new educational and cultural setting. In the American society, for example, as Crawford (2004) claims,

> cultures other than those of the dominant group are treated as sub-standard, primitive, threatening, exotic, or at best irrelevant to American life. Limited English speakers placed in all-English programs inevitably perceive a negative message about the language they brought from home. (p. 199)

Indeed, in some of the studies reviewed in this chapter (e.g. Hunter, 1997), ELLs did not want to be identified as ESL students in schools and rejected this identity. History related to African Americans, Jews, and other ethnic and religious groups indicates that "stereotypes develop in one context with particular meanings and continue as unquestioned fact down through the ages" (Adams et al., 1997, p. 6). If ELLs enter into classrooms with pre-assigned, non-powerful identities, which obviously limit their access to power, how can they become active agents of change and social justice in their lives, communities, and education? Drawing on Cummins (2000), Crawford (2004) argues that

> schooling must counteract the power relations that exist within the broader society. That is, it must remove the racial and linguistic stigmas of being a minority child. Power and status relations between minority and majority groups exert a major influence on school performance. (p. 198)

Adams et al. (1997) further suggest that "oppression circumstances can change through the efforts of human actors" (p. 9). I believe that it is the teachers who play perhaps the most significant role in changing those undesirable circumstances to the advantage of ELLs in classrooms. This is possible, as evidenced by Yoon's study, when classroom teachers appreciate bilingual identities of ELLs, their cultural practices, and sociocultural backgrounds. A number of researchers (e.g., Kayi-Aydar, 2013; Menard-Warwick, 2008; Miller, 2007) argue that language learning and positioning occur simultaneously in classrooms, and teachers can best facilitate learning when they constantly assign powerful positions to learners and provide them with multiple learning opportunities. This way, ELLs can positively construct their L2 voices and gain power. Classroom teachers can accomplish this goal by encouraging participation of ELLs in classroom activities, accepting and valuing their contributions to class discussions, highlighting ELLs' strengths in language use, and focusing more on the content of their written and oral production rather than the language itself; thereby positioning them as legitimate participants rather than incompetent language learners. Teachers can also teach ELLs effective conversational strategies, which would enable them to equally access to classroom talk and resist their marginal positions assigned by non-ELL peers (Kayi-Aydar, 2013).

Education for multicultural social justice begins by increasing one's awareness of power differentials and inequality in society (Einfield & Collins, 2008). Teacher educators can help pre-service and in-service teachers increase their awareness of social inequality and power differentials ELLs experience in regular classrooms through critical class discussions and strong exposure to the relevant literature and practices. By highlighting the multiple dimensions of diversity, teacher educators can help teachers question their own values, culture, and assumptions and increase their sensitivity to and understanding of multiculturalism and social justice. Through an increased awareness of social inequality, teachers can feel empowered and committed to working toward social justice in linguistically and culturally diverse classrooms (Einfield & Collins, 2008). As a teacher educator, I build such discussions in the classes I teach by using data from my own or other scholars' work. For example, one participant, Ana, an ESL student in Yoon's study (2004) said,

> I like being in ESL class. There are people who don't speak English very well. Everybody is same. My friends are there. But in other class, everybody looks at me. I don't like it. (p. 178)

Ana's silence and powerlessness in a middle school class were obviously context dependent. To help my students, who are pre- and in-service teachers, understand critically differential positionings of Ana, I pose questions, such as "What makes this student non-powerful or quite? What might be the causes at the micro level; is it the language used by teachers or peers, if so, how? How about at the macro level—curriculum, ideologies, etc.?" By asking such questions, my goal is to show what marginalizes ELLs and how they are marginalized. ELLs' silence and marginalization are complex and obviously beyond their limited language skills. These conversations are eye-opening for teachers and teacher candidates. Teacher educators can also use videos to show ELLs' participation and interactions with others in classroom settings. Providing transcripts of the video and audio recordings and teaching and doing conversation or positioning analysis also teach pre- and in-service teachers the power of language in classroom talk. Such analyses will hopefully result in their personal transformation and critical self-reflection.

Furthermore, various pedagogical and curricular practices, either tacitly or explicitly, "create the boundaries and strengthen the hierarchies that define the immigrants' marginal location" within classrooms or schools (Olneck, 1995, p. 316). One of those common pedagogical practices in K-12 classrooms is the teacher—whole class instructions in which the teachers spend most of the class time with lecturing or calling on students and asking them questions. Olneck (1995) argues that

> reliance on whole class instruction and on public student participation renders immigrants whose skills in English are limited, and who are reluctant participants, problematic to teachers. [...]. Even in lower ability-level classes, immigrants may be seated apart, encouraged to rely upon one another, and graded for effort alone, resulting in isolation from mainstream students and ongoing classroom activities. (p. 316)

Indeed, constantly having whole-class instruction and calling on ELLs can provoke anxiety in those students. In return, ELLs may struggle in actively participating. In such situations, chances are high that their classmates and teachers position ELLs as low-performing students, or poor language users. In order to help ELLs position themselves in more powerful ways, they can be given multiple opportunities to collaborate with peers, by receiving the scaffolded linguistic assistance whenever needed both from peers and the teacher. Additionally, class activities that recognize and value ELLs' home cultures and mother tongues can easily lead to the empowerment of linguistically and culturally diverse learners and encourage them to be proud of their sociocultural backgrounds (Crawford, 2004).

Conclusion

The literature shows that ELLs are assigned non-powerful positions by their teachers and peers in regular or mainstream classroom interactions and activities. Classroom practices that marginalize ELLs do not allow them the opportunity to access to power in educational settings. In light of the literature, in this chapter, I revisit the notion of multicultural social justice education and suggest ways to empower linguistically and culturally diverse learners in classroom settings. In order to create more socially educational policies and practices in K-12 classrooms, teachers, teacher educators, and policy and curriculum makers should constantly seek ways to assign ELLs powerful positions. It is only when ELLs are positioned in powerful, agentic ways, that they can contribute equally and positively to the societies that they live in and are part of.

References

Abasi, A., Akbari, N., & Graves, B. (2006). Discourse appropriation, construction of identities, and the complex issue of plagiarism: ESL students writing in graduate school. *Journal of Second Language Writing, 15*(2), 102-117.

Adams, M., Bell, L. A., & Griffin, P. (1997). *Teaching for diversity and social justice.* New York: Routledge.

Ajayi, L. (2006). Multiple voices, multiple realities: Self-defined images of self among adolescent Hispanic English language learners. *Education, 126*(3), 468-480.

Banks, J. A., & Banks, C. A. M. (Eds.). (2009). *Multicultural education: Issues and perspectives.* Hoboken, NJ: John Wiley & Sons.

Bashir-Ali, K. (2006). Language learning and the definition of one's social, cultural, and racial identity. *TESOL Quarterly, 40,* 628-639.

Block, D. (2009). *Second language identities.* London: Continuum.

Crawford, J. (2004). *Educating English learners: Language diversity in the classroom* (5th ed.). Los Angeles: Bilingual Educational Services.

Cummins, J. (2000). *Language, power and pedagogy: Bilingual children in the crossfire.* Clevedon, UK: Multilingual Matters.

DaSilva Iddings, A. C. (2005). Linguistic access and participation: Second language earners in an English dominant second grade Classroom. *Bilingual Research Journal, 29*(1), 165-183.

DaSilva Iddings, A. C., & Katz, L. (2007). Integrating home and school identities of recent-immigrant Hispanic English language learners through classroom practices. *Journal of Language, Identity, and Education, 6*(4), 299-314.

Davies, B., & Harré, R. (1999). Positioning and personhood. In Harré, R., & Langenhove, L. V., (Eds.), *Positioning theory* (pp. 32-52). Oxford: Wiley-Blackwell.

Davies, B., & Harré, R. (1990). Positioning: The discursive production of selves. *Journal for the Theory of Social Behavior, 20*(1), 43-63.

Deaux, K. (2001). Social identity. In Worell, J. (Ed.), *Encyclopedia of women and gender* (pp. 1-9). San Diego: Academic Press.

Duff, P. (2002). Pop culture and ESL students: Intertextuality, identity, and participation in classroom discussions. *Journal of Adolescent and Adult Literacy, 45*, 482-487.

Einfeld, A., & Collins, D. (2008). The relationships between service-learning, social justice, multicultural competence, and civic engagement. *Journal of College Student Development, 49*(2), 95-109.

Erickson, F. (2004). *Talk and social theory: Ecologies of speaking and listening in everyday life.* Cambridge: Polity Press.

Fernsten, L. (2008). Writer identity and ESL learners. *Journal of Adolescent and Adult Literacy, 52*(1), 44-52.

Gee, G. P. (2008). *Social linguistics and literacies: Ideology in discourses* (3rd ed.). New York: Routledge.

Gordon, D. (2004). "I'm tired. You clean and cook." Shifting gender identities and second language socialization. *TESOL Quarterly, 38*(3), 437-457.

Hackman, H. W. (2005). Five essential components for social justice education. *Equity & Excellence in Education, 38*(2), 103-109.

Harklau, L. (2000). From the "good kids" to the "worst:" Representations of English language learners across educational settings. *TESOL Quarterly, 34,* 35-67.

Holland, D., Lachicotte, Jr., W., Skinner, D., & Cain, C. (1998). *Identity and agency in cultural worlds.* Cambridge: Harvard University Press.

Hunter, J. (1997). Multiple perceptions: Social identity in a multilingual elementary classroom. *TESOL Quarterly, 31*(3), 603-611.

Kayi-Aydar, H. (2013). 'No, Rolanda, completely wrong!' Positioning, classroom participation and ESL learning. *Classroom Discourse, 4*(2), 130-150.

Kim, T. Y. (2007). The dynamics of ethnic name maintenance and change: Cases of Korean ESL immigrants in Toronto. *Journal of Multilingual and Multicultural Development, 28*(2), 117-133.

Maloch, B. (2005). Moments by which change is made: A cross-case exploration of teacher mediation and student participation in literacy events. *Journal of Literacy Research, 37*(1), 95-143.

Mantero, M. (2007). *Identity and second language learning: Culture, inquiry, and dialogic activity in educational contexts.* Charlotte, NC: Information Age.

McCarthy, C., Giardina, M. D., Harewood, S. J., Park, J.-K. (2003). Contesting culture: Identity and curriculum dilemmas in the age of globalization, postcolonialism, and multiplicity. *Harvard Educational Review, 73*(3), 449-465.

McKay, S. L., & Wong, S. (1996). Multiple discourses, multiple identities: Investment and agency in second-language learning among Chinese adolescent immigrant students. *Harvard Educational Review, 66,* 577-608.

Martin-Beltrán, M. (2010). Positioning proficiency: How students and teachers (de)construct language proficiency at school. *Linguistics and Education, 21*(4), 257–281.

Menard-Warwick, J. (2008). "Because she made the beds. Every day." Social positioning, classroom discourse, and language learning. *Applied Linguistics, 29*(2), 267-289.

Miller, J. (2007). Inscribing identity: Insights for teaching from ESL students' journals. *TESL Canada Journal, 25*(1), 23-40.

Miller, J. (2000). Language use, identity, and social interaction: Migrant students in Australia. *Research on Language and Social Interaction, 33*(1), 69-100.

Norton, B. (2000). *Identity and language learning: Gender, ethnicity and educational change*. Harlow, England: Longman/Pearson Education Limited.

Olneck, M. R. (2005). Immigrants and education. In Banks, J. A., & Banks, C.A.M.G., (Eds.), *Handbook of research on multicultural education* (pp. 310-327). New York: Macmillan

Pavlenko, A. (2002). Poststructuralist approaches to the study of social factors in second language learning and use. In Cook, V. (Ed.) *Portratis of the L2 user* (pp. 277-302). Clevedon: Multilingual Matters.

Pavlenko, A., & Norton, B. (2007). Imagined communities, identity, and English language learning. In Cummins, J., & Davison, C., (Eds.), *International handbook of English language teaching* (pp. 669-680). New York: Springer.

Reeves, J. (2008). Teacher investment in learner identity. *Teaching and Teacher Education, 25*, 34-41.

Ricento, T. (2005). Considerations of identity in L2 learning. In Hinkel, E. (Ed.), *Handbook of research in second language teaching and learning* (pp. 895-911). Mahwah, NJ: Lawrence Erlbaum.

Yoon, B. (2004). Uninvited guests: The impact of English and ESL teachers' beliefs, roles, and pedagogies on the identities of English language learners (Doctoral dissertation, University at Buffalo, 2004). *Dissertation Abstracts International, 65*, 885.

Yoon, B. (2007). Offering or limiting opportunities: Teachers' roles and approaches to English-language learners' participation in literacy activities. *Reading Teacher, 61*(3), 216-227.

Yoon, B. (2008) Uninvited guests: The influence of teachers' roles and pedagogies on the positioning of English language learners in the regular classroom. *American Educational Research Journal, 45*(2), 495-522.

CHAPTER 9

SOCIAL JUSTICE THROUGH CRITICAL LANGUAGE PEDAGOGY IN THE HERITAGE LANGUAGE CLASSROOM

N. Ariana Mrak
University of North Carolina Wilmington

Introduction

When faced with social injustice through language use—i.e., populations that are marginalized because of their ways of speaking—Spanish heritage speakers get penalized twice. Their bilingualism is denigrated for being circumstantial, not elite, while their ability to speak Spanish marks them as imperfect speakers of English (Mrak, 2010; Pomerantz, 2002; Valdés, 2005; Wolford & Carter, 2010). The heritage language (HL) classroom is the perfect place to find a vast continuum of bilinguals with varying degrees of abilities in the two languages. While most of these students are competent speakers of English, they have been led to believe their Spanish is substandard. This was easily explained when courses for this population started in the 70's with a subtractive approach of eradicating their home varieties to impose a *standard* or *academic* variety. Since then, however, the profession moved to an additive bidialectalism or second dialect acquisition (SDA) approach, an expansion based model pioneered in Spanish by Valdés (1997). It focuses on adding the prestige variety of the language to students' linguistic repertoire while validating their home variety under an *appropriateness* model that suggests each of the varieties has a context of use. A second and more recent approach is premised on Fairclough's model (1992) of critical language awareness (CLA), and is represented for Spanish in Gutiérrez (1997), Carreira (2000), Martínez (2003), Leeman (2005), and Correa (2011). Here, classroom discussions encompass linguistic variation, issues of language prestige and subordination in order to demonstrate to students that these constructs have no validity in science and they are of a social, political, and/ or economic nature. Suggestions for implementation include: adequate teacher training (Gutierrez, 1997), improvement of students' linguistic self-esteem (Carreira, 2000), dialect awareness that includes the functions, distribution, and evaluation of dialects (Martínez, 2003), instruction on language subordination and options to accept or fight the dominant group's position (Leeman, 2005), and reactive syllabi and multiple dialect acquisition (Correa, 2011). The rationale behind this approach advocates that students must understand linguistic variation and its social and political implications in order to make informed language choices and be able to fight against linguistic prejudice.

Criticism has been levied on both of these approaches. SDA is premised on the concept of appropriateness, the notion that varieties have a place and an interlocutor. However, this idea encourages the marginalization of non-prestige varieties by deeming them adequate only for certain types of exchanges (Fairclough, 1992). Trying to convince students that there is a prestige variety they should strive for does not prepare them to be active participants in the linguistic choices they make; it indoctrinates them into the status quo. Meanwhile, the problem with the critical approach is that sociolinguistic explanations of the equal value of all varieties of a language and the use of the students' home language as the language of the classroom may leave them without the opportunity to acquire the prestige dialect. Favoring the non-prestige varieties does not give students who decide acquiring the academic variety could be beneficial to them ample time to learn it (Correa, 2010; Leeman, 2005; Mrak 2011a). Furthermore, while both methodologies attempt to provide them with the tools to participate in the society that tries to exclude them, many CLA proponents continue to grapple with the question of how to change the balance of power, how to ensure that the linguistic rights of these students are observed. As such, they suggest going beyond descriptions of linguistic variation that include sociolinguistic, sociocultural, sociohistorical, political, and affective awareness—and questions of overt and covert prestige—to analyze the reasons behind linguicism and to ask how to bring about change (Alim, 2005; Train, 2003). A critical language pedagogy needs to include explanations of how language is used, how it can be used against a group, and it should inform students' of the options available to them, whether they wish to conform or contest the existing norms (Alim, 2005, 2010; Correa, 2011; Leeman, 2005; Schwarzer & Petrón, 2005); thus, allowing them to decide whether to participate in, or fight against, current linguistic practices. As Alim (2005) points out, CLA must go beyond thinking about issues of power to doing something about them.

This paper posits that these two approaches are not mutually exclusive tasks in university courses for heritage speakers. Quite the contrary, in order to empower students to understand and decide of their own free will if they want to accept current discriminatory practices or if they choose to work at overturning them, they must know their options (Mrak, 2011a). However, if the point is to allow students to decide whether they want to participate in maintaining the prestige variety, then there must be room in the methodology for them to gain access to it. This entails designing a curriculum that combines the two approaches—SDA and CLA—in order for heritage language learners (HLLs) to clearly see the benefits and consequences of their choices and for both of these options to be available to them. The challenge resides in preparing teachers and laying out a plan for instruction that can be managed within the limitations of a one-semester course. Students taking their first Spanish class at the post-secondary level must be exposed to the sociolinguistic background that is required to understand the complexities of linguistic discrimination. At the same time, they should be given the option to acquire an academic variety of the language as they do in English. This would contribute to an informed decision on their part and prepare them to fulfill curricular expectations were they to choose to continue their studies in Spanish. The proposal put forth here for a critical language pedagogy combines an additive, second dialect acquisition approach with critical language awareness in order to give students the tools they need to decide whether they are interested in participating in the current paradigm of heritage languages as deficit, of HL speakers as imperfect speakers of both English and Spanish; whether they wish to acquire an academic variety of Spanish or whether their choice is to maintain and defend their variety as worthy of any and all situations.

The question we would like to answer here is how to do this in a beginner course for bilinguals[1] at the post-secondary level. The intent is to bring together critical linguistic awareness while exposing HLLs to the options available to them. These students all speak English—they have been admitted to American universities—if they have a foreign language requirement and they choose to complete it and not continue studying Spanish, it should be their choice. There is enough research showing that being bilingual is not perceived by American society as an asset in the circumstantial bilingual, only in the elite bilingual (Pomerantz, 2002; Valdés, 2005; Wolford & Carter, 2010) and that oftentimes HL speakers go to work in their own communities, obviously requiring their own variety of the language (Potowski, 2005); or that their motivation may be quite different from that of second language learners (Benjamin, 1997; Reynolds et al., 2009). The option of what variety to speak, to study, belongs to the HLL.

The Class

The question of how to incorporate CLA and proficiency in academic Spanish into the classroom grounds us to the reality of having enough time to do both, to have the sociolinguistic discussions while making room for the reading, writing, listening, and speaking tasks that will allow students to augment their knowledge of the language. Whether the institution offers a beginner track for receptive bilinguals, an intermediate track for students with speaking abilities, one course, or multiple courses is usually determined by the student body and administrative limitations. Students have to be placed appropriately, via an exam or an interview (for a thorough discussion on placement exams for HLLs see, Beaudrie, 2012b; Fairclough, 2012; MacGregor-Mendoza, 2012; Potowski et al., 2012; Wilson, 2012). The proposal that follows is for an intermediate Spanish HL class but it can be modified for a beginner-level course.

It is crucial that from the very first day of class, students understand what is expected of them and what the course entails. This sounds like typical, first day introduction to the course but when it comes to HLLs, they usually enter the class with a great deal of insecurity. Depending on the HL population, some will feel that they are ill-prepared for the rigors of the course while others will expect to be over-prepared (Potowski, 2002). A reading, DVD, or class discussion on linguistic variation—be it geographic, social, contextual—is necessary, along with explanations of what is a language and its many manifestations or dialects, where the notion of standard or academic variety fits in and why in the same way that English-speaking students enroll in

English courses and major in English, Spanish-speaking students enroll and/ or major in Spanish. This will require some instructor preparation since, unfortunately, the lack of professional training in the area of HL Education that García Moya highlighted in 1981 lingers to this day (Gutierrez, 1997; Potowski, 2003; Schwarzer & Petrón, 2005). Sociolinguistic training must include explanations of linguistic biases and linguistic sensitivity and provide definitions of concepts like language and dialect (Train, 2003). Teachers must go beyond knowing the culture of their students and participate in it, not just empathize with it (Ellison, 2006; Lacorte & Canabal, 2003). They must understand that just speaking about the right to use non-standard forms and code-switching is not enough; they must take part in them and classroom materials must include them if they are to be tools of empowerment to students (Gutiérrez Spencer, 1995). Otherwise, we fall into what Osborn calls 'paternalistic empowerment', 'a strategy of condescension' which will not effect change (2000, p. 161). This means that different dialects, with all their phonetic, lexical, morphological, and syntactic variation must be welcome in the classroom (Aparicio, 1993). HLLs belong to bilingual communities and bilingualism is the norm for them (Anderson, 2008; Correa, 2010). If exclusion of the L1 in the L2 classroom has not been proven to improve learning (Macaro, 2001); how could it possibly make sense to eliminate it from students who grew up with both languages simultaneously?[2] Quite the contrary, bilingualism should be embraced in the HL classroom (García, 2009). As daunting a task as this may seem, especially for an instructor that is not yet a member of the students' linguistic community, it starts with taking the role of facilitator, allowing students to share what they already know about their own language, and more importantly, what they want to learn (Ducar, 2008). An open discussion on language varieties will uncover all the ones that are present in the classroom and it will reveal students' perceptions of their own varieties versus others. This type of data gathering must be part of every HL classroom in order for the instructor to be able to adjust the curriculum and the discussions to accommodate the needs of the students.

The Curriculum

It is vital for HLLs to be aware of class expectations. It is a frightening thought for most of them to see on a syllabus that they will be asked to write a composition when they have never done this before or to do an oral presentation when they have so often been criticized for their Spanish. A set of student learning outcomes (SLOs) or goals needs to be in place. For a course that brings together critical language awareness and the addition of an academic variety, the outcomes in this proposal have been divided into two groups. The first set—sociolinguistic goals—are the ones that will cover notions of language variation and change, linguistic prejudices, dominant and subordinate varieties. The second set—grammatical goals— will vary depending on the level of the course. While a beginner HL course will introduce HLLs to the four skills in the target language, an intermediate course will most likely have a more heterogeneous group of students and will have to offer a more reactive curriculum. These students will need to expand their communicative skills to domains that go beyond the family and interpersonal communication to include interpretive and presentational modes in areas of interest to them, be it school, business, medicine, law, etc. They will also have to develop command of written norms if they want to continue with upper-level courses in order to major or minor in the language. The SLOs presented here tie in with the World-Readiness Standards for Learning Languages or 5 C's (American Council on the Teaching of Foreign Languages[3]). What follows are suggestions for activities to assist students in obtaining each of these SLOs.

SLO 1: Appreciate Inherent Nature of Language Variation and Change
ACTFL Standards: Comparisons, Connections, Cultures
The purpose of the first goal is to get students to see that everyone speaks a dialect; that there is no one version of any language that is better than the others and that this is true for all languages. Sociolinguistic surveys have long been recommended as a way for HLLs to go into the community and collect lexical information (Rodríguez Pino, 1997). A similar task and one that can be incorporated into many a larger activity in the classroom is simply a variation on ¿Cómo se dice? 'How do you say it?' (Smith et al., 2011). In the original version, students are shown a picture of an artifact known to have many variations throughout the Spanish-speaking world and are asked for the word. Taking this activity a step further, any time we come across a referent with multiple synonyms in Spanish—while reading, writing, or listening to the language—there is the chance to include all of the class members and their varieties by asking them what word each of them uses to

refer to it and to explain that they are all equally correct. Carreira (2000) has pointed out, however, that highlighting lexical differences could give students the impression of vast distinctions among the varieties and even more so when compared to the standard. To avoid this, these activities need to be accompanied by class discussions and explanations. For example, letting students know that words like *banana, banano, plátano, guineo, mínimo, cambur* all seem to refer to 'bananas' or 'plantains' but oftentimes they reference various members of the same family of fruits. A different situation arises with words like *cacahuate* and *maní*—both refer to 'peanut'—but one entered Spanish from Náhuatl and the other from Taíno; or that *aguacate* and *palta* both mean 'avocado', that the first is the word in Náhuatl while the second in Quechua. If we point out that words from Quechua entered into Andean Spanish and words from Náhuatl entered Mexican Spanish then we can follow the analysis to how words from English enter U.S. Spanish and how this is a normal process in languages. Comparisons with English are effective since students come into the classroom with the perception that these are phenomena that only occur in Spanish. A discussion on the different varieties of English across the world, including Outer Circle countries—in Kachru's (1992) terminology—and perceptions of them in the United States help students make connections and understand why and how prestige gets assigned to a particular variety. The same analysis can be applied to varieties within the United States, including—but not limited to—Southern English, African-American English, Chicano English, etc. These activities allow students to make *Comparisons* between varieties of the language and between *Cultures* as well as *Connections* on social, economic, and cultural perspectives.

SLO 2: Understand Linguistic Prejudices
ACTFL Standards: Communication, Cultures, Connections, Comparisons, Communities
The second learning outcome focuses on getting HLLs to understand linguistic prejudice, to get them to talk about the preconceptions and misconceptions that exist about U.S. Spanish. A personal literacy trajectory (Smith et al., 2011) or linguistic autobiography (Aparicio, 1997) asks students to think about when they learned their first and their second languages. They write down the locations where learning took place, the

person(s) involved in this experience with them, the mode of interaction: speaking, reading, listening, or writing. They should think about experiences with Spanish and in Spanish that stand out in their memories and the same for English. This type of exercise allows students to reflect on how these two paths towards acquisition were different or similar. Both of these activities should be followed by class discussions where students can share their own experiences with the entire class. This format allows for *Communication* in interpretive and presentational modes. If any of the students had monolingual experiences in Spanish—growing up in a Spanish-speaking country—the perfect opportunity presents itself to compare the experiences of a monolingual individual and a bilingual and their respective *Communities*. It will be helpful to reflect on the differences between someone who had all or most of their schooling in Spanish with someone who had none. Encourage students to think about other language contact situations—friends, acquaintances—and how they are similar to or different from their own, thus making cultural *Connections* and *Comparisons*. When discussing code-switching—the infamous Spanglish—students most often think of this as a purely Spanish/English phenomenon but when quizzed about people they know or have come across, they are quick to realize they have encountered it in other language contact situations as well. This will lead into the reasons why U.S. Spanish is so reviled and by whom; students will be able to talk about their experiences as circumstantial bilinguals and they will begin to see themselves as competent bilinguals.

SLO 3: Be Able to Decide Whether to Conform or Contest the Linguistic Status Quo
ACTFL Standards: Cultures, Connections, Comparisons, Communities

The third desired outcome follows from HLLs understanding the first two and deciding whether to accept or fight the imposed standard. The goal is to get students to ask themselves whether they want or need to participate in the acquisition and promotion of academic Spanish as the prestige variety. Input from them on what they consider the prestige variety of English and when and why they aim for it, if ever, provides valuable insight. This knowledge provides the kind of information necessary to allow them to make an informed decision on what is the prestige variety of Spanish for them. Questions about whether speaking a standard variety of Spanish affects them in the same way as speaking a standard variety of English should be posed. Determining how U.S. Spanish is no different from any other variety in the changes it faces will help students perceive that matters of prestige are not linguistic but social, political, and economic. An eye-opening activity presents them with three articles, one from Latin America, one from Spain, and one from a Spanish-language newspaper in the United States. The class—as a whole or in small groups—looks for English words or expressions, cases of transfer from English. The point of this exercise is for students to realize how many lexical borrowings appear in Spanish-language papers, not just in the United States but also in Spanish-speaking countries (Mrak, 2011b). Students will need help discovering transfer beyond the lexical level; classroom time devoted to this is fruitful. It opens up the question of why U.S. Spanish receives such biting criticism for its use of English while other varieties do not. Another useful assignment is to send students beyond the classroom into the local community to find the language in action. A community language map, where students take pictures of signs throughout the community, billboards, store signs, community bulletin boards, and other environmental print opens the door to address the realities of a bilingual community (Smith et al., 2011). Students can show their collection in the form of a PowerPoint presentation and thus, share their findings with the rest of the class. This lends itself to discussions as to why someone would choose an English word over a Spanish one or vice versa, phonetic spelling, literal translations, etc. Realizing these are carefully chosen decisions—and not errors—empowers students about the strength of their bilingualism and the value of both of their languages. All of these activities provide the *Cultural Comparisons* and *Connections* necessary to foster respect for all the Spanish-speaking *Communities*.

SLO 4: Expand Communicative Skills
ACTFL Standard: Communication
The next two SLOs involve the expansion of lexical domains and of all three communicative modes. Everyone lacks vocabulary for topics not accessed on a regular basis; therefore, having opportunities to use Spanish in areas related to the university, business, medicine, law, travel—any area of interest to the students—will help them with their interpersonal communication. Oral presentations related to these fields will provide practice in the presentational mode while related readings and these same presentations

will enhance interpretive communication for the whole class. A situation that takes on particular importance in the case of bilingual communities and their speakers is that of audience. When bilinguals are speaking to other bilinguals, they know they can do it in either language or in both of them simultaneously (Grosjean, 1997). When a student does a presentation in front of the class, s/he is speaking to bilinguals. As García (2002) has pointed out, students need a real purpose and a real audience to progress in their acquisition of literacy. The class is a real audience, and a bilingual one, so a first oral presentation could involve sharing with the class plans for after graduation. Since the group is bilingual, bilingual modes of speaking would be expected. The next activity could be a letter to a grandparent, aunt or uncle that does not speak English. A pre-writing activity in which the class discusses what limitations their readers may have is a useful way of encouraging students to consider their reader. Asking HLLs to think about situations in which they were misunderstood or not understood by a monolingual Spanish speaker is useful. Because writing allows for more editing than speaking does, the students can have more control on this type of task. The idea of preparing for a fictitious Spanish monolingual interlocutor will, over time, help students include the listener/reader; and taking into account the audience is an important task in any speaking or writing activity. A second oral presentation could cover preparing a description of university life to share with a student in a Spanish-speaking country who would like to come to the United States to learn English. Again, this should be prefaced by a discussion of possible topics to cover and how they would be described in Spanish. Internet articles or webpages from universities in Spanish-speaking countries would show students pertinent vocabulary. Brief translation exercises throughout the semester—when chosen from different fields—give students the chance to add to their lexicon. An online dictionary available in class is a great resource that should be shared with the class; students need to learn how to use a dictionary, how a bilingual and a monolingual dictionary are both needed as they provide different types of assistance. Throughout these activities, the subject of register should be broached. Recognizing how we want to address our reader/listener gives students a chance to think about their own voices and how they want to express their ideas.

SLO 5: Demonstrate Command of Written Norms
ACTFL Standard: Communication

The second SLO related to acquisition of the academic variety of the language is command of written norms. For students, this always means correct accent placement. Research in this area indicates that students need to work on sight recognition of commonly used words (Samaniego and Pino, 2000) and that amplified phonetic cues can assist them in locating the stressed syllable (Carreira, 2002). By all reports, what does not seem to work is giving students the rules of accent placement in one, lump-sum lecture (Beaudrie, 2007, 2012a). Suggestions for introducing correct accent placement include both of the above mentioned techniques with the addition of a breakdown of the rules into manageable components. For example, when the regular forms of the Preterite are introduced, it is important to signal to students the accents on first and third person singular—*yo* and *él/ella/usted* in students' terms, '*I*' and 'he/she/you-formal, singular'. From there, ask students what other words they know that end in a stressed vowel. It will not be very challenging to get *mam*á 'mom' and *pap*á 'dad' and perhaps with some help from the instructor, *café* 'coffee' and bebé 'baby' (this last one is paroxytone in some dialects). These words will become recognizable fairly easily and putting additional phonetic stress on them makes the required accent mark more obvious. All written work at this point should focus on this stress pattern.[4] Even though accent placement has absolutely nothing to do with the linguistic discrimination HLLs are subjected to, if we ask students on the first day of class what they want to get out of the class, just about every one of them will respond that accents are their weakness. Therefore, I agree with Carreira (2002) that when students discover that they can learn accents, it gives them a real sense of empowerment. However, having as the primary interest a student-based curriculum, every instructor will have to decide how much or how little time to devote to these types of activities. Other orthographic difficulties that students encounter involve multiple graphemes represented by a single phoneme, 'b/v', 's/c/z', 'll/y'.[5] It is important to explain to students that pairs like 'b/v' or 's/z' are different phonemes in English; hence, our ability to distinguish them and choose the correct one in writing. In Spanish, the two letters in each pair represent the same phoneme so it makes it impossible to ascertain which one is required, and that this is not a difficulty limited to heritage speakers but to all speakers of Spanish. All of this necessitates reading with focused noticing (Ellis, 1994, p. 361) and writing with peer-reviewing and self-reviewing that selects specific areas for the task. Again, while most of the spelling requires ample practice to produce sight recognition, some explanations can alleviate students' frustrations. It is important that HLLs are introduced to the features of word processing software that will simplify their writing in Spanish. From setting the language to Spanish in their documents to changing the keyboard to easily access diacritics, these are experiences they will not have had. They also need time to review a composition in class so spell-checking software can be explained. If the software indicates that the word is spelled incorrectly, is the option offered correct? It is good practice for students to look at a definition of the word offered by *Spellcheck* to make sure that it is the one they need. They should have access to a dictionary in class so they can look up words as the need arises. These reviewing exercises also help students see writing as a process, with multiple edits and rewrites. Some instructors may be reluctant to let students write with these aides but as Potowski (2005) points out, integrating readily available technology from the students' inventory of tools creates a real-life writing situation. This is applied learning at its best.

Additional Considerations

Readings for the class should include texts written by U.S. Hispanics, as well as Latin American and Peninsular authors. Time constraints will most likely not permit book length readings so short stories or newspaper articles will work best. The benefit of newspaper articles is that they will allow students to observe a variety of dialects, but most importantly, the influence that English has on Spanish, whether in the United States or abroad (Mrak, 2011b). Listening to radio broadcasts will also serve this purpose. Follow these with discussions on which words are borrowed into Spanish; what type of borrowing it is; why the need to borrow it—is there a preexisting Spanish word? This will help students see their varieties are just like everyone else's. Continuously allow for students to add to the lexical inventory that exists in the classroom and explain that they are synonyms, one no more correct than the other. Furthermore, provide them with sources of new material, with texts they have not had a chance to experiment so they can expand their vocabulary to new domains (Fairclough & Mrak, 2003). Research has shown that HLLs may need focused grammar instruction and contrastive analysis

(Potowski et al., 2009). Free voluntary reading has been shown to be a good resource for this student population (McQuillan, 1996); a book club where students select their own material and discuss it in groups or through journals is a good way to introduce them to literature. Providing a list of selected titles can be helpful to students, even if the option to pick their own still exists, as they may feel overwhelmed by all the choices. Take into account the student body when designing the curriculum, since the varieties of the language will be different every semester and every student will have different curricular needs. A constantly changing syllabus—depending on the discoveries in the classroom—will create the type of reactive curriculum that will assist students most (Correa, 2011; Lacorte & Canabal, 2003). Crucially, as Alim suggests, 'if critical pedagogies are to be relevant and effective, they must be locally situated and constantly negotiated (2010, p. 213).

Conclusion

The importance of empowering students to see themselves as competent bilinguals cannot be overly emphasized. They already speak two languages. The challenges they encounter are also found in monolinguals (and the latter only speak one language!), whether it is placing accents or deciding between 'v' and 'b', or speaking a non-prestige variety. For students who have been made to feel deficient for taking Spanish classes, as if they were cheating by doing so, they need to realize that it is no different than taking English classes. The idea of code-switching as a problem must be dispelled and awareness of it as a common phenomenon in bilingual communities needs to be embraced while the use of the term *Spanglish*, due to its negative connotation as a hybrid spoken by imperfect speakers of English and Spanish, must be stopped (Otheguy & Stern, 2010).

Notes

1. While the term heritage language learner/speaker continues to have currency in the profession to refer to speakers who grew up in a home where a language other than English was spoken, it remains questionable among Hispanic students (and some academics) and thus I prefer the term bilingual to refer to them (Mrak, 2010). Throughout the paper, the two terms are used interchangeably.
2. For many HL speakers, English and Spanish are both L1s. Of course, this is not true for all of them.

3. For a discussion on how the Common Core State Standards fit into Heritage Language Education see Beaudrie, 2012c.
4. For a more detailed look at this approach to teaching accents, see Mrak and Padilla, 2007.
5. 'll' and 'y' share the same phoneme in most varieties of American Spanish as do 's', 'z', and 'c', the latter only when followed by 'e' or 'i'. This is not the case in Peninsular Spanish.

References

Alim, H. S. (2005). Critical language awareness in the United States: Revisiting issues and revising pedagogies in a resegregated society. *Educational Researcher, 34*(24), 24-31.

Alim, H. S. (2010). Critical language awareness. *Sociolinguistics and Language Education, 1,* 205-231.

American Council on the Teaching of Foreign Languages. (n.d.). *World-readiness standards for learning languages.* Retrieved from https://www.actfl.org/publications/all/world-readiness-standards-learning-languages

Anderson, J. (2008). Towards an integrated second-language pedagogy for foreign and community/heritage languages in multilingual Britain. *Language Learning Journal, 26*(1), 78-89.

Aparicio, F. R. (1993). Diversification and pan-latinity: Projections for the teaching of Spanish to bilinguals. In Roca, A. and Lipski, J. M. (Eds.), *Spanish in the United States: Linguistic contact and diversity* (pp. 183-198). Berlin: Mouton de Gruyter.

Aparicio, F. R. (1997). La enseñanza del español para hispanohablantes y la pedagogía multicultural [The teaching of Spanish by Spanish speakers and multicultural pedagogy]. In Colombi, M. C. and Alarcón, F. X. (Eds.), *La enseñanza del español a hispanohablantes: praxis y teoría* [The teaching of Spanish to Spanish speakers: Praxis and theory] (pp. 222-232). Boston: Houghton Mifflin.

Beaudrie, S. (2007). La enseñanza del acento ortográfico en español y su relación con la percepción de la sílaba tónica [The teaching of the accent mark in Spanish and its relationship to the perception of the tonic syllable]. *Hispania, 90*(4), 809–823.

Beaudrie, S. (2012a). A corpus-based study on the misspellings of Spanish heritage learners and their implications for teaching. *Linguistics and Education, 23,* 135-144.

Beaudrie, S. (2012b). Language placement and beyond: Guidelines for the design and implementation of a computerized Spanish heritage language exam. *Heritage Language Journal, 9*(1). Retrieved from http://hlj.ucla.edu/

Beaudrie, S. (2012c). Common core state standards and heritage language education: How do they match? *National Capital Language Resource Center, Crossroads in the Classroom.* Retrieved from http://www.nclrc.org/about_teaching/Crossroads-Beaudrie-swc1.pdf

Benjamin, R. (1997). What do our students want? Some reflections on teaching Spanish as an academic subject to bilingual students. *ADFL Bulletin, 29*(1), 44-47.

Carreira, M. (2000). Validating and promoting Spanish in the United States: Lessons from linguistic science. *Bilingual Research Journal, 24*(4), 423-442.

Carreira, M. M. (2002). When phonological limitations compromise literacy: A connectionist approach to enhancing the phonological competence of heritage language speakers of

Spanish. In Hammadou Sullivan, J. (Ed.), *Literacy and the second language learner* (pp. 239-260). Greenwich, CT: Information Age Publishing.

Colombi, M. C., & Alarcón, F. X. (Eds.). (1997). *La enseñanza del español a hispanohablantes: praxis y teoría* [The teaching of Spanish to Spanish speakers: Praxis and theory]. Boston: Houghton Mifflin Company.

Correa, M. (2010). Heritage language learner programs and life after the classroom: A not so critical approach. *Journal of Linguistic and Language Teaching, 1*(2), 221-240.

Correa, M. (2011). Advocating for critical pedagogical approaches to teaching Spanish as a heritage language: Some considerations. *Foreign Language Annals, 44*(2), 308-320.

Ducar, C. M. (2008). Student voices: The missing link in the Spanish heritage language debate. *Foreign Language Annals, 41*(3), 415–433.

Ellis, R. (1994). *The study of second language acquisition*. Oxford: Oxford University Press.

Ellison, V. R. (2006). Cultural awareness knowledge and the teaching of Spanish to native speakers. *Hispania, 89*(1), 133-146.

Fairclough, M. (2012). A working model for assessing Spanish heritage language learners' language proficiency through a placement exam. *Heritage Language Journal, 9*(1). Retrieved from http://hlj.ucla.edu/

Fairclough, M., & Mrak, N. A. (2003). La enseñanza del español a los hispanohablantes bilingües y su efecto en la producción oral [The teaching of Spanish to bilingual Spanish speakers and its effect on oral production]. In Roca, A. & Colombi, M. C. (Eds.), *Mi lengua: Spanish as a heritage language in the United States, research and practice* (pp. 198-212). Washington, D.C.: Georgetown University Press.

Fairclough, N. (1992). The appropriacy of "appropriateness." In N. Fairclough (Ed.), *Critical language awareness* (pp. 33-56). London: Longman.

García, O. (2002). Writing backwards across languages: The inexpert English/Spanish biliteracy of uncertified bilingual teachers. In Schleppegrell, M. J. & Colombi, M. C. (Eds.), *Developing advanced literacy in first and second languages: Meaning with power* (pp. 245-259). Mahwah, NJ: Lawrence Erlbaum Associates.

García, O. (2009). Education, multilingualism and translanguaging in the 21st century. In Skutnabb-Kangas, T., Phillipson, R., Mohanty, A. K. & Panda, M. (Eds.), *Social justice through multilingual education* (pp. 140-158). Bristol: Multilingual Matters.

García-Moya, R. (1981). Teaching Spanish to Spanish speakers: Some considerations for the preparation of teachers. In Valdés, G., Lozano, A., & García-Moya, R. (Eds.), *Teaching Spanish to the Hispanic bilingual in the United States: Issues, aims, and methods* (pp. 59-70). New York: Teachers College.

Grosjean, F. (1997). Processing mixed language: Issues, findings, and models. In de Groot, A.M. B. & Kroll, J. F. (Eds.), *Tutorials in bilingualism: Psycholinguistic perspectives* (pp. 225-254). Mahwah, NJ: Lawrence Erlbaum Associates.

Gutierrez, J. R. (1997). Teaching Spanish as a heritage language: A case for language awareness. *ADFL Bulletin, 29*, 33–36.

Gutiérrez Spencer, L . (1995). Reading and vocabulary: Recommendations for Spanish for native speakers materials. *Bilingual Review, 20*(2), 176-87.

Kachru, B. B. (1992). Teaching world Englishes. In Kachru, B. B. (Ed.), *The other tongue: English across cultures* (pp. 355-366). Champaign, IL: University of Illinois Press.

Lacorte, M., & Canabal, E. (2003). Interaction with heritage language learners in foreign language classrooms. In Blyth, C. (Ed.), *The sociolinguistics of foreign-language classrooms:*

Contributions of the native, the near-native, and the non-native speaker (pp. 107-129). Boston: Thomson Heinle.
Leeman, J. (2005). Engaging critical pedagogy: Spanish for native speakers. *Foreign Language Annals, 38*(1), 35-45.
Macaro, E. (2001). Analysing student teachers' codeswitching in foreign language classrooms: Theories and decision making. *The Modern Language Journal, 85*, 531-48.
MacGregor-Mendoza, P. (2012). Spanish as a heritage language assessment: Successes, failures, lessons learned. *Heritage Language Journal, 9*(1). Retrieved from http://hlj.ucla.edu/
Martínez, G. (2003). Classroom based dialect awareness in heritage language instruction: A critical applied linguistic approach. *Heritage Language Journal. 1*(1). Retrieved from http://hlj.ucla.edu/Journal.aspx
McQuillan, J. (1996). How should heritage languages be taught? The effects of a free voluntary reading program. *Foreign Language Annals, 29*(1), 56-73.
Mrak, N. A. (2010). Empowering Spanish/English speakers in the Unites States: Reclaiming their bilingualism. In Watzke, J., Mantero, M. & Reece-Miller, P. C. (Eds.), *Readings in language studies, volume 2: Language and* power (pp. 23-37). New York: International Society for Language Studies.
Mrak, N. A. (2011a). Heritage speakers and the *standard*: Fighting linguistic hegemony. In Ortiz-López, L. A. (Ed.), *Selected proceedings of the 13th Hispanic linguistics symposium* (pp. 161-168). Sommerville, MA: Cascadilla Press.
Mrak, N. A. (2011b). Lexical transfer from English to Spanish: How do bilingual and monolingual communities compare? *Southwest Journal of Linguisitcs, 30*(1), 95-115.
Mrak, N. A., & Padilla Aponte, E. K. (2007). ¡Conozcámonos!: Curso práctico de español *para el estudiante bilingüe en los Estados Unidos*. Boston: Thomson Heinle.
Osborn, T. A. (2000). *Critical reflection and the foreign language classroom*. Westport CT: Bergin and Garvey.
Otheguy, R., & Stern, N. (2010). On so-called Spanglish. *International Journal of Bilingualism, 15*(1), 85-100.
Pomerantz, A. (2002). Language ideologies and the production of identities: Spanish as a resource for participation in a multilingual marketplace. *Multilingual, 21*(2/3), 275-302.
Potowski, K. (2002). Experiences of Spanish heritage speakers in university foreign language courses and implications for teacher training. *ADFL Bulletin, 33*(3), 35-42.
Potowski, K. (2003). Chicago's "Heritage Language Teacher Corps": A model for improving Spanish teacher development. *Hispania, 86*(2), 302-311.
Potowski, K. (2005). *Fundamentos de la enseñanza del español a hispanohablantes en los E.E.U.U.* [Fundamentals of the teaching of Spanish to Spanish speakers in the United States]. Madrid: Arco Libros.
Potowski, K, Jegerski, J., & Morgan-Short, K. (2009). The effects of instruction on linguisitc development in Spanish heritage language speakers. *Language Learning, 59*(3), 537-579.
Potowski, K., Parada, M., & Morgan-Short, K. (2012). Developing an online placement exam forSpanish heritage speakers and L2 students. *Heritage Language Journal, 9*(1). Retrieved from http://hlj.ucla.edu/
Reynolds, R. R., Howard, K. M., & Deák, J. (2009). Heritage language learners in first-year foreign language courses: A report of general data across learner subtypes. *Foreign Language Annals, 42*(2), 250-269.
Rodríguez Pino, C. (1997). La reconceptualización del programa de español para hispanohablantes: Estrategias que reflejan la realidad sociolingüística de la classe [The

reconceptualization of the Spanish program for Spanish speakers: Strategies that reflect the reality sociolignuistic class]. In Colombi, M. C., & Alarcón, F. X. (Eds.), *La enseñanza del español a hispanohablantes: praxis y teoría* [The teaching of Spanish to Spanish speakers: Praxis and theory] (pp. 65-82). Boston: Houghton Mifflin Company.

Samaniego, F., & Pino, C. (2000). Frequently asked questions about SNS programs. In American Association of Teachers of Spanish and Portuguese (Eds.), *Professional development series handbook for teachers K-16: Spanish for native speakers* (pp. 29–63). Fort Worth, TX: Harcourt College.

Schwarzer, D., & Petrón, M. (2005). Heritage language instruction at the college level: Reality and possibilities. *Foreign Language Annals, 38*(4), 568-578.

Smith, H. L., Sánchez, P., E. L. D., & Machado-Casas, M. (2011). From linguistic imperialism to linguistic concientización: Learning from heritage language speakers. In Schwarzer, D., Petrón, M., and Luke, C. (Eds.), *Research informing practice—practice informing research: Innovative teaching methodologies for world language teachers* (177-199). Greenwich, CT: Information Age Publishing.

Train, R. W. (2003). The (non)native standard language in foreign language education: A critical perspective. In Blyth, C. (Ed.), *The sociolinguistics of foreign-language classrooms: Contributions of the native, the near-native, and the non-native speaker* (pp. 3-39). Boston: Heinle.

Valdés, G. (1997). The teaching of Spanish to bilingual Spanish-speaking students: Outstanding issues and unanswered questions. In Colombi, M. C., & Alarcón, F. X. (Eds.), *La enseñanza del español a hispanohablantes: praxis y teoría* [The teaching of Spanish to Spanish speakers: Praxis and theory] (pp. 8-39). Boston: Houghton Mifflin Company.

Valdés, G. (2005). Bilingualism, heritage language learners, and SLA research: Opportunities lost or seized? *The Modern Language Journal, 89*(3), 410-426.

Wilson, D. V. (2012). Discrimination is the key: Item analysis and learner characteristics. *Heritage Language Journal, 9*(1). Retrieved from http://hlj.ucla.edu/

Wolford, T. E., & Carter, P. M. (2010). Spanish-as-threat ideology and the sociocultural context of Spanish in South Texas. In Rivera-Mills, S. V. & Villa, D. J. (Eds.), *Spanish of the U.S. Southwest: a language in transition* (111-131). Madrid: Iberoamericana.

CHAPTER 10

NON-NATIVE TEACHERS AND ENGLISH LANGUAGE TEACHING:
Critical Social Choices in the Mexican Context

Gerrard Mugford
Universidad de Guadalajara, Mexico

Introduction

In Mexico, as with many other countries, teaching English as a Foreign Language (EFL) largely reflects pedagogical trends and instruction patterns of the United States and the United Kingdom—or what Kachru (1992, 1995) deemed the Inner Circle. Consequently, there is little or no development of local pedagogical approaches which respond to particular and specific needs (Widin, 2010). Not only is scant attention given to identifying and satisfying the social, economic and political objectives of Mexican students in learning a foreign language but teacher training methodology is far more concerned with adopting and replicating methods and techniques emanating from commercial British, Australasian and North American (BANA) private language schools (Holliday, 1994, 2005) or what Widin identifies as "NABA (North American, British and Australian) language teaching methodologies" (2010, p. 20). Few Mexican EFL teacher trainers analyse whether these methodologies and practices are appropriate for the Mexican context. In this chapter I specifically focus on how teacher trainees view their role in the EFL classroom.

First of all, I want to encourage Mexican EFL teachers to view English language learning in relation to the local surroundings and context. To achieve this, I adopt Pennycook's (2010) view of "language as local practice". He maintains that "languages are a product of the deeply social and cultural activities in which people engage" (2010, p. 1) and, therefore, I would argue that EFL teaching and learning should respond to the local environment rather than try to engage students in decontextualised language routines.

Following Bowles and Gintes (1976), I adopt a critical perspective to education and argue that ELT should reflect an "egalitarian and liberating educational system" that places non-native teachers and their students on an equal footing with Inner Circle native speakers. To identify the theory and underlying principles that influence actual teaching practice within the context of the classroom, I revisit Clark's (1987) value systems of classical humanism, reconstructionism and progressivism which, he argues, reflect the educational strategies of society in trying to achieve its goals. To examine current teaching training practices specifically in Mexico, I review the applicability of Appleby's three educational agendas for the spread of English: "modernisation and development', 'imperialism and class interests' and 'appropriation and disinvention" (2010, pp. 34-35).

To investigate teacher trainees' attitudes and motivations towards English-language teaching in terms of local needs, educational agenda and pedagogical values, I interviewed 115 teacher trainees studying at a public university in Guadalajara, Mexico. I then contrasted these results with the answers from 201 English-language students to determine whether the teacher trainees had the same aims and perspectives. Besides analysing the results, I also attempted to triangulate the findings by asking another group of 26 teacher trainees to scrutinize and reflect on the results. The results indicate that EFL teaching methodology in Mexico is heavily influenced by BANA and NABA practices and that urgent critical work needs to be undertaken in order to develop pedagogic practices that truly respond to local needs.

Literature Review

An overview of teaching practice and methodology needs to be analysed within a larger pedagogical framework especially in ideological terms which reflect "the important relationships among power, meaning and interest" (Giroux, 1997, p. 75). This is to say, in promoting the teaching of a particular pedagogy, there are interests at work which aim to give specific actors increased economic and political power. Whilst concentrating on their professional development and progress, EFL teachers may not be aware of the commercial interests at work (e.g., EFL industry of publishers, international examination boards and language schools) or the political agencies (e.g., government departments or international bodies). Therefore, it is important to raise language teachers' awareness of the aims and objectives of ELT in terms of "the production, consumption, and representation of ideas and behavior, all of which can distort or illuminate the nature of reality" (Giroux, 1997, p. 75). One way of doing this is to understand teaching and learning at the local level and trying to generate ideas which are relevant and reflect, in this case, realities in Guadalajara, Mexico.

Teaching and learning language as local practice involves examining "the practices of everyday life" (Pennycook, 2010, p. 1) rather than solely positioning ELT in future instrumental terms e.g. gaining better employment or studying abroad. Pennycook argues that language should not be delivered in terms of prepackaged functions and need to be seen as "doing" and involves "speakers, histories, cultures, places, ideologies" (p. 6) as "part of social and local activity" (p. 128).

As local practice in the EFL scenario, language users need to appropriate the target language for their own uses–being creative, breaking norms of use–and moving away from "nation-based models of English and take on board current understandings of translingual practices across communities other than those defined along national criteria" (Pennycook, 2010, p. 84). Therefore, EFL teachers need to identify and respond to language as local practice and adopt appropriate pedagogic approaches and practices.

Besides trying to encourage teachers to take into consideration their local surroundings, teacher trainers need to help teachers to define what they are trying to achieve rather than be led by external interests. Bowles and Gintes (1976) argue that the educational system should be "in the process of reproducing society, vigorously promotes personal development and social equality" (p. 265). Therefore, EFL teachers need to examine their teaching goals in terms of students' roles in society, how learners wish to progress and language learning as a way of promoting social equality. These aims are mirrored in Clark's (1987) value systems of classical humanism, reconstructionism and progressivism. Classical humanism "is knowledge-oriented and is concerned with promoting intellectual and cultural values". In terms of ELT, classical humanism parallels Freire's (1993) "banking model" of education where teachers transmit existing norms, values and "commonsense" and taken-for-granted understandings, or as Clark (1987) puts it: "The teacher is seen as someone who possesses knowledge and whose task it is to pass it on to the learners in his/her charge" (p. 5). This approach runs the danger of casting the teacher in a dominating and subordinating role unless she sees her responsibility in helping her students to appropriate the system and use it to their own advantage. Meanwhile, giving students skills so they can make a useful contribution to society is found in reconstructionism which "is society-oriented and is concerned with the promotion of agreed social goals" (p. 1). EFL teachers who forward reconstructionism values are interested in making students functional members of their community and achieving "an effective communicative ability in learners as their ultimate goal" (p. 23). In the Mexican context, reconstructionism in language teaching means to help learners get jobs that require English language skills and helping students complete their university studies, since English is becoming more and more a graduation requirement. With a focus of personal self-actualisation, progressivism "is concerned with the development of individuals, and with the value of diversity" (p. 1). Within the progressivist curriculum, "learners must be considered as individuals with differing learning histories, aspirations, interests, personalities, and learning styles" (p. 81). Programmes are "above all learner-centred" (p. 70) and acknowledge the learners' "differing background experiences, attitudes, and personalities that they bring to the classroom" (p. 81).

Clark's (2010) categorisation of curriculum values allows teachers to take a more critical stance towards EFL pedagogy and links up closely with Appleby's identification of the reasons for the spread of English as a foreign language. Appleby's modernisation and development categories are often cited as key reasons for promoting English in the curriculum especially due to Mexico's close economic ties with the United States and to a lesser extent with Canada. However, reflecting Appleby's identification of "imperialism and class interests", the reality for many language users is that English if used at all is only employed in low-status jobs such as in call centres, assembly lines or in tourism. There is little identification in BANA or NABA teacher training methodology for teaching English to encourage 'appropriation and disinvention' (pp. 34-35).

A key problem in Mexico is that whilst there is a growing demand for English, there is a serious lack of teachers. Writing in the Houston Chronicle, Marion Lloyd in 2009 interviewed Fernando Gonzalez, an official in the

Secretariat of Public Education in Mexico who said that, in addition to the 35,000 existing teachers, a further 85,000 English-language teachers were needed. Teacher training programmes are being implemented throughout the country. For instance, in the local context of this study in Guadalajara, there are three B.A. and three M.A. programmes in TEFL, along with a host of basic and proficiency training courses. However, little research has been carried out as to whether they respond to local needs or are merely replicating global teacher training courses. This paper looks at the teacher attitudes and values on one of these B.A. programmes.

Research Problem and Research Questions

In surveying the overall objectives, curriculum values and motivations related to English-language pedagogy in Mexico, I am asking whether teacher-training programmes adequately prepare teachers to respond to students' social, cultural and educational needs. I want to ascertain whether ELT training programmes encourage teachers to respond to local needs and, as a result, promote meaningful learning within the Mexican context. To pursue this line of inquiry, I examine the views, beliefs and attitudes of the teacher trainees at a public university in Guadalajara. The overarching research question that I am pursuing is: How critically do Mexican teacher-trainees view the objectives and purposes of teaching English as a foreign language? To seek out possible answers to this overarching research question, I have developed three specific research questions.

First of all, I want to find out the teacher trainees' stated objectives in teaching English as a foreign-language. Therefore, my first specific research question is:

> What do BA TEFL undergraduates consider to be the purpose behind their students learning English?

Answers to this question will help me identity the aims, curriculum values and motivations that guide the teacher trainees' pedagogic practices in the classroom context. Replies will assist me in determining whether Clark's (1987) categorisation of curriculum values—classical humanism, reconstructionism and progressivism—do indeed underscore educational approaches in the Mexican EFL context.

To know whether trainee teachers' objectives correspond with those of their students, I designed my second specific research question:

What are specific learning objectives of EFL students?

By asking language students their aims and objectives, I am in a position to evaluate whether teacher trainees are responding to their students' wants and needs at a local level especially in Pennycook's (2010) terms of "language as local practice".

Since I am also interested in assessing the critical awareness of Mexican teacher-trainees with regards to the role of English as a foreign language in the local context, my third specific research question is:

Do BA TEFL undergraduates view English as important within Mexican society?

By reflecting on the usefulness of knowing and using English in the local context, Mexican teacher-trainees are being encouraged to reflect on the educational realities of studying English, especially in Appleby's (2010) terms: modernisation, linguistic imperialism and class interests and appropriation.

Methodology

To carry out this investigation, I divided the research into two stages. In the first stage I collected information on the purposes and aims of teaching and learning English from both teacher trainees and students. In the second stage, I asked teacher trainees to reflect on the findings from the first stage.

In stage one, 115 BA TEFL undergraduates were invited to complete a questionnaire which asked them to consider the usefulness of English and hence the reasons for teaching and learning English. All 115 respondents were middle-class Mexicans between 18 and 25 years old. There were 71 women respondents as opposed to 44 men—the greater amount of female respondents reflects the predominance of women on the BA programme.

The questionnaire asked the teacher trainees to react to a series of statements which covered aspects of EFL pedagogy raised by Clark's curriculum values (classical humanism, reconstructionism and progressivism), Appleby's three educational agendas (modernisation, linguistic imperialism and class interests and appropriation) and Pennycook's view of language as local practice:

Classical humanism: *Knowing and using English helps students develop intellectual and cultural values.*

Reconstructionism: *Knowing and using English is part of an international reality if you really want to succeed in life; Knowing and using English will help students become useful and productive members of society; and Knowing and using English provides work and educational opportunities.*

Progressivism: *Knowing and using English helps students express and develop themselves in their own way.*

Modernisation: *Knowing and using English help with the modernisation and development of Mexico.*

Class interests: *Knowing and using English helps reduce social inequality by giving people a better chance in life.*

Appropriation: *Knowing and using English helps students achieve own individual professional and personal goals.*

Language as local practice: *Knowing and using English allows students to understand how English is used locally in Guadalajara.*

Respondents were given the choice of: *strongly agreeing, agreeing, disagreeing* or *strongly disagreeing*. The questionnaire was applied in English and can be viewed in Appendix 10A.

To compare the trainee teachers' perceptions regarding the reasons and motivations for learning, 201 English-language students were given a roughly similar questionnaire. The statements were developed after extensive piloting which pinpointed which statements were more relevant in reflecting the language learners' motivations:

Classical humanism: *Knowing English, I will become an educated person; Knowing English, I will be able to appreciate English speaking countries' literature, music and film.*

Reconstructionism: *English will provide me more opportunities to get a job; I will be able to use English at work; English will increase my salary significantly; and English will allow me to do business abroad.*

Progressivism: *English will allow me to grow professionally; English will permit me to study abroad; and Knowing English, I will improve personally.*

Modernisation: *English will facilitate me the use of new technologies such as the internet.*

Class interests: *Knowing English, I will be part of a higher social class.*

Appropriation: *Knowing English I can communicate when travelling abroad; English will let me make friends. Knowing English, I will be able to communicate with people from other countries.*

Language as local practice: *English will allow me to interact through social networks; English will let me communicate with my relatives from the USA.*

Respondents were given the choice of: *definitively, probably, probably not,* or *definitively not*. The questionnaire was applied in Spanish and an English-language translation can be viewed in Appendix 10B.

After analysing the results, I designed a second stage in which I asked a group of 26 teacher trainees from the same university to critically comment on the findings and reflect on the attitudes expressed by the teacher trainee respondents. This stage added a degree of triangulation to the study as the respondents' peers examined the findings. To prepare the second group of teacher trainees to critically analyse the results, I gave them a short presentation on the critical pedagogy that surfaced after the Mexican Revolution especially during the 1934-1940 presidency of Lazaro Cardenas del Rio. During this period of political and educational upheaval, teachers tried unsuccessfully to relate pedagogy more closely to their students' needs. By describing these past attempts, I tried to get the trainee teachers to examine whether their peers' reflections were critically responding to the English-language needs of the country and of language students. Following a group discussion, the teacher trainees submitted their views and opinions in writing. Although they were not required to do so, the respondents gave their analyses and interpretations in English. In quoting from these evaluations, I have used pseudonyms in order to protect the identity of the teacher trainees.

Results

In this section I present the results of both questionnaires given to the teacher trainees and the language students with the aim of comparing the findings and ascertaining the degree of correlation between their educational values.

The study of teacher trainees revealed the following: By adding together the *strongly agree* and *agree* answers, the results indicate a range of educational values that are important to the teacher trainees (see Table 10.1). They considered statement number 5, *work and educational opportunities*, to be the major reason for studying English with 113 answers, reflecting reconstructionist values. In second place was statement number 8, *helps students achieve own individual professional and personal goals*, with 108 answers which indicates the appropriation of English. In the third place was statement number 7, *develop intellectual and cultural values*, with 105 answers which reflects classical humanism. In fourth place was statement number 1, which claimed that English is part of an international reality if you really want to succeed in life, with 103 answers which also reflect reconstructionism. The teacher trainees' answers appear to focus principally on reconstructionist values, appropriation of English and classical humanism. As can be seen in Table 1, answers reflecting progressivism, modernisation and class interests were given less importance.

The teachers' answers contrast with the language students' replies. Taking the definitively agree answers in consideration, the results show that Statement 6, *Knowing English I can communicate when travelling abroad*, with 187 replies was the most popular answer emphasising the importance of appropriation of language. In second place, statement number 7, *English will permit me to study abroad* with 165, reflects progressivism. In third place, statement number 2, *English will provide me more opportunities to get a job*, received 161 responses and reflects reconstructionism. In fourth position, statement number 1, *English will allow me to grow professionally* with149 responses again reflects progressivism. In fifth place, statement number 10, *Knowing English, I will be able to communicate with people from other countries* received 148 responses and reflects appropriation.

The language students' answers reflect a strong orientation towards appropriation of the language and progressivism. As I will argue in the

Table 10.1
Teacher trainees' responses regarding the useful of learning and knowing English (N=115)

Knowing and using English....	Strongly Agree	Agree	Disagree	Strongly Disagree	Other
is part of an international reality if you really want to succeed in life.	30	73	10	2	-
will help with the modernisation and development of Mexico.	29	68	17	-	1
will help students become useful and productive members of society.	18	73	20	3	1
helps reduce social inequality by giving people a better chance in life.	14	73	26	2	-
provides work and educational opportunities	61	52	2	-	-
helps students express and develop themselves in their own way	12	76	25	2	-
helps students develop intellectual and cultural values	43	62	8	1	1
helps students achieve own individual professional and personal goals	46	62	7	-	-
allows students to understand how English is used locally in Guadalajara	14	65	34	2	-

next section, these results contrast with the teacher trainees' perceived objective for learning and knowing English which principally focused on reconstructionism values, appropriation of English and classical humanism.

Data Analysis

In this section, I engage in a critical analysis of the findings where I triangulate my evaluation and understandings with that of the 26 teacher trainees. The teacher trainees' interpretations and conclusions provide an important local perspective to the study.

In my analysis of the study, I would argue that the teacher trainees' principal focus is on helping to build a modern Mexico and therefore language students need to be trained to be useful and productive members of society. Such an interpretation suggests that teachers' see their major role as being part of what Bowles and Gintis (1976, p. 265) identify as the "process of reproducing society" and promoting reconstructionism which Clark (1987) identified as "society-oriented and is concerned with the promotion of agreed social goals" (p. 1). At the same time, teacher trainees do recognise that students may want to appropriate English for their own benefit which Appleby (2010) identified as using English for "appropriation and disinvention" (pp. 34-35). The trainee teachers also promote classical humanism by saying that the target language was useful to developing intellectual and cultural values.

These results, however, contrast quite heavily with the language students' identification of language appropriation as their key motivation followed by progressivism which Clark argues focuses on personal self-actualisation. These values reflect a much more individualistic motivation towards the learning of English and there appears to be less interest in learning English in order to help with the development of the country. Therefore, it appears that the teacher trainees are not fully aware of, or attuned to, learners' reasons for wanting to learn and use English.

When presented with the teacher trainees' stated values in teaching English, their peers offered three explanations for the attitudes and beliefs expressed by the teacher trainees. First of all, some teacher trainees took a non-critical stance to the results and argued that instrumental motivation is in reality a key factor for both teachers and students. For instance, Samantha said "the reality is that many people only want to learn or teach English in order to have a better job." Such views would support the notion that English teaching and learning should be influenced by reconstructionism values. This perception was reiterated by Bernardo: "People want to learn English in chase of the American Dream, by studying and completing a degree in the hope that it will help them get a good job and work from the bottom using English as a tool on their way."

Some teacher trainees felt that research instruments were not the most appropriate and that more qualitative methods should have been used such as unstructured interviews and more personalised approaches rather than an anonymous questionnaire.

Other teacher trainees took a critical view of the results and argued that the findings results reflect the educational realities in Mexico. Vanessa argued that language teachers have forgotten their educational role: "I think the research has a lot of true things. I think that English teachers forget the real reason why they are teaching EFL." Teresa put this attitude down to conformity with the status quo: "I think that the results reflected the real situation that we are facing in this moment in terms of education. If the teachers seem to be less interested on changing education I believe it's because it's just the way it is...." Finally, in a revealing comment Julieta felt that over the years:

> less importance was given to EFL teaching. I think it is because English teachers themselves don't see the way they can help people in this specific Mexican context. They don't see the relevance of learning English in a non-English speaking country.

Julieta's comment would suggest that Mexican teacher training programmes need to help teacher trainees identify and reflect on why they are teaching English and not just solely concentrate on reproducing BANA and NABA teaching methods, procedures and techniques.

Conclusions

Freire (1993) provides a very powerful model for foreign-language education by emphasising the concept of praxis: 'human activity consists of action and reflection: it is praxis; it is transformation of the world' (p. 106). Teachers and learners need to reflect on their specific context and engage in dialogic action which Freire argues involves cooperation and communion which leads interactants 'to focus their attention on the reality which mediates them and which—posed as a problem—challenges them' (p. 149). In such a context dialogical action will lead to transformation as English-language learners and users shape their learning to respond to their needs and aspirations.

In contrast, the results suggest that Freire's (1993) "banking model" of education is prevalent among Mexican EFL teachers. Teachers teach English as a foreign language with the aim of helping students get better jobs whilst failing to recognise that their students may have much more personal, individual and local goals. They appear to be far more concerned in adopting and replicating methods and techniques emanating from commercial British, Australasian and North American (BANA) private language schools. Teacher trainees need to be helped to critically reflect on the educational values that they are pursuing and whether they are in accordance with the students' needs and interests. Whilst this study only examined one local context with relatively few participants, these findings and the subsequent implications should be relevant to other ELT contexts. Therefore, in response to my first specific research question, BA TEFL undergraduates do consider the purpose behind their students learning English, but their answers may not always coincide with that of their students.

My second specific question identified detailed learning objectives of EFL students which may have a much more local and personal focus than the economic objectives identified by teachers. At the same time, there appears to be little recognition among the teacher trainees that English may have an important role to play as a local practice or even perhaps in changing people's lives beyond that of merely seeking better employment opportunities.

In answer to my third specific research question, BA TEFL undergraduates only view English as important within the Mexican society in economic and employment terms. Whilst students are aware of the importance of appropriation of language, this is recognised to a much lesser degree by the teacher trainees. If Mexico is to develop its methodologies and trends, rather than follow BANA and NABA trends, a concerted effort needs to be made to make English responsive to local needs and reflect language as local practice.

So, the answer to my overall research question is on the whole 'no'. Teacher-training programmes in this instance in Mexico do not appear to adequately prepare teachers to respond to their students' social, cultural and educational needs. As a result, there is little or no development of local pedagogical approaches. The teaching and learning of English need to respond to specific wants and to language as local practice: 'To look at language as practice is to view language as an activity rather than as a structure, as something we do rather than a system we draw on, as a material part of the social and cultural life rather than an abstract entity" (Pennycook, 2010, p. 2). In the Mexican context, English-language classroom activities that reflect a local and personal focus include studying intercultural differences (Canagarajah, 1999), such as reacting and responding to negative or rude/impolite incidents in the target language and examining attitudes towards potentially sensitive topics that are all too often avoided in EFL textbooks such as racism and cultural stereotypes (Cook, 2000 p. 158).

References
Appleby, R. (2010). *ELT, gender and international development*. Bristol: Multilingual Matters.
Bowles, S., & Gintes, H. (1976). *Schooling in capitalist America: Educational reform and the contradictions of economic life*. London: Routledge & Kegan Paul.
Canagarajah, S. (1999). *Resisting linguistic imperialism in English teaching*. Oxford: Oxford University Press.
Clark, J. L. (1987). *Curriculum renewal in school foreign language learning*. Oxford: Oxford University Press.
Cook, G. (2000). *Language play, language learning*. Oxford: Oxford University Press.
Freire, P. (1993). *Pedagogy of the oppressed*. New York: Continuum.
Giroux, H. A. (1997). *Pedagogy and the politics of hope: Theory, culture and schooling*. Boulder, CO: Westview.
Holliday, A. (1994). *Appropriate methodology and social context*. Cambridge: Cambridge University.
Holliday, A. (2005). *The struggle to teach English as an international language*. Oxford: Oxford University Press.
Kachru, B. J. (1992). Teaching world Englishes. In Kachru B. J. (Ed.), *The other tongue: English across cultures* (Second ed., pp. 355-365). Urbana: University of Illinois Press.
Kachru, B. J. (1995). World Englishes: Approaches, issues, and resources. In Brown H. D. & Gonzo, S. (Eds.), *Readings on second language acquisition* (pp. 229-261). Upper Saddle River, NJ: Prentice Hall Regents.
Lloyd, M. (2009, Feb 1). Mexico launches effort to teach its students English. *Houston Chronicle*. Retrieved from http://www.chron.com/news/nation-world/article/Mexico-launches-effort-to-teach-its-students-1620945.php
Pennycook, A. (2010). *Language as local practice*. London: Routledge.
Widin, J. (2010). *Illegitimate practices: Global English language education*. Bristol: Multilingual Matters.

Appendix 10A

Name: _____

Can you please respond as a language teacher to the following statements regarding the use of English? All answers will be treated in the strictest confidence.

Please underline/circle only one option.

Knowing and using English....

is part of an international reality if you really want to succeed in life.

strongly agree   agree   disagree   strongly disagree

will help with the modernisation and development of Mexico.

strongly agree   agree   disagree   strongly disagree

will help students become useful and productive members of society.

strongly agree   agree   disagree   strongly disagree

helps reduce social inequality by giving people a better chance in life..

strongly agree   agree   disagree   strongly disagree

provides work and educational opportunities.

strongly agree   agree   disagree   strongly disagree

helps students express and develop themselves in their own way.

strongly agree   agree   disagree   strongly disagree

helps students develop intellectual and cultural values.

strongly agree   agree   disagree   strongly disagree

helps students achieve own individual professional and personal goals.

strongly agree   agree   disagree   strongly disagree

allows students to understand how English is used locally in Guadalajara.

strongly agree   agree   disagree   strongly disagree

Thank you for answering this questionnaire. Please write yes, if you agree that your answers can be used for academic purposes: _____

Appendix 10B

Questionnaire Results	Definitely	Probably	Probably not	Definitely Not	Total
1 English will allow me to grow professionally.					
2 English will provide me more opportunities to get a job.					
3 I will be able to use English at work.					
4 English will increase my salary significantly.					
5 English will allow me to interact through social networks.					
6 Knowing English I can communicate when travelling abroad					
7 English will permit me to study abroad.					
8 English will let me make friends.					
9 English will let me communicate with my relatives from the USA.					
10 Knowing English, I will be able to communicate with people from other countries.					
11 English will facilitate me the use of new technologies such as the internet.					
12 Knowing English, I will become an educated person.					
13 Knowing English, I will be able to appreciate English speaking countries' literature, music and film.					
14 Knowing English, I will improve personally.					
15 Knowing English, I will be part of a higher social class.					
16 English will allow me to do business abroad.					

CHAPTER 11

A TRANSFORMATIVE EDUCATIONAL EXPERIENCE IN SAN ANDRÉS, COLOMBIA

María Cristina Montoya
Carol Dean
Diane Mancini
SUNY College at Oneonta

Introduction

Our college has a mission to develop a strong sense of values that distinguish the institution as a center for excellence in teaching. Faculty members strive to be leaders in nurturing the development of individuals who contribute to local and global communities, and engage students in exceptional learning experiences, within and beyond the classroom. To address the College's mission, two collaborating faculty members in the field of foreign language teaching designed a course that included service learning and study abroad providing an educational platform within the context of social justice.

The new course, "Faculty Led Off-Campus Experience in San Andrés, Colombia," offered students a cultural immersion experience and understanding of the living conditions of the population on this Caribbean island. Two primary goals of the course were: 1) cultural research through a participant ethnographic approach using service-learning pedagogy, and 2) increased and meaningful use of Spanish. The outcomes provided us with more than expected. Upon returning and listening to our students' reflections, we realized that this pedagogical practice targeted social justice leadership within the global context. The group of students was immersed in cross-cultural interactions, which allowed them to develop a new vision of cultural competence.

Students learned about the sociolinguistics of a multidialectal community, gained an appreciation for the idiosyncrasies and history of the people from San Andrés, and practiced their Spanish oral skills all within the context of service-learning. Many of the College students were pre-service teachers, though students from a wide variety of disciplines participated. They worked with children and teenagers from underprivileged "barrios" of San Andrés, and visited the elderly. Included in the visits were two educational institutions where undergraduates had the opportunity to interact with secondary level students and others with special needs. College students interacted daily with residents of San Andrés, taking notes in their field journals, engaging in socio-linguistic research, and taking first steps as observers and analysts becoming ethnographers of the world around them. As a result of the pedagogical and socio-cultural immersion approach of the course, students reflected on a transformative and life-changing experience. The students' feedback was unanimous that the course had been successful in meeting its initial goals, and that it had led to an overwhelming perception of self-transformation.

Why San Andrés?

San Andrés is part of an archipelago that consists of three major islands: San Andrés, Providencia, and Santa Catalina (Parsons, 1964). The islands' oldest inhabitants refer to themselves as the Raizal, or roots in Spanish. They have been in San Andrés since the 1600's when their ancestors were brought from West Africa to the islands by English-speaking Puritan colonists to work as slaves on their farms. British colonizers who developed the island as an agricultural resource were the first inhabitants of the island, but Spanish colonizers soon forced the Puritans off the islands, leaving behind the Raizal community.

Over the next two hundred years, the islands were disputed, conquered, and forgotten by almost all the major imperial powers, until they were finally annexed by Colombia in 1831. This population acted independently from any external interference for many years, even after annexation to the Colombian territory. They spoke English-based Creole and enjoyed their autonomy until the Colombian government secured control in the 1950s. The Free Port Decree in 1953 by the Colombian central government and construction of the airport on San Andrés—the largest island of the three-part archipelago—generated massive immigration from continental Colombians. The overwhelming immigration, mostly from the Caribbean coast, transformed the composition of the population on this island. Along with this change, Spanish indisputably became the language of education and business on the island (Ross, 2007).

After the Colombian continental invasion, the Raizal community was "forced" to remain in certain areas, and officials from the central government of Colombia questioned their religious and linguistic practices. Public schools implemented Spanish as the official language for instruction, and Catholicism became a community practice. This transformation progressed unquestionably until the 1990s when the Colombian constitution was amended, and the value of respecting the language and cultures of indigenous groups was recognized, the Raizal being one of these groups (Falkenberg, 2006).

After the Colombian constitution amendment in 1991, the Raizal community group gained their importance within the island priorities, and processes of identity and language recovery were initiated; however, forty years of unrestricted immigration from the mainland and imposition of Spanish had already shaped the lives of new generations. This socio-economic transformation into a multilingual/multicultural society was what we found upon arriving to experience our pedagogical service-learning practice.

The island provided us with a rich environment for sociolinguistic research and immersion into the Spanish language for our students. They found common roots with islanders in neighborhoods where English was the ancestral language, and interacted with Spanish speakers in tourism, business and educational settings. The San Andrés experience allowed the students to study culture from an ethnographic approach. They researched the island's history and studied the living conditions of the populations on the island, practiced their Spanish oral skills, learned about the sociolinguistics of a multidialectal community, and gained an appreciation for the cultural practices and history of the people of San Andrés, all through an intercultural service-learning activity.

The College Students

Demographics of our college student population reveal that the majority of our students are predominantly white within different urban/rural growing up experiences in the northeast of the United States. The college has a reduced international student population and the Spanish speaking population is mostly of heritage origin from the urban areas with big clusters of Hispanic immigrants or the migrant workers from the east north of the country. Our students did not have much previous knowledge of the history and evolution of the Hispanic speaking world in the Caribbean region. Therefore the course and immersion experience in San Andrés was a novelty for the majority of them. The students enrolled were from different majors: some from education, a strong program in our college, the future teachers varied from foreign language, English, Human Ecology, and Math; other students were double majoring or minoring in Spanish on pair with a social science degrees in psychology, criminal justice, anthropology, and sociology. Few came from the child and family studies programs. Four had Hispanic heritage background and orally fluency in Spanish. Their ages ranged from 19 years old to 24, from all different class levels. The group was composed of 18 female and two male. The diversity of our student group and the variety of their topics of interest enriched the discussion and nurtured a variety of perspectives in support of social justice leadership.

Immersion through Service-Learning

Anyone who has ever participated in or overseen a study abroad program would likely agree with Goldoni's (2013) finding that simply being in the target culture, whether short-term or long-term, does not, in and of itself, lead to meaningful learning or improved proficiency in the target language (TL). In fact, study abroad has been viewed as nothing more than "…a vacation in the 'Grand Tour' tradition" (p. 360). This concern has prompted many studies aimed at improving the experience so that students return with increased proficiency in the TL and a great appreciation for the target culture (Cadd, 2012; Di Silvio, Donovan, & Malone, 2014; Goldoni, 2013; Reynolds-Case, 2013). One common finding for achieving this goal is the need for engaging students in authentic interactions with native speakers; there is enough research in the field that proves how designing a meaningful lesson abroad achieves high impact learning. Cadd's (2012) study examined whether incorporating requirements for students abroad to interact with native speakers had a positive outcome. Di Silvio et al. (2014) explored how study abroad homestay experiences fostered language development. Reynolds-Case (2013) examined whether short-term study abroad experiences could produce any measurable development in students' command of the language. In addition, Falce-Robinson and Strother (2012), and Goldoni (2013) found that intentional interactions with native speakers through service-learning can greatly enhance the likelihood that students will experience improvement both in speaking the target language, and further their understanding of cultural practices, products, and perspectives. Designing a short or long term experience abroad with the integration of service-learning is one way to ensure the likelihood that students will have regular and substantive interactions with native speakers. In fact, Goldoni (2013) concluded that it is "the most direct and successful strategy for creating a rich, authentic, meaningful, and effective cultural and linguistic experience" (p. 370). In a similar approach, Thompson (2012) recognizes that service-learning pedagogy is essential to the achievement of ACTFL's five Cs—Communication, Communities, Cultures, Comparisons and Connections (National Standards in Foreign Language Education Project, 2006), and identifies six key elements in every successful service-learning practice: 1) reciprocity 2) reflection 3) development 4) meaningful service 5) civic responsibility, and 6) diversity. Service-learning provides culturally authentic opportunities where students are able to experience all six of these. The various best practices and theories described above are aligned with Gerstl-Pepin and Aiken's (2012) claim which support leadership in higher education and prioritize social justice issues while understanding and valuing diversity and multiculturalism as essential knowledge base for world leaders.

Both service-learning and pre-departure preparations were key components of this faculty led off-campus course. Three learning objectives were targeted in the course design to intersect service-learning and immersion with foreign language teaching standards:

1. Provide the students with an authentic cultural and linguistic setting to understand the diversity within the Spanish/ English speaking Caribbean region.
2. Encourage sociocultural comparisons that allowed students to reflect about their position as U.S. citizens in other communities.
3. Allow for opportunities to use Spanish and negotiate meaning with native speakers of the language.

This service-learning pedagogical approach provided us with the educational practice needed to achieve our learning outcomes, not only in alignment with ACTFL's Five C's, but also in pursuit of the 6th C, "Compassion" (ACTFL, 2013). Through its initiative focused on global giving, ACTFL is fostering awareness of the responsibility we all have with the rest of the world to make it a more equitable and inclusive place for human beings. This compassion component aligns well with our second learning objective above. The key elements of service-learning pedagogy were accomplished. While students were practicing their language skills and obtaining multicultural competence, the community abroad had the opportunity to express their needs, promote awareness of their social-economic conditions to the rest of the world, and use the educational material and sports equipment we brought to their neighborhoods and schools. Reflection was a main component of the students' assignments; cognitive and affective aspects of the experience recorded by each student transformed their practices into learning; our students engaged in deep reflection about their positions of class, race and free speech privilege when they observed the limitations that other people experience outside of the United States. One common idea in the students' reflection was how they observed happiness and friendliness among the people from the island in spite of their lack of economic resources for basic survival. Our college students had the opportunity to re-evaluate the meaning of "need" and "want" within their own privileged class and citizenship. Development of different stages through the course allowed students to grow and transform (preparing, observing, interacting, reflecting, discussing). Two years have passed since our first encounter with the San Andrés community, and we have observed the evolution of our students; those who graduated or were juniors during our trip, are applying to graduate programs that involve bilingual education and English as a Second Language practices. Several of them are planning to return to San Andrés and take part in the second stage in collaborating with the San Andrés bilingual education initiative. The discussion still goes on and serves as a platform to promote other similar courses in our college campus. The experience offered meaningful service—the service was challenging, and required problem solving skills in order to provoke critical thinking. The undergraduate students who lacked oral Spanish fluency were required to be creative as they met the people and interacted through a variety of educational activities. Students and community members understood each other through the act of service-learning and created bonds that continue through social media networks. The course promoted civic responsibility since students felt empowered to work for social justice and improve the quality of life of the community. Our students returned with an heightened sensitivity about their own positions in society, eager to create awareness and promote change for a more equitable society. The experience allowed various populations and distinct communities to interact and work for a common goal. Being placed in situations where they were able to observe inequities between communities, the college students came to appreciate how some benefited more than others. Our students came back with an enhanced understanding of the concept of diversity and how important it is when considering human collaborations for a more just world.

The Experience
Planning and Teaching the Course

Pre-departure preparation is an important factor in the design of service-learning as part of a successful study abroad experience—it is one of what Falce-Robinson and Strother (2012) list as the "five core components of service-learning" (p. 85), developing a vision and community partnerships, setting a time-line, and determining methods of evaluation.

For this experience, it all began with a contact—a family relative who moved from mainland Colombia to "La Isla de San Andrés" thirty years ago. Without her help this never could have been possible. She made all the contacts and arrangements for us with the local communities, schools and neighborhoods. We asked her for sites to develop our service-learning assignments, and she provided us with information about tangible needs of the communities. Prior to arrival on the island, our contact was organizing our interactions with the residents of the different neighborhoods on the island while we were preparing our students for the encounter.

The course itself met once a week throughout an entire semester, with the trip to San Andrés over the spring break in the middle of the semester. The course included intensive reading and research about San Andrés. Students read the history related to the conquest and colonization of the Caribbean, discussed the history of the slave trade and its impacts on modern Caribbean peoples in collaboration with a guest lecturer from the Africana and Latino studies department. Virtual tours of parts of the islands were presented to the students to get a feel for its look and layout. Additionally, students had opportunities to role-play interactions, practice transactions with pretend money, and collect school supplies, books, arts and crafts materials, paint, brushes and hygiene products which they would later give directly to the members of the island communities. Students also were required to plan educational workshops in order to facilitate meaningful interactions between them and the islanders through sports, literacy, and arts and crafts activities. They even practiced packing fifty pounds of luggage efficiently, and were ready for the immersion that would give them the opportunity to use their Spanish in an authentic environment. All these course activities and requirements served not only to prepare the students academically, but also to engage and involve them in creating what Goldoni (2013) identifies as "...a strong and genuine commitment to a serious, profound, and durable investment in the target language, people, and culture" (p. 371). Even with all this preparation prior to our arrival on the island, we still had no certainty about the extent to which this immersion and service-learning experience would change our students' views of the world.

Cultural Immersion in San Andrés

The class spent ten days on the island. The trip was mandatory in order to pass the course, and upon returning students met again once a week to discuss their observations and learning while abroad. Within only a few days of arriving on San Andrés, the students were able to experience first-hand the real living conditions on the island, the socio-linguistic issues of a multidialectal community, the islanders' identity struggles, and economic needs. Students who had some proficiency in Spanish were able to directly obtain information for their research by interviewing and negotiating meaning with the community members. Students who were not proficient in Spanish and had not experienced the creole dialect, found the communication act intriguing and gained a brief insight into the real life struggles faced by those unable to use spoken language as a form of communication. Many of them realized how vital it was to communicate in the target language in order to meaningfully interact with the local people.

While in San Andrés, one day was dedicated to learning about the schools and educational systems. The morning was spent at Orange Hill, a school dedicated to special needs students. Some of the less severe students came to Orange Hill before or after their regular school to receive extra help with their course work. Other students who could not attend a mainstream school were taught life skills that they could use to find work outside of the school. Our college students were incredibly moved by the dedication of Orange Hill's faculty and pupils; many of them even bought handmade crafts made by the Orange Hill students. In the afternoon the students had the opportunity to visit Flowers Hill Bilingual School, one of the three bilingual high schools on the island. Here the students were able to spend several hours talking with the high school students about everything from their favorite movies to what their plans were for after high school. It was an opportunity for both groups of students to learn how their peers lived in another part of the hemisphere.

In addition to the school visits, our group also spent several days visiting many of the different San Andrean communities. In the Raizal communities of Loma Barak and San Luis, we watched youth perform traditional island dances, and played customary games. In the Atlántico continental immigrant community we saw dances from mainland Colombia, and learned how to make crafts from coconuts. In Santa Ana, one of the most impoverished communities, our students were asked to help the children paint the wall of their basketball court. The students were deeply touched by the level of love and hospitality the communities shared with them and were quick to return the favor. Some students formed close bonds with a particular child. We even met up with the youth from one community for lunch on a later date.

We also had the opportunity to meet with the Governor and other public officials. Everyone was very welcoming and allowed the students to ask them questions that would help them complete their research. We even were interviewed by Colombian television and radio. We were highly recognizable as our large group trudged around the streets of San Andrés—everyone seemed to know who we were! This kind of attention made our students feel empowered to promote change, important factor for leadership and social justice advocacy.

While on the island, we stayed together at an all-inclusive resort. Though not a culturally authentic experience, for our first attempt at this course, it relieved us of the added complication of coordinating meals and housing for over twenty people scattered across an island where public transportation could be unreliable and where many of our students would find it difficult to communicate urgent matters without the help of their professors or a Spanish-speaking classmate. Though we ate breakfast and dinner at the hotel and slept there each night, our days began bright and early on foot or in a shuttle bus to spend long, hot days working in neighborhoods. Each day we visited a different neighborhood or institution to try to get the most holistic view possible of what life is like for the people of San Andrés. The unplanned contrast between the lifestyles of people in the various communities we visited, and the plush comforts of our hotel provoked a meaningful reflection from the students: for sometimes of the day, college students were experiencing the luxuries of their privilege class, and an hour later they were immersed in a community that lacked of basic survival needs, students puzzled and were able to see "the wrong" "the inequality". We gathered each evening at the hotel lobby and talked about our day's journey. Some of the students expressed their realization that they complain even when they have everything, and yet the people they met on the island were happy with even less of the minimum required to survive. Students and community members felt empowered from their mutual collaboration. They were able to scrutinize their place in the social reality, combine voices, and create dialogue, which is the argument developed by Gilbridge-Brown's (2011) in the author's examination of service-learning as a critical pedagogy. She claims, it is essentially experiential, focusing on reflection and seeking action in order to enacting social change.

Students' Evaluation of the Course

Self-reflection through meaningful encounters is a difficult task to accomplish if we do not take our students out of the classroom and their comfort zones. Our students' written comments at the end of their experience confirm that with only ten days in the target culture was possible to expect transformative experiences for our students. This was a concern that had challenged us from the beginning, but our students' feedback at the end of the course, as well as their well thought-out and developed research projects proved that only a few days of immersion could be enough when combined with service-learning pedagogies. Students reported later during campus presentations and course evaluations reflections such as:

I can only hope I touched them as much as they touched me.

To work with such happy and welcoming people has taught me that there is more to life than material things.

Visiting San Andres was a life changing experience.

I got the opportunity to go outside of my comfort zone, and it was the best decision of my life.

Spending one week doing all that we did changed my outlook on life completely. There are truly no words to describe how much of an incredibly rewarding, humbling experience this trip was for me, and I would love to go back in the future.

Students' Research Projects

Students were required to carry out a research study while on the island, so during the weeks leading up to the trip, and while studying the history of the island and its people, they planned a topic related to the island. This included forming key points of inquiry and identifying which demographic would be the best to help them answer their questions. These research projects were, in fact, what Goldoni (2013) calls "ethnographic projects…designed to help students learn and apply a cultural framework that focuses on the practices, products, and perspectives of culture" (p. 372), thereby maximizing their learning process and chances of success.

Students read about the islands' past, reviewed the few research articles that exist about this island and watched YouTube videos, while constructing a reality that they were preparing to compare upon arriving to what is the island today. For several of them, their research plans changed when they observed a reality they were not able to foresee from the readings before the trip.

One student quickly perceived the sociolinguistic conflict lived between the continental immigrants and the Raizal community, and immediately prepared to investigate the phenomenon. Two students who were dog lovers were disturbed by the amount of street dogs, and wanted to investigate the situation of domestic animals in this particular community; something that they could never have seen prior to immersion. Future teachers found the visits to the schools extremely helpful in their data collection in order to compare U.S. and San Andrés curricula. Family and child studies majors used the visits to the different communities to engage with mothers and children, and talk about the family structure common in their community. Fashion majors took pictures of every individual and compared dress and appearance to ethnic background and social position. Food majors photographed and tasted every delicatessen they encountered despite our warning about street food and the possibility of illness. Overall, students were attentive to the information they needed to collect for their research; each one of them looked at a different aspect.

Upon returning to the States, each one of them was tasked with composing a ten-page paper and an accompanying fifteen-minute presentation about their topic. Spanish majors were encouraged to write their papers in Spanish, though all presentations were given in English so that all the students could understand them. During the last days of the semester, they presented final research projects, revealing details of life on the island they could not possibly have noticed simply through our course readings. Their discoveries were eye opening, not just about life in San Andrés, but also about the students' own lives and academic potential. Students additionally were able to cite numerous examples of the relationships between and among San Andrean products, practices and perspectives; for example, music (product) is used daily (practice), and seen as something happy (perspective).

At the end of the course, students were required to complete a course evaluation and express commentaries of their perception of instruction. The commentaries assured the significance of the immersion/service-learning academic experience.

> Besides loving the trip, I enjoyed doing the research and even writing about it.

> Best class ever! Not only getting to visit a tropical island, but learning about the culture and interacting with the people of the island and how the past affected the present situation of the people.

So transformative was the experience, that one student, with a double major in Spanish and Anthropology, returned that summer for a full month to continue her research on the Raizal community. She collected a great amount of recorded hours interviewing islanders, and was able to publish an article in an undergraduate journal based upon her research in San Andrés (Mancini, 2013). Her main research goal was to study contemporary Raizal ideologies, policies and practices through their linguistic expression. This student investigated the situation of the Raizal community through history to be able to understand their current use of the English language. She described in her research how, since the 1950s, the Raizal community was not only obligated to adjust to sharing their island with the continentals, but also with a growing tourism industry from which they feel largely excluded (Ross, 2007). Environmental changes have made it impossible for the Raizal to continue harvesting fruits such as coconuts and oranges, which had been one of the islanders' chief sources of income for over a century (Parsons, 1964). She conducted interviews and participant observations to examine how these factors affected the Raizal as a community. She went beyond what she had gained from our course, and took the experience a step further as a researcher demonstrating that the pedagogical approach to the course was successful in generating self-reflection and transformative action, not just for the Oneonta students, but also for this community in need of allies who could present the Raizal identity and territorial re-claim to the attention of others outside of the island.

Outcomes of Service-Learning in Higher Education

The main activities of this course aligned with the various definitions discussed about service-learning and its role in higher education (Strait & Lima, 2009). While it was a credit-bearing educational experience, it allowed the students to participate in an organized service activity outside of the classroom and, more importantly, took the students abroad to a community with a different language and cultural practice. College students from different socio-economic backgrounds and with a wide range of interests engaged in authentic interaction and observed communities with various essential needs; this generated personal and professional transformative re-action. This group of students was not just servicing, but learning by critically examining their positions within the various communities. The integration of service generated a practice for cross-cultural collaborations, which challenged traditional power relationships. It humbled the students through their understanding that this was a reciprocal process where they were learning how to be agents of change. Various scholars whose practice is embedded in service-learning pedagogies (Gilbridge-Brown, 2011; Kistler, 2011; Vaccaro, 2011) have stated how this educational practice empowers students and community members through their mutual collaboration. The authors explain how students are able to scrutinize their place in social reality, combine voices, and create dialogue. These are difficult tasks to accomplish if we do not take our students out of the classroom and their comfort zones.

Students described the service-learning experience as "humbling" and "life changing." At the airport on our last day, as we were preparing to leave the island, we noticed that something had changed in the students' perceptions of reality, and that they were already missing contact with the islanders. This pedagogical practice had reduced stereotyping about "upper middle class gringos" from the community members abroad and stereotyping about poverty from the college students' privileged perspectives. Consequently, this service-learning course has accomplished for the undergraduate students what Vaccaro (2011) describes as reflection upon their class privilege. It also increased the students' capacity for advocacy, in that it has developed their sense of responsible citizenship and has encouraged deep reflection about personal biases, assumptions, and deficit thinking.

Language Immersion and Second Language Acquisition

Drawing upon the research cited earlier in this chapter, this experience was intentionally designed with the integration of service-learning to promote and necessitate students' use of Spanish with local residents.

At the conclusion of the course, students were asked to complete a simple survey in an attempt to gather some quantifiable data about their experience, in particular about their use of Spanish as a result of the service-learning project. While on the island, those students who already had some level of oral proficiency in Spanish (e.g., Spanish majors and heritage speakers) engaged in conversations regularly with local residents, socializing, negotiating meanings, providing and obtaining information, and even teaching. They further served to facilitate conversations for students who had little to no proficiency in the language, serving as linguistic and cultural bridges throughout the service learning experience. Even students with limited proficiency had opportunities to learn basic Spanish through these interactions, and, more surprisingly, the experience motivated many of the students to pursue learning more Spanish, by declaring minors and majors in Spanish upon their return. Overall, the students' responses revealed a strong positive correlation between their service-learning and their use of Spanish.

The Future of the Educational Relationship between San Andrés and Oneonta

The government of San Andrés is interested in promoting the use of English and recovering the Creole heritage identity, and it is precisely within the context of this official language planning where we, college students and faculty, become part of their team. We came to the island, not as U.S citizens imposing our ideologies of freedom and democracy, but as English speakers to participate in a dynamic plan for language recovery. The people of San Andrés want to make English an important part of their practices. Their motivation is instrumental, so that they can progress and compete in the Caribbean tourism industry, and offer continental Colombians a less expensive option for studying English abroad. It provides integrative motivation as they seek to recover the language of their ancestors as part of an identity distinct from continental Colombians. Oneonta students are developing global citizenship through the use of their native language while learning Spanish and understanding the complexities of languages in contact.

The first course taught in San Andrés accomplished the initial stage of this service-learning curriculum-based project, which was mainly to introduce both communities, and to recognize community needs. The second stage will be to return with a defined co-educational plan that engages our students from New York in a constructivist communal project with the schools and neighborhoods in San Andrés. The action accomplished in spring 2012 provides our Oneonta campus community an opportunity to carry on its mission to promote learning, change, and social engagement working towards justice in society.

Consequently, the success of this learning experience has inspired us to expand upon it and return for a more extended collaboration with our new friends in San Andrés. In the summer of 2014, we will be partnering with Flowers Hill public school to organize workshops for local teachers about bilingual teaching methodologies, and our students will serve as bilingual teaching assistants in a local school. Local teachers and college students will conduct team teaching during a period of three weeks within various curricula. At the end of the teaching period San Andrés teachers and students, along with Oneonta students, will be able to present bilingual projects that hopefully have impacted the recovery of English for the Raizal community and the acquisition of it as a second language for the continental population.

Now that we have first-hand knowledge of the island and have established some contacts, during the second visit, we will be staying in *Posadas Nativas*, living among the residents of Isla San Andrés. Our group of students will be a mixture of English speakers from other majors as well as Spanish majors. The plan is to stay at different Posadas where they can practice their Spanish or, for those with no Spanish proficiency, with members of the Raizal community. The immersion experience is targeting not only language, but also culture, and both types of students will gain from the interaction.

San Andrés presented for us a particular scenario where we were able to fit in and generate reciprocity in learning and service between the undergraduate students and the island's community; however, educators do not need to find perfect given environments to obtain successful results. Any scenario or course content may be appropriate if instructors design courses with an experiential learning component by looking at the course planning holistically and interweaving teaching, research and service. Taking students out of the classroom and empowering them with the responsibility of their own learning is key in turning a common learning experience into a transformative one. Students need to ask questions and become researchers for their own inquires, and educators must open the doors of the classroom and lead their students out.

References

ACTFL. (2013). In pursuit of the 6th "C"—Compassion. *The Language Educator, 8*(4), 20-21.

Cadd, M. (2012). Encouraging students to engage with native speakers during study abroad. *Foreign Language Annals, 45*(2), 229-245.

D'Amico, M. L. (2012). L2 fluency and willingness to communicate: The impact of short-term study abroad versus at-home study. *US-China Foreign Language, 10*(10), 1608-1626.

Di Silvio, F., Donovan, A., & Malone, M. E. (2014). The effect of study abroad homestay placements: Participant perspectives and oral proficiency gains. *Foreign Language Annals, 47*(1), 168-188.

Falce-Robinson, J., & Strother, D. (2012). Language proficiency and civic engagement: the incorporation of meaningful service-learning projects in Spanish language courses. *Interdisciplinary Humanities, 29*(3), 73-87.

Falkenberg, M. (2006). El significado del otro y la etnoeducación: otro reflejo de San Andrés, isla [The significance of the other and ethnoeducation: Other reflections from San Andrés Island]. *Cuadernos del Caribe, 8*, 28-41.

Gerstl-Pepin, C., & Aiken, J. A. (Eds.). (2012). *Social justice leadership for a global world.* Charlotte, NC: Information Age Publishing.

Gilbride-Brown, J. (2011). Moving beyond the dominant: Service-learning as a culturally relevant pedagogy. In Stewart, T. & Webster, N. (Eds.), *Exploring cultural dynamics & tensions within service-learning* (pp. 27-44). Charlotte, NC: Information Age.

Goldoni, F. (2013). Students' immersion experiences in study abroad. *Foreign Language Annals, 42*(3), 359-376.

Kistler, S.A. (2011). Engaging culture: Ethnography as a model for service-learning practice. In Stewart, T. & Webster, N. (Eds.), *Exploring cultural dynamics & tensions within service-learning* (pp. 3-26). Charlotte, NC: Information Age.

Mancini, D. (2013, Spring). "English is my language": The importance of incorporating the study of linguistic identity in field research. *Journal of Undergraduate Anthropology, 3*, 77-82.

National Standards in Foreign Language Education Project. (1999). *Standards for foreign language learning in the 21st century.* Yonkers, NY: Author.

Parsons, J. (1964). *San Andrés y providencia: Una geografía histórica de las islas Colombianas del Mar Caribe Occidental* [San Andrés and providence: A historical geography of the Columbian Islands of the Western Caribbean Sea]. Bogotá: Banco De La Republica.

Ross, J. (2007). Routes for roots: Entering the 21st century in San Andrés Island, Colombia. *Caribbean Studies, 35*, 3-36.

Reynolds-Case, A. (2013). The value of short-term study abroad: an increase in students' cultural and pragmatic competency. *Foreign Language Annals, 46*(2), 311-322.

Strait, J. R., & Lima, M. (Eds.). (2009). *The future of service – learning new solutions for sustaining and improving practice.* Sterling, Virginia: Stylus Publishing, LLC.

Thompson, G. (2012*). Intersection of service and learning. Research and practice in the second language classroom.* Charlotte, NC: Information Age.

Vaccaro, A. (2011). Challenging privileged paradigms through service-learning: Exposing dominant ideology, unlearning deficit thinking, and debunking the myth of meritocracy. In Stewart, T. & Webster, N. (Eds.), *Exploring cultural dynamics & tensions within service-learning* (pp. 45-62). Charlotte, NC: Information Age Publishing.

CHAPTER 12

COLLEGE ENGLISH INSTRUCTORS' AND STUDENTS' PREFERENCES FOR TYPES OF WRITTEN CORRECTIVE FEEDBACK

Janet Oab
Palawan State University

Introduction

Communication skills are essential for career advancement. More specifically, writing is a vital part of almost every job. In fact, effective writing may help one obtain a job, perform one's duties more successfully, and earn promotions. However, effective writing skills are not acquired overnight. These skills are honed over the years through formal education, patience, and discipline. Hence, academic writing and technical writing courses are offered in college to prepare students for the writing tasks in their chosen profession. Accordingly, teachers are expected to help students develop the critical skills of brainstorming, researching (through print and online sources), drafting, revising, editing, formatting, and proofreading. In the process of developing these skills, teachers give feedback on students' written output. This feedback aims to guide students on the improvements that they should make both on the content and the mechanical aspect of their output. Corrective feedback in general is a long-standing educational practice that can arguably be linked to almost everything we learn. According to Russel and Spada (2006), in language learning "the term corrective feedback refers to any feedback provided to a learner, from any source that contains evidence of a learner's error of language form" (p. 134).

However, there is no single perception about the value of providing corrective feedback in second language (L2) writing. Differences in opinion exist regarding the efficacy of written corrective feedback. Truscott (1996, 1999), reflecting the views of teachers who adhere to process theories of writing, advances that correcting learners' errors in a written composition may enable them to eliminate the errors in a subsequent draft, but has no effect on grammatical accuracy in a new piece of writing. Hence, Truscott (1996) stressed that grammar correction has no place in writing courses and should be abandoned. Similarly, Kepner (2005) maintains that there is no convincing research evidence that error correction has ever helped student writers improve the accuracy of their writing. He even stressed that error correction is harmful because it diverts time and energy away from the more productive aspects of a writing program.

On the contrary, Ferris (1999) argues that Truscott's arguments were premature and overly strong given the rapidly growing research evidence pointing to ways in which effective error correction can and do help at least some student writers, provided it is selective, prioritized and clear. In addition, he maintains that there are equally strong reasons for teachers to continue giving feedback, not the least of which is the belief that students have regarding its value.

In addition, Ellis (1994) pointed out that another distinction of greater theoretical and practical significance is between "direct" and "metalinguistic" feedback. Direct feedback entails supplying learners with the correct target form. Metalinguistic feedback involves providing some kind of metalinguistic clue as to the nature of the error that has been committed and the correction needed. He further stressed that metalinguistic feedback then appeals to learners' explicit knowledge by helping them to understand the nature of the error they have committed.

According to Amrhein and Nassaji (2007), with the increasing research evidence both for and against the effectiveness of Written Corrective Feedback (WCF), researchers have looked for ways to explain why different amounts and types of WCF might be ineffective. In their research, they suggested that one major problem is the perspective from which WCF is provided. For example, when teachers correct errors, they often change students' language according to what they think learners want to or should say, but there is at times a mismatch between the idea that a student wants to express and that which a teacher assumes is correct. Furthermore, the effectiveness of WCF has also been suggested to hinge upon students' preferences for it. In other words, students' opinions and preferences for certain types and amounts of WCF affect the results of the students' learning outcomes.

Acquiring another language means learning everything about the system. As Sanz (2000) mentions, second language learners are demonstrated to have developed metalinguistic awareness that facilitates them in learning another language. This claim implies that ESL learners can easily adapt or acquire a new language because of the exposure to the language and that for this acquisition to take place, it is necessary to communicate. Taking this into account may suggest that there are both positive and negative influences in acquiring skills in the target language. However, learners tend to develop personal strategies in the use of their L1 skills in engaging in L2 activities; in most cases involving a prevailing language in an ordinary conversation, the communicator tends to codeswitch or use their L1 along with the L2. Nonetheless, using the benefits of previously learned skills, specifically the first language, leads to transfer in the use of the latter. Hence, this observation merits an instructional intervention that could possibly address this phenomenon. One of the most universal and helpful techniques is to raise consciousness among the learners about their difficulties. Although this technique might resolve such difficulties, when transfer is allowed to continue, there is the risk of fossilization, making error correction more difficult. Ellis (1994) pointed out that the distinction of greater theoretical and practical significance is between "direct" and "metalinguistic" feedback. Direct feedback entails supplying learners with the correct target form. Metalinguistic feedback involves providing some kind of metalinguistic clue as to the nature of the error that has been committed and the correction needed. He further stressed that metalinguistic feedback then appeals to learners' explicit knowledge by helping them to understand the nature of the error they have committed.

Most frequently, students learning a second language face tremendous cognitive processing in order to perform well in any activities that require them to exhibit their linguistic knowledge in the newly learned language. Specifically, in writing tasks, students tend to make a word for word translation of the sentence from their L1 in the L2, in which this manner is not applicable. The ESL classroom in specific must be interactive to permit students to take part personally in the process. Designing meaningful activities is a large component of the teachers' duties. Apart from this task, teachers' recognition of both weaknesses and strengths has an impact on students' behavior towards learning a second language. This simply summons the teachers to give attention to errors that surface in their writing tasks.

Needless to say, students should learn the conventions of writing like organizing ideas, choosing the right vocabulary, and using grammatical devices to become more proficient and effective writers. More often, the difficulties range from generating and developing ideas that communicate a clear message to translating these ideas into a readable text with a good choice of vocabulary and grammatical patterns that are appropriate to the subject matter (Hogue, 2008). Given that this is a complex skill to master, students are prone to committing errors in writing, which teachers fervently address through the use of strategies in treating them. Although teachers respond to the works of the students by providing appropriate feedback with the expectation that students will accept the corrections/feedback, the teachers' intention may not be communicated uniformly to students. What is more, Ammar and Spada (2006) express that students' uptake of any corrective feedback technique depends also on their proficiency level. This proficiency may affect students' perception on the error correction strategy that the teacher utilizes, especially in how they would interpret the markings or comments that the teacher indicated in the written output. This idea suggests a problematic relationship between the teacher's intention of treating the errors and the students' perception on how the errors are being addressed by the teacher. A possible mismatch is viewed to be a source of miscommunication that eventually defeats the purpose of developing awareness of errors among students. Lasagabaster and Sierra (2003) remark that if teachers want to establish credibility of any pedagogy, they have to discover what the learners have to say about their learning and what they think could benefit them. In so doing, establishing a common ground may lead to better learner participation and teacher insight.

The purpose, therefore, of this study is to examine and compare the preferences of ESL students and teachers with regard to WCF. I examine what types of WCF do ESL teachers and students consider useful and whether there are differences between the two participants. In fact, as Lee (2008) describes, studies comparing both the teachers and students responses as to their preferences are relatively few. Interested in investigating whether the teachers and students are in agreement, this chapter describes both the attitudes and preferences of teachers and students toward written feedback. Specifically, this study answers the following questions:

- What forms of errors in students' expository compositions do the instructors and the students think warrant corrective feedback?
- What types of WCF do the instructors and the students find most useful for the latter's expository composition?
- Is there a significant difference between the instructors and the students' respective preferences for the forms of errors requiring WCF and the types of WCF applied to students' errors in their expository composition?

Framework of the Study

In this paper, the term "corrective feedback" is comprehended as a form of treating errors in students' writing. This follows the definition of Lightbrown and Spada (1999) that describes teachers' feedback as an indication that the learners' use of the target language is incorrect. Thus, WCF includes various forms of feedback that the teachers are using as a response to erroneous usage of the target language. Throughout the study, the terms corrective feedback techniques, written feedback/correction and error correction method/style are interchangeably used. The examination of teachers' and students' attitudes and perceptions on written feedback is anchored on Owens (2009) who states that the effectiveness of written feedback is ascertained if preferences of both teachers and students matched and that differences determine the need to reconcile both sides to establish a common ground. Exploring the students' preferences in error correction, and their beliefs about effective feedback vis-à-vis the teachers' intentions in writing corrective feedback are at the center of the study's investigation. The results clearly show that teachers and students are in agreement in almost all aspects of error correction methods included in the study, therefore providing the idea that the teachers' ways, styles, and preferences are interpreted, comprehended and responded to positively by students. Hence, mutuality between the students' and teachers' preferences brings about communication of the former and the latter. In effect, corrective feedback serves its purpose of raising the students' consciousness in terms of modifying errors and awareness on correct usage of the target language.

Diab (2005) examined students' attitudes towards error correction and their expectations regarding teachers' feedback on their writing. Trying to ascertain the effectiveness of feedback, the study examined the techniques used by writing teachers in responding to errors in students' written output. Comparing both preferences is the core of the study with the purpose of determining whether the error correction and paper-marking techniques of the teachers are congruent with the expectations of the students. A similar study was conducted by Amrhein and Nassaji (2007) on the effectiveness of written corrective feedback matching the teachers' and students' preferences, and like most of the findings, the paper confirmed areas of agreement but regarded discrepancies as potential implications of the kind of pedagogy that teachers believed to be helpful. Such a pronouncement seems to call for the reconsideration of the kind of corrective feedback techniques that the teachers incorporate. Nonetheless, students' preferences could be re-examined for they perhaps exaggeratedly put impact on more individualized form of feedback. This means that sometimes students will just tick their own preferences that are so individualistic or one sided and that the teachers will no longer be given the chance of airing their own preferences as well. Even so, Owens (2010) suggests that teachers have to adjust their own claims and discover what the learners prefer. Correspondingly, Hyland & Hyland (2006) express that teachers' responses should center on the person writing the text, an approach that is favored by more students.

In the study of Lasagabaster and Sierra (2005), when they examined students' perception versus teachers' error correction techniques, it was found that a significant number of students unintentionally noticed what the teachers used in correcting the errors. This may indicate a gap between what the teachers believed to be beneficial to students and students' unawareness or unfamiliarity with the method or technique the teachers were using when addressing errors. As noted by Ammar and Spada (2010), the proficiency level underlies the percentage of students' uptake to any instructional intervention. These empirical observations suggest the need for a study linking teachers' intention with students' perceptions, as these two elements are inseparable. This chapter aims, therefore, to examine both the teachers' and students' responses both sides with the hope to uncover similarities and differences that will lead to the reconciliation of any gap between them.

Methodology
Research Design
This paper employed both quantitative and qualitative design to determine

students' and teachers' opinions about the usefulness of different types and amounts of WCF, and also the reasons for their responses. Specifically, a close-ended questionnaire with items in Likert Scale format consisting seven (7) questions was developed. To allow the participants to describe in their own words the reasons for their preferred feedback choices, open-ended questions were also included in the questionnaires. To quantify the significant differences between the participants' preferences on written corrective feedback, a t-test was run and p-values were calculated.

Participants
This study was conducted at a state university in South-east Asia, particularly in the College of Engineering, Architecture and Technology, College of Business and Accountancy, College of Sciences and College of Nursing in this institution. One writing class with 25 students was taken from each of the colleges mentioned. In totality, there were one hundred (100) students, 65 females and 35 males. They were identified through random sampling. Their ages ranged from 17 to 18 years old. The students were currently enrolled in their Writing for Specific Purposes course, whose prerequisites were two specific English courses: English 11-Communication Arts and Composition, which focuses on the basics of English grammar with an integration of writing composition, and English 12-Speech and Oral Communication, which zeroes in on the basics of oral communication with the inclusions of public speaking activities. Normally, students who are enrolled in English 21 are second-year students.

Aside from the students, thirty writing teachers from the Department of English of the university participated in the study. These teachers are non-native speakers of English, yet their field of specialization is teaching English. These teachers regularly handle academic writing courses aside from other English courses. Specifically, twenty-five of them were regular faculty with ten to twenty years in service while the other five had less than five years teaching experience.

Instrument
The data were gathered using a questionnaire based on that of Amrhein and Nassaji (2010), which was accessed online with a minute modification made by the researcher in order to fit the main objective of this study. Specifically,

the questionnaire elicited the opinion of the second year college students and English teachers of the university, in order to understand their impressions of the usefulness of the different types and amounts of WCF and also the reasons for their responses. There were two questionnaires for the intended participants: one for the students and one for the teachers. The instrument has two parts, the first part is a close-ended item in which the respondents just need to tick their preferred answers to the questions; and the second part is an open-ended questionnaire in which they have to explain their answers in the first part of the instrument.

Data Gathering Procedures
With permission from the Deans of the colleges, the questionnaires were administered in each of the different English classes. The purpose of the study and instructions for completing the questionnaire were explained. The questionnaires were retrieved after all the students answered them. Likewise, the instructors/professors participating in this study were given the instrument, and these were answered during their free time. After the administration of the questionnaires, the researcher conducted a focused-group discussion (FGD) with the respondents to validate their responses.

Method of Analysis
Frequency count, percentage and ranking were used to obtain the results of the participants' responses in the questionnaire. A *t*-test was also used to find out if there is a significant difference between the students' and teachers' responses. Likewise, for the qualitative analysis, the participants' answers to the open-ended questions were summarized and categorized according to common or prevailing themes and then compared between teachers and students. The coding was first completed by the researcher and then reviewed by a colleague acting as an inter-rater.

To answer the items in the questionnaire, it was categorized using a five-point Likert scale. And to arrive at the total responses made by the respondents, the researcher made use of the computed mean with the following descriptions: 1.0-1.5 *useless*; 1.51-2.5 *not useful*; 2.51-3.5 *doesn't matter*; 3.51-4.5 *quite useful* and 4.51-5.0 *very useful*.

Results and Discussion

Table 12.1 shows the forms of errors in students' expository compositions as observed by the students and instructors. As can be seen, out of 100 students, nearly 70 percent maintained that their teachers should point out grammatical errors while nearly sixty five percent believe that teachers should identify spelling and vocabulary errors. It can be derived from the students' responses that there is high awareness of the need to correct mechanical errors in writing. The fact, however, that organization and content were ranked lower reflects their inability to recognize the significance of these areas that should receive more emphasis in writing.

Table 12.1
Frequency and mean rating as observed by the students and teachers

ITEMS The teacher …	Students' Responses Rating					Mean Rating	Teachers' Responses Rating					Mean Rating
	1	2	3	4	5		1	2	3	4	5	
1. Should point out organization errors.	1	3	11	36	49	4.29 quite useful	3	0	5	6	16	4.07 quite useful
2. Should point out grammatical errors.	1	0	5	26	68	4.6 very useful	0	0	2	20	8	4.20 quite useful
3. Should point out content/ideas errors	1	6	13	45	35	4.07 quite useful	0	2	0	7	21	4.57 very useful
4. Should point out punctuation errors	1	2	20	47	30	4.03 quite useful	0	3	2	15	10	4.07 quite useful
5. Should point out spelling errors.	2	1	8	26	63	4.47 quite useful	2	2	0	12	14	4.13 quite useful
6. Should point out vocabulary errors.	1	1	7	28	63	4.51 very useful	0	0	0	10	20	4.67 very useful
Over-all Mean Rating						4.33 quite useful						4.29 quite useful

LEGEND:
1.00 – 1.5 not useful at all (useless)
1.51 – 2.5 not useful
2.51 – 3.5 doesn't matter
3.51 – 4.5 quite useful
4.51 – 5.0 very useful

Similarly, although teachers stressed the significance of pointing out shortcomings in the content of students' output, more teachers emphasized the importance of choice of words, which is, of course, mechanical in nature while less emphasis is given on the importance to point out organizational errors. Ideally, teachers should have considered content and organization as the areas that should have received more attention when correcting students' output. More specifically, organization is important in achieving coherence in writing.

What is more, students are not writing teachers; hence, their beliefs on what should be corrected in their output most probably emanates from their past experiences in their writing courses (e.g., elementary and high school). This means that if they were not properly oriented as to how their written output is scored, they are confident that a similar technique of scoring will be applied just like in their first two English courses they had previously taken. Hence, their responses are based on their previous experiences. The mismatch between students' and teachers' responses suggests a need for teachers to review what should be prioritized to ensure better writing output in their students.

Table 12.2 shows the participants' evaluation of the types of instructors' written corrective feedback in the students' expository composition as perceived by both the students and teachers. As can be seen, nearly half of the students identified error correction with comments as the most common feedback followed by giving clues or directions on how students may correct their errors. Similarly, nearly 35 percent of the teacher respondents identified error correction with comments as the most common feedback given by teachers, followed by just providing comments/clues on how errors may be corrected. The match between students and teachers' responses shows that whether the focus of error corrections was on mechanics or content or both.

Recall that in Table 12.1, the data show a mismatch between the areas that teachers believe should be given importance when correcting students' output from students' perceptions. A computation of a t-value of students' and teachers' responses in Table 12.3 reveals however, that the two groups' responses do not differ significantly ($t = 0.309$, $p = 0.770$), which is higher than the alpha level of .05. This could have resulted from the fact that the mean ratings were very close to each other, only ranging from quite useful to very useful. This shows that even though error correction in content and organization was not especially highlighted by teachers, it does not mean that they were taken for granted as part of the correction criteria.

Table 12.2
Frequency and ranking of written corrective feedback observed by the students and teachers

ITEMS	Students' Responses			Teachers' Responses		
	Frequency (n = 100)	Percentage	Rank	Frequency (n = 30)	Percentage	Rank
1. He/She gives clues or directions on how you can correct your work.	41	41	2	8	26.7	2
2. He/She points out where your errors occur but not necessarily indicating the correction.	5	5	3	4	13.3	3.5
3. He/She corrects your errors and makes comment.	49	49	1	10	33.3	1
He/She just corrects your errors.	2	2	4.5	2	6.7	5.5
5. He/She gives feedback by giving comments about your error/s but not correcting it.	2	2	4.5	4	13.3	3.5
6. He/She doesn't need to give any feedback on the errors you have committed.	0	0	7	0	0	7
7. He/She makes feedback by giving comments on the ideas or content but no errors are corrected.	1	1	6	2	6.7	5.5
	100	100		30	100	

Table 12.3
T-test for the forms of errors of students and teachers

	Students' Mean Rating	Teachers' Mean Rating	T-value	P-value	Interpretation
Forms of Errors	4.33	4.28	0.309	0.770	Not Significant

To further support the findings in Table 12.2, the difference between the preferred applied written corrective feedback by the students and teachers in the students' expository composition was computed, and the result of the t-test shows no significant difference between the two groups ($t = 1.23$, $p = 0.24$). The results imply that students' perceptions regarding how feedback should be given by teachers matches that of their teachers, as shown in Table 12.4.

Table 12.4
T-test of preferences of the students and teachers

ITEMS	Students' Responses (n = 100) Frequency	Teachers' Responses (n = 30) Frequency	T-value	P-value
1. He/She gives clues or directions on how you can correct your work.	41	8		
2. He/She points out where your errors occur but not necessarily indicating the correction.	5	4		
3. He/She corrects your errors and makes comment.	49	10		
4. He/She just corrects your errors.	2	2	1.23	0.24
5. He/She gives feedback by giving comments about your error/s but not correcting it.	2	4		
6. He/She doesn't need to give any feedback on the errors you have committed.	0	0		
7. He/She makes feedback by giving comments on the ideas or content but no errors are corrected.	1	2		

Qualitative Results and Analysis

The benefits of the most useful types of written corrective feedback were addressed in the open-ended questions. For the purpose of this chapter, I focused on the top three types of feedback, based on the first three items got the high frequency of responses (see Table 12.4). In terms of the benefits identified for correcting the errors and making comments, the majority of the students maintained that it is an effective way of giving feedback in order to be aware of their errors, and through the given comments they can avoid making the same mistakes again. On the part of the teachers, this was also their first choice, for most of them said that this would let the students know what errors they committed. The belief is that knowledge of their errors increases their ability to self-correct in the future which will result in better written output.

Similarly, both groups identified *Gives clues or directions on how one can correct his work* as the most effective feedback that can be given by teachers. According to the students, the common reasons were they felt they would be guided to see their errors and how to check their composition from the beginning to end, and to learn the proper techniques in writing. Likewise, the teachers acknowledged that giving clues or directions encourages students to self-correct with the aid of clues from their teachers.

The third most common feedback identified by both students and teachers was to point out where the errors occur but not necessarily indicating the correction. Students perceive that compared to the first two types of feedback, this approach allows them to reflect, self-correct and develop insights. Similarly, teachers believe that through this type of feedback students will be more conscious of their errors to the extent that they would discover why and how they would correct them.

The survey conducted shows ample indication of the preferences of the students and the teachers on written corrective feedback. Data revealed that while students generally perceived that pointing out grammatical, spelling and vocabulary errors were very useful, error correction in organization and content/ideas was important as well. On the other hand, while teachers placed emphasis on content, vocabulary and organization, grammatical and spelling error corrections were considered quite useful. The t-test identified no overall significant difference between the responses of the two groups. With regard to the most useful feedback, both groups identified the same type of feedback as the most useful such as (1) correcting errors and making comments, (2) giving clues or directions as to how it will be corrected and (3) pointing out where the errors occur and not necessarily indicating the correction.

Conclusions/Implications for Language Teaching

Based on these results, it can be gleaned that students have a clear expectation as to the specific written corrective feedback that they prefer and find important. Hence, teachers can likewise focus on how to respond to student output and to guide them in improving their writing. Firstly, it would be easier to explain to students how they earn their scores in their compositions. Secondly, assessing written output is quite tedious, but making the specific criteria to be considered in the corrections are clear to the students would make the evaluation easier. Through these measures, questions will be avoided and scoring would be credible in the eyes of the students.

This study is limited by the small sample of respondents. The findings are directional but not conclusive, which simply means that the results of this paper can be used as a guide as to the formulation of WCF but it will still depends on the types of learning objectives. Besides, the instruments used surveyed only the respondents' beliefs. Owing to time constraints, no actual data (e.g. students' written output) were collected containing teachers' feedback in order to verify whether teachers really practice their beliefs about error correction. Future research should employ a broader sample and wider scope.

References

Ammar, A., & Spada, N. (2006). One size fits all? Recasts, prompts, and L2 learning. *Studies in Second Language Acquisition, 28*, 543-574.

Amrhein, H., & Nassaji, N. (2007). Written corrective feedback: What do students and teachers prefer and why? *Canadian Journal of Applied Linguistics, 13*, 95-127.

Diab, R. (2005). EFL university students' preferences for error correction and teacher feedback on writing. *TESL Reporter, 38*(1), 27-51.

Ellis, R. (1994). *The study of second language acquisition*. Oxford: Oxford University Press.

Emmons, R. H. (2003). *An effective writing formula for unsure writers*. Retrieved from http://www.airpower.au.af.mil/airchronicles/aureview/1975/sept-Oct/Emmons.html

Hyland, K., & Hyland, F. (2006). Interpersonal aspects of response: Constructing and interpreting teacher written feedback. In Hyland, K. and Hyland, F. (Eds.), *Feedback* in second language writing: Contexts and issues (pp. 206-224). Cambridge: Cambridge University Press.

Houge, A. (2008). *First steps in academic writing: Level 2*. New York: Pearson Longman.

Kepner, C. G. (1991). An experiment in the relationship of types of written feedback to the development of second-language writing skills. *Modern Language Journal, 75*, 305-313.

Lasagabaster, D., & Sierra, J. M. (2003). Students' evaluation of CALL software programmes. *Educational Media International, 40*(3–4), 293–304.

Lasagabaster, D., & Sierra, J. M. (2005). Error correction: students' versus teachers' perceptions. *Language Awareness, 14*(2-3), 112-127.

Lightbown, P., & Spada, N. (1999) *How languages are learned*. Oxford: Oxford University Press.

Lee, I. (2008). Student reactions to teacher feedback in two Hong Kong secondary classrooms. *Journal of Second Language Writing, 17*, 144-164.

Owens, J. (2009). *Feedback in second language writing: Teacher and student attitudes and preferences*. Retrieved from http://www.academia.edu/1885384

Russell, J., & Spada, N. (2006). The effectiveness of corrective feedback for the acquisition of L2 grammar: A meta-analysis of the research. In Norris, J. M., & Ortega, L. (Eds.), *Synthesizing research on language learning and teaching* (pp. 134-164). Amsterdam: John Benjamins.

Sanz, C. (2000) Bilingual education enhances third language acquisition: Evidence from Catalonia. *Applied Psycholinguistics, 21*(1), 23–44.

Truscott, J. (1996). The case against grammar correction in L2 writing classes. *Language Learning, 46*, 327-369.

Truscott, J. (1999). The case for "the case for grammar correction in L2 writing classes": A response to Ferris. *Journal of Second Language Writing, 16*, 255-272.

CHAPTER 13

DOING CRITICAL PEDAGOGY IN NEOLIBERAL EFL SPACES:
Negotiated Possibilities in Korean Hagwons

Gordon West
University of Hawai'i at Mānoa

Introduction

Reports of critical pedagogy in action have come from all over the world and from many different contexts, including East Asia (Crookes, 2013; Devince, 2012; Eberhardinger, 2011) and South Korea in particular (Kang, 2009; Shin & Crookes, 2005a/b; Sung & Pederson, 2013;). This report builds on those earlier works to include work in a neoliberal context, specifically private language institutes (*hagwons*). The historical context that gave rise to the prominence of hagwons in South Korean English as a Foreign Language (EFL) will briefly be sketched along with a description of the hagwon that was the site of this study, Universal Language School (ULS). A personal account of teacher research and evolution toward critical pedagogy in the form of negotiating syllabi and participatory curriculum development will be given, supported by examples of artifacts collected from the teacher research. Finally, an argument will be drawn not only for the possibility, but the necessity for such praxis in neoliberal contexts, and insights from the experience shared, that future teachers may also follow this path.

South Korea is in the middle of an English language education boom. In the past decade the number of foreign EFL teachers working in South Korea increased 73% from 6,414 in 2000 to 23,600 in 2010 (KIS, 2011). Only 3,477 are employed by public schools (EPIK, 2012). This leaves the vast majority of foreign EFL teachers in Korea employed by hagwons. The number of hagwons has increased from 1,421 in 1970 to 70,213 in 2008 (Moon, 2009). Hagwons are a major site of language learning and intercultural contact, and therefore one that we cannot afford to ignore.

Despite having been controlled by a number of right wing dictators after the Korean War, South Korea had, during that period, followed a largely egalitarian approach to education. An example of this policy is the 1974 High School Equalization Policy (HSEP) which had the goal of eliminating "elite" schools and competition between schools and was fairly successful (Byun & Kim, 2010). Also, in 1980, private tutoring (including most forms of hagwons and public school teachers selling their services as after school tutors) was banned to further equalize education (Park, 2007). A shift began in the mid-1990s, however, toward neoliberal education policies (Byun & Kim, 2010; Jeon, 2009; Lee, 2011; Park, 2010).

Reforms to the education system were affected by the financial crisis of 1997. The crisis was disastrous, reducing per capita GNP by almost half (Koo, 2007). While the cause of the crisis was attributed to monetary policies applied to Asian financial markets by the International Monetary Fund (IMF) (Stiglitz, 2002), the bailout given to South Korea by the IMF to overcome the crisis was conditioned by further structural adjustment policies designed to implement neoliberal economic reforms (Crotty & Lee, 2005). Neoliberal reforms were sold by leaders using rhetoric that essentially made those principles synonymous with freedom and democracy in Korea (Park, 2007; Seth, 2002).

Changes to the education system followed fast on the heels of those neoliberal reforms. The ban on private teaching was overturned in 2000 by the Constitutional Court (Korea's highest court) as part of this new interpretation of freedoms guaranteed by the constitution where choice is given prominence above all other rights (Park, 2007). The "shadow education" market inhabited by hagwons brought in $10 billion on private English language education in 2006 alone (Koo, 2007).

By 2008 the HSEP had been three times revised to weaken its egalitarian aims, construed as overregulation in neoliberal discourse (Byun & Kim, 2010). At the same time, leading public figures called for public schools to adapt to the market by creating afterschool programs to compete with hagwons (Lee, 2011). This drove the marketization and competition of schools in Korea, though public schools are losing. Percentages of students participating in hagwons jumped from 15% in 1980, to 54% in 1997, and 72.6% in 2002 (Yang, 2003, as cited in Park, 2007, p. 102) before rising even higher to 80% in Byun & Kim's (2010) study.

Hagwons follow a "business capital strategy" of English language education, specifically in recruiting teachers who are "young, flexible, temporary, inexpensive to train at the beginning, un-pensioned at the end… and replaceable wherever possible by technology" (Hargreaves & Fullan, 2012, p. 2). The only teaching qualifications required to teach EFL at a hagwon are to have a BA degree in any subject, a clean criminal background check, and be from a "native speaking" country. I arrived as just such a teacher in 2009. I had only a BA in Global Studies, some minor tutoring experience, and little expectation that I would a have long-term career in English Language Teaching (ELT).

Universal Language School

The school that I landed in was ULS, a large English language hagwon with just over 1000 students in Seoul. The hagwon employed 19 foreign teachers from North America (18) and the United Kingdom (1) along with 22 Korean teachers and 31 to 38 support staff (teaching aides, bus drivers, cooks, administrative support staff, etc., whose exact number was always in flux) during the years of this study 2009-2012, with slight variations. ULS is a chain hagwon, meaning that there are many other ULS branches around Korea, with this being one of the larger branches.

Typically foreign teachers are expected to teach between 6 and 7 40-minute periods per day, for a total of 35 contact hours per week, along with five hours of prep time per week. From March 2010 to May 2012, the period I focus on in this chapter, I worked as an afternoon middle school teacher with a 1:30 – 9:00/9:30 schedule. Even as an afternoon teacher, my day started by teaching a special activity lesson to kindergarten students. The class sizes were small, capped at just 12 students, and teachers were assigned to a class for usually the entire year. Often times, I had students for multiple years, or their siblings in my classes. This resulted in being able to build close connections with the students that would be important in establishing trust with the students.

My focus in this chapter is work with three different classes. The first is a second grade class of six students in the Returnee Advanced Placement (RAP) program at ULS. These students were in their fifth year of study at

ULS by second grade. They had advanced proficiency and were also highly valued by the institution as returning customers. The curriculum for the class was specialized. I taught reading and writing classes to them while a second American teacher taught integrated skills and a third Korean teacher taught grammar. The specialized curriculum meant that I had more control since it was supposed to be tailored to the class.

The other two classes I report on are Middle A and H. These were two of the more advanced proficiency middle school classes at ULS; however the linguistic levels of the students varied widely. The middle school classes were less stable, often fluctuating between 8 to 12 students. ULS specialized in kindergarten and elementary programs, the curriculum for which was mostly developed by their franchising corporation. This left the middle school curriculum as in flux as the student population, with each director of the program setting the curriculum. This relatively loose curriculum also left openings for interventions in an otherwise tightly controlled environment.

Teacher Research

For the two years I focus on for this report, I engaged in systematic investigations into my teaching. As I had a wide variety of classes (kindergarten, elementary, and middle school at different proficiency levels), my research and the projects also varied widely according to my needs and the needs of the students. I term these investigations collectively as teacher research in opposition to action research or exploratory practice (Allwright, 2003). I do this because for much of the time I was teaching, I had little access to research methodology materials or training that was directly related to my field. Teacher research remains a form of rigorous inquiry, even though teachers' knowledge has been marginalized in relationship to academic researchers in the past (Crookes, 1993). I have, with the luxury of returning to an academic setting, been able to synthesize and analyze my data in a way that provides a contribution to knowledge in the field of critical pedagogy.

My data collection and research design shared at times many traits of action research as it has been popularized (i.e., Burns, 2009), but my research was first and foremost a response to resistance I saw from my students to my teaching. It was in this sense also similar to Allwright's (2003) concept of exploratory practice as focusing on improving the quality of life in the classroom. I echo other scholars' critiques of formalized action research though as something that requires time and expertise beyond the means of most classroom EFL/ESL teachers (Aoki & Hamakawa, 2003).

In addition to student resistance, my research was prompted by my own growing realization that my teaching style did not match my personal values. As an untrained teacher, my teaching style could best have been described my first year as the "banking method" (Freire, 2000), where I was there to give knowledge of English to my students. This dictatorial approach did not fit with my personal politics, and my sympathy was with my students when they resisted. My search for another way brought me to critical pedagogy as articulated by Cowhey (2005) and Freire (2000). In adopting critical pedagogy, I was able to theorize my teaching. I was also able to theorize the resistance I was seeing as very similar to the "weapons of the weak" described by Scott (1985) in his landmark study that I had encountered as an undergraduate. These frameworks of resistive agency by my students and of the pedagogy of hope offered by critical pedagogy guided my inquiries. My biggest problem then became that none of the accounts of critical pedagogy did anything to help me understand how it could be applied to my situation.

In this chapter, I will present one narrative example of my evolution as supported by evidence from my teacher research. My example focuses on my systematic progression in applying principles of participatory or negotiated syllabi as an attempt to conceptualize what problem-posing education could be in my context. While I also attempted other aspects of critical pedagogy (i.e., using codes, participatory assessment, dialogical learning, and using learner-created materials), they are beyond the scope of this chapter. I discuss negotiated syllabi because it is where I began my transformation as a teacher, and the narrative provides a clear path for other teachers to follow in beginning their journeys toward critical pedagogy.

Negotiated Syllabi

One of the main characteristics of critical pedagogy is that the class should be shaped in dialogic fashion with the students. This can be done in part through negotiating the syllabus. This process is also referenced as part of the process of creating democratic classrooms (Weiner, 2005; Wolk, 1998). This process has been previously described in East Asian contexts (i.e., Hashimoto & Fukuda, 2011), and with young learners (i.e., Wolk, 1998), although not in clear practical terms. In this section, I use classroom artifacts to demonstrate a gradual increase in student input as I became more comfortable and more convinced in the necessity of negotiating the syllabus.

Both Nation and Macalister (2010) and Crookes (2013) draw on Breen and Littlejohn's (2000) work to describe possible processes of negotiating syllabi. Nation and Macalister describe the process in terms of increasing learner-centeredness, but as an essentially apolitical process. Crookes notes this limitation in Breen and Littlejohn's work, and draws more on the Freirian notion of a period of listening in which the teacher must spend time with the students and understand their context and problems before the class or curriculum can begin to be formed. Practically this process is not possible in most situations, but may become possible if viewed as occurring over several different classes during time teaching at the same institution. In my situation at ULS, I built relationships with the students over years in different classes and got to understand their problems and context. Eventually, we were able to begin to define why we were there for ourselves, not just as their parents or ULS defined the reason for their learning. Reaching that understanding through numerous dialogues gave me the confidence to allow them to negotiate the "how" and "what" of our classes.

Figure 13.1 shows my first narrow negotiation of the syllabus with my Returnee Advanced Placement second grade class (RAP2) class. In the beginning, I simply asked them what topics they wanted to talk or write about in class. I had them write their answers on ballots and then collected and analyzed them. After ranking the most popular topics, I shifted the curriculum or used supplementary materials to focus on the most popular topics. In doing this, several mistakes were made. First, this was only a democratic process in the shallowest sense. There was no transparency in how I determined what the most popular topics were or on which days we would talk about which topics. When I surveyed the students to see how this process was going, they were surprisingly in agreement that they did not like the topics of discussion or writing in class. I had assumed that what second grade students said they were interested in the first week of class was what they would be interested in three months later. This was *not* the case.

This beginning is inauspicious. Many teachers have done similar things with their classes, and done it better. I start here because it can help show teachers who want to negotiate that they do not need to start big, and from here there are smaller steps to take before fully negotiating the syllabus.

Doing Critical Pedagogy in Neoliberal EFL Spaces

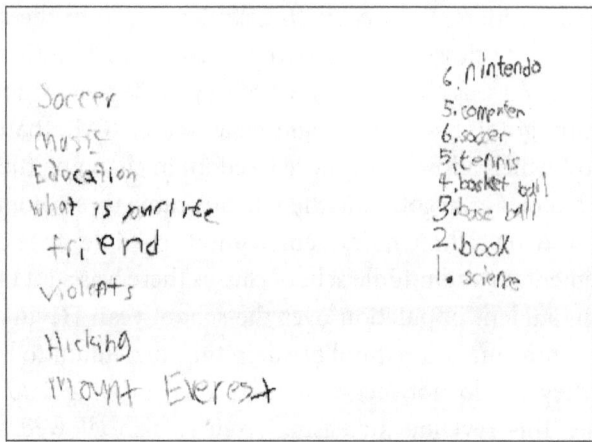

Figure 13.1. RAP 2 topic interest survey (2 surveys shown). March 2011

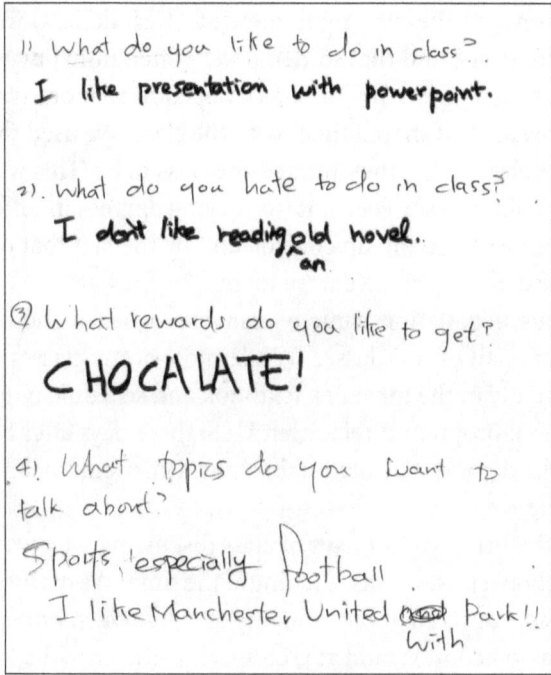

Figure 13.2. Student interest survey, Middle A. June 2011

My first small attempt at negotiating student input to the syllabus was done across all of my classes. Topics were something I felt fairly comfortable with integrating and was able to do so with varying degrees of success across classes. Some programs had a more rigid syllabus (i.e., RAP) than others (i.e., middle school) which allowed for more freedom in changing the content.

My next attempt at negotiating the syllabus came three months after the first. Classes were on a three month curriculum schedule since especially in the upper elementary and middle school classes there was a lot of movement and change in student population over the school year. Having a level test every three months made a natural break in the curriculum to bring in new students so they would not feel as if they were jumping into the middle of the course. This revenue increasing strategy also allowed a chance to readjust curriculum and shift directions with classes. This took the form of renegotiation as my teaching evolved.

Figure 13.2 shows the next generation of ballot. I increased student input on classroom activities. My inclusion of reward choice is problematic, but came as a response to the directly monetized (ULS dollars) form of reward that I wanted to escape and that students were often unhappy with.

Figure 13.3 then shows my process of becoming more transparent as I compiled the results and shared them with the class. We used this handout to start a dialogue about what they wanted the class to be. This was still limited by the set curriculum to some extent (to varying degrees in different classes), by my own comfort in giving up control, and by the fact that our discussion did not include defining why we were there.

Full syllabus negotiation came a year after I began the process, but it did not happen in all of my classes. While most of my classes retained a set curriculum, usually in the form of a textbook and schedule of pages to cover, the middle school program director left ULS, three days after being hired, in March 2012. She departed before establishing a curriculum, and so I was left with an opening.

We spent the first two full days of class discussing why we were there in both middle school classes I was teaching at the time. We discussed the things the students and I disliked about studying as it had been done in general, in the Korean hagwon context, and at ULS specifically, since the local context is where you are able to make the most impact. We then worked through what we could do to change the class. The openness of these dialogues was possible

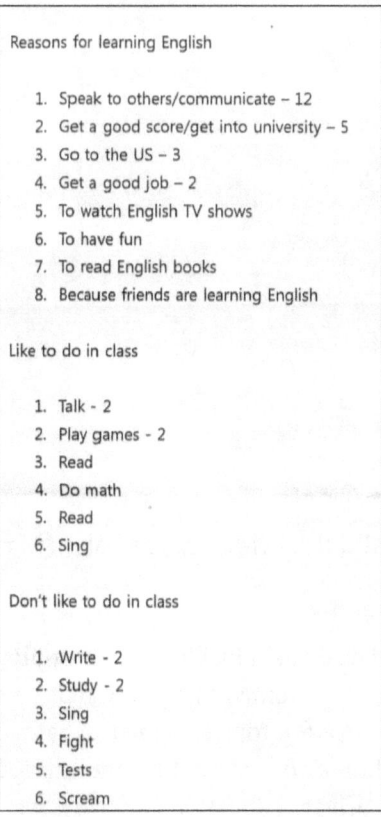

Figure 13.3. Compilation of survey results prepared for students, Middle A. June 2011

because I knew many of the students before and had gained their trust as someone who would not betray their complaints to administration or their parents.

Once we were able to work through why we were in the class together and what our goals were, we were able to negotiate the content of the class. Figure 4 shows a ballot for which the task we would take on as the central focus of the class for our first three month period together. The items on the ballot are a result of discussions held in class. Both of my middle school classes ended up choosing debate as their activity for the first three-month period. Middle H had done debate before and had enjoyed it. Middle A wanted to do debate

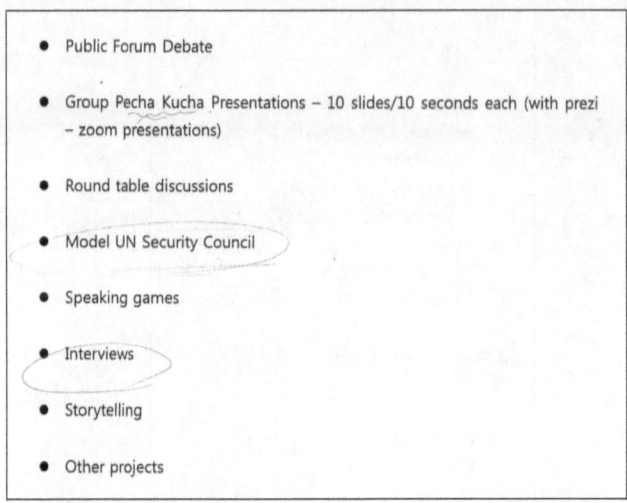

Figure 13.4. Middle H class activity ballot. March 2012

because it had been previously held by ULS as a prestigious special class only for the highest level, and they wanted to tap into that prestige.

The students then chose the topics of their debates. Middle A chose to debate whether or not homework should be abolished. Middle H chose to debate the relevance of private education and whether or not it should be abolished. The topics of the debates highlighted things in their lives that they deemed to be severe and immediate problems—too much homework, and too much time in school due to competition furthered by private afterschool education. The fact that the projects were debates also highlighted the conflicting views they had on these subjects and their desire not to be seen too readily by other teachers at the school or their parents as openly in defiance of the system. They wanted to fight, but in a way that seemed balanced and which they thought would be the most legitimate form of argument. In this, debate was a shrewd choice. My role then was to guide them through the process and rules of debate, research, and help keep the class on a schedule to complete tasks in a timely fashion. I was also a language resource, helping the students with the language they would need to debate.

Figure 13.5 shows an example textbook evaluation from the Middle A class. When a new middle school director was found in May 2012, she knew

> **Writing to Learn: The Essay**
>
> 1. Find 2 of the writing topics (ex. "Sports," "My Day," etc...) What are they?
>   Talking about school, Jobs for the future
> 2. How difficult is the book?
>   Very Easy   Very Difficult
>   1   ②   3   4   5
>
> 3. How interesting is the layout (how does the book look to you?)
>   Very boring   Very interesting
>   ①   2   3   4   5
>
> 4. How interesting are the topics?
>   Very boring   Very interesting
>   1   2   3   ④   5
>
> 5. Do you like the book? Why or why not?
>   I don't like dark, but this book decorated only black
>   so this looks dark and borning
>   book

Figure 13.5. Middle A textbook evaluation form. May 2012

of the negotiated process my middle school classes were operating and was outwardly supportive. Although she insisted that we use a textbook going forward, she agreed to allow me to choose the textbooks we would use. I, in turn, brought the possible textbooks to the class and we discussed how to evaluate and choose which book to use. The students were disappointed by the fact that they had to again use a textbook, but were sincere in their desire to choose one that was a good fit. As the comment on Figure 13.5 demonstrates, a lot of the focus was on ascetics, although they were careful to not ignore content either.

In the end, the textbook we choose collectively was approved by the director. On the day we received the new textbooks, though, a different book arrived. While outwardly supportive, the director did not trust the students, in dialogue with me, to choose a book. This betrayal was devastating to the class morale.

Wolk (1998) writes of his own obstacles and the derision he faced from colleagues in running democratic classes. He mentions the stereotype, in an American context, that "serious" learning can only occur under in a highly structured, teacher-created environment (Wolk, 1998). This stereotype applies to the Korean context as well. While negotiated syllabi are linked to increasing learner motivation through involvement in even the most apolitical terms (Nation & Macalister, 2010), they are also a political tool. Simply negotiating the syllabus in an otherwise highly controlled, autocratic environment is an act of creative resistance. It is an opening of space.

Democratic teaching involves not just "doing" democracy, but reimagining democracy (Weiner, 2005). It can be transformative and resistant to the material structures of neoliberalism in the form of textbooks and corporate curriculum that limit democracy in schools. It takes time, though, and in a neoliberal model of education where time is money, this is a major obstacle. Just as teachers might be limited initially by their "apprenticeship of observation" (Lortie, 1975), students also need time to overcome their past experiences in school. If students have no experience with democratic learning, and if the imaginary of education has been colonized (Crookes, 2013), it takes time to imagine new forms of education. As critical praxicioners, our job is to guide them to this new understanding, slowly if necessary, and be ourselves transformed by the process.

Discussion

Negotiating the syllabus in and of itself is not necessarily part of a critical praxis. It is however, an opening, and a way for teachers to begin the shift to problem-posing education. My own experience as detailed in my examples was far from a direct path toward critical pedagogy. There were important issues, like the faux-monetary reward system for students, and even the student-as-customer paradigm that I left largely unchallenged, at least initially. The point for sharing the failures and short-comings, as well as my perceived successes, is to help show other teachers in contexts that might seem unlikely locations for critical pedagogy that it only needs to start with small interventions, and even then, it is a complicated process. It took time not only for me to evolve and become comfortable in my own critical praxis, but also for the relationships I needed for this transformation to be possible to develop.

The neoliberal space of the private language institute allowed me openings and opportunities that many teachers in other contexts do not have. I was able to develop close rapport with the students in small classes and in a setting where I got to know siblings and families over a few years of teaching. I also worked hard to build close relationships with my co-teachers at the school. My Korean co-teachers, as the person of contact for the parents of my students, were also invaluable in helping me build trust among the parents. Finally, I was able to win the trust of the administrators. In an environment where customer service takes prominence many times over educational process and English as a product is prized support from my students and their parents cast me as a valuable asset in the eyes of the administration.

There are two common criticisms that I have faced in discussing this work with others. The first pertains to practicing critical pedagogy as an American in an EFL context, and especially working with young(er) learners. Am I not imposing my cultural values on my students? This is an old critique that critical pedagogues face, but is rooted in a basic misunderstanding of critical pedagogy and teaching in general as a political process, having been termed the question of imposition by Crookes (2013). This assumption is reached under the false belief that teaching is a neutral process. Teaching is a highly political process, all the more so fraught in the contentious case of English language education in Korea. Not acknowledging the political nature and values being privileged in this educational context is dangerous because it preserves and reifies repressive structures in the status quo. Critical praxis, in contrast, acknowledges the explicitly political nature of education and the stance of the teacher is made clear rather than obscured.

A more serious critique is related to doing critical pedagogy in neoliberal spaces. This concern is founded in the fact that doing any work in these spaces serves only to legitimize them and put public, state-sponsored education at risk (Lipman, 2009). This position, in my view, overvalues state education, and fails to problematize the fact that such education also already exists in a neoliberal paradigm. While public education must remain a site of struggle in Korea and elsewhere, other sites of struggle cannot be ruled out. In EFL contexts in particular, where larger social movements may not exist or be possible for teachers to participate fully in, we must teach in the cracks (Hartlep, 2012). This means that we must work to raise consciousness and build communities as a way of creating space for support of social justice and resistance to neoliberal values in whatever context we find ourselves in.

Conclusion

This chapter has attempted to illuminate the neoliberal paradigm in which much of Korean EFL education exists. It has also attempted to show through teacher research, the possibilities for negotiating syllabi and participatory curriculum design as a way for teachers to begin making interventions with the goal of evolving toward critical pedagogy. The challenges involved with this evolution have been shared, along with the successes, to illustrate the difficulty of doing critical pedagogy in particular contexts but also the ultimate possibility and need for it. Arguments have also been made against some critiques of practicing critical pedagogy in EFL and neoliberal contexts. Further research is needed to explore the largely unexamined, but hugely important, hagwon sector in Korea for its impact on EFL education. Until further research or political movements find a way to challenge this neoliberal model of EFL, teachers should continue to find ways to resist, and open spaces for critical practice wherever they find themselves.

References
Aoki, N., & Hamakawa, Y. (2003). Asserting our culture: Teacher autonomy from a feminist perspective. In D. Palfreyman, & R. C. Smith (Eds.). *Learner autonomy across cultures: Language education perspectives* (pp. 240-253). New York: Palgrave Macmillan.
Allwright, D. (2003). Exploratory practice: Rethinking practitioner research in language teaching. *Language Teaching Research*, 7(2), 113–141. doi:10.1191/1362168803lr118oa
Breen, M. P., & Littlejohn, A. (2000). *Classroom decision-making: Negotiation and process syllabuses in practice.* Cambridge: Cambridge University Press.
Burns, A. (2009). *Doing action research in English language teaching: A guide for practitioners.* New York : Routledge.
Byun, S., & Kim, K. (2010). Educational inequality in South Korea: The widening socioeconomic gap in student achievement. *Research in the Sociology of Education*, 17, 155–182. doi:10.1108/S1479-3539(2010)0000017008
Carr, W., & Kemmis, S. (1986). *Becoming critical: Education, knowledge, and action research.* London: Falmer Press.
Cowhey, M. (2005). *Black ants and Buddhists: Thinking critically and teaching differently in the primary grades.* Portland, ME: Stenhouse Publishers.
Crookes, G. (1993). Action research for second language teachers: Going beyond teacher research. *Applied Linguistics*, 14(2), 130–144. doi:10.1093/applin/14.2.130
Crookes, G. (2013). *Critical ELT in action: Foundations, promises, praxis.* New York: Routledge.
Crotty, J., & Lee, K.-K. (2006). The effects of neoliberal "reforms" on the post-crisis Korean economy. *Review of Radical Political Economics*, 38(4), 669–675. doi:10.1177/0486613406290903
Derince, Z. M. (2012). Reflections on teaching practices through conditionings in Turkey. *Journal for Critical Education Policy Studies*, 10(1), 248-264.
Eberhardinger, M. J. (2011). Critical pedagogy overseas. (Unpublished academic paper). Greensboro, NC: University of North Carolina at Greensboro.
English Program in Korea. (2012). Seoul: Author. Retrieved from http://www.epik.go.kr/
Freire, P. (2000). *Pedagogy of the oppressed.* New York: Continuum.

Hargreaves, A., & Fullan, M. (2012) *Professional capital: Transforming teaching in every school.* New York: Teachers College Press.

Hartlep, N. (2012). Teachers' pet projects versus real social justice teaching. In A. Honigsfeld, & A. Cohan (Eds.). *Breaking the mold of education for culturally and linguistically diverse students: Innovative and successful practices for the 21st century* (pp. 13-21). New York: Rowman & Littlefield Publishers.

Hashimoto, N., & Fukuda, S. (2011). Reaching for their own goals: A more democratic classroom. *The Language Teacher, 35*(1), 17-22.

Jeon, M. (2009). Globalization and native English speakers in English Programme in Korea (EPIK). *Language, Culture and Curriculum, 22*(3), 231–243. doi:10.1080/07908310903388933

Kang, M. O. (2009). Berstein's pedagogic device and teachers'relatively autonomous praxes in South Korea. *Curriculum and Teaching Dialogue, 12*(1), 105-119.

Koo, H. (2007). The changing faces of inequality in South Korea in the age of globalization. *Korean Studies, 31*(1), 1–18. doi:10.1353/ks.2008.0018

Korean Immigration Service. (2011). *Tonggyeowolbo* [Monthly Statistical Data Report]. Seoul: Ministry of Justice.

Lee, J. (2011). The policies on supplemental education in Korea. *IIAS Newsletter, 56*(2), 16-17.

Lipman, P. (2009). Paradoxes of teaching in neo-liberal times: education "reform" in Chicago. In S. Gewirtz, P. Mahony, I. Hextall, & A. Cribb (Eds.), *Changing teacher professionalism: International trends, challenges and ways forward* (pp. 67 – 80). New York: Routledge.

Lortie, D. C. (1975). *Schoolteacher: A sociological study.* Chicago: University of Chicago Press.

Moon, G. (2009, December 15). Statistics paint Korean picture. *Korea Joongang Daily.* Seoul Korea. Retrieved from http://koreajoongangdaily.joinsmsn.com/news/article/article.aspx?aid=2913964

Nation, I. S. P., & Macalister, J. (2010). *Language curriculum design.* New York: Routledge.

Park, J. S. (2007). Educational manager mothers: South Korea's neoliberal transformation. *Korea Journal, 47*(3), 186-213.

Park, J. S.-Y. (2010). Naturalization of competence and the neoliberal subject: Success stories of English language learning in the Korean conservative press. *Journal of Linguistic Anthropology, 20*(1), 22–38. doi:10.1111/j.1548-1395.2010.01046.x

Scott, J. C. (1985). *Weapons of the weak: Everyday forms of peasant protest.* New Haven: Yale University Press.

Seth, M. J. (2002). *Education fever: Society, politics, and the pursuit of schooling in South Korea.* Honolulu, HI: University of Hawaii Press.

Shin, H., & Crookes, G. (2005a). Indigenous critical traditions for TEFL?: A historical and comparative perspective in the case of Korea. *Critical Inquiry in Language Studies, 2*(2), 95-112.

Shin, H., & Crookes, G. (2005b). Exploring the possibilities for EFL critical pedagogy in Korea: A two-part case study. *Critical Inquiry in Language Studies, 2*(2), 113-,138.

Stiglitz, J. E. (2002). *Globalization and its discontents.* New York: W.W. Norton.

Sung, K., & Pederson, R. (Eds.) (2013). *Critical ELT practices in Asia: Key issues, practices, and possibilities.* Rotterdam: Sense Publishers.

Weiner, E. (2005). *Private learning, public needs: The neoliberal assault on democratic education.* New York: Peter Lang.

Wolk, S. (1998). *A democratic classroom.* Portsmouth, NH: Heinemann.

CHAPTER 14

CROSS-CULTURAL EQUITY:
Pathway for Impoverished and Marginalized Students in Two-Way Bilingual Immersion Programs

Ana M. Hernández
Annette Daoud
California State University San Marcos

The purpose of this study is to analyze the cross-cultural equity of peer interactions between Native Spanish Speakers (NSS) and Native English Speakers (NES) in Two-Way Bilingual Immersion (TWBI) programs. This will be accomplished by examining student dispositions during classroom instruction. The researchers will examine the sociolinguistic and sociocultural relationships between White, middle class NES students and low socioeconomic (SES) NSS Hispanics/Latinos residing in impoverished urban and suburban environments. The immersion program is designed to facilitate the attainment of bilingual and biliteracy skills of both groups of students without the risk of native language loss (Cummins, 1994; Lindholm-Leary, 2001, 2005). Students learn academic content in both languages, as well as cross-cultural awareness. However, while the fundamental role of TWBI programs is to ensure positive social interactions between NSS and NES in learning environments (Howard et al., 2007; Lindholm-Leary, 2001, 2005), the sociolinguistic and sociocultural dispositions between NSS and NES students continue to be a challenging goal for educators and students. Concerns include the matter in which the NES students disrespected the academic spaces of NSS students by cutting off classmates during class discussions and dominating oral contributions (Palmer, 2008). Similarly, other studies confirm the status quo of equity in the TWBI and outline the challenges of NSS conforming to subordinate roles (De Jong, 2006; Fitts, 2006; Hernandez, 2011; Palmer, 2008).

In many countries, the notion of linguistic equity can be challenging in bilingual education contexts. For example, the language situation in Finland, an official Finish and Swedish bilingual nation in Northern Europe, poses parallel findings. Finland's immersion programs have a multilingual orientation goal where all citizens study three languages, including English, in addition to the mother tongue before the age of 10 (Björklund & Mard-Miettinen in Tedick et al., 2011). Questionnaires about the student language use within and outside of school revealed that the majority of the students in grades 4-6 felt confident to use all their languages in the classroom (Björklund, 2005). However, when students were asked about language preference, the majority of students ranked English as more important than Swedish in grades 2 and 6. Results of this study suggest that English is perceived as more prestigious than Swedish among upper primary immersion students. The study suggests devoting more instructional time to Swedish, since time spent on English may be negatively impacting the development of the Swedish language.

This research study examines NSS and NES interactions in a TWBI middle school program (grades 6-8) in southern California, USA. The intent of the study is to examine the social and linguistic implications of low SES Hispanic/Latino students (NSS) and White, middle class (NES) students' dispositions. We define cross-cultural dispositions as the conscious acts of equity and justice used by students when interacting in a social settings and/or academic situations. Dispositions allow students to understand, connect with, and express learning within each student's cultural background and academic strength within the context of teaching, learning and schooling (Gallavan, 2011). We identify and examine both sociolinguistic and sociocultural dispositions in the interactions across student groups to determine how cross-cultural equity is attained. We define sociolinguistic dispositions as students exhibiting behaviors of being respectful towards others' contributions during interactions, and being social or easily engaging in a conversation. Additionally, we identify the following sociolinguistic dispositional roles: A negotiator—a student who can reach consensus during group work; a facilitator—a student who seeks engagement from others; a listener —a student who pays attention to other speakers. Sociocultural dispositions are identified as behaviors such as being democratic, understanding, supportive, compassionate, and unprejudiced during student interactions. We also identify and examine the role of a collaborator, a student who can work with others to complete a task, as a sociocultural dispositional role. We propose in this paper that the degree to which students exhibit these sociolinguistic and sociocultural dispositions lead to cross-cultural equity in TWBI programs.

The following research questions guide this inquiry: 1) What cross-cultural dispositions are evident in the interactions between low SES Hispanic/Latino (NSS) and White middle class (NES) students in their Spanish academic context? 2) What are the social and linguistic implications for cross-cultural equity between these students?

Theoretical Framework

This inquiry draws from the theoretical foundations of critical theory/pedagogy to develop consciousness of authoritarian tendencies by the dominant groups in traditional education. Students of impoverish communities, who are linguistically and culturally diverse, need to connect knowledge to power and freedom of oppression in order to achieve social reconstruction (Freire, 1970; Giroux, 1988). It is important for teachers to view educational opportunities for students who have been historically disenfranchised by inequitable systems. Teachers can transform students into thinkers for social change and active learners in their communities. Structures that allow dominant social relations create a "culture of silence and oppression" for groups of students who are perceived as subordinates in social stratifications. This theory permits teachers to re-examine and reconstruct peer interactions as a critical process for transformation, rather than to allow a place of complacency in the classroom.

Improving educational experiences through understanding and respect of all students is the foundation of the theories and practices of multicultural education (Banks, 2003; Gallavan, 2011; Nieto & Bode, 2008). Peer interactions that are rooted in cross-cultural equity are paramount in TWBI programs, particularly in California where over 25% of students in public schools (K-12) are classified as English learners, either immigrants or the sons and daughters of immigrants living in poverty or below poverty level (California Department of Education, 2011). Finding pathways in cross-cultural dispositions, will allow low SES Hispanic/Latino (a historically underserved and marginalized group of students in American schools) to gain better access to the distribution of power and equity during peer interactions. Educators must understand student attitudes and behaviors towards peers in order to become fully aware of how these dispositions impact each group's academic and social schooling experiences. August and Hakuta (1997, p. 346) point out in their review of programs for English learners, neglecting to fully understand intergroup or social relations is unfortunate because "the social climate in schools can undermine even the best of academic programs."

Sociolinguistic and Sociocultural Perspectives
Through a sociolinguistic lens, researchers study how language is used by students and for what purpose. The social context affects production as well as the perception of a language, for example how students perceive the status of their primary language (L1) and the target language (L2) they are learning (Tarone, 2007). Often, when the target language has status over the primary language, the target language becomes the institutional language of academic discourse while the primary language is used for peer-to-peer social discourse (Tarone & Swan, 1995). The "politics of language" influences the decision-making process that a student undergoes while choosing which language to speak in a given context. Even in instructional programs that positively promote dual language development, students are often taught to value English over their native or primary language (McCollum, 1999).

From a sociocultural perspective, student learning can be understood through a critical examination of social relationships and the teacher-student and student-student power relations. Learning occurs through meaningful interactions among individuals, and the relationships students form directly impact their knowledge base and attainment (Vygotsky, 1978). Strategies that students use to learn a language (L2) are determined by multiple contextual factors that are "embedded in institutional, interactional and instructional practices" used by teachers and peers in the classroom (Jang & Jimenez, 2011, p. 147). Individual, social and societal factors impact teacher-student and student-student interactions that directly influence learning. Looking broadly at the sociocultural contexts of schooling, one must examine student social, emotional, and academic needs as well as external societal factors such as perceptions and stereotyping of a student's culture (Collier, 1995).

Cultural, Social, and Linguistic Capital

Bourdieu (1986, 1991) identifies forms of capital; cultural, social and linguistic, as a means of explaining how knowledge, beliefs, relationships and language of a "preferred" group in a society are recognized as having dominance over the knowledge, beliefs, relationships and language of other groups in that society. Cultural capital refers to the "ways of talking, acting, moving, dressing, socializing, tastes, beliefs, likes and dislikes, competencies, and forms of skills and knowledge that distinguish one group from another" (Bourdieu & Passeron, 1977 as cited in DeMarris & LeCompte, 1999). The distinctions between the cultural capital different groups possess in society depend on the economic status that each group has in that society. How and why individuals come to belong to a particular group in society, and why one group has power over others is determined by the social capital they possess.

Social capital refers to "the aggregate of the actual or potential resources which are linked to possession of the durable network of more or less institutionalized relationships of mutual acquaintance and recognition" (Bourdieu, 1986, p. 249). Social capital then is determined by an individual's group membership as well as the availability of real or potential resources that a group has access to in a society. An individual group member possesses social capital based on how expansive her/his network of connections is, and to whom s/he is connected. Individuals who are "well-connected" have an expansive network with other "well-connected" individuals who have access to economic and cultural capital. Conversely, in a society divided by social classes, members of the lower class who possess the least amount of social capital also have the least access to economic and cultural capital. Bourdieu refers to "a space of relations which is just as real as a geographical space" to explain how the size of the networks created by individual group members depends on the group's social place in society (Bourdieu, 1986, p. 249). Groups with the most social capital have more expansive networks which give them more pathways to economic and cultural capital. These pathways are also shorter in distance to economic capital than pathways of any other group in society. Lower class groups in a society not only have less access to these pathways, but must travel greater distances to attain economic and cultural capital (Bourdieu, 1991). As is the case with cultural capital, the symbolic power that the upper classes has in society play an important role in sustaining their control of social capital. Cultural and social capital, along with the underlying symbolic power which perpetuates or limits access to each of them, are transmitted in part through the language practices and preferences of groups in society.

The language of the dominant culture not only represents the dominant authority, but also manifests and symbolizes it through discourse practices and preferences (Bourdieu, 1991). In keeping with the economic terminology, Bourdieu states that the language which is used in the "linguistic market" of the dominant group is defined by "distinction and correctness" as compared to other languages or discourses. Consistent with the use and transmission of other forms of capital, the language of the dominant culture imposes itself as the legitimate language in society. Other languages or dialects in a society are measured against how members of the dominant culture determine their legitimate use in society. When a society wants to establish a standard language, the dominant culture will unify different dialects that may not be seen as "correct" in order to distinguish the standard language from languages used by other members of society (Bourdieu, 1991). Whether a society seeks to establish a standard language or to establish preferences for certain dialects or discourse practices, schools play a key role in transmitting the legitimate practices and uses of language. The status given to one language over another within schools is an important issue because "this institution has the monopoly in the large-scale production of producers and consumers" (Bourdieu, 1991, p. 49). How well a person can communicate in the labor market, i.e. convert cultural and social capital into economic capital depends in part on the access s/he has in school to the legitimate language uses of the dominant culture. English is the legitimate language in schools in the United States. The forms of English students have access to in schools can improve or limit their success in schools as well as have consequences for their access to all other forms of capital.

Methods

This research examined cross-cultural equity during English and Spanish peer interactions inside, as well as outside, classroom contexts in TWBI programs. The analysis represented "an empirical inquiry that investigates a contemporary phenomenon in depth and within its real-life context, especially when the boundaries between phenomenon and context are not clearly evident" (Yin, 2009, p. 18). The researchers examined the data through a Glaserian approach to grounded theory in which open coding strategies and constant comparison of incidents allowed answers to emerge and generate or reframe theory (Grbich, 2007). The constant comparative method allowed for the development of categories through theoretical sampling, as a significant feature of grounded theory.

Contexts for Study
The research guided the collection and analysis of data through a naturalistic approach (Miles & Huberman, 1994). The intent of the study was to examine the social and linguistic dispositions of low SES Hispanic/Latinos (NSS) and White, middle class native speakers of English. Data collected for this inquiry represented a TWBI middle school program (grades 6-8) in southern California, USA.

Students in this research study participated in a 90/10 TWBI program during elementary school. Instruction in a 90/10 program begins in kindergarten where the target language, in this case Spanish, is taught 90% of the day with 10% of the instructional time dedicated to learning English. Instruction in the target language then decreases through the grade levels, until it reaches 50% of the day in English and the other half in the target language. In middle school, the program only offers Social Studies in Spanish and all other subject matter is taught in English. At the time of the study, TWBI program model configurations met the criteria established by the Center for Applied Linguistics (CAL, 2012).

The middle school located in San Diego County was originally known as a western-type farming community, but had evolved through the years into an affluent residential area. This middle school was the only feeder school to the district's TWBI program. The school's student demographics included: 48% White, 20% Hispanic/Latino, 17% Asian, 11% other ethnic groups, and 4% African American. Participants in this study were identified as 46% NSS Hispanic and 49% of a low socioeconomic status (SES).

Sampling of Participants
One middle school bilingual teacher participated in the research. She taught all three TWBI Social Studies classes in grades 6-8. Students in the study represented low SES Hispanic/Latino NSS and White middle class NES

students. Majority of Hispanic/Latino NSS students qualified for free and reduced lunch. TWBI middle school students (n=69) participated in the study through an anonymous survey administered by their bilingual teacher. Surveys collected were as follows: 6th grade (n=15), 7th grade (n=28) and 8th grade (n=26). The survey was optional to the students at each grade level. Numbers of participants included 39 NSS Hispanic/Latinos and 30 White middle class NES students.

Data Sources

The researchers analyzed qualitative and quantitative data for triangulation, including classroom observations of student interactions, student surveys, and a teacher reflection.

Instrumentation. The instruments used to measure peer interaction of NSS and NES students were as follows: a) 5 hours of classroom observations of student interactions during their instructional time (Spanish social studies), b) student surveys for one class at each grade level (grades 6-8), and c) a teacher reflection completed after the teacher reviewed the student survey data. Lesson observations were helpful in documenting the student engagement during classroom instruction. The researchers wrote field notes on student interactions during five-one hour social studies sessions during spring semester. Middle school students completed an optional survey pertaining to their sociolinguistic and sociocultural interactions in class (See Appendix A). This survey was administered by their bilingual teacher. The teacher completed a reflection after examining the student surveys for her three classes (grades 6-8).

The instruments for this research study represented tools currently used in the field to collect information about peer interactions. The tools were appropriate to the context of the research, as well as the populations and settings represented in the study. The teacher was familiar with the use of classroom observations and reflecting on student outcomes. None of the instruments used during the data collection phase were of foreign nature to the teacher or intrusive to the student learning environment. The purpose was to minimize disruption to normal classroom practices and routines. The middle school teacher administered the optional student surveys.

Results and Discussion
Student Surveys
Results from student surveys demonstrated preferences for language use. Overall, students in all grade levels had a preference for using both languages in their daily interactions. However, for the NES students, the use of English was mostly preferred in their oral communication with no references made to using only Spanish. While the NSS preferred to communicate in both languages, they conversed in Spanish-only less than 25% of the time, although this decreased through the grade levels as the preference for English use increased (see Figure 1). By 8th grade, the Spanish-dominant students reported speaking in Spanish-only conversations about 6% of the time. A summary of student survey statements follows:

English Proficient Middle School Students
- To think in another language makes me a better student (6th grade NES student).
- It is not a chance; it is an honor to learn another language (7th grade NES student).
- I love learning Spanish and English (8th grade NES student).

Spanish Proficient Middle School Students
- When you know two languages, you open up to the world more and are less ignorant (6th grade NSS student).
- Both languages will help you get further in life (7th grade NSS student).
- Learning two languages makes me more valuable (8th grade NSS student).

It is evident from the findings that the middle school students value learning two languages. In their statements, students alluded to becoming better students, understanding more about the world and prospering in life by knowing two languages. Although all students preferred to use both languages when speaking, it is evident that they also overwhelmingly preferred to use English more often than Spanish (see Figure 14.1).

Other data reported by the students included *who they liked to work with during class time*. Students had the following choices on the survey: English Speaker, Spanish Speaker or the language does not matter. When students were asked about their language preference when working with their peers on class assignments, 68%-100% of the students in all grade levels selected "language does not matter" (See Figure 14.2). English-dominant students

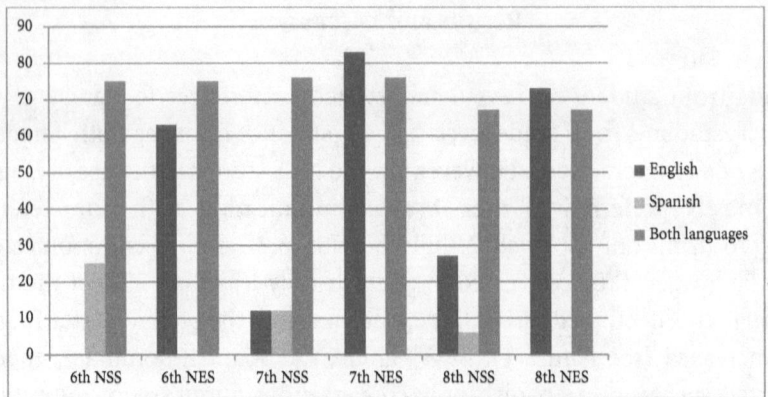

Figure 14.1. I Prefer to Speak...

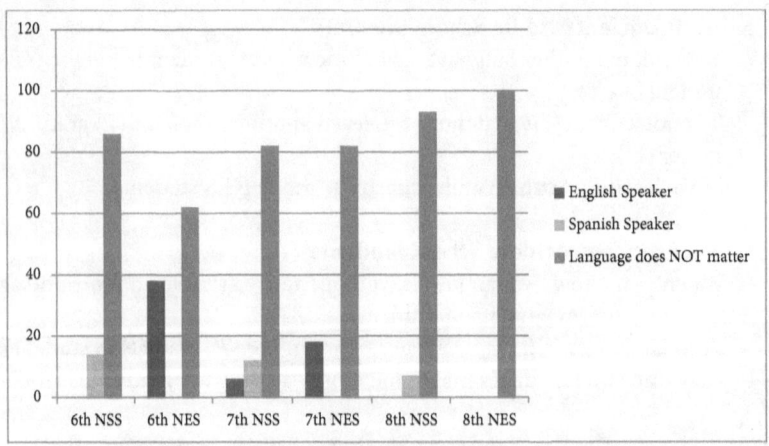

Figure 14.2. I Like to Work With a Student Who is...

also preferred to work with English speakers 18%-38% of the time, while Spanish-dominant students selected to work with Spanish-speakers 7%-14% of the time. This preference also decreased through the grade levels. The students wrote the following statements on their surveys about each other:

Middle School Students - Native English Speakers
- Spanish speakers will have a good job and life and I hope they continue to work hard (8th grade NES student).
- It's a bond that we will always have (7th grade NES student).

- I feel English speaking people are smarter (7th grade NES student).
- People who speak Spanish make fun of people (7th grade NES student).
- I don't care about people who speak another language (7th grade NES student).

Middle School Students – Native Spanish Speakers
- It is hard when there is nobody to help you (8th grade NSS student).
- I can communicate with them in any language (8th grade NSS student).
- People now understand what I say (7th grade NSS student).
- I am jealous of English speakers—they know the language better than me (7th grade NSS student).
- You have more in common (7th grade NSS student).
- They are hard workers, and will get far in life (6th grade NSS student).

After examining the student comments, the researchers concluded that there appeared to be positive comments about one another, but also noticed some innuendos related to strained perceptions towards each other. Most comments made by the students seemed very positive towards the program's cross-cultural goals, such as students stating that they were developing a bond between them, had more in common, and wished each other well in life. However, there statements also referred to one group being more intelligent than the other, not caring for speakers of other languages, Spanish speakers making fun of others, or being jealous of one another.

Teacher Reflection
The students' bilingual teacher wrote a reflection after examining the survey data. The teacher believed all students (NSS and NES) were respectful and patient with one another during class discussions by listening attentively to the speakers and allowing sufficient wait time to allow speakers to communicate an idea. The teacher reported that all students collaborate during group time by distributing the responsibilities of the task evenly and demonstrating a sibling-like attitude towards each other. Usually, one to two students lead or facilitate a group activity and are willing to help struggling students with the task. The teacher also stated students tended to support one another by keeping each other in check with the assignments and mentoring a classmate that needs extra assistance. Due to the nature of their collaboration and support for others, the teacher reported that she tends to nominate her students for leadership roles in school service clubs, such as

the Associate Student Body (ASB), Where Everybody Belongs (WEB), and Community Kindness. She felt her TWBI students (both NSS and NES) had a better sense of working and mentoring linguistically and culturally diverse students than non-TWBI students in her other classes. The teacher wrote in her reflection, "TWBI students set an example for student leadership on our campus." Additionally, she stated, "I saw in the data that almost half of the students said they felt proud or very proud of speaking another language and using the language to help others."

The nature of the TWBI student sociolinguistic and sociocultural interactions also sets them apart from others, because they tend to be very social and talkative in class. The teacher stated, "If for any reason there is a substitute in class, they will use the time to socialize rather than work. I normally receive a note that will say 'class chatty & off-task' even though they are typically hard workers." The teacher reported that all TWBI students tend to have a democratic nature, "If one student proposes an idea, then others will feel like they either get to vote on the new idea or can propose an idea themselves." Teacher noted, "Although they tend to socially group themselves as native and non-native Spanish speakers, they are unprejudiced and recognize injustice more easily than my non-TWBI students."

Researchers' Observations

Through open coding comparison of data (reflection and open-ended questions on the student surveys), categories emerged. Researchers grouped the topics by characteristics to generate four main themes related to student dispositions of cross-cultural equity (See Table 14.1). Two main arching themes identified as sociolinguistic and sociocultural interactions served as the headings for the following categories: 1) Conscious *positive* behaviors of discourse; 2) Conscious *negative* behaviors of discourse; 3) Valuing social justice in group interactions; 4) Resistance to/lack of social justice in group interactions.

In positive behaviors of discourse, students were highly engaged in their group activities making conscious efforts to communicate clearly with one another, facilitated conversations in either language to clarify concepts, and assisted one another in completion of the tasks. During the negative behaviors of discourse, the students were shifting languages for their own purposes. This shifting was not intended to facilitate interactions, but seemed

Table 14.1
Student Dispositions on Sociolinguistic and Sociocultural Interactions

Students ELs/EP	Sociolinguistics: Conscious **positive** behaviors of discourse	Sociolinguistics: Conscious **negative** behaviors of discourse	Sociocultural: **Valuing** social justice in group interactions	Sociocultural: **Resistance to/lack of** social justice in group interactions
EP	Clarification of vocabulary Facility in expressing viewpoints Preference to use both languages when speaking	Domination of conversation Argumentative at times Language shift (Spanish to English) Difficulties in maintaining high levels of Spanish Lack of respect for Spanish language	Interest to complete work together in Spanish Waiting their turn during group work	Preference to complete work alone when in English Controlling of group activity Competiveness in group Seeking teacher attention Lack of interest in learning Spanish in upper grades Lacking democratic decision-making Some appreciation of multiple perspectives
EL	Willingness to collaborate ideas Primary language use Translating for others	Reverting use of L1 for L2 Conforming to power language (English) Allow EP to dominate conversations Jealousy towards others' languages	Democratic attitude Respectful to others' contributions	Assimilation to dominant cultural ways Adhering to subordinate roles Complacency
EP & EL	Negotiation of task Opportunities to practice languages with each other Analyzing similarities in languages Safe environment to take risks in languages Authentic opportunities to use language Demonstrating engagement in biliteracy tasks	Lacking strategies on how to manage conversation in small group interactions Need to create a safe climate for conversations View English as language of power	Engaging in cooperative learning strategies Alternating group roles Taking turns Listening to others Joint projects/goals Cooperation to complete tasks (co-construct knowledge) Making cultural connections to personal lives Learning about themselves and others Learning community Sharing leadership	Not getting along during small group structures Lack cultural knowledge of others Interacting inappropriately with students unlike themselves Thinking about bias, prejudice and/or stereotyping Needing compassion for learning community Need for conflict management

argumentative during the tasks, and revealing a need for strategies on how to facilitate group interactions in the target language.

Results also demonstrated student value of social justice in their group interactions when they had a vested interest to complete the tasks together, democratic and respectful attitudes towards everyone, and work to establish a sense of community. Characteristics of resistance or lack of social justice during group engagement became apparent when students controlled group activities or demonstrated competitiveness, dominant groups emerged and disrespected others, students refused to work with a group or seek teacher help. More detailed descriptions of the dispositions can be found on Table 14.1.

Data analysis revealed ways in which students created cross-cultural pathways towards equity, particularly when students used personal dispositions around the distribution of power during interactions. Findings examined peer interactions as a critical process for transformation and the potential for change in students who have been historically marginalized in their own learning communities. The following dispositions emerged through constant comparison of data sources pertinent to equity (see Figure 14.3). Students who exhibited positive sociolinguistic dispositions had excellent interpersonal and communicative skills and also demonstrated sociocultural dispositions by their ability to develop a community of practice. The process indicated that both sets of dispositions could theoretically affect cross-cultural equity.

Sociolinguistic and Sociocultural Dispositions

The researchers defined the following terms around the student dispositions necessary to attain cross-cultural equity based on the results of the surveys and the teacher's reflection. The researchers identified five dispositions listed under sociolinguistics (negotiator, respectful, facilitator, social and listener) and six outlined for sociocultural (democratic, understanding, supportive, collaborator, compassionate and unprejudiced). The dispositions are described as the following:

Sociolinguistic Dispositions
- *Negotiator*—is a student who confers with another or others in order to come to terms or reach an agreement or consensus during group work. This student allows others to provide their perspectives. Negotiations are conducted in a respectful manner.

- *Respectful*—is a student who is characterized by demonstrating politeness and respect towards others' contributions, their native language and/or cultural ways. This student will listen to others and wait his/her turn without dominating the group activity or conversation.
- *Facilitator*—is a student who makes progress easy in a group by encouraging others, prompting students, seeking engagement from others, and sustaining the conversation in the target language and topic. This student is key to the group dynamics, leadership, and monitoring interactions.
- *Social*—is a student who can easily engage others in a conversation and encourages participation from the group. This student enjoys the company of others and is friendly towards diverse students.
- *Listener*—is a student who listens to others and pays attention while others are speaking. This person confirms others through body language (eye contact, shaking head in agreement, smiling, taking notes, etc.)

Sociocultural Dispositions
- *Democratic*—is a student who advocates democracy for others, believes in practicing social equality, seeks benefits for everyone.
- *Understanding*—is a student who is compassionate, appreciates or shares the feelings and thoughts of others; demonstrates sympathy, can come to mutual agreement on something, sees others' perspectives, is tolerant.
- *Supportive*—is a student who provides emotional support or assistance to others in groups, displays affirmation or acceptance towards other students, has a positive attitude
- *Collaborator*—is a student who can work together, especially in a joint intellectual effort, and joins with others in some activity or endeavor to complete a task.
- *Compassionate*—is a student who feels or shows compassion; expresses sympathy towards others; feels genuine concern and interest in others, kind, tender-hearted
- *Unprejudiced*—is a student who is free from prejudice or bias; impartial; without preconception of others, open-minded, uninfluenced by others

Educational Significance
This study examines peer interactions as a critical process for transformation of power between impoverished and middle class students. Examination of the interpersonal dispositions of students in TWBI programs demonstrates

the difficulty of attaining cross-cultural equity and equal status of languages during student engagement. At times, students in this study experienced challenges maintaining social equity.

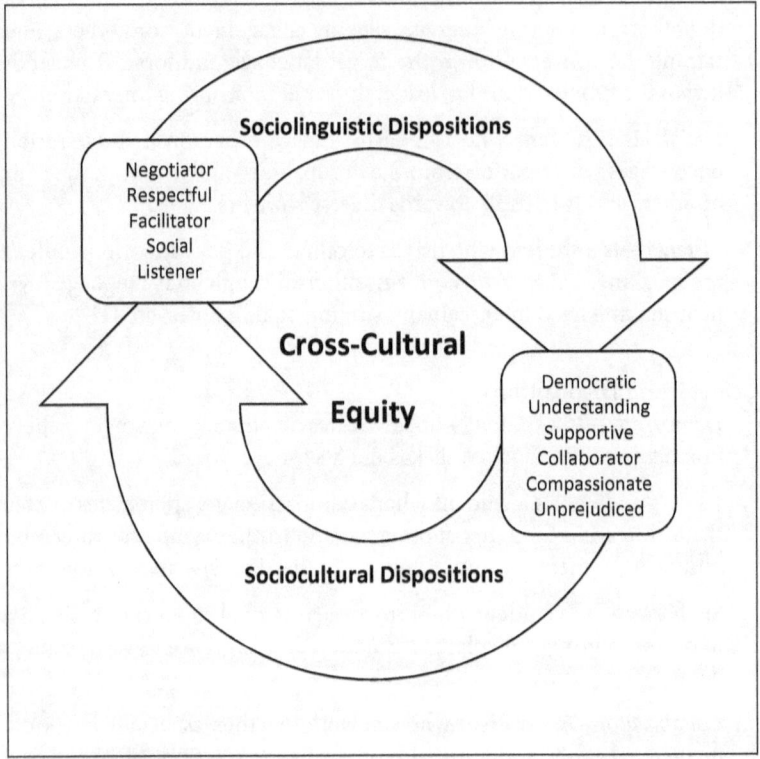

Figure 14.3. Cross-Cultural Equity Dispositions

Results from this study document the social and linguistic implications of interactions between low SES Hispanic/Latino NSS and White middle class NES students in TWBI. Although the stated goal of TWBI programs is to ensure positive social interactions and cultural appreciation across diverse groups of students, it is clear from this research that the goal is far from achieved. The findings indicate some inequities in cultural and linguistic capital between NSS and NES peers in TWBI programs. These inequities further limit pathways to forms of capital that the impoverished and marginalized students who are classified as English learners already experience. Giroux (1988, p. 94) explains that student "discourse of cordial relations" must come from pedagogical practices around the goal of encouraging healthy expression and harmonious social relations in school. Freire (1970) stresses the importance of teaching students how to read the word and the world. In TWBI programs, NSS and NES students have the opportunity to learn from one another, and together learn about the world they live in from multiple perspectives. By addressing cross-cultural equity in students' dispositions, TWBI can cultivate global citizens who can apply the knowledge they learn to their experiences both in the classroom and beyond (Banks, 2003; Lindholm-Leary & Genesee, 2010).

The unique findings from this study addressed teacher perceptions of language status and peer interactions in a TWBI middle school program through an inside look at student perspectives about language and social interactions in grades 6-8. The teacher also seemed concerned that English and Spanish speakers could perceive the status of Spanish as subordinate to English. One of the implications of this study is that educators can further examine student discourse and analyze new strategies to foster a more culturally relevant pedagogy in their programs (Ladson-Billings, 1995). Additionally, understanding how students think about both languages and perceive their peer interactions may inform programs on how to better serve their needs.

Policy and Instructional Implications

Emphasis on state and district assessments and language policies that promote English as the prestigious language in schools can create barriers for motivating students to acquire higher levels of Spanish. The study notes a need to develop strong sociolinguistic aptitudes in TWBI programs to augment the vigor of the target/heritage language use in the classroom. Programs must encourage strong academic participation from Spanish speakers by providing a nonthreatening environment without dominance of one linguistic group over another. Hence, teachers need to ensure positive participation of Spanish speakers and encourage vitality of the native language in group interactions.

Examining student sociolinguistic and sociocultural dispositional behaviors lead to several instructional implications. By identifying these behaviors, teachers can encourage positive behaviors of discourse between NSS and NES students. For example, creating group activities in which students can develop negotiation and facilitatation skills in Spanish can lead to greater equity of the use and perception of Spanish by students. Similarly, by identifying positive sociocultural dispositional behaviors, teachers can create instructional strategies and group activities that help students value social justice and equity in their interactions. Activities that foster positive sociocultural behaviors, such as understanding, being supportive, and compassionate and unprejudiced, allow students to interact in a democratic way where both NSS and NES student contributions are valued in Spanish and English. By explicitly addressing student sociolinguistic and sociocultural dispositions in their instruction, teachers are building a classroom in which cross cultural equity can flourish.

Further Research Needed
There is the need for more research on the impact of language status in the classroom and how it can affect positive and negative issues of social justice and equity for both language groups. Social capital and group empowerment should be further explored in TWBI. More research needs to be conducted on language status attributes and possible associations to marginalization of culturally and linguistically diverse groups in the classroom.

There is scant research on middle school education in TWBI. Future studies conducted in this area could also inform educators of linguistic and cultural capital amongst native English and native Spanish speakers. Lindholm-Leary and Genesee (2010) viewed TWBI programs as systems that are essential to reducing prejudice and discrimination as they provide modes of cultural and social interactions to facilitate relationships in diverse settings and prepare students as global citizens with a competitive edge. TWBI programs provide immense possibilities to combat marginalization and stigmatization of linguistically diverse populations, by raising the status of the target/heritage language in their school communities.

References
August, D., & Hakuta, K. (1997). *Improving schooling for language minority children: A research agenda*. Washington, DC: National Academy Press.
Banks, J. (2003). Teaching literacy for social justice and global citizenship. *Language Arts, 81*(1), 18-19.

Björklund, S. (2005). Toward trilingual education in Vaasa/Vasa, Finland. *International Journal of the Sociology of Language, 1*, 23-40.

Björklund, S., & Mard-Miettinen, K. (2011). Integrating multiple languages in immersion: Swedish immersion in Finland. In Tedick, D. J., Christian, D., & Fortune, T. W. (Eds.) *Immersion education: Practices, policies, possibilities* (pp. 13-35). Bristol, England: Multilingual Matters.

Bourdieu, P. (1986). The forms of capital. In Richardson, J. (Ed.), *Handbook of theory and research for the sociology of education* (pp. 241-258). New York: Greenwood Press.

Bourdieu, P. (1991). *Language and symbolic power*. Cambridge, MA: Harvard University Press.

California Department of Education. (2011). *Educational demographics unit*. Retrieved on http://www.cde.ca.gov/dataquest

Center for Applied Linguistics. (2012, July). Directory of two-way bilingual immersion programs in the U.S. Retrieved from http://www.cal.org/twi/directory

Collier, V. (1995). Directions in language education. *National Clearinghouse for Bilingual Education, 1*(4), 1-8.

Creswell, J. (2008). *Educational research: Planning, conducting, and evaluating quantitative and qualitative research* (3rd ed.). Boston: Pearson.

Cummins, J. (1994). Primary language instruction and the education of language minority students. In Leyba, C. (Ed.) *Schooling and language minority students* (2nd edition, pp. 3-50). Los Angeles: Evaluation, Dissemination and Assessment Center.

De Jong, E. (2006). Integrated bilingual education: An alternative approach. *Bilingual Research Journal, 30*(1), 23-44.

DeMarrais, K. B., & LeCompte, M. D. (1999). *The way schools work: A sociological analysis of education*. New York: Addison Wesley Longman.

Fitts, S. (2006). Reconstructing the status quo: Linguistic interaction in a dual-language school. *Bilingual Research Journal, 29*(2), 337-365.

Freire, P. (1970). *Pedagogy of the oppressed*. New York: Continuum International Publishing Group Inc.

Gallavan, N. (2011). *Navigating cultural competence in grades 6-12: A compass for teachers*. Thousand Oaks, CA: Corwin.

Giroux, H. (1988). *Teachers as intellectuals: Toward a critical pedagogy of learning*. Massachusetts: Bergin & Garvey Publishers, Inc.

Grbich, C. (2007). *Qualitative data analysis: An introduction*. Thousand Oaks, CA: Sage.

Hernández, A. (2011) *Successes and challenges of instructional strategies in two-way bilingual immersion*. Unpublished doctoral dissertation, University of California, San Diego.

Howard, E., Sugarman, J., Christian, D., Lindholm-Leary, K., & Rogers, D. (2007). *Guiding principles of dual language education rating template: Strand 3, instruction, action plan*. (2nd ed.). Washington, DC: US Department of Education and National Clearinghouse for English Language Acquisition. Retrieved from http://www.cal.org/twi/guidingprinciples.htm

Jang, E., & Jimenez, R. (2011). A sociocultural perspective on second language learner strategies: Focus on the impact of social context. *Theory Into Practice, 50*, 141-148.

Ladson-Billings, G. (1995). Toward a theory of culturally relevant pedagogy. *American Educational Research Journal, 32*(3), 465-491.

Lindholm-Leary, K. (2001). *Dual language education*. Clevedon, England: Multilingual Matters.

Lindholm-Leary, K. (2005). *Review of the research and best practices on effective features of dual language education programs*. Washington, DC: Center for Applied Linguistics and the

National Clearinghouse for English Language Acquisition on Education, Diversity and Excellence.

Lindholm-Leary, K., & Genesee, F. (2010). Alternative educational programs for English learners. In California Department of Education (Eds.) *Improving education for English learners: Research-based approaches* (pp. 323-382). Sacramento, CA: CDE Press.

McCollum, P. (1999). Learning to value English: Cultural capital in a two-way bilingual program. *Bilingual Research Journal, 23*(2&3), 113-134.

Miles, M., & Huberman, M. (1994). *Qualitative data analysis.* (2nd ed.). Thousand Oaks, CA: Sage.

Nieto, S., & Bode, P. (2008). *Affirming diversity: The sociopolitical context of multicultural education* (5th ed.). Boston: Pearson Education, Inc.

Palmer, D. (2008). Diversity up close: Building alternative discourses in the two-way immersion classroom. In Fortune, T. W. and Tedick, D. J. (Eds.) *Pathways to multilingualism: Evolving perspectives on Immersion Education* (pp. 97-116). Clevedon, England: Multilingual Matters.

Preskill, H., & Catsambas, T. (2006). *Reframing evaluation through appreciative inquiry.* Thousand Oaks, CA: Sage.

Tarone, E. (2007). Sociolinguistic approaches to second language acquisition research – 1997-2007. *The Modern Language Journal, 91*, 837-848.

Tarone, E., & Swain, M. (1995). A sociolinguistic perspective on second language use in immersion classrooms. *The Modern Language Journal, 79*, 166-178.

Vygotsky, L. (1978). *Mind in society: The development of higher psychological processes.* Cole, M. (Ed). Cambridge, MA: Harvard University Press.

Yin, R. (2009). *Case study research: design and methods* (4th ed.). Thousand Oaks, CA: Sage.

Appendix 14A

Student Survey: Dual Language Immersion, Middle Level, Grades 6-8

1) Write your grade level: _____

2) My native language is…   ___English ____Spanish ____other language (_____)

3) At home, I speak mostly…   ___English ____Spanish _____ both ____other (_____)

4) At school, I speak mostly…   ___English ____Spanish _____ both ____other (_____)

5) I prefer to speak…. ____English ____Spanish _____ both _____ other (_____)

6) When I speak with my friends outside of class, I prefer to use… __English __Spanish __both __other (_____)

7) This is how I feel about my culture and language… __very proud __proud __somewhat proud __not proud

8) This is how I feel about learning a second language & culture… __very proud __proud __somewhat proud __not proud

9) During **Spanish** activities in class, I speak in **Spanish** to my *group or partner*… (select one answer)
  ____ all the time   ____most of the time   ____some of the time   _____not at all

10) During **English** activities in class, I speak in **English** to my *group or partner*… (select one answer)
  ____ all the time   ____most of the time   ____some of the time   _____not at all

11) I pick my friends by… (select one answer) __ language __race/culture __what we like to do __how we get along ___popularity

12) During nutrition or lunch time, I like hanging out with …. (select one answer)
  ___ students who are like me ___ students who are different than me ____ doesn't matter
  ____ no one

13) When I need help in **English**, I usually…
  _____ a) Ask a student who speaks English
  _____ b) Ask a student who speaks Spanish
  _____ c) Ask a student who is bilingual
  _____ c) Ask the teacher
  _____ d)Look around the room
  _____ e) None of the above, I usually_____

14) When I need help in **Spanish**, I usually…
  _____ a) Ask a student who speaks Spanish
  _____ b) Ask a student who speaks English
  _____ c) Ask a student who is bilingual
  _____ c) Ask the teacher
  _____ d) Look around the room
  _____ e) None of the above, I usually_____

15) In class, I like to work with a student who is …. (select one answer)
  _____English speaker   _____Spanish speaker   _____ the language does not matter

16) When I am working with a group in **Spanish**…
_____a) I listen and wait for my turn.
_____b) I interrupt the group in order to speak.
_____c) I do most of the talking in the group.
_____d) I let the group talk and tell me what to do.
_____e) I switch from Spanish to English.
_____f) none of the above, I usually _____

17) When I am working with a group in **English**…
_____a) I listen and wait for my turn.
_____b) I interrupt the group in order to speak.
_____c) I do most of the talking in the group.
_____d) I let the group talk and tell me what to do.
_____e) I switch from English to Spanish.
_____f) none of the above, I usually _____

18) This is my **strongest** language(s) when I … (put an **X** under your choice for each one)

	Spanish	English	Both	Other language (_____)
a) read	_____	_____	_____	_____
b) write	_____	_____	_____	_____
c) speak	_____	_____	_____	_____
d) think	_____	_____	_____	_____

19) I feel the most **important** language(s) is … (put an **X** under your choice for each one)

	Spanish	English	Both	Other language (_____)
a) at home	_____	_____	_____	_____
b) at school	_____	_____	_____	_____
c) in your neighborhood	_____	_____	_____	_____
d) to you	_____	_____	_____	_____
e) for your future	_____	_____	_____	_____

20) During class activities in **English**, I prefer to work … (select one answer)
____with the whole class   ____in a small group   ____with a partner   ____by myself

21) During class activities in **Spanish**, I prefer to work … (select one answer)
____with the whole class   ____in a small group   ____with a partner   ____by myself

22) I get along with other students in class… (select one answer)
____all the time   ____most of the time   ____some of the time   ____not at all

23) I care about what my friends in class think about me.   ____Yes ____No

24) I feel supported in class by… ___ Spanish speakers   ___ English speakers   ___ everyone
____no one

25) I like helping… ___ Spanish speakers ___ English speakers   ___ either (doesn't matter)
____no one

On a separate piece of paper, please write about…

26) What are your feelings about learning **English, Spanish or both** languages?

27) What are your feelings about students who speak **English, Spanish or both** languages?

LANGUAGE POLICY AND SOCIAL JUSTICE

CHAPTER 15

LANGUAGE RIGHTS FOR MEXICAN AMERICANS AND THE TREATY OF GUADALUPE HIDALGO

Eduardo D. Faingold
University of Tulsa

Several indigenous minorities inhabit the United States and its territories. One indigenous minority is the Mexican American, who trace their lineage to the Mexicans who were living in the American Southwest at the time of annexation by the United States of more than half of the Mexican territory (this includes the states of Arizona, California, Nevada, New Mexico, Utah, and parts of the states of Colorado, Kansas, Wyoming, and Oklahoma). Other indigenous groups include Puerto Ricans, American Indians, native Hawaiians, the Chamorro people of Guam, and other Pacific Islanders. None of these groups voluntarily joined or became a territory of the United States. Yet although from time to time some of them have raised the issue of independence, especially in Puerto Rico, they generally have been content with signing treaties that granted them some degree of autonomy or special rights within the United States. With the exception of the Mexican Americans of the Southwest, all of the conquered minorities mentioned above have obtained special powers of self-government, including language rights. For example, in both the State of Hawaii and Guam, the indigenous languages, Hawaiian and Chamorro respectively, have equal status with English in schools, courts, and other dealings with government. Similarly, in Puerto Rico, Spanish and English are co-official languages (Kilty & Vidal de Haymes, 2000; Kymlicka, 1995).

It was not for lack of trying that Mexican Americans failed to obtain language rights in the Southwest. The historical record demonstrates that since the beginning of the occupation of the Southwest, Mexican Americans fought to obtain language rights for Spanish speakers. For example, in 1848 in California, Mexican Americans succeeded in passing a constitutional measure to have all state laws and regulations translated into Spanish. But only a few years later, in 1855, the California legislature refused to provide for the translation of laws into Spanish (Weber, 2003).

In New Mexico, because Mexican Americans were numerically dominant, they successfully opposed public schools and opted instead for parochial schools, where Spanish was the language of instruction. Thus, in 1890 Mexican Americans in New Mexico voted strongly against statehood because a new constitution threatened the parochial school system. In 1912, when New Mexico gained statehood and its 1910 constitution took effect, Spanish speakers obtained the constitutional right to vote, hold public office, have access to bilingual teachers, and sit in juries regardless of their ability to speak, read, or write in English. The Mexican Americans of New Mexico succeeded in making these language rights permanent because at the time of enactment, the New Mexico constitutional assembly made these provisions difficult to amend. On the other hand, in Arizona and Texas, Mexican Americans, who were numerically inferior and consequently lacked political power, were unable to produce language legislation to protect their right to use Spanish in public (Weber, 2003).

A consensus exists among academics and activists that the language rights of Mexican American speakers of Spanish in the Southwest are protected by the Treaty of Guadalupe Hidalgo (hence, the Treaty). This idea has been accepted not only by leading scholars of the Treaty (e.g., Flores & Murillo, 2001; Martinez-Brawley & Zorita, 2001; San Miguel & Valencia, 1998), but also by important Mexican American activists (e.g., Lopez Tijerina, 2000; Rendon, 1971) and influential theorists in language policy (e.g., Kymlicka, 1995).

This paper argues that those who advocate for the language rights of Mexican Americans in the southwestern states of the United States are protected by the Treaty are mistaken. I demonstrate that a close reading of the Treaty reveals that it cannot be used in an American court of law to protect the linguistic rights of Spanish speakers. This is because the text of the Treaty, as ratified by both the U.S. and Mexican governments, makes no mention of civil rights, or even language or culture rights. Thus, I submit that the Treaty is not the correct legal instrument to argue in favor of linguistic rights for Spanish speakers in the United States. Rather, more sound arguments can be made under more modern civil rights legislation, such as Titles VI and VII of the Civil Rights Act of 1964 (Faingold 2006; 2011; 2012a; 2012b; 2013a; 2013b).

Violations of and Modifications to the Treaty of Guadalupe Hidalgo
Article VIII of the Treaty of Guadalupe Hidalgo ("Treaty of Guadalupe Hidalgo", 2013) granted U.S. citizenship to Mexican Americans living in the Southwest at the time of annexation. However, a large part of the population in the annexed territories included Mexican Americans who had Indian ancestry. In violation of the Treaty, these individuals were not granted U.S. citizenship, nor did they receive the constitutional protections of Article VIII of the Treaty, which were automatically given to all Mexican Americans of European ancestry living in the annexed territories (Luna, 1999; Meeks, 2007; Nieto-Phillips, 1999).

> **Article VIII**
> ... those who shall prefer to remain in the said territories may either retain the title and rights of Mexican citizens, or acquire those of citizens of the United States. But they shall be under the obligation to make their election within one year from the date of the exchange of ratifications of this treaty; and those who shall remain in the said territories after the expiration of that year, without having declared their intention to retain the character of Mexicans, shall be considered to have elected to become citizens of the United States.
>
> In the said territories, property of every kind, now belonging to Mexicans not established there, shall be inviolably respected. The present owners, the heirs of these, and all Mexicans who may hereafter acquire said property by contract, shall enjoy with respect to it guarantees equally ample as if the same belonged to the United States.

In California, the Indian tribes were deprived of the protections specified in the Treaty, and they became the victims of murder, slavery, and starvation. Their population declined by more than 100,000 in twenty years as white people overran their tribal lands and committed genocide. Moreover, many Mexican Americans guaranteed American citizenship under the Treaty had

Indian ancestry or were dark skinned, but in a unanimously-adopted proviso at the first meeting of the California legislature in 1848, the new California constitution restricted suffrage to white citizens exclusively (Wilson Moore, 2003). Similarly, in the Territory of New Mexico, where most of the Indian population lived, citizenship was limited to white people until statehood in 1912 (Griswold del Castillo, 1990; Nieto-Phillips, 1999). As early as 1863, the Arizona legislature limited voting rights to "white men and white Mexican men," thereby excluding Mexican Americans of Indian ancestry (Glenn, 2002, p. 159). In these ways, within a generation of the Treaty, Mexican Americans of Indian decent in the annexed territories became a disenfranchised, poverty-stricken minority (Anna, 1993; Griswold del Castillo, 1990).

Soon after the Treaty's ratification, the U.S. legal system was used to violate whatever meager protections the Treaty provided to protect the property and civil rights of Mexican Americans in the territories. Local laws were deemed to supersede the Treaty (Griswold del Castillo, 1990). Most importantly, the Supreme Court, in violation of the U.S. Constitution (Article VI.2, Article III.2.1), which gives international treaties that have been ratified by the U.S. Senate and the President of the United States the same status as the Constitution, incorrectly claimed that U.S. laws take precedence over international treaties (Griswold del Castillo, 1990). As a result, the Treaty was not enforced when the property and civil rights of Mexican Americans were at stake.

The intent to deny rights to Mexican Americans living in the territories was evident even as the Treaty was being ratified. For instance, Article X protected land grants made by Mexico to its citizens in the annexed territories but was entirely stricken by the U.S. Senate during the ratification process.

Draft of Article X Before Ratification
All grants of land made by the Mexican Government or by the competent authorities, in territories previously appertaining to Mexico, and remaining for the future within the limits of the United States, shall be respected as valid, to the same extent that the same grants would be valid, if the said territories had remained within the limits of Mexico .... (Griswold del Castillo, 1990, pp. 180-181)

That the Treaty was modified to deny property rights to Mexican Americans holding land grants in what is today the Southwest of the United States comes as no surprise, because the U.S. Army effectively was occupying more than half of Mexico, including Mexico City, at the time. And yet, the United States was following its own legislation to the letter, since according to the U.S. Constitution, the U.S. Senate has the power to amend a treaty, and strike and change articles at will ("U.S. Constitution", 2009).

Mexico could have refused to ratify the Treaty after the U.S. Senate amended it, but the Mexican government chose to ratify it. Obviously, Mexico had little choice in the matter. The Treaty was in fact a *diktat*, rather than a negotiated agreement between equals, as indicated by the fact that during negotiations, the U.S. Army was occupying most of Mexican territory, including Mexico City, the nation's capital.

The deletion of Article X created chaos among Mexican American holders of land titles in California, resulting in promulgation of the Federal Land Act of 1851, which opened Mexican American lands to litigation in American courts. Thus, as a result of fraud, manipulation, and indebtedness, nearly 40 percent of the land held by Mexican Americans in California before 1840 was transferred to American ownership, forcing marginalized Mexican Americans into wage labor and ultimately, poverty (Wilson Moore, 2003).

Similarly, when the draft of Article IX, which aimed to protect the civil rights of Mexican Americans, was submitted to the U.S. Senate for ratification, the words "civil rights" were replaced by the word "religion" and the phrase "admitted as soon as possible" was replaced by the expression "at the proper time." Also, at the time of ratification, the U.S. Senate deleted from Article IX of the draft Treaty ("Treaty of Guadalupe Hidalgo", 2013) legal wording granting Mexican Americans political rights equal to those obtained by French and Spanish citizens in Louisiana and Florida in the aftermath of the Louisiana Purchase from France (1803) and the Adams-Onis Treaty with Spain (1819), respectively. Clearly for the U.S. Senate, to paraphrase George Orwell, in the treaty-making process, some nations were more equal than others.

Draft of Article IX Before Ratification
The Mexicans who, in the territories aforesaid, shall not preserve the character of citizens of the Mexican Republic, conformably with what is stipulated in the preceding Article, shall be incorporated into the Union of the United States, and **admitted as soon as possible**, according to the principles of the Federal Constitution, to the enjoyment of all the rights of citizens of the United States. In the meantime, they shall be maintained and protected in the enjoyment of their

liberty, their property, **and the civil rights now vested in them according to the Mexican laws**. (Griswold del Castillo, 1990, pp. 179-80)

Article IX
The Mexicans who, in the territories aforesaid, shall not preserve the character of citizens of the Mexican Republic, conformably with what is stipulated in the preceding article, shall be incorporated into the Union of the United States and be **admitted at the proper time** (to be judged of by the Congress of the United States) to the enjoyment of all the rights of the citizens of the United States, according to the principles of the Constitution; and in the meantime, shall be maintained and protected in the free enjoyment of their liberty and property **and secured in the free exercise of their religion without restriction.**

Not surprisingly, Mexican historians have used the Treaty of Guadalupe Hidalgo to argue that the United States purposely violated the civil rights of Mexican Americans in the annexed territories. A study of the Mexican War and the Treaty of Guadalupe Hidalgo by the well-known Mexican historian Gastón García Cantú notes that the Mexican government at the time was deeply concerned about the rights of its citizens remaining in the United States. He notes that Mexican diplomats at the time of signing the treaty were very much aware that the destiny of thousands of its citizens in the United States would be discrimination and contempt, but the Mexican diplomats had no means to stop the Americans from violating the rights of Mexican Americans in the annexed territories (García Cantú, 1971).

Language Rights and the Treaty of Guadalupe Hidalgo
A close reading of the Treaty reveals that neither Article IX nor any of its articles ("Treaty of Guadalupe Hidalgo", 2013) are designed to protect the linguistic rights of Mexican Americans in the territories annexed by the United States after the Mexican-American War. That is, the text of the Treaty, as ratified by both the U.S. and Mexican governments, makes no mention of civil rights, let alone language and culture rights.

Nevertheless, there is broad consensus among scholars of the Treaty of Guadalupe Hidalgo that Spanish speakers in the Southwest are protected by it, especially by Article IX. For example, San Miguel & Valencia (1998) misquote the Treaty when they argue that the right of Spanish speakers to maintain their language through bilingual education, and the right to use Spanish in public are protected by Article IX of the Treaty:

> The subtraction of Spanish from public education was accomplished through the enactment of English-language policies at the state and local levels, which not only prescribed English as the medium of instruction in the schools, but also discouraged, inhibited, or prohibited the use of Spanish. [...] They also violated the Treaty of Guadalupe Hidalgo, which guaranteed Mexican Americans "the enjoyment of all the rights of citizens of the United states," *including the right to maintain their language* [emphasis added].

Freeman (1975), admits that "the treaty does not explicitly refer to either culture or language"; yet without offering any arguments to support his claim, he states that "the Treaty of Guadalupe Hidalgo can be interpreted as *protecting the colonists' and their descendants' use of Spanish* [emphasis added]" (p. 26). Similarly, Flores & Murillo (2001) state, also without offering any arguments to support their claim or citations from the Treaty, that "[t]he Treaty of Guadalupe Hidalgo [...] *accorded to protect the language rights* of Mexicans living in the newly annexed and conquered territories of the U.S. Southwest [emphasis added]" (p. 202). Similarly, Rendon (1971) states that "culture, *language* and religion [emphasis added]" are rights due to Mexican Americans under the Treaty (p. 71). In the same vein, Martinez-Brawley & Zorita (2001) argue that the "Treaty of Guadalupe Hidalgo guaranteed the right of the former Mexican citizens to *maintain their culture and, by extension, their language* under the flag of the USA [emphasis added]" (p. 59).

Finally, and most importantly, the consensus that the Treaty protects the language rights of Mexican Americans in the Southwest has made its way to authoritative language policy works. Thus, for example, Kymlicka (1995) mistakenly states that "[l]anguage rights were also guaranteed to Chicanos [Mexican Americans] in the south-west [sic] under the 1848 Treaty of Guadalupe Hidalgo" (p. 12).

In spite of the fact that the Treaty of Guadalupe Hidalgo, as we have seen, lacks the necessary legal language to protect the language rights of Mexican Americans in the United States, in 1969, in Tijerina v Henry (48 F.R.D 274), Reies Tijerina, using the Treaty as a legal instrument, brought a class-action lawsuit against New Mexico's State Board of Education on behalf of poor Mexican Americans of Indian ancestry in The United States District Court of New Mexico. In his lawsuit, Reies Tijerina demanded a reapportionment of boards of education as well as the teaching of all classes in both English and Spanish (see further, Lopez Tijerina, 2000). The District Court ruled against Reies Tijerina. In its ruling, the Court found that he had misinterpreted the scope of the Treaty when basing his suit for bilingual education on Articles VIII and IX of the Treaty (see above). The court ruled (48 F.R.D. 274) that the "Treaty between the United States and Mexico did not contemplate administration of public schools or confer any proprietary right to have Spanish language and culture preserved in public schools, and did not furnish basis for purported class action to have all subjects and all classes taught in both English and Spanish."

In 1970, soon after the ruling by the District Court, Reies Tijerina appealed his case to the United States Supreme Court (398 U. S. 922 90 S. Ct. 1718). The Supreme Court dismissed the case, stating that the "Appellant's claim that 'the Treaty of Guadalupe Hidalgo specifies that a certain class of individuals are entitled under it to the preservation of their language and culture'... is wholly unsubstantiated by the Treaty itself. Even if the Treaty read as Appellants wish it did, it could not, under any stretch of the imagination, be so construed..."

In a dissenting opinion, Justice Douglas argued that, although the Treaty was not the right legal instrument in Reies Tijerina's case, the case could have merit on civil rights grounds, especially under the Thirteenth and Fourteenth Amendments to the United States Constitution (398 U. S. 922 90 S. Ct. 1718; see, also, Delgado & Palacios, 1975).

As one expert in civil rights legislation explains, long after the signing of the Treaty,

> The Civil Rights Act [of 1964] transformed the legal landscape by outlawing discrimination and by creating legal remedies to battle discrimination. The Act enabled Mexican Americans to pursue a strategy both more likely to win substantive results and more likely to lead to cooperation with other minorities ... Civil rights legislation, enabled, for example, a new push for bilingual educational services. (MacLean, 2007, pp. 125-130)

Language Rights for Spanish Speakers in the United States

The lack of linguistic protections in the Treaty does not mean that Mexican Americans and Spanish speakers in general lack legal recourse to argue for language rights in the Southwest or elsewhere in the United States. Language discrimination cases have been argued using the U.S. Constitution and the

Civil Rights Act of 1964 (see Faingold 2006; 2011; 2012a; 2012b; 2013a; 2013b; and references therein); the Voting Rights Act of 1965, which outlaws English literacy tests ("Voting Rights Act", 2009); the Bilingual Education Act of 1968, which was allowed to expire in 2002 under President George W. Bush; and Executive Order 13166 given by President Clinton in 2000 to federal agencies which says that people who are LEP (limited English proficient) should have meaningful access to federally-conducted and federally-funded programs and activities ("Executive Order #13166", 2013).

A significant number of language discrimination cases have been won by Spanish speakers under Titles VI and VII of the Civil Rights Act of 1964. For example, in 1974 the Supreme Court held that school districts receiving federal funds have an obligation under Title VI of the Civil Rights Act of 1964 to assure that students are not excluded from meaningful participation in school programs on the basis of national origin.

Title VII of the Civil Rights Act has provided the grounds on which many linguistic- rights cases have been won. In 1999 a District Court in California ruled against Lenox Health Care and Vencor, who prohibited employees from speaking languages other than English in a nursing home. In 2000 a District Court in Texas ruled against Premier Operator Services for firing Hispanic employees who refused to sign an English-only agreement to prevent them from speaking Spanish at any time, including breaks. In 2000 the Federal Court in Illinois settled in favor of Hispanic employees of Watlow Batavia, which had disciplined workers for speaking Spanish with co-workers on an assembly line. In 2006 the 10th Circuit settled in favor of Hispanic employees of the City of Altus, Oklahoma, which had prohibited Hispanic employees from speaking English at all times (Faingold, 2006; 2011; 2012b; and references therein).

Conclusion

As a result of the Mexican-American War (1846-1848), Mexico lost more than half of its territory to the U.S. through the Treaty of Guadalupe Hidalgo (1848). As I show in this paper, the consensus among scholars of the Treaty is that the language rights of Mexican Americans in the Southwest are protected by it, especially by Article IX. However, a close reading of the Treaty reveals that neither Article IX nor any other article is designed to protect the linguistic rights of Mexican Americans in the annexed territories. Thus, the

Treaty of Guadalupe Hidalgo is deemed to be the wrong legal instrument to protect the language rights of Mexican Americans. Rather, this work suggests that stronger arguments in favor of language rights for Mexican Americans can be made under the 14th Amendment of the U.S. Constitution ("U.S. Constitution", 2009) and more modern civil rights legislation, such as Titles VI and VII of the Civil Rights Act of 1964 ("Civil Rights Act of 1964", 2009; see, also, Faingold, 2012b).

Acknowledgements

Revisions of this paper have benefited from comments by audiences at the 40th Annual meeting of the Linguistics Association of the Southwest, Brownsville, Texas, October 2011, and the International Society for Language Studies, San Juan, Puerto Rico, June 2013. This research was supported in part by two University of Tulsa Faculty Grants in 2010 and 2013.

References

Anna, T. E. (1993). Demystifying early nineteen-century Mexico. *Mexican Studies / Estudios Mexicanos, 9*, 119-37.

Civil Rights Act of 1964. Retrieved from http://usinfo.state.gov.usa/info/laws/majorlaw/civilr19.htm

Delgado, R., & Palacios, V. (1975). Mexican Americans as a legally cognizable class under rule 23 and the Equal Protection Clause. *Notre Dame Law Review, 50*(3), 393-203.

Executive Order #13166. Retrieved from http://www.stpaul.gov/FAQ.aspx?QID=878

Faingold, E. D. (2006). Expert witness report: Code-switching in the workplace. *Maldonado v. City of Altus*, 433 F. 3d 1294 (10 Cir. 2006).

Faingold, E. D. (2011). Code-switching in the work-place: The linguistic rights of Hispanics in the United States. In Comisión de Lingüística (Eds.), *Comunicación Social en el Siglo XXI* (Vol. 1) [Social communication in the 21st century]. Santiago de Cuba, Cuba: Centro de Lingüística Aplicada.

Faingold, E. D. (2012a). Official English in the constitutions and statutes of the fifty states in the United States. *Language Problems and Language Planning, 36*, 136-148.

Faingold, E. D. (2012b). Language rights in the United States Constitution and the Civil Rights Act of 1964. In Miller, P. C., Watzke, J. L., & Mantero, M. (Eds.), *Readings in language studies (Volume 3): Language and identity* (pp. 447-457). Grandville, MI: International Society for Language Studies.

Faingold, E. D. (2013a). Devolution in Wales as a road map for the Southwest of the U.S. Paper presented at the 24th Conference on Spanish in the United States and 9th Conference on Spanish in Contact with Other Languages. McAllen, TX. March 6-9, 2013.

Faingold, E. D. (2013b). Official English in the constitutions and legislative statutes of the 50 states in the United States. Paper presented at the 19th International Congress of Linguists. Geneva, Switzerland. July 22-27, 2013.

Flores, S. Y., & Murillo Jr., E. G. (2001). Power, language and ideology: Historical and contemporary notes on the dismantling of bilingual education. *The Urban Review, 33,* 183-206.

Freeman, L. D. (1975). The students' rights to their own language: Its legal bases. *College Composition and Communication, 26,* 25-29.

García Cantú, G. (1971). *Las invasiones Norteamericanas en México* [The North American invasions in Mexico]. Mexico, D.F: Ediciones Era.

Glenn, E. N. (2002). *Unequal freedom: How race and gender shaped American citizenship and labor.* Cambridge: Harvard University Press.

Griswold del Castillo, R. (1990). *The treaty of Guadalupe Hidalgo: A legacy of conflict.* Norman, OK: University of Oklahoma Press.

Kilty, K. M. (2000). Racism, nativism, and exclusion: Public policy, immigration, and the Latino experience in the United States. *Journal of Poverty, 4,* 1-25.

Kymlicka, W. (1995). *Multicultural citizenship.* Oxford: Oxford University Press.

Lopez Tijerina, R. (2000). *The called me "King Tiger": My struggle for the land and our rights.* Houston, TX: Arte Público Press.

Luna, G. T. (1999). On the complexities of race: The Treaty of Guadalupe Hidalgo and Dredd Scott v. Sandford. *University of Miami Law Review, 53,* 691-716.

MacLean, N. (2007). The Civil Rights Act and the transformation of Mexican American identity and politics. *Berkeley La Raza Law Journal, 18,* 123-134.

Martinez-Brawley, E. E., & Zorita Paz, M. B. (2001). Latino immigrants in the borderlands: Transcultural lessons from the academy. *International Social Work, 44,* 55-73.

Meeks, E. V. (2007). *Border citizens: The making of Indians, Mexicans, and Anglos in Arizona.* Austin: University of Texas Press.

Nieto-Phillips, J. (1999). Citizenship and empire: Race, language, and self-government in New Mexico and Puerto Rico. *Centro Journal, 11,* 51-74.

Rendon, A. B. (1971). *Chicano manifesto.* New York, NY: Collier Books.

San Miguel, Jr., G., & Valencia, R. (1998). From the Treaty of Guadalupe Hidalgo to Hopwood: The educational plight and struggle of Mexican Americans in the Southwest. *Harvard Educational Review, 68,* 353-412.

Treaty of Guadalupe Hidalgo. Retrieved from http://www.ourdocuments.gov/doc.php?doc=26&page=transcript

U.S. Constitution. Retrieved from www.senate.gov/artandhistorycommon/briefings/treaties.html

Voting Rights Act of 1965. Retrieved from http://www.ourdocuments.gov/doc.php?flash=true&doc=100

Weber, D. J. (2003). *Foreigners in their native land. Historical roots of the Mexican Americans.* Albuquerque, NM: University of New Mexico Press.

Wilson Moore, S. A. (2003). "We feel the want of protection". The politics of law and race in California, 1848-1878. *California History, 81,* 96-125.

CHAPTER 16

LANGUAGE POLICY AND SOCIAL JUSTICE IN QUÉBEC

Patrick-André Mather
Universidad de Puerto Rico, Rio Piedras

Québec is a predominantly French-speaking province within Canada, and its language policies have evolved over the past 40 years from official bilingualism to French monolingualism. Most prominent among language laws adopted by the government is the Charter of the French Language ("Bill 101"), which imposes the use of French in virtually every sphere of activity in the province. This law has had a profound effect on Québec society, enabling Francophones to have access to jobs that, traditionally, had been occupied mainly by the English-speaking elite (Bourhis, 1984). On the other hand, some of the articles of Bill 101 have been denounced as discriminatory against English-speakers, for example the ban on the use of English in commercial signs or restrictions on access to English-language public education. These perceived injustices have been blamed for the exodus of over 100,000 English Québeckers in the late 1970s and early 1980s, mainly toward Ontario. This paper discusses issues related to the social and economic consequences of language legislation in Québec over the past four decades, with reference to the economics of language framework developed by scholars such as Grin (1996, 2003), which identifies and measures economic benefits and drawbacks of specific language policy decisions.

Legal Framework of Québec's Language Policies
The language legislation of Québec represents an attempt to strike a balance

between the linguistic communal rights of Francophones, and individual linguistic rights as guaranteed by the Canadian Constitution. After a century of official bilingualism, in 1973, French was adopted as the official language of Québec by the Liberal (federalist) government of Robert Bourassa, under Bill 22. Even though this measure was largely symbolic, it created considerable resentment among the English-speaking community, who perceived it as an attempt to limit Anglophone rights in the province and restrict the use of their language in the workplace and in public service. This discontent contributed to the defeat of the Liberal government in the 1976 provincial elections.

In 1977, following the election of the separatist Parti Québécois, the Charter of the French Language (Bill 101) imposed the French language in all spheres of public life, with some exceptions for the English-speaking minority such as English-language public schools and hospitals, and a bilingual status for English-majority municipalities. This new law went considerably further than Bill 22, since it imposed French as the sole language in public and commercial signs, required all immigrants to send their children to French-medium public schools, and required all members of trade corporations (such as doctors, lawyers, notaries, etc.) to pass a French-language exam. While English-speakers were allowed to keep their institutions (e.g. public schools and universities, hospitals), the number of English-language schools decreased significantly over the following decades due to the new restrictions on enrollment. Universities and hospitals were not affected since no restrictions were imposed at that level.

Throughout the 1980s, Québec's language laws were challenged in Federal courts, which invalidated some articles of Bill 101, including the restriction on the use of languages other than French in commercial signs. In 1987 however, the federalist Liberal Party of Québec adopted a new law (Bill 178), which overrode the Canadian Constitution (using the "Notwithstanding clause") by maintaining French-only requirements on commercial signs. This measure sent shockwaves throughout Québec and Canada, since the law was adopted not by the separatist Parti Québécois, which was defeated in the 1985 provincial elections, but by the federalist Liberal Party. Again, English-speakers felt betrayed by the party which had traditionally defended their interests, but seemed to be siding with the Parti Québécois on linguistic issues. This suggests that even though Francophones were and remain divided on the issue of independence, there appears to be greater consensus on the need to protect and promote the French language.

On the federal level, Canada's official policy of bilingualism and multiculturalism, adopted under Prime Minister Pierre Trudeau's government by virtue of the 1969 "Official Languages Act", contrasts sharply with Québec's assimilationist policy of French monolingualism and integration of immigrants to the French-speaking community. In principle, the federal law provides each Canadian citizen the possibility of using French or English anywhere in Canada, which includes access to public education and government services in his/her language. In particular, federal law provides specific protections for official-language minorities (Anglophones in Québec and Francophones in the rest of Canada). Québec language laws, by contrast, seek to impose a territorial view of language rights, where French is the only official language in Québec, and where English-language rights are restricted to specific areas such as bilingual municipalities. This tension is reflected in the various challenges to Québec's language laws before the Canadian Supreme Court, by Anglophones who feel humiliated by restrictions on public signs, but also by some Francophones who feel that they are discriminated against for not having the right to send their children to English public schools in Québec.

It should be noted that Québec-style monolingualism policies are common in several European countries like Belgium, and even in the United States where, even though there is no official language at the federal level, English monolingualism policies have been adopted in 30 American states (Bourhis, 2010, p. 785). Nevertheless, within the Canadian context, Québec's language laws remain very controversial and, in some respects, incompatible with both the Canadian Charter of Rights and the Canadian Official Languages Act.

Some researchers have discussed the notion of Linguistic Human Rights (e.g., Grin, 2005), which are meant to protect minority speakers whose linguistic heritage is threatened. Should Francophones in Québec be viewed as a linguistic minority within the Canadian context, in which case language legislation such as the Charter of the French Language seems appropriate, or should they be viewed as a majority within the Québec context, in which case French-only language laws can be viewed as oppressive toward the Anglophone linguistic minority in that province? The next section deals with the issue of economic and social justice, and how these are related to language policies in Québec.

Economic Differences Between Francophones and Anglophones

Over the past decades, the socio-economic status of English and French speakers in Québec has evolved (Vaillancourt, 1996) and the income gap between these communities has been greatly reduced since the implementation of Bill 101 in the late 1970s. Language policy has also impacted relations between speech communities in Québec (Larrivée, 2003).

Within the Interactive Acculturation Model (IAM), Bourhis (2010) analyzes societies where immigrants have to choose between competing host communities, and more specifically the city of Montreal where, even though Anglophones are technically a minority, they represent a majority within the wider Canadian context and thus represent a challenge to the Francophone community's ability to attract and integrate immigrants. Typically, immigrant groups are torn between the desire to maintain their own language and identity, and the need to integrate into the host community in order to reap the economic benefits of speaking the majority language, to achieve upward social mobility.

In Québec, and particularly in Montreal, immigrants face a more difficult choice given the competition "at the top" between Francophone and Anglophone host communities. Many immigrants become functionally trilingual, but eventually choose between French and English as their main language of daily interaction. Even though English-speakers represent only 8% of the Québec population (their numbers have declined steadily over the past 30 years—see Table 16.1), they remain a substantial minority in Montreal, and even an outright majority in some of the upscale Western suburbs of the City which have official bilingual status, an exception permitted under Québec law. The most striking contrast in Table 16.1 below is the fact that the Anglophone population has fallen between 1971 and 2001, not only as a percentage of the Québec population, but also in absolute numbers. This is due in large par to the exodus of some 150,000 Anglophones in the late 1970s, following the election of the first separatist government in 1977.

In his work on the economics of language, Grin (1996) shows how income (the dependent variable) is related to the linguistic background of speakers (the independent variable). In particular, he demonstrates that income differences between Anglophones and Francophones have decreased in the 1970s, although bilingual Francophones still earn more that French monolinguals. This suggests that English remains a vector for economic progress in Québec, including among Francophones, and that despite efforts by the government to "francize" the workplace, English has not been displaced by French, but is competing with it on a more equal footing than in the previous decades. This is consistent with the dominant position of English in North America as a whole, and explains why, for example, bilingual Latinos in the United States have an economic advantage over monolingual Spanish speakers, even in heavily Hispanic cities like Miami or Los Angeles (Chiswick and Miller, 1992).

Table 16.1
Approximate English-Speaking Population of Québec, 1765–2001 (Canada 1871–2001)

Date	Population	Percentage of Québec total
1765	1,000	1.3
1792	10,000	5.8
1851	221,000	24.0
1881	260,000	19.1
1911	315,000	15.9
1941	460,000	14.0
1971	790,000	12.0
2001	627,000	8.7

Note. Source: Dickinson (2007, p. 13).

In Québec province, the income gap between French and English speakers has decreased dramatically between 1970 and 2000, which suggests that Francophones have made some important headway towards employment equality. In fact, some researchers (Nadeau, 2010) suggest that, in the Québec public sector, Anglophones may have been discriminated against, since Francophones in that sector enjoyed a wage premium that may reflect more than a higher relative demand for French skills. Nadeau goes further and suggests that this premium may have also been present in Québec's private sector in 2000, meaning that Québec's Anglophones in 2000 were in a similar position as Francophones in 1970 (i.e., that becoming bilingual does not guarantee equal access to the market premium for each group). This being said, in 2010 Anglophones still earned, on average, more than Francophones in Québec.

An Evaluation of Québec's Language Policies Over Forty Years
Despite the risks and drawbacks for the English-speaking community, language policy and planning in Québec has had a positive impact in terms of social justice, education and economic opportunities for the population as a whole, as measured in terms of median income, level of education, language proficiency, and cross-cultural communication. One benefit is the fact that the intergenerational maintenance of immigrant languages (56%) is twice as high in Québec than in the rest of Canada, suggesting that the competition between host languages favors multiculturalism. If one of the goals of language policies is to promote linguistic diversity and protect minorities, then the effect of Québec's French-only language policies over the past 40 years can be viewed as positive, even though these effects were not necessarily foreseen by those who drafted the policies, who had a more assimilationist agenda.

Ironically, after almost 40 years of languages policies favoring French monolingualism, Québec is more bilingual and multicultural than ever: many English-speakers send their children to French immersion schools (voluntarily), and young Francophones are learning English at higher rates thanks to increased access to higher education, including access to English-language colleges and universities. This may not be the explicit goal sought by successive nationalist governments in Québec, but French-only language policies have not only promoted greater opportunity for Francophones, but also a higher rate of bilingualism and multilingualism among Francophones, Anglophones and Allophones (speakers of languages other than English and French). This is shown by sociolinguistic studies such as Bourhis (2010).

Québec's language laws have been criticized because of their supposed negative economic impact. In terms of the overall cost of language policies, Vaillancourt (1978, 1987) shows that, contrary to popular belief, the economic cost of Québec's language policies is modest, below 0.5% of the province's GDP. Grin estimates the total economic cost of implementing

Québec's language policies at between 0.28% and 0.48% of GDP (Grin, 2005, p. 454). These numbers are important factors in the overall assessment of language policies, since detractors often mention the economic cost as an argument against the implementation of such policies. Given the consensus among Francophones on the need for some legal protection of the French language, it seems that, as a whole, the Québécois are willing to pay the (modest) economic price of implementing language policies.

Conclusion

Despite the risks and drawbacks for the English-speaking community, language policy in Québec has had a positive impact in terms of social justice, education, economic opportunities, and cross-cultural communication. The stated objectives of Québec's language laws, in particular the Charter of the French Language (1977), was to promote French as the sole language of Québec. By this benchmark, the policy has failed, since the rate of bilingualism and multilingualism has increased over the past decades, and English remains an important language in education and in the workplace, especially in bilingual/multicultural Montréal. However, if the policy is evaluated against different criteria, in short, if bilingualism, social justice and cultural diversity are seen as a positive outcome, then one can argue that Québec's Charter of the French Language is a resounding success.

References

Bourhis, R. (Ed.). (1984). *Conflict and language planning in Québec*. Clevedon, England: Multilingual Matters.

Bourhis, R. (2001). Reversing language shift in Québec. In Fishman, J. A. (Ed.), *Can threatened languages be saved?* (pp. 101-141). Clevedon, England : Multilingual Matters.

Bourhis, R. (2010). Acculturation in multiple host community settings. *Journal of Social Issues*, 66(4), 780-802.

Chiswick, B., & Miller, P. W. (1992). Language in the labor market: The immigrant experience in Canada and the United States. In Chiswick, B. (Ed.), *Immigration, language and ethnicity, Canada and the United States* (pp. 229-296). Washington: American Enterprise Institute.

Dickinson, J. (2007). The English-speaking minority in Québec: A historical perspective. *International Journal of the Sociology of Language*, 185, 11-24.

Grin, F. (1996). Economic approaches to language planning. *International Journal of the Sociology of Language*, 121, 1-16.

Grin, F. (2003). Language planning and economics. *Current issues in language planning,* 4(1), 1-66.

Grin, F. (2005). Linguistic human rights as a source of policy guidelines: A critical assessment. *Journal of Sociolinguistics*, 9(3), 448-460.

Larrivée, P. (Ed.). (2003). *Linguistic conflict and language laws: Understanding the Québec question*. Basingstoke: Palgrave Macmillan.

Nadeau, S. (2010). Another look at the Francophone wage gap in Canada: public and private sectors, Québec and outside Québec. *Canadian Public Policy / Analyse de politiques, 36*(2), 159-179.

Schmid, C., Zepa, B., & Snipe, A. (2004). Language policies and ethnic tensions in Québec and Latvia. *International Journal of Comparative Sociology, 45*(3-4), 231-252.

Shapiro, D., & Stelcner, M. (1997). Language and earnings in Québec: Trends over twenty years, 1970-1990. *Canadian Public Policy, 23*(2), 115-140.

Vaillancourt, F. (1996). Language and socioeconomic status in Québec: Measurement, findings, determinants, and policy costs. *International Journal of the Sociology of Language, 121*, 69-92.

CHAPTER 17

ANALYSING LANGUAGE POLICY TEXTS:
A Two-Pronged Approach

Dilhara D. Premaratne
The Australian National University

A new trend emerged in language policy (LP) research in recent years with the recognition that relevant decision making is influenced by socio-political and economic factors rather than by purely linguistic reasons (Cooper, 1989; Ricento, 2000; Tollefson, 1991; Wiley 1999; Williams, 1992). The new approach views language planning as not "ideologically neutral" (Pennycook, 1995, p. 39; Williams, 1992, p. 123), or "empty of ideological content" (Tollefson, 1991, p. 11). As language policies are seen as safeguarding the interests of powerful groups in society and promoting their views and ideologies, the new trend looks for ideologies, values, and views that may lurk behind language policies disguised as solutions to language problems (Hornberger, 2006, Tollefson, 1991).

Social Justice Issues Caused by LP Decisions

A characteristic feature of the new approach to LP is focusing on social justice issues that have been caused by specific views and ideologies that influenced LP decisions. Chief among these is the theory of modernization which specified "modern" as having features of the western states to which the researchers belonged, while "traditional" was identified as lacking in these features (Williams, 1992). Therefore, most LP practitioners saw traditional languages as requiring modernization (Eastman, 1983). A related theory concerns the spread of English to non-English speaking countries, which is based on the widely accepted belief that English is a tool for modernization. This belief fails to take into account the inequality and exploitation that the spread of English causes in developing countries (Tollefson, 1991).

Linguistic unification, language standardization and monolingualism have also been usually prescribed "as panaceas for socio-economic ills" (Wiley, 1999, p. 17). However, when a language or a language variety functions as a gatekeeper for employment and/or higher education, it becomes "a key marker of socio-economic class and power" (Tollefson, 1991, p. 136). This leads to the marginalization of certain dialects and minority languages, the destruction of linguistic diversity, the loss of language rights, and the creation and sustenance of socio-economic inequality (Bokhorst-Heng, 1999; Chen, 1996; Donahue, 1995; Wiley, 1999; Williams, 1992).

In addition to examining the inequality and exploitation caused by certain language policies, scholars have also focused on how ideological processes are produced and reproduced in societies and how they impact language policies (Auerbach, 1995; Blommaert, 1999; Lo Bianco, 1999; Pennycook, 2001; Van Dijk, 1989, 1998). Reproduction of ideologies is seen as leading to normalization, that is to say a hegemonic pattern in which the ideological claims are seen as normal ways of thinking and acting. As discourse is identified as central among social practices that reproduce ideology, looking for manifestations of ideology in discourse is seen as an important role of the LP researcher.

Solutions for Social Justice Issues Caused by LP Decisions

The new LP research has also explored possible solutions to issues of social justice brought about by LP measures. An important step in this direction is empowering those affected by LP processes in various ways. The new research suggests that this can be done by providing knowledge and opening up opportunities for people to participate in the decision making process. First, agents at the micro- and meso-levels should be empowered to enable them to play a more proactive role in the decision-making process. Second, the target populations for whom particular policies are formulated should be enabled to participate in discussion and negotiation (Lo Bianco, 1999; McCarty, 2002; Ricento and Hornberger, 1996).

As factors that affect the participatory policy-making approach exist in many socio-political contexts, various strategies have been suggested to overcome such influences. The strategies are mostly in relation to empowering people to stand up against oppression by educating the public about the potential damage that can be caused by macro policies. Bringing to light issues of social justice caused by language policies is an important way in which LP scholars and researchers can make a contribution in this regard. One important way that this can be achieved is by analysing LP texts, such as official documents which explain or promote language policies, and media texts that review language policies, to surface social justice issues lurking beneath the texts (Donahue, 2002; Lo Bianco, 1999; Tollefson, 2002).

This paper views rigorous text analysis as necessary to reveal how information is controlled in language policy texts and how communication is used strategically to manage public opinion. To this end, the paper looks at two analytical frameworks—Cooper's language planning accounting scheme (1989) and Fairclough's critical discourse analysis framework (2003)—that can be used together effectively to reveal how public opinion is shaped in language policy texts to bring about policy change.

The Language Planning Accounting Scheme

Cooper's language planning accounting scheme (Cooper, 1989) is a robust framework that allows researchers to systematically assess the adequacy of the information given about a language planning situation. It is a comprehensive framework that helps to analyse a language policy under eight LP categories: the actors who did the planning, the behaviours they attempted to influence, the population they targeted, the ends that motivated them, the conditions under which they operated, the decision-making rules they used in policy formulation, the means they used to implement the policies, and the effect they achieved or hoped to achieve.

Cooper's LP accounting scheme helps to assess the adequacy of information provided in LP documents in two important ways. Firstly, it brings to light the extent of any inadequacy by surfacing the number of categories in a policy document that are not covered at all or are only partially covered. Secondly, the language planning accounting scheme identifies the categories on which adequate information is not provided and also exactly where they occur by pinpointing the sub-categories or other aspects that are lacking in information. Cooper's language planning accounting scheme can therefore be called an information-sensitive tool.

The CDA Framework

Fairclough's (2003) Critical Discourse Analysis (CDA) framework is shaped by a hybrid approach to discourse analysis. It brings together approaches that pay close attention to the linguistic features of texts and those that focus on the historical and social context of texts. The key features of the framework relevant for language policy analysis are Genre, Discourse, and Style. Genre concerns ways of (inter)acting, or relating, that is, what writers are doing discoursally, such as reporting, explaining, and persuading. Discourse concerns ways of representing or representations (i.e., how aspects of the world are represented). Style concerns ways of being, or social identities (i.e., how writers identify themselves in discourse).

The CDA framework helps to identify how genre is exploited in policy texts to bring about consent for policies. The genre that is commonly used in policy documents is the report genre. This genre entails a generalised description and is commonly used to limit policy options and portray the socio-economic order as simply given (Fairclough, 2003).

The report genre stands in contrast to exposition, a description of concrete events or processes, which is a genre that is rarely used in policy discourse. It gives concrete details about the exact times of events, how exactly they came about and where they happened. Inclusion of these elements makes the expository genre more concrete than the report genre previously discussed.

Persuasion is another genre that is commonly used in policy texts. A type of persuasive genre that is increasingly used in policy documents is the hortatory report genre. It is used to create merely an impression of a current situation rather than a concrete picture of the situation. Policy texts that use this genre often appear to be promotional than analytical, and is concerned more with persuading people that the proposed policies are the only practicable policies than with opening up dialogue (Fairclough, 2003).

The CDA framework also helps to surface how discourses are used as an effective strategy in policy documents. Discourses are powerful as they have the potential to achieve hegemony. It may be essential for a particular group that particular discourses gain hegemony and are assimilated into the target population (Fairclough, 2005a). The CDA framework facilitates the deconstruction of a developing hegemony of a discourse through inter-discursive analysis. Analysing the hegemonic construction of a discourse helps to expose the strategies used by particular groups to bring about changes in certain ways (Fairclough, 2005b).

The CDA framework also helps to expose how discourses are structured to achieve consensus. A common strategy that is used to win public approval is the exclusion of elements usually found in the representation of concrete events, such as social actors, times, places and the means of events. Such abstract representation helps to manufacture consent as it makes an undesirable situation appear as something that happens to people rather than something that is done to people (Fairclough, 2003). A similar effect is created by the use of nominalization which excludes participants in clauses, and shifts agency to abstract processes or entities that operate as nouns (Fairclough, 2003).

The CDA framework also makes apparent how identities are textured in policy documents. By analysing linguistic features such as vocabulary and metaphor, it helps to surface how writers commit themselves to truth claims (modality) and values (evaluation). One way that writers commit themselves to strong truth claims is by making predictions. The power of futurological predictions commonly made by influential people in policy texts is significant because injunctions about what people must do or not do now can be legitimised in terms of such predictions about the future.

Combined Use of the LP Accounting Scheme and the CDA Framework

The LP accounting scheme and the CDA framework can be used together to enrich the analysis of language policy discourse. The two analytical tools complement each other in several ways. The following section illustrates these by analysing four examples from a language policy text. The policy text that is analysed relates to the new Chinese script reform introduced in the People's Republic of China (China hereafter) in 2009. The analysed text was published by the Ministry of Education (MOE), which is responsible for the new script reform. The text will therefore be referred to as the MOE document. The new policy has introduced many changes to the existing script policy that are likely to be undesirable for the public and can be anticipated as one that will be difficult to sell. Information about the new policy is given below.

Script reform became necessary in China in modern times when the Chinese script began to pose challenges due to their logographic nature. The Chinese script is particularly challenging for mass literacy and computer use as it has a large number of characters. While it is difficult for ordinary people to recognise and produce characters, the number of characters required for contemporary writing vastly exceeds the number of keys on a standard computer keyboard.

To address some of the issues related to mass literacy, the Chinese script was simplified in 1956 by reducing the number of strokes in a large number of commonly used characters. An official list of characters, consisting of 7,000 characters was introduced later based on this initiative. To address the issues related to computer use, the Chinese script was simplified again in 2009 by reducing the number of characters that people can use. An official list of characters consisting of 8,300 characters was introduced for this purpose.

Although the previous list of characters had only 7,000 characters, this initiative did not restrict the use of characters to just those on the official list. This is because people had the opportunity to use any characters outside the official list as long as they did not have simplified versions. The new list, however, is based on a more stringent initiative for two reasons. First, it is implemented through a new law introduced for the purpose called the Language Law. Second, it restricts the use of characters to the specified characters on the list, and does not allow characters outside the list unless official permission has been obtained.

The list is likely to affect many sectors of society negatively. For example, the list will affect a large number of family names and place names, as some characters required for these names are not on the list. It will also affect the expressive power of the language, as characters necessary for certain words are not included on the list. If the new list applies to hand-written characters, it will affect writing in the public space because at present many characters outside the list are used for this purpose. Finally, it requires people to learn a large number of new characters in place of characters they had previously learnt.

One advantage of using the LP accounting scheme and the CDA framework together to analyse policy discourse is that the former exposes lapses in information provision in a policy document that are not picked up by the latter. For example, an LP document may prove to be expository and concrete when analysed by applying the CDA framework. Consequently, a researcher who uses this analytical tool may conclude that no attempt was made to manage public perceptions when presenting the policy. However, the document may lack vital information about certain aspects of the policy because it is to the advantage of certain groups to withhold that information. A researcher who uses the two analytical tools together will therefore be in a better position to judge whether public perceptions are managed in a language policy document. The description of the new character list in the MOE document is an example.

According to the CDA framework, the description of the character list uses exposition in terms of genre. Exposition is a description of concrete events or processes. While policy texts that use exposition can be seen as providing information without using persuasive techniques to manage public perception, texts that do not use exposition can be seen as limiting policy options and portraying the socio-economic order as simply given (Fairclough, 2003). Therefore, according to the CDA framework, exposition usually helps to open up dialogue in policy documents. As exposition is the genre used in the above description, it means that no attempt has been made to cover up any social justice issues caused by the policy.

However, when the LP accounting scheme is applied to the description of the new character list, it shows that the information provided is not wholly comprehensive. This can be seen in terms of two categories in the LP accounting scheme—the category of Behaviour and the category of Decision Making. Under the former, information needs to be provided about the structural properties and the functions of the planned behaviour. This information is important because it shows the extent of the changes made to existing policy. Under the latter, information needs to be provided about the reasons for the decisions made in relation to a particular policy, which includes information about how language planners select alternatives in an effort to standardize terminology, orthography, and so forth. This information is important because it is vital to an understanding of the inclusion and exclusion of items. However, the description of the new character list provides only some information under the above categories.

Under the category of Behaviours, the description specifies the number of tiers in the new list, the total number of characters, the type of characters, the number of characters contained in each tier and the function/purpose of the new list. Although it is stated that the new list will be implemented as the standard for character use in areas of common use in society, the status of hand-written characters is left to speculation. As hand-written characters are used in calligraphy and in public spaces, having to use only standard characters in these areas can have strong ramifications in Chinese society. Therefore, leaving this issue ambiguous and unclarified is in the interest of the policy makers who are keen to win public approval for the new policy.

Under the category of Decision Making, the description of the new character list provides information in relation to the selection of characters only for the new third tier. The public does not have any information as to why familiar characters were deleted from the other two tiers. As 500 characters have been deleted from the previous list, the information that is withheld relates to a substantial portion of the character list.

Another advantage of using the two analytical tools together is that the CDA framework exposes discursive strategies used to manage public perceptions that are not picked up by the LP accounting scheme. For example, an LP document may prove to be comprehensive in the provision of information about a policy. Therefore, a researcher who uses this analytical tool may conclude that a policy text or a particular section of a policy text is presented satisfactorily when essential information is provided. However, when the CDA framework is applied to the same section of the policy text, it may become apparent that discursive strategies were used to manage public perceptions. Using the two analytical tools together would therefore provide a more reliable way of uncovering any social justice issues caused by language policies. The following extract from the MOE document illustrates the ability of the CDA framework to pick up issues that the LP accounting scheme is not able to pick up.

The implementation of the List is an important measure that will facilitate the smooth implementation of the language law. This will be achieved by unifying and improving existing character standards, eliminating inconsistencies between various standards and unifying scattered standards, making a standard character policy and its legal impact clear and establishing the extension of the concept of "standard characters" mentioned in the Law to areas of common use. This will have the effect of spreading "the standard characters" mentioned in the Law of Common Language Use throughout general levels of society.

The above extract provides information about one of the benefits of the new policy. According to the description, the benefit is the unification of the many different character standards that are in use in Chinese society at present. According to the LP accounting scheme, this information belongs to the category of Effects and provides adequate and appropriate information under the given category. However, applying the CDA framework to the description brings about a different finding.

An inter-discursive analysis done under the CDA framework shows that a popular discourse is drawn upon in the above description, and is used skilfully to win public consent. The discourse that is drawn upon is that of character standardization which represents standardization as the solution to the challenges posed when adapting the archaic Chinese writing system to modern times.

The discourse of character standardization is identified by the word "standardization" which is used repeatedly in a number of different forms, such as "standardization", "standard" (as both noun and adjective), and "standards", used in combination with a variety of words (e.g., character standardization, script standardization, language standardization, a social standard, a new standard, past standards, character standards, scattered standards, various standards, standard characters, a standard character booklet, a standard character policy).

Semantic relations between words also help to distinguish discourses as they show how different discourses structure the world differently (Fairclough, 2003). In this description, semantic relations of equivalence and difference are created through a process of classification. This strategy helps towards creating and proliferating differences between objects, entities, groups of people, and so forth, and collapsing or subverting differences by representing them as equivalent to each other (Fairclough, 2003).

In the extract above, a relation of equivalence is first created between concepts related to past standards and then between concepts related to the new standard. Then, a relation of difference is created between the two categories. Both collocation (the pattern of co-occurrence of words) and hyponymy (the re-wording of a particular word or expression) are used to create a relation of equivalence between concepts related to past standards. For example, words such as "existing", "scattered" and "various" occur in collocation with the word "standards". Hyponomy is used to re-word "existing standards" as "scattered standards" and "various standards". Through re-wording, a relation of equivalence is textured between concepts that are not normally associated with each other (Fairclough, 2003), suggesting that standards established in the past and still existing today are diverse and not streamlined and therefore need to be replaced by a single uniform standard.

A relation of equivalence is created between concepts related to the new standard through words such as "a standard character policy", "the concept of standard characters", and "spreading the standard characters". The two categories of past and present standards are then placed in a simultaneous contrastive relation of difference. This textual process of meaning-making amounts to building up meaning around the concept of a new standard. It is an important element in the process of seeking to achieve hegemony for the state-approved character initiative.

A third advantage of using the two analytical tools in combination is that the LP accounting scheme can confirm the findings of the CDA framework and vice versa. For example, the LP accounting scheme may find that the information provided in a policy document about a particular category of the policy does not adequately cover that category. At the same time, the CDA framework may find that discursive strategies are used to manage public perceptions when presenting information about that category. As both analytical tools would identify issues in the presentation of this category, each would confirm the findings of the other. The following extract from the MOE document shows how the LP accounting scheme and the CDA framework help to confirm each other's findings.

The National Law of Common Language and Character Use of the People's Republic of China announced in October 2000 stipulates: "The country will promote *putonghua*, and promote standard characters," and also makes clear that "national organizations will adopt *putonghua* and standard characters as the working language and script." "Schools and other providers of education will teach *putonghua* and standard characters through their Chinese language courses. The Chinese resources used will meet the nation's character standards." Additionally, "the hospitality industry will adopt standard characters as the basic working script".

The above extract is a description of the manner in which the new Chinese character policy will be implemented. It sets out the principal means of implementing the policy as the Language Law introduced in the year 2000. The policy will be implemented through national organizations that will adopt *putonghua* (standard speech) as the official working language and the new list of characters as the official script. According to the LP accounting scheme, the above description provides information under the category of Means. However, it also provides information about the target population in an indirect manner. In the LP accounting scheme, Cooper mentions two types of target population. They are primary and secondary targets. As information about the target population is presented within information that belongs under the category of Means, attention is not adequately directed towards the target population. Therefore, while the primary targets come out only indirectly as national organizations, the secondary targets, the people who work in these organizations or use the services of these organizations, come out even less directly. In other words, attention is diverted from the people who will actually experience the consequences of the new policy. The effect this creates is favourable for the policy makers.

When the CDA framework is applied to the above description, it becomes clear that this description is also a strategic section of the policy document. This is achieved by excluding elements usually found in the representation of concrete events, such as social actors (participants in clauses which are not inanimate objects) times and places. The exclusion of social actors particularly helps to manufacture consent in policy documents. This is because diverting the reader's attention away from such actors can make an undesirable situation appear as impersonal (Fairclough, 2003).

In the above description, there is no social actor in the first sentence because the Language Law, which is the key participant, is not a social actor. In addition, the social actors that are included are not represented by name but by category, and as a group instead of as individuals (e.g., "other providers of education", "the hospitality industry"). The representation of social actors is mainly impersonal (e.g., the country, schools, national organizations), and the reference is more generic (e.g., 'the country', 'schools') than specific (e.g., 'our country', 'schools in regional areas'). Due to this abstract representation, no individual or individuals can be held responsible for the formulation or the implementation of the Language Law and the impact that it will have on society.

Finally, when the two analytical tools are used together, the CDA framework can clarify the findings of the LP accounting scheme and vice versa. For example, a researcher using the LP accounting scheme may find that the information provided in a particular area of a policy document is largely acceptable in terms of the existing information though more information could have been provided. The researcher may therefore waver when deciding whether to deem the information as acceptable. The uncertainty posed by such a situation may change if the CDA framework is applied and it reveals that discursive strategies have been used in the section to manage public perceptions. Applying the CDA framework would therefore clarify for the researcher that there is something going on in that particular part of the text that needs critical attention. The following extract from the MOE document illustrates this point:

> In the past 20 years, following the modernization of our country and the rapid development of informatization work, language use in our country changed dramatically. The development of scientific technology and the rise in the standard of education have caused scientific and technical terms to expand and enter people's daily lives. The breadth and depth of the link between language standardization and the development of society is unprecedented. The print industry has replaced mechanical printing with laser printing as the main means of publication. Family registers and dictionary compilers mainly use computers and the lack of characters and the presence of incorrect characters directly affect their publications and the quality of information...... In social life, government departments in charge of household registers, post offices, financial affairs, and insurance and the hospitality industry already use computers for data storage and retrieval. Therefore, non-standard personal and place names and rare characters affect the establishment of information systems in industries, inconveniencing the daily lives of people. Implementing a character standard that facilitates contemporary language use has already become an important event and will be something the masses will demand.

The above extract is a description of the factors that led to the new Chinese character policy. According to the LP accounting scheme, it provides information under the category of Conditions. According to the description provided, the major factor that prompted the new policy is the change that occurred in language use due to the modernization of Chinese society, namely, the expanded use of scientific and technical terms in daily life and the widespread use of laser printing and computer use (which required a new set of characters to be recognised as official characters). Although information has been provided under the category of Conditions, neither the explosion of scientific and technical terms in daily usage nor the extensive use of technology in producing printed documents is supported by evidence.

Therefore, a researcher using the LP accounting scheme may be faced with some uncertainty as to the acceptability of the information. In this situation, the CDA framework can be used for clarification.

When the CDA framework is applied to the description, it becomes apparent that strategies have been used in the section to manage public opinion. First, the description provides an account that merely creates an impression of the current character situation rather than a concrete picture of the situation. This is a feature of the hortatory report genre that is increasingly used in policy documents. To create this effect, time and place are frequently excluded from the description. For example, the social change that is said to be taking place in China is not represented as taking place in specific places or localities of the country (rural/urban, long-established/newly developed, and so forth), and the change in character use is not represented as taking place in specific domains of language use (advertising, fiction, and so forth) or in relation to particular users (scholars, professionals, students, and so forth). Similarly, socio-linguistic changes are not represented in terms of specific points in time or in terms of specific durations of time. In addition, participants in clauses are excluded through the use of nominalization to shift agency to abstract processes or entities that operate as nouns. As discussed before, nominalization is generally used in genres of governance because it can "obfuscate agency, and therefore responsibility" (Fairclough, 2003, pp. 132, 144). The exclusion of time, place and agency thus helps to create just an image of the current situation instead of a concrete picture.

Second, the above description constructs the current socio-linguistic situation in China as a critical problem that is facing the entire nation. Legitimization is used to create this effect. The type of legitimization used is mythopoesis (legitimization conveyed through narrative). This technique helps to conjure up a picture of a transformed China that has been swept over by a new wave of modernization. Although not a narrative, this particular use of legitimization can be considered a form of mythopoesis as it helps to create the impression of a socio-technical upheaval (Fairclough, 2003). The description consists of a number of claims about the changes that have taken place in the language and in the society, none of which are supported by any evidence. As a result, the reader is confronted by one unsupported claim after another within a short stretch of writing. Claims about the socio-linguistic changes that are said to have taken place in contemporary China help to legitimize the proposed policy. In other words, the new character policy is portrayed as inevitable by the way Chinese society now is. This strategy is now commonly referred to as the "TINA principle". The term is derived from the former British Prime Minister Margaret Thatcher's famous expression, "There is no alternative" (Fairclough, 2003, p. 99).

Conclusion

The recent interest generated in LP research about social justice issues caused by language policies and the recognition that a critical public eye needs to be developed to detect such issues early on is demanding critical analysis of policy texts by LP researchers. Sophisticated analytical tools are required to address this demand as equity issues are likely to be concealed in various ways in language policy documents. Withholding or limiting vital information and using special discursive strategies are common ways of managing public perceptions to keep equity issues hidden from the public eye. Cooper's language planning accounting scheme is an information-sensitive tool that is able to discern any attempts made in an LP document to manage the flow of information. Fairclough's CDA framework is a multi-faceted tool that is able to analyse policy discourse both linguistically and socially and bring to light ideologies, values and views that may lurk behind language policies disguised as solutions to language problems. Although they are both robust tools in their own domains, they have limited capacity when used alone as one cannot do the work of the other. Therefore, as argued in this study, using them in combination is an effective way of subjecting policy documents to rigorous textual analysis.

The benefits of the two-pronged approach to policy text analyses proposed in this study are two-fold. First of all, it helps to create a better-informed and more critical public citizenry (Donahue, 2002) by exposing equity issues hidden in language policy documents and how public attention is diverted from such issues through strategic policy discourse. Raising public awareness is a first step in helping the public play a more proactive role in relation to language planning matters.

A more discerning public that questions language policies would induce policy makers to a more transparent approach in policy documents. This would lead to providing information that is adequate for the full understanding of policies. It would also encourage the genuine use of exposition to explain policies rather than promoting them through persuasion or merely presenting them through reporting.

References

Auerbach, E. (1995). The politics of the ESL classroom: issues of power in pedagogical choices. In J. Tollefson (Ed.), *Power and inequality in language education* (pp. 9-33). Cambridge: Cambridge University Press.

Blommaert, J. (1999). The debate is open. In J. Blommaert (Ed.), *Language ideological debates* (pp.1-38). Berlin: Mouton de Gruyter.

Bokhorst-Heng, W. (1999). Singapore's speak Mandarin campaign: Language ideological debates and the imagining of the nation. In J. Blommaert (Ed.), *Language ideological debates* (pp. 235-65). Berlin: Mouton de Gruyter.

Chen, P. (1996). Modern written Chinese, dialects, and regional identity. *Language Problems and Language Planning, 20,* 223-243.

Cooper, R. (1989). *Language planning and social change.* Cambridge: Cambridge University Press.

Donahue, T. (1995). American language policy and compensatory opinion. In J. Tollefson (Ed.), *Power and inequality in language education* (pp. 112-141). Cambridge: Cambridge University Press.

Donahue, T. (2002). Language planning and the perils of ideological solipsism. In J. Tollefson (Ed.), *Language policies in education: Critical issues* (pp. 137-162). Mahawah, NJ: Lawrence Erlbaum.

Eastman, C. (1983). *Language planning an introduction.* San Francisco: Chandler & Sharp.

Fairclough, N. (2003). *Analysing discourse: Textual analysis for social research.* London: Routledge.

Fairclough, N. (2005a). Critical discourse analysis in transdisciplinary research. In R. Wodak and P. Chilton (Eds.), *A new agenda in (critical) discourse analysis* (pp. 53-70). Amsterdam: John Benjamins.

Fairclough, N. (2005b). Discourse analysis in organizational studies: The case for critical realism. *Organization Studies, 26*(6), 914-939.

Hornberger, N. (2006). Frameworks and models in language policy and planning. In T. Ricento (Ed.), *An introduction to language policy: Theory and method* (pp. 24-41). Malden, MA: Blackwell.

Lo Bianco, J. (1999). The language of policy: What sort of policy making is the officialization of English in the United States? In T. Huebner and K. Davis (Eds.), *Sociopolitical perspectives on language policy and planning in the USA* (pp. 39-65). Amsterdam: John Benjamins.

McCarty, T. (2002). Between possibility and constraint: Indigeneous language education, planning and policy in the United States. In J. Tollefson (Ed.), *Language policies in education: Critical issues* (pp. 285-307). Mahawah, NJ: Lawrence Erlbaum.

Pennycook, A. (1995). English in the world/The world in English. In J. Tollefson (Ed.), *Power and inequality in language education* (pp. 34-58). Cambridge: Cambridge University Press.

Pennycook, A. (2001). *Critical applied linguistics: A critical introduction.* Mahwah, NJ: Lawrence Erlbaum.

Ricento, T., & Hornberger, N. (1996). Unpeeling the onion: Language planning and policy and the ELT professional. *TESOL Quarterly, 30,* 401-428.

Ricento, T. (2000). Historical and theoretical perspectives in language policy and planning. *Journal of Sociolinguistics, 4,* 196-213.

Tollefson, J. (1991). *Planning language planning inequality.* London: Longman.

Tollefson, J. (2002). Critical issues in educational language policy. In J. Tollefson (Ed.), *Language policies in education: Critical issues* (pp. 3-15). Mahawah, NJ: Lawrence Erlbaum.

van Dijk, T. (1989). Structures of discourse and structures of power. In J. Anderson (Ed.), *Communication yearbook* (pp. 18-59). Newbury Park, CA: Sage. Retrieved from http://www.discourses.org/OldArticles/Structures%20of%20discourse%20and%20structures%20of%20power.pdf.

van Dijk, T. (1998). *Ideology a multidisciplinary approach.* London: Sage. Retrieved from http://www.discourses.org/OldBooks/Teun%20A%20van%20Dijk%20-%20Ideology.pdf.

Wiley, T. (1999). Accessing language rights in education: A brief history of the US context. In J. Tollefson (Ed.), *Language policies in education: Critical issues* (pp. 39-64). Mahawah, NJ: Lawrence Erlbaum.

Williams, G. (1992). *Sociolinguistics: A sociological critique.* London: Routledge.

CHAPTER 18

THE DISCURSIVE CONSTRUCTION OF PRO-NUCLEAR IDEOLOGY POST-3/11:
A Critical Discourse Analysis of the Oi Reactors Restart Decision

Nicholas Drane
Boston College

Following the March 11th, 2011 earthquake, tsunami, and nuclear disaster in northeast Japan, what has come to be known as a "nuclear village" (Kingston, 2012) of academics, politicians, media figures, business interests, and energy industry officials mobilized to create a discourse legitimizing nuclear power and de-emphasizing the severity of events unfolding in and around the Fukushima Dai-ichi Nuclear Plants. Their aims were clear: to diffuse opposition to nuclear power as a result of the accident, legitimize their careers as agents and supporters of the industry, and stabilize their own positions within this maelstrom. Sensing a backlash against nuclear power, world leaders and major media outlets internationally repeated and broadened the legitimizing claims of the nuclear village to diffuse opposition and normalize the role of nuclear power and its political, economic, and media tributaries throughout the world.

The following is a critical discourse analysis examining a single day of coverage following then-Prime Minister Noda's order to restart the Oi reactors in Fukui Prefecture. This decision was met with widespread resistance within Japan and internationally, including—by some reports—180,000 people demonstrating outside of the Prime Minister's residence in the wake of his decision (Head, 2012; Ryall, 2012). These were eventually the first reactors to go online following the March 11th 2011 earthquake, tsunami, and nuclear disaster. The analysis demonstrates an implicitly pro-nuclear discourse at work to create debate without human agents that goes beyond explicit support for nuclear power in mainstream media, normalizing economic convenience and presenting nuclear accidents as incidental phenomenon outside the purview of human control or interference. These sources implicitly foreground the convenience and economic necessity of the restart and de-emphasize the anti-nuclear movement and its working-class supporters. A matter-of-course "we" is constructed to give an illusion of an imagined "Japan" united on this decision. It is imperative that students and individuals seeking to problematize this crisis understand the public relations agenda embedded in sources they trust and rely on to understand this critical situation.

The author does not expect readers of this analysis to have clearly defined values regarding nuclear power, nor a scientific or technical knowledge of the subject. It is clear that a very complex debate with a vast multiplicity of perspectives exists on this issue (Aldrich, 2012; Kingston, 2012) and mainstream media sources should avoid a discursive preference for a single ideology or enforce a false dichotomy and bracketing of differences.

Positionality

In addition to my research interests in critical discourse analysis, critical pedagogy, and emancipatory approaches to education, I have a number of personal and professional connections to Fukushima, Japan. From 2002 to 2008, I lived and worked as a teacher in Fukushima City, just outside of what was until recently an evacuation zone. I have continuing concern for my former students and colleagues, many of whom have relocated to other parts of the country or overseas as a result of the nuclear crisis. I choose to be explicit about my own role as an anti-nuclear activist who works in solidarity with the people of Fukushima and our movement comrades around the world. I feel fortunate that I can take up these critical issues in my academic work.

Existing Literature

A number of studies and reports related to the Fukushima crisis exist and there are sociological and anthropological perspectives on natural disasters that provide interesting frameworks. However, few have approached the problem of disasters and their worldwide impact at the level of discourse.

Perko et al. (2011) provides a discourse analysis—not necessarily critical—that includes useful insights demonstrating how mainstream media has a responsibility to present accurate reporting while simultaneously abiding by an economic logic that cannot saturate the viewer or reader with too much negativity. Hasegawa (2012) has detailed some sociological lessons of the post-3-11 period that includes media critique. Beelitz and Merkel-Davies' (2012) discourse analysis of "CEO-speak" following a minor German nuclear incident provides useful illustrations of how the managerial class frames their decision-making processes.

Butler et al. (2011) contains a subsection entitled "Framing and Media" wherein the authors identify seven "interpretive packages" or "frames" that media outlets have utilized in their coverage of the Fukushima crisis. I have found these frames to be useful guidelines; however, the authors have applied them to media that is explicitly pro-nuclear, whereas my aim is to uncover the pro-nuclear where it hides in seemingly neutral media registers. Frame analysis also informs Gamson and Modigliani's (1989) work that addresses interpretive packages of nuclear power from 1945 through the 1980s. Doyle (2001) offers a critical discourse analysis that positions the framing of nuclear power within a broader discourse of climate change.

A body of literature exists that addresses the logic of nuclear power within the domain of Science, Technology, and Society Studies (STS). Although the discursive is not at the center of this work, there are a number of classics in the field that supply guiding principles, interpretive frameworks, and rationale for this study. These include Winner (1986), who interrogates the often invisible relationship between emerging technologies and centers of power. He questions deterministic views of technology, which is illustrated in this study, by revealing discursive constructions of technological progress as a neutral social value. Also within STS, Perrow (1984) argues that with increased technological complexity—even technologies related specifically to safety—the risk of accidents rise and we must face the reality that accidents are a "normal" part of living with technologies of increased complexity and scope. In this study, I draw on Perrow by revealing the normalized/naturalized/dehumanized inevitability of nuclear technologies as they are implicitly framed in media. I believe the Oi reactors restart decision will be a critical chapter in the history of the "post-Fukushima" period of nuclear power. My analysis, although small-scale, is one of the first to look at this decision from a discursive angle and I humbly suggest that this analysis be viewed as a possible gateway into the discursive DNA present in other events and texts generated by this crisis.

Data and Rationale

This analysis examines seven online news sources accessed two days after then-Prime Minister Noda's order to restart the Oi nuclear reactors and all originally dated June 16th 2012—the day of the Prime Minister's decision. These sources are: *The Wall Street Journal, Christian Science Monitor, The Japan Times, The Mainichi, Voice of America, Agence France Presse, and BBC News*. These sources were all top ten Google News search hits when searching "Oi reactors restart. Individuals wishing to learn more about this event would likely have viewed some or all of these sources as they were at the top of the search result queue. The nature of online news is such that these search results may have been different just a few minutes (or seconds) before or after my search, nevertheless the sources extracted here are a representative example of the type of sources likely to come up when searching the event on that day. Two of the articles presented in this study were edited a few days later; however, they are presented as I found them on June 16th. I opted to study a single day of coverage as opposed to a longer period to reflect the likely observations of an average reader; someone casually interested in the restart because of the immediacy and timeliness of the event but not necessarily investigating in great detail over time. This type of reader, I argue, will come away with a pro-business or pro-nuclear orientation and consider the case closed without need for further inquiry. More has been written since the Oi decision was made and the reactors themselves have been restarted and again partially shut down, but the articles under analysis here reveal the initial reactions that I argue are the most revealing.

Theoretical Framework

Fairclough (2003) and Chouliaraki and Fairclough's (1999) critical discourse analysis (CDA) is the bedrock of my approach, buttressed by insights from systemic functional linguistics (SFL) and critical theory (CT). CDA is an interdisciplinary mode of theorizing, analysis, and application that rejects the possibility of value-free research. CDA is simultaneously interpretative and explanatory, and functions as social action as it seeks to make implicit power relations explicit. Central to this analysis are Fairclough's notions of intertextuality, difference, and assumptions. The central question of intertextuality is to determine which voices are included and which are excluded. Difference refers to the degree of dialogicality—is there an acceptance and exploration of different points of view or are there false dichotomies and bracketing of differences under artificial consensus? Furthermore, what existential or ideological assumptions are being made?

A major analytical tool of CDA is systemic functional linguistics (Halliday, 1994). SFL views language as "networks of interlocking options" (Halliday, 1994, p. xiv) from which users make particular choices that reflect an ideological position. Transitivity analysis unravels some of the values and beliefs embedded within language choices. Halliday argues that clauses fulfill three conditions: the process—indicated by the verb; participants—the noun typically being acted upon; the circumstantial elements of this interaction. Processes can be material, mental, or relational—referring to concrete conditions in reality, processes of consciousness, and defining processes respectively. With SFL, I attempt to analyze headlines in terms of transitivity to determine who or what are the actors/agents/carriers of a headline and who/what is being acted upon. I also seek to determine what material, mental, verbal, relational, behavioral, or existential processes are implied. Another layer here is thematic foregrounding: what elements of the restart situation are brought to the fore and which are de-emphasized and how this done linguistically.

Critical Theory draws on interdisciplinary methods across the social sciences to critique social structures within a neo-Marxist framework. I particularly rely on the work of Herbert Marcuse (1968) seeking to highlight moments when multiplicity of opinions are "entombed" under broader terms, creating a totalizing and essentialized discourse. These insights are very closely related to Fairclough's notion of difference and in a sense illustrate this concept in clearer terms.

Analysis

Headline Transitivity Patterns

A glance at headline transitivity patterns (Table 18.1) reveals that in six of seven headlines the decision to restart the Oi reactors was without human agency. *Voice of America* and *The Mainichi* give agency to "Japan." *Christian*

Science Monitor also puts Japan in the agentive position preceded by the circumstantial element "Jitters." In all three of these cases "Japan" is endowed with the power of internal reflection to "OK," "Decide," or otherwise carry out the restart process. The *Christian Science Monitor* headline is particularly interesting as the vast opposition to the restart is collectively entombed in the noun "Jitters." It is worth asking what type of impression the average reader is likely to receive by the word "Jitters" in this context. Would they or would they not have a sense of debate, active opposition, or lively engagement with the issue? The *Wall Street Journal* puts "Nuclear-Restart Plans" in the participant position engaged in the existential process of "dividing" Japan. The *Japan Times* places "Oi Decision" in the participant role as it "draws" international outcry. *Agence France Presse* admits the restart is controversial yet the primary agent is dehumanized within "Work" that simply "Begins."

The sub-headlines are also revealing. In the *Wall Street Journal* the sub-headline reads: "Tokyo Aims to Get Economy Back on Track, but Local Leaders, Some Residents Oppose Atomic Power." Again "Tokyo" appears as an actor engaged in the material process of "aiming." The opposing actors are "Local Leaders" and "Some Residents" who "Oppose." Here "Leaders" and "Residents" are over-lexicalized, a process that mitigates any potential agency or power. Furthermore, the qualifier "Local" is unclear. Does "Local" refer to opposition local to Tokyo (in relation to the previous sentence) or does it mean leaders local to those in Fukui Prefecture surrounding the nuclear plant? It seems more likely that the "Local" designation is included to diminish the status of opposing actors while augmenting the entombing power of "Tokyo" to speak for the entire population. The circumstantial elements in this sub-headline are important: the process "Get Economy Back on Track" as being somehow parallel to "Atomic Power," suggesting that opposition to one implies opposition to the other. The *Japan Times* sub-headline states that "Reactor Restarts" are "hit" by protests. Again, the protests are not directed at a human agent nor are they proposed by conscientious human agents, they appear simply to "hit" the restart process creating a dehumanized terrain. The *Japan Times* excludes human agency from both headline and sub-headline. Only the *BBC* includes a human agent of the restart as "Japan PM Noda orders nuclear reactors back online." Nevertheless, this is still problematic as the restart was likely not exclusively Noda's doing, which we will see later.

Headlines are powerful in the sense that they provide the coordinates of a media outlet's ideological orientation (Van Dijk, 1989). To thoroughly analyze a headline is the first step in unraveling what I call the "ideological DNA" of certain dominant discourses. One interesting exercise within transitivity analysis is to consider what swapping agentive roles would look like. I propose this exercise also for teachers seeking to engage their classes in media critique using critical discourse analysis and systemic functional linguistics as pedagogical tools. Consider again the *Wall Street Journal* sub-headline, *Tokyo Aims to Get Economy Back on Track but Local leaders, Some Residents Oppose Atomic Power*. As stated previously, "Tokyo" is given agency to get the economy "Back on Track," which as argued earlier is presented synonymously with opposing atomic power. Let's consider the likely impression a reader would have if we reversed the relational roles: *Local Leaders, Some Residents Oppose Atomic Power but Tokyo Aims to Get Economy Back on Track*. Here leaders and residents are given a greater sense of agency despite still being over-lexicalized as "Local" and "Some." Nevertheless the switch in relations is important. Students, teachers, or activists using CDA as a tool could debate the power that this switch would have. More could still be done, by identifying the local leaders and residents by name and unpacking the entombed parties contained within "Tokyo." Although the *Wall Street Journal* mentions local leaders and some residents in the plural sense, only a single dissenting voice is quoted within the article, "farmer Ritsuko Watanabe." Further research reveals that "Tokyo" likely refers in this case to a narrow segment of business interests with influence in Japanese government (Kingston 2012b; Nagata, 2012). If we allow ourselves to jump up the ladder of inference and suggest that getting the economy "Back on Track" refers to sustaining business profits, and if we omit the over-lexicalizations, the headline could be adjusted to look something like this: *Leaders and Residents including farmer Ritsuko Watanabe Oppose Atomic Power but Business Interests aim to Sustain Profits*. It is unlikely we would ever see such a headline in print. Nevertheless, it is a mirror image of the original, only with entombed voices and discursively deflected voices reinstated and revealed.

Interrogating the verb "Oppose" in this headline would also be appropriate. Individuals and parties in the anti-nuclear movement do not simply oppose; this entombs the multiplicity of actions that they *propose,* ranging from alternative energy sources to more egalitarian economic arrangements. To conclude this exercise, consider the following: *Leaders and Residents including farmer Ritsuko Watanabe propose Alternative Energy Sources but Business Interests aim to Sustain Profits.*

Table 18.1
Headline transitivity patterns in selected articles

Headline Source	Participant	Process	Participant
VOA	Japan	OK's	Restart for 2 Nuclear Reactors
BBC	Japan PM Noda	orders	nuclear reactors back online
AFP	Work	begins	on controversial Japan nuclear restart
WSJ	Nuclear-Restart Plans	Divide	Japan
Sub-Headline	Tokyo Local Leaders, Some Residents	Aims to Get Oppose	Economy Back on Track but Atomic Power
JT	Oi decision	draws	international outcry
Sub-Headline	Reactor restarts	hit by	protests from Europe, America, Asia
TM	Japan	to restart	2 reactors for 1st time since Fukushima crisis
CSM	Jitters as Japan	decides to restart	nuclear reactors

Discursive Deflection of Anti-Nuclear Voices: Entombing Multiplicity

Quotation patterns and assignments of agency shed considerable light on Fairclough's categories of intertextuality, difference, and assumptions. Non-mainstream voices opposed to the restart are either omitted or mitigated linguistically by being presented as temporal actors in the shadow of immovable entities. Differences are bracketed within broader groups and pro-nuclear voices are largely dehumanized and allowed to speak on behalf of the entire nation.

Beyond headlines the bodies of articles reflect an implicit ideological leaning toward pro-nuclear voices. Table 18.2 reflects quoted voices and parties given agency by the respective sources. As you can see, parties supportive of or responsible for the reactor restart are quoted with much greater frequency than others. However, the discursive landscape goes beyond mere numbers. Table 18.2 reflects three levels of opinion on the issue: individuals or parties opposed to the reactor restarts; those whose opinions are ambiguous or neutral; and those supportive of or responsible for the restarts.

Of the seven articles, four identify opposing parties by name. Of these, the *Christian Science Monitor* gives the most voice—naming two—to those opposed; however the agent responsible for the restart is referred to as "Japan." In *Agence France Presse* and *Voice of America*, the Japan branch of Greenpeace is given agency. This is crucial as the multiplicity of voices within the anti-nuclear movement is entombed by this organization, not to mention the likely multiplicity of voices within the organization itself. In both of these cases "Prime Minister" has supportive agency, and in the case of *Voice of America*, like *Christian Science Monitor*, "Japan" is given agency.

Individuals or groups responsible for or supportive of the reactor restart are referred to as "Japan," "The Japanese Government," the "Prime Minister," and "Tokyo", among others. In some cases the agents of the decision are omitted altogether and referred to simply as "the decision," while anti-nuclear parties are referred to as "the opposition" or "widespread opposition." Again, being designated as "opposition" removes the human voice from a movement that *proposes* as much as it *opposes*. Individuals or groups opposed are referred to as "protestors," "activists," "Greens," "critics," and "opponents," verbs that suggest action, but no pro-active actions are detailed. Furthermore, any action would be mitigated in the shadow of all-encompassing opponents such as "Tokyo" or "Japan." "Green" generally has a positive connotation although it is a limiting term because it implies someone politically or personally pre-occupied with environmental concerns and not representative of the general population. "Opponent," "protestor," and "critic" are negative terms, in the sense that they are "negating" the preferred status quo discursively constructed in the headline and article.

Table 18.2
Quotation patterns in selected articles

Reference	Quoted Source: Individuals or Parties opposed to restart *Names as designated in article*	Quoted Source: Individuals or parties neutral or ambiguous on restarts *Names as designated in article*	Quoted Source: Individuals or Parties supportive of or responsible for restart *Names as designated in article*
The Mainichi	(None)	(None)	-Prime Minister Yoshihiko Noda -Fukui Gov. Issei Nishikawa -Kansai Electric President Makoto Yagi -Economy, Trade, and Industry minister Yukio Edano
The Japan Times	(None)	(None)	(None)
The Wall Street Journal	-farmer Ritsuko Watanabe	-Kazumi Mizukami, deputy chairman of a group representing 424 Nagahama neighborhood associations	-Industry Minister Yukio Edano -Nuclear and Industrial Safety Agency spokesman Gyo Sato -Hiromi Nakaya, a 59-year-old lifelong resident
Agence France Presse	-Japan branch of environment watchdog Greenpeace	(None)	-Prime Minister Yoshihiko Noda -Issei Nishikawa, the pro-nuclear power governor of Fukui Prefecture
BBC News	(None)	(None)	-Prime Minister Yoshihiko Noda -governor of Fukui prefecture, Kazumasa Nishikawa
Voice of America	-Japan branch of the environmental group Greenpeace	(None)	(None)
The Christian Science Monitor	-Masahito Kodama, an anti-nuclear power plant campaigner -Jiku Miyazaki, a local Buddhist priest and anti-nuclear campaigner	-Mitsuhiko Watanabe of Toyo University in Tokyo -residents such as Miwako Inoue -Hiromichi Muramatsu is typical of many local business owners	(None)

Limitations

As stated, my research agenda is to generate evidence of the nuclear village at work; however, there are some limitations, which I recognize. I am unable to point at a specific source of pro-nuclear ideology. It is a constellation of many powerful individuals and organizations forming a complex genealogy difficult to untie. Some suggest there is some kind of conspiracy or that media outlets are directly controlled by certain business interests. I do not disagree with this possibility but I have not attempted to establish these connections in this chapter. I simply assert that a problem exists and it should be interrogated. Furthermore, "entombing" practices are common across countless media registers, sources, and topics. If these practices are problematic here, it can be argued that they are promoting unequal power relations elsewhere as well. However, this is beyond the scope of my present analysis. I strongly argue that discursive framing has the power to give a certain impression to the reader, but I cannot illustrate precisely how this happens cognitively. Although I have not attempted to determine the cognitive effect of these discursive strategies, there are studies (Li, 2011) that point the way toward doing so.

Conclusion

Work presented in this chapter is a snapshot of a single day of coverage, of a single event, in the chain of events that has unfolded since March 11th, 2011. If we are to look at the Oi reactors restart decision as a single stitch in a tapestry of the "post 3-11" period, we can see that the ideological thread running through these media discourses is representative of the broader media picture. The processes of disarming the ideologies that invisibly inform the discourses of our daily lives is not easy, but I believe that CDA as a tool for teachers, students, and activists seeking to problematize and interrogate popular perceptions of this process is an avenue of possibility. Not only can we seize upon the semiotic data that perpetuates a pro-nuclear ideology, we can also use it as a tool to reflect inwardly. If the language of activists becomes the language of the *Wall Street Journal,* we have already lost the battle. It is easy to internalize the logic that "Japan" speaks for all Japanese or that a "Local" leader is a minor player essentially without geography. It is easy to assume that economic convenience is the most crucial guiding principle in our decision making and in media coverage of the nuclear power debate. CDA allows us to reinvent and perpetuate our own ideologies and common sense within this debate, with working-class people as agents, and the health and safety of our children as the only inviolable principle.

References

Aldrich, D. (2012). Networks of power. In Kingston, J. (Ed.), *Natural disaster and nuclear crisis in Japan* (pp. 127-139). London: Routledge.

Butler, K., Parkhill, K. A., Pidgeon, N. F. (2011, November/December). Nuclear power after Japan: The social dimensions. *Environment*. Retrieved from http://www.environmentmagazine.org

Chouliaraki, L., & Fairclough, N. (1999). *Discourse in late modernity: Rethinking critical discourse analysis*. Edinburgh: Edinburgh University Press.

Doyle, J. (2011). Acclimatizing nuclear? Climate change, nuclear power and the reframing of risk in the UK news media. *International Communication Gazette, 73*(1-2), 107-125.

Fairclough, N. (2003). *Analysing discourse: Textual analysis for social research*. London: Routledge.

Gamson, W., & Modigliani, A. (1989). Media discourse and public opinion on nuclear power: A constructionist approach. *The American Journal of Sociology, 95*(1), 1-37.

Halliday, M. A. K. (1994). *An introduction to functional grammar*. London: Edward Arnold.

Hasegawa, K. (2012). Facing nuclear risks: Lessons from the Fukushima nuclear disaster. *International Journal of Japanese Sociology, 21*(1), 84–91.

Head, M. (2012, July 3). Japanese nuclear reactor re-activated despite mass protest. *World Socialist Web Site*. Retrieved from http://www.wsws.org

Herman, S. (2012, June 18). Japan OK's restart for 2 nuclear reactors. *Voice of America*. Retrieved from http://www.voanews.com

Japan PM Noda orders nuclear reactors back online. (2012, June 18). *BBC News*. Retrieved from http://bbc.co.uk

Japan to restart 2 reactors for 1st time since Fukushima crisis. (2012, June 18). *The Mainichi*. Retrieved from http://www.mainichi.jp

Johnston, E. (2012, June 17). Oi Decision draws international outcry: Reactor restarts hit by protests from Europe, America, Asia. *The Japan Times*. Retrieved from http://www.japantimes.co.jp.

Kingston, J. (2012a). Japan's nuclear village. *The Asia-Pacific Journal, 10*(37). Retrieved from http://www.japanfocus.org/site/make_pdf/3822

Kingston, J. (2012b). Power politics: Japan's resilient nuclear village. *The Asia-Pacific Journal, 10*(43). Retrieved from http://www.japanfocus.org/site/make_pdf/3847

Li, J. (2011). Collision of language in news discourse: A functional–cognitive perspective on transitivity. *Critical Discourse Studies, 8*(3), 203-219.

Marcuse, H. (1968). *Negations: Essays in critical theory*. Boston: Beacon.

McCurry, M. (2012, June 18). Jitters as Japan decides to restart nuclear reactors. *Christian Science Monitor*. Retrieved from http://www.csmonitor.com

Merkel-Davis, D., & Beelitz, A. (2012). Using discourse to restore organisational legitimacy: "CEO-speak" after an incident in a German nuclear power plant. *Journal of Business Ethics, 108*(1), 101-120.

Nagata, K. (2012, July 28). Keidanren pans government's three nuclear energy proposals. *The Asahi Shimbun*. Retrieved from http://ajw.asahi.com

Obe, M., & Dawson, C. (2012, June 18). Nuclear-restart plans divide Japan: Tokyo aims to get economy back on track, but local leaders, some residents oppose atomic power. *The Wall Street Journal*. Retrieved from http://www.wsj.com

Perko, T., Turcanu, C., Geenen, D., Mamani, N., Van Rooy, L. (2011). Media content analysis of the Fukushima accident in two Belgian newspapers. Mol, Belgium: SCK-CEN. Retrieved from http://publications.sckcen.be/dspace/bitstream/10038/7502/1/blg_mediaanalysisfukushimabelgianmedia.pdf

Perrow, C. (1984). *Normal accidents: Living with high-risk technologies*. New York: Basic Books.

Ryall, J. (2012, June 28). Japan ignores protests to resume nuclear power. *The Telegraph*. Retrieved from http://www.telegraph.co.uk

Van Dijk, T. A. (1989). Critical news analysis. *Critical Studies, 1*(1), 103-126.

Winner, L. (1986). *The whale and the reactor: A search for limits in an age of high technology*. Chicago: University of Chicago Press.

Work begins on controversial Japan nuclear restart. (2012, June 18). *Agence France Presse*. Retrieved from http://www.afp.com

INDEX

A

ability xi, 35, 88-89, 98, 110-112, 119, 121, 125, 140-141, 157, 161, 171, 182, 227, 260, 272, 286, 298
ableism 140
accommodations xii, 70, 121, 130-146
acquisition xii, 9, 101, 109, 111-112, 119, 125-127, 136, 161-163, 168, 170-171, 175, 192, 211, 217, 228-229, 266
advocacy xi, xv, 129-130, 132, 134, 143, 146, 205, 210, 272
amendment xiv, 278, 280
analysis xiii-xv, 41, 43, 57, 61, 64, 77, 78, 86, 95, 102, 114, 126, 146, 157, 167, 172, 177, 189, 222, 229, 252, 253, 260, 265, 266, 293, 294, 295, 299, 304, 305, 307, 308, 309, 310, 311, 313, 317, 318, 319
Anglo x, xiv, 3, 6, 8-10,13-15, 18, 284-286
assessment 115, 118, 176, 235, 263, 265, 289
attitudes xi, 8, 26, 31, 53, 62-63, 86, 99, 109, 126-127, 131, 133, 140, 144-146, 152, 154, 180, 182, 183, 186, 189, 192, 219, 229, 250, 260
awareness xii, 60, 65, 70, 75, 78, 131, 136, 139, 141, 143, 156, 161-163, 166, 173-176, 181, 184, 202-203, 217-219, 223, 247, 304

B

Banks 148-149,158, 160, 249, 263-264
bilingual x, xiii, , 3, 4, 6-11, 13, 15-19, 77-78, 108, 127, 156, 229, 158, 164-165, 168-170, 173-177, 202, 205, 211, 247-248, 253-254, 257, 265-266, 272, 276, 278-279, 281, 284-289
bilingualism xiv, 9, 18, 19, 78, 161, 165, 169, 175-177, 283-285, 288-289
biliteracy 175, 247, 259
Bourdieu 5, 21, 62, 77, 89-90, 101, 108, 112, 126, 251-252, 265

C

Canagarajah 57, 192
capital xi, 53, 72, 89-90, 107-109, 111-114, 119, 123-127, 152, 233, 245, 251-252, 262, 264-266, 275
charter school x, 3-4, 7, 8, 12, 20
classroom xi-xiii, 4, 7, 17, 60, 77, 88, 89, 99, 116, 125, 134, 140, 143, 145-149, 151-162, 164-167, 169, 172-173, 175-176, 179-180, 182-183, 192, 197, 206, 209-210, 212-213, 217, 234-235, 238, 245, 247-250, 252, 254, 263-264, 266, 305
college x-xiii, 20, 24, 31-33, 35-37, 89, 91-92, 94, 96, 99, 130-131, 144-146, 177, 197, 199-200, 202-203, 205-206, 210-211, 215, 222

communication xiv, 24, 37, 84, 86, 90, 99, 102, 108, 114, 118, 121, 166, 169-170, 204, 219, 221, 255, 280, 288-289, 293

community x-xv, 4, 11, 12, 14, 18-20, 23, 24, 48, 50, 53, 57, 78, 85, 89, 107, 108, 112, 114, 118-119, 121, 123-124, 127, 129, 144, 146-147, 150, 154-155, 160, 164-166, 169-170, 173-174, 176, 181-182, 197-199, 201-212, 243, 249, 253, 259, 260, 264, 284-286, 288, 289

constitution 199, 232, 272, 274

critical language xii, 161-163, 166

critical pedagogy xii-xiii, 23, 36, 176, 186, 206, 231, 234-235, 242-245, 265, 308

cross-cultural xiii, 197, 209, 247-249, 252, 257-258, 260, 262-263, 288-289

cultural background 248

culture x, xii-xiii, 8, 21, 24-25, 33, 35, 37, 48-50, 53-54, 57, 77, 61, 80, 84, 87, 89-90, 99, 101-102, 108-109, 111-114, 119-125, 127, 131, 149-151, 153-156, 158-159, 165, 167-168, 179, 181, 183, 185, 187-189, 191-193, 197-201, 204, 206-210, 212-213, 243-244, 247-252, 257-265, 273, 276-278, 288-289

Cummins 155, 158, 160, 247, 265

curriculum xiii, 6, 9, 10, 23, 36, 60, 78, 99-100, 153, 157-159, 163, 165-166, 171, 173, 182-184, 211, 231, 234, 236, 238, 242, 244-245

D

Delpit 60, 77

development xi-xiii, 37, 78, 107, 109, 110-114, 118, 122, 124-125, 127, 133, 140-144, 146-147, 151, 155, 176, 177, 179-182, 185, 188-189, 191-193, 197, 201, 229, 231, 248, 250, 253, 266, 302

dialect xii, 60, 66, 69, 75, 78, 81, 161-166, 171-172, 176, 204, 252, 292, 305

discourse x, xiv-xv, 61, 62, 67, 70, 72, 75, 77-78, 147, 154, 159, 232, 250, 252, 258-259, 263, 292-296, 299, 304-311, 313, 318

dual language 19, 250, 265

E

educational policy 60

English xi-xiii, 5-6, 8-9, 11-17, 21, 31, 35, 44-45, 49-50, 54-56, 57, 59-61, 64, 69-70, 72-75, 77-79, 87-88, 92, 98-102, 107, 110, 113, 115-117, 120, 122, 129, 147, 150, 152-161, 163-173, 175-176, 179-195, 198-202, 208-209, 211-213, 221-222, 224, 231-233, 235, 243-245, 247-250, 252-253, 255-257, 259, 262-266, 271-272, 277-280, 283-289, 291-292, 305

English as a foreign language xiii, 179-184, 190-192, 228, 231, 233, 235, 243-245 179, 231

English as a second language 49, 202

environment 13, 15, 32, 52, 54, 112-114, 119-121, 123, 132, 145, 149, 180, 199, 204, 234, 241-243, 254, 259, 263, 316

equity xiii, 26, 39, 148, 247-250, 252, 258, 260-264, 304

expression 4, 12-13, 23, 25, 47, 68, 72, 87, 89, 95, 98-99, 115, 117, 208, 263, 275, 299, 304

F

Fairclough xiv, 61-62, 77, 161-162, 164, 172, 175, 293-295, 297, 299, 301, 303-305, 310-311, 314, 318

feedback xiii, 198, 206, 215-229

foreign-language 175, 177, 183, 190

foreign language education 127, 177, 190, 201, 213

Foucault 62, 77

Freire 23, 36, 181, 190-192, 235, 244, 249, 263, 265

G

gap xiv, 131, 144, 220, 244, 286-287, 290

Gee 150, 159

Giroux 23, 36, 180-181, 192, 249, 263, 265

H

hegemony x, 5, 8, 176, 292, 294, 300

heritage language xii, 36, 37, 161, 163, 173, 174, 175, 176, 177, 263, 264

Hispanic v, 6, 24-25, 27, 31-33, 37, 127, 152, 158, 173, 175-176, 200, 248-249, 253-254, 262, 279, 287

I

identity ix-xi, 4, 12-13, 21, 31, 36, 48, 54, 56-57, 67-69, 77, 107, 111, 114, 119, 121, 123-125, 127, 147, 150-151, 153-155, 158-160, 183, 187, 199, 204, 209, 211, 213, 280-281, 286, 305

ideology x, 3-5, 6-8, 12, 16-17, 20-21, 60, 76, 78, 89-90, 157, 176-177, 181, 208, 211, 213, 281, 291-292, 304, 308, 317
immigrant x, vi, 31, 33, 48-58, 150, 153, 157-159, 200, 205, 207, 249, 281, 284-286, 288-289
immigration x, 37, 48-57, 199, 281
impoverished 205, 247, 261-262
injustice x, 16, 17, 132, 136, 161, 258
interaction xi-xiii, 18, 23, 62, 76, 108, 111, 118, 120-121, 124-125, 147, 150-151, 154, 157-158, 160, 168, 197, 200-201, 203-204, 209-210, 212, 247-250, 252, 254-255, 258-265, 286, 311
interdisciplinary ix, xi, 130, 141, 144, 310-311
interviews x-xi, 48, 59, 61-63, 107, 112-114, 119-125, 190, 209

J

Japan ix, xiv-xv, 307-308, 310-312, 314, 315-319
Japanese 152, 313, 315, 317-318

K

Kachru 167, 175, 179, 192
Korea xiii, 38, 231-233, 243-245
Korean viii, 159, 231-234, 238, 241, 243-245

L

language minorities 285
language policy xiv, 77-79, 272, 277, 283, 286, 288-289, 291, 293- 295, 297, 304-306
language rights xiv, 271-272, 277-280, 285, 292, 306
Latina 15-16, 21, 36-37
Latino xiii, 6, 12, 36, 203, 247-249, 252-254, 262, 281, 287
legal xiv 130, 134, 138, 142, 273-274, 275, 277-278, 280-281, 289, 298
legitimation x, 4, 59-62, 64, 68
linguistic x-xii, xiv, 3, 5, 7-8, 12-13, 16-18, 21, 25, 35, 54, 57, 60, 62, 64, 68, 70, 76-80, 84-86, 91, 99, 101-102, 107-110, 125, 145, 149, 152-155, 157, 161-167, 169, 171, 174, 176-177, 184, 192, 198-199, 201, 204, 208, 210, 213, 217, 234, 248-249, 251-253, 262-264, 272-273, 276-280, 284-286, 288, 291-292, 294-295, 303
linguistic identity 213

M

marginalized 130-131, 152, 154, 157, 161, 234, 249, 260, 262, 275
media 62, 88-89, 101, 153, 155, 203, 293, 307-309, 313, 317, 318
Mexican xii, xiv, 12-13, 25, 151, 167, 179, 182-184, 186, 190-192, 271-281
Mexico xii, xiv, 24, 34, 38, 127, 151, 179-183, 185, 188-193, 271-272, 274-275, 277-281
multicultural education 130, 160, 249, 266

N

narrative xiii, 20, 54-55, 57, 235, 303
native speakers iii-v, 87-88, 99, 101, 111-112, 118, 121-122, 124-125, 150, 175-177, 180, 200-201, 212, 221, 253
neoliberal xiii, 231-232, 242-245
non-native xii, 87, 108, 110, 112, 117, 121, 124-125, 127, 176-177, 180, 221, 258
Norton 150, 152, 160, 245
nuclear viii, xiv, 307-310, 312-319

P

pedagogy xi-xiii, 23-24, 35-37, 102, 158, 162-163, 174, 176, 180, 182-184, 186, 197, 201-202, 206, 213, 218, 220, 231, 234-235, 242-245, 249, 263, 265, 308
Pennycook 179, 181, 184-185, 192, 291-292, 305
Philippines vii, 83-84, 102
political xiii, 5, 73, 83, 162, 169, 179-181, 186, 242-244, 272, 275, 291-292, 307
positional identities xii, 149-150
positioning theory xii, 154
power ix, xi, xiii, 5, 21, 23, 49, 65, 77, 86, 90, 108, 124, 147-152, 155-158, 162-163, 175-176, 180, 209, 249-252, 259-261, 265, 272, 275, 292, 295-296, 305-309, 311-313, 316-319
praxis v, 126, 146, 174-177, 190, 231, 242-244
pre-service teachers 198
program xiii, 6, 7, 15, 16, 18, 20, 21, 24, 25, 26, 109, 112, 125, 126, 135, 141, 145, 176, 177, 200, 216, 233, 234, 238, 247, 248, 253, 257, 263, 266
Puerto Rican x, 59-65, 66-72, 76, 80, 271
Puerto Rico x, vii, 31, 38, 59, 61-63, 69, 70, 76-78, 80, 271, 280-281

Q

Québec viii, xiv, 283-290

R

race 4, 17, 21, 25-26, 31, 36-37, 102, 129, 148, 202, 281
readiness xi, 36, 130, 133-134, 136, 140, 144, 174
real life xi, 118, 122, 124, 125, 172, 204, 252
reflection ix, xiii, 85, 125, 157, 176, 190, 201-202, 206, 209-210, 254, 257-258, 260, 312
Russia x, 38, 48-49, 53, 55-57
Russian vii, x, 47-51, 53-58, 126, 134

S

service-learning xii-xiii, 159, 197-199, 201-204, 206, 208-213
social capital xi, 107-109, 111-114, 119, 123-127, 251-252, 264
social class xi, 85-86, 89-91, 96-99, 102, 148, 186, 195, 251
socialization xi, 17, 107, 109, 112, 114, 119, 120, 124-125, 127, 159
social justice ix-xv, 6, 16, 20, 23-27, 35, 36, 39-40, 62, 129, 131-133, 135, 140-143, 145-146, 148-150, 155-156, 158-159, 197, 200-201, 203, 205, 243, 245, 258-260, 264, 286, 288-289, 291-293, 297-298, 304
sociocultural 57, 156, 158, 162, 177, 201, 247-250, 254, 258, 260, 263-265
Spanish x-xiii, 6, 8-18, 21, 24-25, 27-28, 31-35, 38-40, 44, 59-64, 68-72, 74-78, 80-81, 107, 110, 112-120, 122, 123-127, 134, 161, 163-177, 186, 197-202, 204, 206, 208, 210-212, 247, 249, 252-259, 263-264, 271-273, 275-280, 287
study abroad xi, 107, 113, 115, 118, 123, 125-127, 186-187, 195, 197, 200-201, 203, 212-213
system xiii, 23, 28, 30, 55, 89-90, 121, 141, 143, 180-182, 192, 217, 232, 240, 242, 272, 274, 299

T

teacher-training iv, 183
teaching assistants iii, 137, 145, 146, 211
theory iv, vii, 3, 20-21, 36, 67, 85-86, 90, 101-103, 126, 154, 159, 174, 175, 177, 180, 249, 253, 265, 291, 310, 318

transformative educational v, viii, 197-213
treaty viii, xiv, 272-281

U

United States iv, x, 24-25, 27-30, 35, 37-38, 40, 49-50, 55, 59-61, 69-70, 73, 77-78, 83, 149, 152, 154, 167, 169-170, 172, 174-176, 179, 182, 200, 202, 252, 271-278, 280-281, 285, 287, 289, 305

V

van Leeuwen 62, 78
Vygotsky 23, 37, 250, 266

W

writing 8, 10-11, 25, 27, 35, 37, 43-44, 47-49, 57-58, 67, 117-118, 124, 151, 153, 158, 164, 166, 168, 170-172, 186, 208, 215-224, 227-229, 234, 236, 296, 299, 303

ABOUT THE EDITORS

Miguel Mantero, Ph.D., is Professor of Educational Linguistics and Director of the program in Second Language Acquisition and Teaching at the University of Alabama. His research focuses on cognition in second language acquisition, and identity and discourse processes in language education.

John L. Watzke, Ph.D., is Professor and Dean of the School of Education at the University of Portland. His research focuses on beginning teacher pedagogical development and teacher professional identity formation.

Paul Chamness Miller, Ph.D., is Associate Professor in the English for Academic Purposes program at Akita International University in Akita, Japan. His research interests include instructed SLA and social justice issues of English Language Learners and LGBTIQ teachers and students.

ABOUT THE CONTRIBUTORS

Carey L. Busch, M.Ed., Assistant Dean of Student Accessibility, Student Accessibility Services, Ohio University, Athens, Ohio, United States

Ashlee Dauphinais Civitello, Doctoral Student in Linguistics, The Ohio State University, Columbus, Ohio, United States

Annette M. Daoud, Ph.D., Professor of Multilingual / Multicultural Education, School of Education, California State University, San Marcos, San Marcos, California, United States

Carol S. Dean, Ed.D., Associate Professor of Secondary Education, State University of New York College at Oneonta, New York, United States

Nicholas Drane, M.A., Doctoral Student in Curriculum & Instruction, Boston College, Chestnut Hill, Massachusetts, United States

Eduardo D. Faingold, Ph.D., Associate Professor of Spanish, University of Tulsa, Tulsa, Oklahoma, United States

Aline Ferreira, Ph.D., Post-Doctoral Research Fellow of Psychology, Wilfrid Laurier University, Waterloo, Ontario, Canada

Muriel Gallego, Ph.D., Associate Professor and Language Program Director of Spanish, Department of Modern Languages, Ohio University, Athens, Ohio, United States

Ana M. Hernández, Ed.D., Assistant Professor of Multicultural and Multilingual Education, School of Education, California State University San Marcos, San Marcos, California, United States

Malathi Iyengar, Ph.D. Candidate, Ethnic Studies, University of California - San Diego, San Diego, California, United States

Hayriye Kayi-Aydar, Ph.D., Assistant Professor of TESOL, Department of Curriculum and Instruction, University of Arkansas at Fayetteville, Fayetteville, Arkansas, United States

Diane M. Mancini, B.A., Undergraduate student of Spanish Language and Literature and Anthropology, State University of New York at Oneonta, New York, United States

Patrick-André Mather, Ph.D., Professor of French and Linguistics, University of Puerto Rico at Rio Piedras, San Juan, Puerto Rico

María Cristina Montoya, Ph.D., Assistant Professor of Foreign Languages and Literatures, State University of New York College at Oneonta, Oneonta, New York, United States

N. Ariana Mrak, Ph.D., Associate Professor of Spanish Linguistics, University of North Carolina Wilmington, Wilmington, North Carolina, United States

Gerrard Mugford, Ph.D., Professor, Department of Modern Languages, Universidad de Guadalajara, Guadalajara, Mexico

Bettina P. Murray, Ph.D., Assistant Professor, Department of Communication and Theatre Arts, John Jay College of Criminal Justice, City University of New York (CUNY), New York, New York, United States

Janet Bacuel Oab, M.A.T., Faculty, Department of English, Palawan State University, Puerto Princesa City, Palawan, Philippines

About the Contributors

Dilhara Darshana Premaratne, Ph.D., Australian National University, Canberra, Australia

John W. Schwieter, Ph.D., Associate Professor of Spanish and Linguistics, Wilfrid Laurier University, Waterloo, Ontario, Canada

Elaine M. Shenk, Ph.D., Associate Professor of Spanish and Linguistics, Saint Joseph's University, Philadelphia, Pennsylvania, United States

Yulia (Julia) Stakhnevich, Ph.D., Professor and Co-Coordinator of TESOL, Bridgewater State University, Bridgewater, Massachusetts, United States

Yvonne Velasco, Assistant Professor of English, Carlos Hilado Memorial State College, Negros Occidental, Philippines

Gordon Blaine West, M.A. Candidate, Lead Reading Instructor, The English Language Institute at the University of Hawaii at Manoa, Honolulu, Hawaii, United States

Also Available from ISLS!

READINGS IN LANGUAGE STUDIES
VOLUME 1
Language across Disciplinary Boundaries

Edited by
Miguel Mantero, University of Alabama
Paul Chamness Miller, Akita International University
John L. Watzke, University of Portland

Available at all bookstores and online vendors:
ISBN-10: 0977911411
ISBN-13: 978-0977911417
Paperback: 652 pages; 35 Chapters
Average price: $39.00 paperback; $55.00 hardcover

READINGS IN LANGUAGE STUDIES
VOLUME 2
Language and Power

Edited by
John L. Watzke, University of Portland
Paul Chamness Miller, Akita International University
Miguel Mantero, University of Alabama

Available at all bookstores and online vendors:
ISBN-10: 097791142X
ISBN-13: 978-0977911424
Paperback: 466 pages; 23 Chapters
Average price: $45.00 paperback; $60.00 hardcover

READINGS IN LANGUAGE STUDIES
VOLUME 3
Language and Identity

Edited by
Paul Chamness Miller, Akita International University
John L. Watzke, University of Portland
Miguel Mantero, University of Alabama

Available at all bookstores and online vendors:
ISBN-10: 0977911446
ISBN-13: 9780977911448
Paperback: 467 pages; 32 Chapters
Average price: $50.00 paperback; $63.00 hardcover

Publications of the International Society for Language Studies, Inc.

To learn more about ISLS and its mission, visit our website at

www.isls.co

ISLS retains a low membership fee that includes:
a quarterly journal, monthly newsletter, and conference registration reduction.

www.ingramcontent.com/pod-product-compliance
Lightning Source LLC
Chambersburg PA
CBHW032000220426
43664CB00005B/88